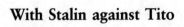

With Stalin against Tito

Also by Ivo Banac:

*The National Question in Yugoslavia:
Origins, History, Politics*

WITH STALIN AGAINST TITO

Cominformist Splits in Yugoslav Communism

Ivo Banac

Cornell University Press

Ithaca and London

First published 1988 by Cornell University Press

International Standard Book Number 0-8014-2186-1
Library of Congress Catalog Card Number 88-47717
Printed in the United States of America
Librarians: Library of Congress cataloging information appears on the last page of the book.

The paper in this book is acid-free and meets the guidelines for permanence and durability of the Committee on Production Guidelines for Book Longevity of the Council on Library Resources.

WAYNEO S. VUCINICH ET JOSEPHO TOMASEVICH

DE CULMEA ET DE PUNCTA STAGNI

MAGISTRIS AMICISQUE

HAS HISTORIAS

DIVISIONUM ILLYRICARUM

RECENTIORIS AETATIS

DEDICAT

A.

Contents

Illustrations

Preface

In the spring of 1948 Stalin struck at the Communist Party of Yugoslavia, thereby transforming his ire at Tito's leadership into an abrupt and unintended schism. Though only four decades separate us from the promulgation of the Cominform Resolution, Stalin's bill of divorcement, this first split in the Communist state system might as well have occurred in another eon of Communist history.

Stalin's rule was based on an absolutely concentrated apparatus of power, which was independent of society and wholly legitimated by the elliptical ideology of Marxism-Leninism, itself an extension of Stalin's *prāgma*. Though this system fabricated numerous enemies, thereby amassing ideological arguments for its monopoly of power, it was largely impervious to internal challenge. But whereas active opposition became almost inconceivable in the Soviet Union, dissent and even open defection were not uncommon in the foreign Communist parties. However noisy, these minisplits amounted to very little in practice and, in a sense, actually strengthened the legitimacy of Moscow. Indeed, for every organization that proclaimed itself "genuinely Communist"—such as the Leninbund of Ruth Fischer and Arkadi Maslow, Tan Malaka's Partai Republik Indonesia, M. N. Roy's Revolutionary Party of the Indian Working Class, and even Trotsky's grandly named Fourth International—Stalin could count on frequently large, usually resourceful, and fully "bolshevized" Comintern sections that did his bidding without demur.

The Moscow-centered Communist movement of Stalin's day evinced a certain severe symmetry that is now difficult to retain in the proscenium of memory. Polemics between Communist parties (along the lines of the Sino-Soviet split) were inconceivable, not to mention shooting wars between Communist states (as in China's campaign to "punish Vietnam" in 1979). Moreover, in 1948 Stalinism enjoyed enormous intellectual prestige, and many eminent writers, artists, and scientists were members of Communist parties outside the bloc. In these circumstances, Stalin's failure to overpower Tito's leadership had vast significance for Soviet ideological and political hegemony in both the bloc and the international movement: here was an alternative communism.

The impact of the Stalin–Tito rift on world communism has been a subject of so much scholarly interest that it is generally assumed that the main issues of the events of 1948 have been thoroughly dissected. In fact, the Yugoslav, Western, and, indeed, Albanian accounts of the rupture in Soviet–Yugoslav relations (Soviet and allied works on the subject do not exist) have concentrated on the sources of the dispute, the strategic and tactical nature of the Soviet encounter with Belgrade after the Cominform Resolution, and the effects of the split on the evolution of the Yugoslav political system and on the Titoist ideology. One looks in vain for some analysis of the vast inward dimension of the crisis—the social history of Yugoslav society during the split. According to Branko Petranović, a noted Serbian historian, "historical science has said nothing about 1948. Though thirty-five years separate us from these events, they still seem immersed in contemporaneity."

Among the important subjects that have been excluded from scholarly studies of the Soviet–Yugoslav dispute are the differentiation process within the Communist Party of Yugoslavia and the origin of the segment of Tito's party that supported the Cominform Resolution. These *ibeovci*, as they were called in Yugoslavia—the term derives from the initials IB, for Informburo, better known as the Cominform (Communist Information Bureau), Stalin's postwar coordinating body of nine European Communist parties—were not just a few notable party leaders and military commanders; according to recently published statistics, they represented a significant section of the Yugoslav party, perhaps as much as a fifth of its membership. Nevertheless, Yugoslav scholarship has paid little serious attention to this group. By and large, the *ibeovci* are treated in a derogatory way that may be expedient but cannot enlighten. Moreover, the Yugoslav party prefers to downplay the strong hand that Moscow held. The downgrading of the Cominformist threat also plays a part in the Yugoslav effort to disown the party's Stalinist past. The consequent dearth of scholarly work, compounded by the hesitancy of historians in Yugoslavia and elsewhere to claim any degree of confidence when they tackle the postwar history of Eastern Europe, has precluded a full and unbiased analysis of the motives that propelled the pro-Soviet forces.

In this book, I seek to reconstruct those motives, to discover whom the Cominformists appealed to and what internal differences (if any) existed within their ranks, to establish whether all persons tarred with the Cominformist brush actually considered themselves to be adherents of the movement (if such it was), and to explain why the *ibeovci* of 1948 failed in their mission. These questions cannot be explored fully without reference to the history of factional struggles in Yugoslav communism. The Cominformists, after all, constituted only one of the latter-day hotbeds of internal party dispute, as their evolution in many ways continued the old rifts of the years before and during World War II. Hence my secondary aim in this book, to determine the place of Cominformism within the developed typology of factional struggles in the Communist Party of Yugoslavia. This endeavor should be of benefit not just to students of Yugoslav politics but to specialists in comparative communism. Finally, the stratagems the Soviets devised to deal with Yugoslav Cominformism constitute an excellent case study of a tactic that has been followed to our day (Ignacio Gallego's Partido Comunista de los Pueblos de España, Taisto Sinosalo's Democratic Alternative in Finland). Investigation of those stratagems can contribute to the exploration of Soviet policy in the international Communist movement during the twilight of Stalinism.

The Cominformists have held my interest for a very long time. From 1969 to 1971, while working on other projects at the collections of the Hoover Institution in Stanford, I started systematically to assemble sources on Cominformism, though I had no immediate research plans in mind. In 1978, thanks to a two day conference on the thirtieth anniversary of the Stalin–Tito split organized by Wayne S. Vucinich at Stanford, I started to work on a synthetic paper on the subject. That paper, actually a sizable manuscript, is significantly revised and expanded in this book.

The history of the Cominformists is extremely difficult to study because most of the pertinent primary sources remain inaccessible. Yugoslavia's Law on the Use of Archival Sources (1963) bars access to archival documents more recent than 1947. Yugoslavia may well release such materials at some point in the future, but the Soviet Union, the Eastern Bloc countries, and Albania are much less likely to do so. Moreover, according to Vladimir Dedijer, the well-known Yugoslav chronographer, writing in his newest volume of sources on Tito's biography (Belgrade, 1984), "A serious obstacle to the work of future historians of this period in our history is the fact that a great part of the documents was *destroyed,* not only during the evacuation [the war scare in the summer of 1949] but also because special orders for the destruction of archival sources were [occasionally] issued. For example, many interrogations of Cominform adherents, analyses of their reasons for coming out for the Cominform, and the like in the archives of the Administration of State Security [UDB-a] were destroyed . . . in 1966. An order for the destruction of file cards with data on individuals was issued separately" (p. 107).

Despite these difficulties, a rich vein of available evidence— official publications, newspapers and journals (including many issued by Cominformist émigrés), memoirs, and an occasional archival collection—can be mined to great advantage, with results that are more than provisional. To this evidence one must add an unusual but extremely perceptive source—imaginative literature, which, in Yugoslavia at least, has contributed much more than historiography to the evaluation of the Cominformist phenomenon. Ever since 1968, when Dragoslav Mihailović wrote his novel *When the Pumpkins Blossomed,* but especially in the early 1980s, Yugoslav writers, playwrights, and filmmakers (Puriša Djordjević, Ferdo Godina, Branko Hofman, Antonije Isaković, Dušan Jovanović, Dragan Kalajdžić, Žarko Komanin, Krsto Papić, Slobodan Selenić, Abdulah Sidran, Aleksandar Tišma, Pavle Ugrinov, and others) have taken up the theme of the Cominform conflict, creating what Predrag Matvejević, a leading Croat literary and social commentator, has called the "Goli Otok literature," after the Adriatic island-prison where Cominformists were confined. Andrej Inkret, a Slovene critic, has rightly noted that in Yugoslavia novelists and poets must still discharge the sort of task that in the nature of things would more fittingly be undertaken by historians or essayists. Mladen Markov, the Serbian author of a re-

markable novel about the forced collectivization of agriculture in
Yugoslavia, was more to the point when he noted that Yugoslav
"historiography has been pushed aside, not to say suffocated. Its
themes were taken over by literature. What could not stand out as
plain fact was being covered with the garb of literature and thereby,
as they say, passed." Hence the historian's responsibility to consider
the findings of literary colleagues with the same seriousness that they
have brought to the task of doing away with political taboos.

My research has profited from an additional important source. I
had the good fortune to obtain the exclusive use of a collection of
documents, currently in the Hoover Institution Archives, compiled
during the 1950s by Dinko A. Tomašić (1902–1975), professor of
sociology and of East European studies at Indiana University, Bloomington. Tomašić was preparing a study of postwar Yugoslavia (some
of his findings were published in *National Communism and Soviet
Strategy* [Washington, D.C.: Public Affairs Press, 1957]) and in the
process acquired some valuable sources. These documents have
proved very important for my study, though no more so than other
sources. Among the most important documents in the Tomašić Collection are interviews with ninety emigrants from Yugoslavia conducted by American authorities in Trieste and Austrian Carinthia. As
most of these exiles probably are still alive, I have withheld their
names to avoid violating their privacy. Appendix I, however, should
provide insight into the kind of person who was interviewed. I am
especially grateful to Carol Tomašić for authorizing access to her late
husband's collection. Her purpose was to honor Professor Tomašić's
memory through new research on the topics to which he devoted his
fertile scholarly life. I join her in this endeavor.

This work has benefited from the generous assistance of the staffs
of the Hoover Institution Library at Stanford University, the Sterling
Memorial Library at Yale University, and the Library of Congress, as
well as the University and National Library (Sveučilišna i nacionalna
knjižnica), the Institute for the History of the Workers' Movement of
Croatia (Institut za historiju radničkog pokreta Hrvatske), and the
Miroslav Krleža Yugoslav Lexicographical Institution (Jugoslavenski
leksikografski zavod "Miroslav Krleža"), all of Zagreb. Other persons helped me to acquire rare journals and documentary materials,
offered valuable suggestions on various aspects of my work, or read
all or parts of the several versions of my manuscript. As I cannot

mention them all, I mention none, but all have my sincere thanks. Special thanks are very much in order, however, to Barbara Salazar, who copyedited the manuscript, and to Florence Stankiewicz, who corrected the proofs. In the end, as Antonije Isaković's Cominformist in the novel *Tren 2* (Moment 2) would have it, "History comes in chunks. Each event has a separate box. And only later is a connection sought; the writing of history begins. Events are set even without you."

IVO BANAC

New Haven, Connecticut
January 1988

Abbreviations

AVNOJ	Antifašističko vijeće narodnog oslobodjenja Jugoslavije (Antifascist Council of People's Liberation of Yugoslavia)
BRP	Bəlgarska rabotničeska partija (Bulgarian Workers' Party)
CC	Central Committee
Cominform	Communist Information Bureau (Informburo)
Comintern	Communist International
CPSU	Communist Party of the Soviet Union
DAG	Democratic Army of Greece
FTT	Free Territory of Trieste
HIA-TC	Hoover Institution Archives, Dinko A. Tomašić Collection
IMRO	Internal Macedonian Revolutionary Organization
JA	Jugoslovenska armija (Yugoslav Army)
KKE	Kommounistikón Kómma Elládas (Communist Party of Greece)
KOS	Kontraobaveštajna služba (Counterintelligence Service)
KPH	Komunistička partija Hrvatske (Communist Party of Croatia)
KPJ	Komunistička partija Jugoslavije (Communist Party of Yugoslavia)
KUNMZ	Kommunisticheskii universitet natsional'nykh men'shinstv Zapada (Communist University of Western National Minorities)
NFJ	Narodni front Jugoslavije (Popular Front of Yugoslavia)
NOF	Narodnoosloboditelniot front (National Liberation Front)
PCI	Partito Comunista Italiano (Italian Communist Party)
PKSH	Partija Komuniste Shquiptare (Albanian Communist Party) or Partia Komuniste e Shqipërisë (Communist Party of Albania)
SKJ	Savez komunista Jugoslavije (League of Communists of Yugoslavia)

SKOJ	Savez komunističke omladine Jugoslavije (League of Communist Youth of Yugoslavia)
SRPJ(k)	Socijalistička radnička partija Jugoslavije (komunista) (Socialist Workers' Party of Yugoslavia [Communist])
UDB-a	Uprava državne bezbednosti (Administration of State Security)
ZAVNOH	Zemaljsko antifašističko vijeće narodnog oslobodjenja Hrvatske (Land Antifascist Council of People's Liberation of Croatia)

PART I

DIVISIONS

Constituent areas of Yugoslavia

1

Sources

Drug nam Staljin iz Rusije piše:
partizani, ne bojte se više!
a mi njemu otvoreno pismo
mi se nikad ni bojali nismo!

Comrade Stalin writes to us from Russia,
O Partisans, be afraid no more!
But we send him an open letter,
We were never afraid at all!
Sreten Žujović-Crni, 1941

Stalinism has been defined as the top-down radical bolshevism of the Civil War period which imbued Soviet political culture with "martial zeal, revolutionary voluntarism and *élan,* readiness to resort to coercion, rule by administrative fiat (*administrirovanie*), centralized administration, summary justice, and no small dose of that Communist arrogance (*komchvanstvo*) that Lenin later inveighed against."[1] Neither a bureaucratic Thermidor nor orthodox Leninism, Stalin's revolution from above to a greater or lesser extent was fixed, too, in the international Communist movement. The Komunistička partija Jugoslavije (KPJ, Communist Party of Yugoslavia) was no exception to this rule. Though some features of Yugoslavia's war for national liberation, which the KPJ led to a victorious conclusion against the Axis occupiers and domestic opponents from 1941 to 1945, strongly militated against acquiescence to Stalinism, Yugoslavia's postwar recovery was nevertheless pursued on the Stalinist model: the "iron rule" of a proletarian dictatorship dominated

---

1. Robert C. Tucker, "Stalinism as Revolution from Above," in Robert C. Tucker, ed., *Stalinism: Essays in Historical Interpretation* (New York, 1977), p. 92.

by the party, whose historical mission was to overcome the class enemy and to organize the new socialist economy by a centralist system of state management. Small wonder, then, that Stalin's attack on the KPJ in 1948 came as a "terrible surprise" to Tito. All the same, he assured the Fifth Congress of the KPJ in July 1948, he was confident that the Yugoslav party's "unwavering loyalty to the science of Marx-Engels-Lenin-Stalin [would] prove in practice that it did not deviate from the path of that science."[2]

Tensions between the KPJ and the Soviet leadership were evident from the beginning of the war, which swept Yugoslavia's national groups into grim disaster. After the Axis aggression in April 1941, the royal government of Yugoslavia, headed by King Petar II, fled the country and ultimately established itself in London as an Allied government in exile. After the Yugoslav armed forces capitulated to the Germans on April 17, the territory of Yugoslavia was either partitioned outright among the Axis partners and their satellites (Germany, Italy, Hungary, Bulgaria) or incorporated into special occupational zones (Serbia, Banat).[3] The unannexed portions of Croatia (with Bosnia-Hercegovina) formally became a new Axis ally—the Independent State of Croatia. This was, in fact, an Italo-German condominium, garrisoned by the two conquering powers, and ruled through the profascist Ustašas (Insurgents), a minuscule Croat nationalist organization headed by Ante Pavelić.

The Soviet government agreed to respect the sovereignty and territorial integrity of Yugoslavia in a friendship and nonaggression pact with Belgrade, signed in Moscow at 2:30 A.M. on April 6, 1941—that is, only hours before the Axis attack on Yugoslavia. After Moscow's effort to prevent the extension of the war in the Balkans ended in failure, the Soviets, still bound by the nonaggression pact with Germany, gave way to German pressure and, on May 8, terminated

2. Vladimir Dedijer, ed., *Dokumenti 1948* (Belgrade, 1980), 1:376.
3. The Yugoslav spoils, in the main, were shared in the following way: Germany occupied and planned to annex northern Slovenia. Italy annexed southern Slovenia, portions of Croatia's coastline (Sušak and its hinterland, central Dalmatia, and eastern Konavle), practically all of the Adriatic islands, and the Bay of Kotor. Italy also occupied Montenegro, and its satellite kingdom of Albania acquired Metohia, most of Kosovo, and portions of Montenegro (Ulcinj), the Sandžak, and western Macedonia. Hungary got the Yugoslav portions of Baranja and Bačka, as well as Prekmurje (Slovenia) and Medjimurje (Croatia). Most of Macedonia and a portion of Kosovo and southeastern Serbia (Pirot) went to Bulgaria.

diplomatic relations with the exiled government of Yugoslavia. The Soviets may well have been toying with the idea of recognizing the partition of Yugoslavia that spring; earlier, in 1939, they had established a separate Slovak Communist Party and recognized the independence of Slovakia. Moscow sent out feelers to the diplomatic representatives of Pavelić's Croatia, suggesting that mutual recognition was possible.[4] As late as July 9, the Comintern instructed Josip Kopinič (b. 1914), a Slovene Communist and the head of the chief Soviet intelligence center in Zagreb, to establish in Croatia a "second center," really a nucleus of a new party organization independent of the KPJ.[5] Tito also had troubles with Ivan Srebrenjak (Antonov), a Croat Communist and the head of a rival Soviet intelligence network, also in Zagreb. In April the KPJ regional committee in Macedonia, under Metodij Šatorov (Šarlo) (1879–1944), had acceded to the Communist Bəlgarska rabotničeska partija (BRP, Bulgarian Workers' Party), effectively recognizing Bulgaria's acquisition of Vardar (Yugoslav) Macedonia. Šatorov, who supposedly had the Comintern's mandate, denounced Tito as an "Anglophile" for having characterized Yugoslavia (Macedonia included) as enslaved by the occupiers.[6] Despite Tito's protests, the Comintern waited until September to inform the BRP that the KPJ must continue to exercise organizational control in Macedonia for "practical and appropriate reasons."[7] The policy of Blagoje Nešković (1907–1984), the secretary of the KPJ's regional committee for Serbia, has also been cited as evidence of the Soviets' intent to partition the KPJ. Nešković's espousal of urban insurgency on the Bolshevik model, it is said, appealed to the dogmatist element in Moscow.[8]

Tito's discomfiture with the ambiguous Soviet moves increased with the beginning of armed resistance, which he enthusiastically supported, though the party had only 6,600 members in October 1940 and some 17,800 additional members in the Savez komunističke omladine Jugoslavije (SKOJ, League of Communist

4. Stephen Clissold, ed., *Yugoslavia and the Soviet Union, 1939–1973: A Documentary Survey* (London, 1975), p. 11 and n. 35, p. 96.

5. Vjenceslav Cenčić, *Enigma Kopinič* (Belgrade, 1983), 1:226–27.

6. Josip Broz Tito, *Sabrana djela*, 20 vols. (Belgrade, 1977–1984), 7:114.

7. Ibid., n. 311, p. 237.

8. Vladimir Dedijer. *Novi prilozi za biografiju Josipa Broza Tita*, vol. 2 (Rijeka, 1981), p. 429.

Youth of Yugoslavia). True, at the outset the resistance was largely spontaneous, as when the Serb peasants rebelled against Ustaša terror in eastern Hercegovina in June and July 1941. In Serbia, and to a lesser extent elsewhere, remnants of the royal Yugoslav army were grouping in the countryside. These guerrillas, or Chetniks, led but hardly controlled by Colonel Dragoljub (Draža) Mihailović, had no plans to lead a mass uprising against the occupiers. Their strategy was to keep the Germans busy with skirmishes and sabotage but to risk no undue losses, especially among the civilian population, which was exposed to brutal German reprisals. They planned no general uprising until the fortunes of war turned against the Axis. The signal for the uprising would come from the government in exile and the Allies. This approach accorded with the expectations of the Allies themselves, notably the British.[9]

Tito proposed a very different strategy. The leader of a militant left faction that had dominated the KPJ since 1937, he did not flinch at human losses and was far less prone than many of his comrades to expect the Russians to arrive by New Year's. As early as the end of June 1941 he sent a wireless message to Grandpa—the party term for the Comintern leadership, ultimately Stalin himself—saying: "We are preparing a popular uprising against the occupiers, because among the people there is a vast readiness for struggle." As if as an afterthought, he asked for Moscow's opinion.[10] However covertly, he aimed to promote a revolutionary seizure of power in Yugoslavia. Somewhat earlier in June he informed Grandpa that he had reached an agreement with Dragoljub Jovanović, the leader of Serbia's Left Agrarians, on the following basis: "(1) Joint struggle against the occupiers. (2) Joint struggle for Soviet power and alliance with the USSR. (3) Joint struggle against English agents and attempts to restore the old order. (4) Joint struggle against the stirring up of national hatred. (5) Joint committees of the worker-peasant alliance. Dr. Jovanović himself recognizes the necessity of our [Communist] hegemony in the struggle for and the defense of captured power."[11]

Though the radical intent of this program was not made explicit,

---

9. Of the immense literature on the Chetniks, the best work, especially valuable for its analysis of Chetnik strategy and tactics, is Jozo Tomasevich, *War and Revolution in Yugoslavia, 1941–1945: The Chetniks* (Stanford, 1975).

10. Tito, *Sabrana djela,* 7:48.

11. Ibid., p. 42.

the symbols adopted by Tito's Partisans made a flagrantly revolutionary statement. While the Soviets invoked traditional symbols as the best means to rally people in the struggle against the Germans, Tito openly embraced the iconography of international communism. In Stolice (Serbia) on September 26–27, the Partisan supreme staff adopted the five-pointed red star as the Partisan emblem and the clenched fist as their salute. And when on December 21, Stalin's birthday, Tito formed the elite First Proletarian National Liberation Shock Brigade, a five-pointed star with a hammer and sickle occupied the middle of its red flag.[12] Moreover, Tito's group, which for years had carefully educated party members to exult in the example of the USSR and to revere Stalin as its leader, now had an opportunity to extol Stalin's cult among new recruits to the resistance, men and women who often had no previous exposure to Communist rites. Hence the impression was created that Stalin was the only antifascist leader and that Tito was his Yugoslav interpreter. The peasant Partisans of Lika (Croatia) sang:

> Oj, Staljine, ti narodni bože,
> Bez tebe se živjeti ne može.
> Hajde, braćo, da mjerimo Drinu,
> Da gradimo ćupriju Staljinu.

> Drug će Staljin i crvena zvijezda
> Uništiti fašistička gnijezda.

> O Stalin, thou people's god,
> Without thee we cannot live.
> Let's go, brothers, let's measure the Drina,
> Let us build a bridge for Stalin.

> Comrade Stalin and the red star
> Will destroy the fascist nests.[13]

In a similar vein, "The Poem about the Fist" by Vladimir Nazor, a major Croat poet who joined the Partisans in 1942, became a marching song. It began:

12. Ibid., pp. 139–40; 8:30.
13. Vladimir Dedijer, *Dnevnik*, 3d ed. (Belgrade, 1970), 1:333.

Uz Tita i Staljina,
dva junačka sina,
nas neće ni Pakao smest . . .

With Tito and Stalin.
two heroic sons,
not even Hell will confound us . . .[14]

Nazor, then sixty-seven years old, had never been a Communist and
was noted for his deep if unconventional religious sentiments. Neither
he nor any other Partisan wrote a song about Churchill or Roosevelt.

Though Tito's revolutionary approach quickly created a mass insurgent base, especially in western Serbia, Moscow opposed these
developments for two reasons. First, the very survival of the Soviet
Union depended on a strong coalition with Great Britain and the
United States. This alliance plainly could not be based on the Popular
Front of the Comintern's Seventh World Congress (1935), which had
held that the fight against fascism was simply a new chapter in the
history of the proletarian struggle against capitalism—fascism being
defined as the "power of finance capital itself."[15] Of course, Stalin
knew that his alliance with Churchill and Roosevelt, despite its practical necessity, did not sit well with his Communist base. In 1942 he
cited the orthodox warnings against the "organic deficiency"
(*organicheskii nedostatok*) of the coalition, namely, that it "was
made up of heterogeneous elements having different ideologies, and
that this circumstance will not allow them to organize joint action
against the common enemy."[16] To offset this liability, Stalin believed,
the coalition must construct a common ideological platform. Whereas the program of the Italo-German Axis included the destruction of
democratic liberties, Stalin's program for the "Anglo-Soviet-American coalition" called for the "restoration of democratic liberties"
(*vosstanovlenie demokraticheskikh svobod*).[17] Here, too, the Soviets

---

14. Ibid., 2:95.
15. Georgi Dimitrov, "The Fascist Offensive and the Tasks of the Communist International in the Struggle of the Working Class against Fascism," in *Selected Works* (Sofia,
1967), 1:563.
16. I. V. Stalin, "Doklad na torzhestvennom zasedanii Moskovskogo Soveta deputatov
trudiashchikhsia s partiinymi i obshchestvennymi organizatsiiami goroda Moskvy 6
noiabria 1942 g.," in *Sochineniia* (Stanford, 1967), 2:72.
17. Ibid., pp. 69–70.

sought to serve their immediate state interests by downgrading the class element in communism.

At least initially, the Soviets wanted the Communist elements in occupied Europe to take the call for the "restoration of democratic liberties" quite literally. In other words, the regimes that fell victim to Hitler were to be restored with Communist help. That policy called for a radical shifting of gears. The Communists were duty-bound to struggle for the thrones of Queen Wilhelmina and King Petar II. As far as the Yugoslav Communists were concerned, nothing was to be done to offend the British, their Yugoslav clients in London, or Draža Mihailović, whom the British recognized as the only legitimate commander of resistance forces in Yugoslavia. Petar had promoted him to the rank of general, named him chief of the supreme command, and appointed him minister of the army, navy, and air force in the royal government in exile. Aware of the KPJ's tensions with Moscow, the London Yugoslavs and the Chetniks tried to influence Stalin by painting Tito in Trotskyist hues. "Moscow does not recognize the Partisans," claimed a Chetnik broadsheet in Lika: the Partisans "renounce all obedience to Stalin (whom they have sentenced to death in one leaflet on account of his pact with England and America), because he ordered them to place themselves under Draža's command and to submit to his will."[18]

"At Grandpa's," wrote Tito in March 1942 to Moša Pijade (1890–1957), his old mentor in Marxism, "they have great regard for the alliance with England." So they did, and hence Moscow's persistent reproof of Tito's leftism. On March 5, Grandpa radioed Tito that "it can be inferred from the documents [received?] from the English and the Yugoslav governments that the Partisan movement is acquiring a Communist character, and that it is being directed at the Sovietization of Yugoslavia. Why, for example, did you feel it necessary to form a special proletarian brigade?"[19] "The defeat of the fascist bandits and the liberation from the occupier," the Comintern lectured Tito during the same period, "is now the main task, the task that stands above all

18. Vladimir Dedijer, *Josip Broz Tito: Prilozi za biografiju* (Belgrade, 1953), p. 338. These accusations forced Tito to bring the equally nonsensical charge that the Chetniks were harboring Trotskyists: "In Montenegro (in Kolašin and other places), the Chetniks, under the protection of the occupiers, have organized some so-called Communist organizations and accepted into them individuals whom we have excluded from the party in the past as Trotskyites" (Tito, *Sabrana djela*, 11:51).

19. Tito, *Sabrana djela*, 9:100, 224.

other tasks. Consider that the Soviet Union has treaty relations with the Yugoslav king and government and that the taking of an overt stand against them would create new difficulties between the Soviet Union on the one hand and England and America on the other. Do not view the issues of your struggle only from your own, national standpoint, but also from the international standpoint of the Anglo-Soviet-American coalition." On March 10, Moscow suggested that Tito change certain passages in the manifesto issued by the Partisan supreme staff to the occupied countries of Europe, a document that the Comintern had solicited from him in February. Among the incriminating passages were references to the KPJ as the organizer of the Partisan movement and cheers for the "uprising of all enslaved peoples of Europe," the Red Army, Comrade Stalin, and the Soviet Union.[20]

Though Tito could "completely agree" to the change in the wording of this or that manifesto, he could not reconcile himself to joint action with Draža Mihailović. True, after Tito's departure from occupied Belgrade to liberated territory in September 1941, he had two meetings with Mihailović. Before the second one, on October 27 in Brajići (Serbia), he tried to interest the Chetnik commander in combined anti-German operations to be directed by a joint operational staff. He called for a new type of civil authority, based on people's committees, and went so far as to offer Mihailović the position of chief of staff at Partisan headquarters.[21] These overtures came to nothing. Only one day after the meeting at Brajići, Mihailović's representatives were seeking German arms against the Partisans and placing the Chetniks at the disposal of the occupiers against the Communist threat. By November the two sides were in armed conflict, and Tito tried to alert the Soviets to the Chetniks' collusion with the occupiers. He sent a message to Moscow on November 25 protesting the "dreadful nonsense" of Soviet radio propaganda in favor of Mihailović. The Chetnik leader, wrote Tito, was the commander of common rabble and at that very moment was turning captured Partisans over to the Germans: "It was only on account of London that we refrained from completely liquidating Draža M., but we shall find

20. Cited in Moša Pijade, "Priča o sovjetskoj pomoći za dizanje ustanka u Jugoslaviji," in *Izabrani spisi*, tome 1, vol. 5 (Belgrade, 1966), pp. 780–81.
21. Tomasevich, *Chetniks*, p. 147.

it difficult to restrain our Partisans from doing the same." He repeatedly sought Soviet military aid, pleaded with Moscow to publicize Partisan actions, rhetorically asked whether "nothing could be done in London against the treacherous policy of the Yugoslav government [in exile]," launched preposterous claims of Anglo-Italian cooperation against the Partisans, and expressed sorrow at the lack of Soviet understanding.22

Tito was angered especially by Moscow's opposition to the political claims of the KPJ. Moscow offset his projected People's Committee of Liberation in August 1941 by restoring diplomatic relations with the Yugoslav government in exile. Reports that Moscow and the London Yugoslavs had agreed in August 1942 to upgrade their respective missions to the rank of embassy made Tito boil with righteous indignation: "Can nothing be done to ensure that the Soviet government is better informed about the treacherous role of the Yugoslav government . . . ? Do you really not believe what we report to you every day? . . . This may have terrible consequences for our whole struggle."23 And in November, when Tito informed Moscow of his plans to form the Antifašističko vijeće narodnog oslobodjenja Jugoslavije (AVNOJ, Antifascist Council of People's Liberation of Yugoslavia), the Comintern instructed him to limit its scope to that of the political arm of the Partisan movement in order to avoid giving it the appearance of a government. "Do not put [this committee] in opposition to the Yugoslav government in London. Do not at this stage raise the issue of the abolition of the monarchy. Do not put forward any republican slogan."24 Moreover, the Soviets blocked Tito's attempt to assume the presidency of AVNOJ. They sent a message to Edvard Kardelj (1910–1979), the second man in the Yugoslav Politburo, asking the party *aktiv* "to take a stand against Tito's attempt to become the president of AVNOJ, which could be interpreted in the West as a Communist effort to make a revolution in [Yugoslavia]."25 They must have been discomfited by Tito's message of October 12, 1943, asking whether Moscow approved the Par-

22. Tito, *Sabrana djela*, 7:198, 10:170, 11:106
23. Ibid., 7:94 and n. 209, p. 226; 12:30.
24. Slobodan Nešović and Branko Petranović, comps., *AVNOJ i revolucija: Tematska zbirka dokumenata, 1941–1945* (Belgrade, 1983), p. 262.
25. Dedijer, *Novi prilozi*, vol. 3 (Belgrade, 1984), p. 196.

tisans' decision to thwart a likely British landing in Yugoslavia: "We shall not allow this landing and are ready to oppose it by force."[26]

Tito, in fact, transformed AVNOJ into the nucleus of his government when, at Jajce in November 1943, he assumed the rank of marshal, explicitly repudiated the government in exile, and forbade the return of King Petar—all without bothering to inform Stalin in advance. Not unexpectedly, the Soviet leader, who at that moment was meeting with Churchill and Roosevelt at Teheran, flew into a rage. Moscow put a blackout on all news of Jajce and censored the radio programs broadcast by Yugoslav Communists in the USSR. As D. Z. Manuil'skii, the top Soviet official in the Comintern, explained to the SKOJ representative in Moscow, "The Khoziain [boss, that is, Stalin] is exceptionally angry. He considers this a stab in the back of the USSR and the Teheran decisions."[27]

The tensions with Tito reminded the Soviets of earlier instances when he had broken discipline. Though not in themselves a sufficient cause for open conflict, they represented extreme presumption, a psychological stumbling block unacceptable to a despot of Stalin's caliber. Stalin and the Soviet leadership could not accept the audacity of "Comrade Val'ter," the hand-picked consignee of the Yugoslav section, in taking on the role of an independent shareholder—Marshal Tito, the rank that the Partisan leader bestowed on himself at Jajce. Worse still from the Soviet standpoint, Tito presumed to make war with limited liability. And indeed, Tito was growing into independence with every Partisan success. At the outset he sought Soviet approval for every significant endeavor. But as he smashed the Chetniks, survived crippling enemy offensives in the spring of 1943, gained British recognition in the role previously assigned to Mihailović, and profited enormously from the capitulation of Italy, Tito increasingly underscored his intention of ruling Yugoslavia, and to Stalin's surprise encountered little resistance from the Western Allies.

26. Tito, *Sabrana djela*, 17:54.
27. Cited in Dedijer, *Josip Broz Tito*, p. 358. Probably as a result of this initiative, AVNOJ's first leadership had a somewhat noncommunist appearance. Its president, Ivan Ribar, the head of Yugoslavia's Constituent Assembly in 1920, was not a party member (though his son Ivo Lolo Ribar was the secretary of SKOJ and a member of the Politburo), nor were two of its vice-presidents. The six remaining members of the presidium were all Communists, but three were of recent vintage (1942), including Vlada Zečević, a Serbian Orthodox priest.

The steady supply of arms and equipment that began to flow to Tito from the British in the second half of 1943 was dictated by the Allied Mediterranean strategy. But, as Churchill quickly realized, beyond the damage that the arming of the Partisans inflicted on the Germans, it had most deleterious effects on Britain's strategy of keeping Yugoslavia within the British sphere of influence, preferably under King Petar. As a result, Churchill increasingly held that the best way to improve Britain's political standing in Yugoslavia—and the king's dynastic chances—was to force the king to jettison Mihailović and cut a deal with Tito.

Churchill's plan had no effect on the bleak future of the Yugoslav monarchy, but it did prompt Tito to pursue a more balanced course toward the Western Allies. As Tito began to adopt the garb of a statesman, he started to cast off his ultraleftism. Sounding more and more like Stalin at the beginning of 1944, Tito now berated the Croat Partisan press for creating the impression that a Communist revolution was taking place in Yugoslavia, canceled plans to celebrate the twenty-fifth anniversary of the KPJ, and even banned the clenched-fist salute in the Partisan army. But Tito's upgrading of the Western Allies was no more than a reflection of his disappointment in the USSR and his increasing preoccupation with statecraft. "Approach all matters," Tito instructed his party leaders on January 30, 1944, "from the standpoint of a new, independent state formation that is nobody's affiliate but a product of the struggle of our peoples."[28]

Despite the arrival of a Soviet military mission at Tito's headquarters in late February 1944, Tito's communications with Moscow declined significantly after Teheran. The steady improvement of his relations with the British, especially after Brigadier Fitzroy Maclean's return to Tito's headquarters in January 1944, did not, however, help the British to make advantage of Tito's revolutionary aspirations. On the contrary, Churchill simply reached beyond his grasp when in the spring of 1944 he forced King Petar to accept a new premier, Ivan Šubašić, an obliging Croat politician, and give him the difficult task of reaching a compromise with Tito. The destruction of Tito's headquarters at Drvar (Bosnia) by the Germans in May 1944 and Tito's transfer to the outlying Adriatic island of Vis, which was under British air cover, was advantageous to British strategy. On June 16, 1944,

28. Tito, *Sabrana djela*, 18:226; 19:109; 20:33, 231.

Šubašić struck an agreement with the Partisan leader at Vis which
was hardly helpful to the monarchist cause. In its essentials, the Vis
agreement committed the London Yugoslavs to recognize Tito's military and political achievements in the country, thus leaving faint
chance for the monarchy should the people want it back after the
war.[29] Nor were the British particularly reassured by Tito's declaration during his meeting with Churchill, on August 12 at Naples, that
he had no desire to introduce communism to Yugoslavia.[30] This was
less than two weeks before Soviet troops entered Romania and one
month before their entrance into Bulgaria. More distressing still, Tito
secretly left Vis for Moscow the night of September 18–19, not bothering to inform the British of his intentions.

The first meeting between Tito and Stalin was quite reserved, with
all the wartime controversies replayed in abridged form. Tito rejected
Stalin's warnings about the strength of the Serbian bourgeoisie and
heatedly resisted any suggestion that the king ought to be returned to
the throne. Stalin was peevishly obstinate: "You don't have to return
him forever. Only for a while, and then slip a knife into his back at
the opportune moment."[31] Nevertheless, the Soviets agreed to Tito's
formula: Marshal F. I. Tolbukhin's Third Ukrainian Front had to
request permission to enter Yugoslavia from Tito's provisional government, the National Committee of Liberation, and accept in advance the Partisans' civil authority in the liberated areas. As the arrangement made no mention of the king and Šubašić, this was as
good as formal political recognition. The British were particularly
vexed by Tito's incorporation of the Bulgarian army, which had just
switched sides in the war, in combined operations for the liberation of
Serbia. Not for the first time, Churchill was impressed to note that
only Stalin could oblige Tito to show more flexibility with the king
and refrain from imposing Communist hegemony in Yugoslavia.

When Churchill and Anthony Eden arrived in Moscow on October
9, the Red Army and the Partisans were already at the gates of
Belgrade. Hence Churchill's plan to pin Stalin down on the exact
limits of Soviet political influence in the Balkans, in which he was
remarkably successful. In the famous "percentages agreement" be-

29. The best study of the origin and consequences of the Vis agreement is Dragovan
Šepić, *Vlada Ivana Šubašića* (Zagreb, 1983).
30. Nešović and Petranović, *AVNOJ i revolucija*, p. 632.
31. Dedijer, *Josip Broz Tito*, p. 385.

tween the two leaders, modified somewhat by Eden and V. M. Molotov during the same meeting, the Soviets agreed to limit their decisive influence to Hungary, Romania, and Bulgaria in exchange for British predominance in Greece. Yugoslavia was to be shared on a fifty-fifty basis, despite Molotov's attempt to increase the Soviet interest to 60 percent.[32] In view of these results, Churchill was not happy when Tito and Šubašić reached a new agreement on November 1 in liberated Belgrade, under which the king would transfer his sovereign rights to a regency made up of three persons approved by Šubašić and Tito and would recognize AVNOJ as the temporary legislative body until an election could be held. Moreover, without consulting King Petar, Šubašić agreed that the king should not return to Yugoslavia before a referendum had been held on the future of the monarchy, and that a joint cabinet of Tito's supporters and neutral London Yugoslavs would be formed even before the referendum.[33]

To assuage the British, the Soviets invited Tito and Šubašić to Moscow, evidently hoping to redress the balance in favor of the royal government. Probably sensing Stalin's intentions, Tito sent Kardelj in his stead. During the meeting with the Yugoslavs on November 22, Stalin was considerate to Šubašić and harsh with Kardelj. The Soviet leader denigrated the Partisan army and its officers ("They have raised their tail") and demanded their obedience to Soviet military advisers in Yugoslavia and their acceptance of old royalist officers in the army. Where he railed at the Yugoslav Partisans, he had only praise for the Bulgarians ("That is a real army"). On political matters, he accused the KPJ of narrowness and sectarianism for refusing to permit the king to return. He praised the constructive role of King Michael of Romania and noted that, in any case, kings no longer mattered, as they were only harmless figureheads with no social role. To Kardelj's astonishment, Stalin then revealed the "percentages agreement" with Churchill, noting by way of introduction that the Yugoslavs were not alone in the world and could not behave as if they were. Šubašić was mostly silent during Stalin's criticism of the KPJ and Kardelj's meek defense. As Kardelj noted in his memoirs, Šubašić

32. On this question see Albert Resis, "The Churchill-Stalin Secret 'Percentages' Agreement on the Balkans, Moscow, October 1944," *American Historical Review* 83, no. 2 (1978): 368–87.

33. Nešović and Petranović, *AVNOJ i revolucija*, pp. 643–45.

"had no need to speak because Stalin defended Šubašić's theses better than Šubašić himself."[34]

Stalin's attempt to balance Tito's dealings with the Yugoslav government in exile probably would have been more fruitful had Britain's policy been more consistent. Churchill reminded Tito in a personal note on December 2 (a copy of which was passed to Stalin) that Britain expected free ballots in Yugoslavia, both for the constituent assembly and in a referendum on the future of the monarchy. Moreover, he pointedly called Tito's attention to the Anglo-Soviet arrangement, which committed the two sides to a joint policy toward Yugoslavia, something that Stalin immediately corroborated.[35] But Churchill was also resigned to the inevitability of Yugoslavia's drift into a leftist dictatorship, as he confided to an unsuspecting Šubašić on January 8, 1945: "Tito holds all power in the country. Tito has the arms and ammunition and he is everything in the country. The real power is in his hands and that of his men. They will carry out the agreement and everything that you signed as they see fit. That is the reality. And that, at the same time, is a leftist dictatorship."[36] Instead of extracting more from the "percentages agreement" with Stalin, Churchill ultimately forced King Petar to accept the second Tito-Šubašić agreement, with all the negative consequences for the future of the dynasty and—far more important—the course of political pluralism in Yugoslavia.

To the end, Western politicians tended to blame Moscow for Tito's actions; the historical record tells quite a different story. At Yalta, Stalin agreed to Churchill's demand that AVNOJ accept all members of the prewar Yugoslav parliament who were not tainted with collaboration and that the legislation passed by AVNOJ be ratified by the forthcoming constituent assembly. This "true crime against Yugoslavia," as Tito understood it,[37] did not prevent him from continuing to pursue his revolutionary policy. By May, his Partisan army was in control of Yugoslavia's western frontiers and pushed farther into Carinthia, Trieste, and Venezia Giulia. There ensued two Soviet inter-

---

34. Edvard Kardelj, *Borba za priznanje i nezavisnost nove Jugoslavije: Sećanja* (Belgrade, 1980), second manuscript page reproduction after p. 32 and pp. 66–68.

35. *Stalin's Correspondence with Churchill and Attlee, 1941–1945* (New York, 1965), p. 285.

36. Cited from Šubašić's notes in Šepić, *Vlada Ivana Šubašića*. p. 365.

37. Dedijer, *Novi prilozi*, 2:913.

ventions. Stalin, fearing that the Yugoslavs were endangering the Soviet-sponsored government of Karl Renner in Vienna, ordered the Yugoslavs out of Austrian Carinthia.[38] And in the crisis over Trieste, he supported the British demand that the Yugoslavs quit the city and its immediate environs (the future Zone A): "Within 48 hours you must withdraw your troops from Trieste," Stalin ordered Tito in early June, "because I do not wish to begin the Third World War over the Trieste question." Small wonder that the Soviets took offense at Tito's defiant speech at the height of the crisis, delivered on May 27 in Ljubljana, in which he declared that "we do not wish to be petty cash used in bribes; we do not wish to be involved in a policy of spheres of interest."[39] Hence it can fairly be held that if Tito's revolution— originally political, later social—could not have been prevented, the arguments against the inevitable, consistently and oddly, were no less forceful in Moscow than in London. Tito, for his part, still held that Stalin, however ungainly his deception, nevertheless promoted the KPJ's interests by excessive falseness to the West. A crafty innocent beheld the innocent craftsmaster.

During Tito's visit to Moscow in April 1945 to sign a friendship treaty with the USSR, Stalin chided the Yugoslavs for their pretension to a Soviet type of government: "No, your government is not Soviet—you have something in between De Gaulle's France and the Soviet Union."[40] In fact, with the possible exception of Albania, which closely followed the Yugoslav lead, Yugoslavia was a lot closer to the Soviet model of proletarian (party) dictatorship than was any of the emerging "people's democracies" of Eastern Europe.[41] Most of the

38. Vojtech Mastny, *Russia's Road to the Cold War: Diplomacy, Warfare, and the Politics of Communism, 1941–1945* (New York, 1979), p. 282.

39. Cited in Dedijer, *Novi prilozi*, 2:917–18. The last sentence is omitted in Josip Broz Tito, *Govori i članci, 1941–1957* (Zagreb, 1959), 1:278. The Soviets protested against Tito's speech. Their ambassador in Belgrade reported that Kardelj, too, opposed Tito's attitude, noting that Tito "was inclined to regard Yugoslavia as a self-sufficient unit outside the general development of the proletarian revolution and socialism," whereas he, Kardelj, hoped that the Soviets would regard Yugoslavia as a future Soviet republic and the KPJ as a part of the Soviet Communist party. See *The Soviet-Yugoslav Dispute* (London, 1948), pp. 37–38.

40. Milovan Djilas, *Conversations with Stalin* (New York, 1962), p. 114.

41. On the communization of Eastern Europe, see Hugh Seton-Watson, *The East European Revolution* (New York, 1951); and François Fejtö, *Histoire des démocraties populaires* (Paris, 1952).

interim East European governments were genuine coalitions, at least for a time: in Romania until the installation of Petru Groza's National Democratic Front government; in Bulgaria until the resignation of the agrarian leader Nikola Petkov from the cabinet in August 1945; in Hungary until the arrest of the smallholders' leader, Béla Kovács, in February 1947; and in Czechoslovakia until the Communist coup of February 1948. But the roles of Šubašić, Milan Grol, and other London Yugoslavs in the united government of Democratic Federative Yugoslavia (the appellation that circumvented the question of monarchy) were decorative from the start, and led to the demission of their office.[42]

The Narodni front Jugoslavije (NFJ, Popular Front of Yugoslavia), from its formal inception in August 1945, was a counterfeit coalition dominated by the KPJ. For conspiratorial reasons that were never fully brought to light, the KPJ kept its membership (and most of its leadership) secret until 1948, preferring to act through the transmission of the NFJ. Tito was its president and Sreten Žujović-Crni (1899–1976), a future Cominformist, was its general secretary. The elections for the Yugoslav constituent assembly, carried out on November 11, 1945, were an uneven match between the NFJ and the unavowed "black box," which received 9.52 percent of the vote. An additional 11.43 percent of all voters abstained. By contrast, the parliamentary elections of November 1945 in Hungary and May 1946 in Czechoslovakia were genuinely free. Moreover, whereas Hungary, Romania, and Bulgaria were formally monarchies until January 1946, September 1946, and December 1947, respectively, Yugoslavia's constituent assembly abolished the monarchy on November 29, 1945, the second anniversary of the AVNOJ meeting at Jajce, and proclaimed the Federative People's Republic of Yugoslavia. The country's first postwar constitution, modeled on the Stalin constitution of 1936, was adopted in January 1946. Later, similar constitutions were embraced by the other "people's democracies"—by

---

42. On the postwar history of Yugoslavia, see three works by Dušan Bilandžić: *Borba za samoupravni socijalizam u Jugoslaviji, 1945–1969* (Zagreb, 1969), *Društveni razvoj socijalističke Jugoslavije* (Zagreb, 1976), and *Historija Socijalističke Federativne Republike Jugoslavije: Glavni procesi* (Zagreb, 1978); see also Branko Petranović and Čedomir Štrbac, *Istorija socijalističke Jugoslavije*, 3 vols. (Belgrade, 1977). For the immediate postwar history, see Branko Petranović, *Politička i ekonomska osnova narodne vlasti u Jugoslaviji za vreme obnove* (Belgrade, 1969).

Albania in 1946, by Poland and Bulgaria in 1947, by Romania and Czechoslovakia in 1948, and by Hungary and the German Democratic Republic (DDR) in 1949.

The radicalism of Yugoslavia's Communists was most evident in the KPJ's policy toward the various shades of opposition. Though their attitude was perhaps understandable in light of the fierce enmities engendered by a war in which no quarter was given, the retribution they took against real and bogus collaborators and anticommunists was nevertheless harsh—much harsher than the putatively severe punishments imposed in Poland and Bulgaria. Various Ustaša and Chetnik leaders were tried and executed in the summer of 1945; Draža Mihailović was captured and shot in 1946. The Yugoslav Communists shunned such expediencies as absorbing local fascists into the party, as the Hungarian and Romanian Communists had done; on the contrary, they elected to extend repressive measures against more and more elements that they perceived as threats.

The arrest of August Košutić, vice-president of the Croat Peasant Party, upon his voluntary arrival in Partisan territory in Croatia in the fall of 1944, was perhaps the first instance of Communist repression directed against an antifascist politician in Eastern Europe during the last phases of the war. The resignation of Šubašić, Grol, and most of the other London Yugoslavs from Tito's cabinet in the summer and fall of 1945 marked one of the first clashes between the Communists and those East European politicians who did not wish to subordinate themselves to a Communist-led umbrella organization. Public activities by Yugoslav parties not allied with the Popular Front ended in the fall of 1945 with the stifling of the opposition press, Zagreb's *Narodni glas* (People's voice, published by the Marija Radić group of the Croat Peasant Party) and Belgrade's *Demokratija* (Democracy, organ of Grol's Democratic Party).[43]

The Yugoslav Communists were the first to institute legal proceedings against church dignitaries of episcopal rank, sentencing Archbishop Alojzije Stepinac of Zagreb to sixteen years in jail in October

43. On the passing of the modicum of political pluralism in postwar Yugoslavia, see Vojislav Koštunica and Kosta Čavoški, *Stranački pluralizam ili monizam: Društveni pokreti i politički sistem u Jugoslaviji, 1944–1949* (Belgrade, 1983), and "Opozicione političke stranke u Narodnom frontu Jugoslavije (1944–1949)," *Istorija 20. veka* 1 (1983):93–116.

1946.[44] They were among the first to arraign politicians of the old parties, including those who collaborated with the Partisans and even participated in Tito's administration, on the charge of spying for the Western powers.[45] They were the first to try, in October 1947, the "opposition within the Popular Front," when they condemned Dragoljub Jovanović, a Serbian left agrarian and a prewar ally of the Communists, for subversive activities on behalf of British intelligence.[46] And they were the first in Eastern Europe to prosecute their own members, in the so-called Dachau trials of April and August 1948 and July 1949. The Dachau trials were on a smaller scale than the Moscow trials of the 1930s in the number of victims, but not in their method.[47]

The Yugoslav Communists were no less zealous in imitating Soviet economic policy. There was never any doubt that the KPJ meant to expropriate the bourgeoisie. Speaking before the party's ideological commission in 1945, Kardelj stressed that to do otherwise would risk turning the KPJ into a "petty bourgeois party"; the "halfway solu-

44. This was one year before the arrest of Bishop Varnava Nastić, administrator of the Orthodox diocese of Dabar-Bosnia in Yugoslavia, and two years before the arrest of Greek Catholic bishops in Romania and the trials of the Lutheran bishop Lajos Ordas and the Catholic primate József Cardinal Mindszenty in Hungary. On the persecution of the Christian churches in Yugoslavia after the war, see Stella Alexander, *Church and State in Yugoslavia since 1945* (Cambridge, U.K., 1979), pp. 53–177.

45. Among the most important of these trials were those of Miša Trifunović of the Radical party and others in January 1947; the trial of Črtomil Nagoda of the Pravda group, which participated in the Slovene Partisans' Liberation front; those of Ljubo Sirc, Franc Snoj of the Slovene People's party and minister of local transportation in the Communist-led first people's government of Slovenia in 1945, and others in July 1947; and those of Tomo Jančiković of the Croat Peasant Party, vice-governor of the Yugoslav National Bank in 1945, and others in February 1948. The first two of these trials predated the prosecution of the agrarian leaders Nikola Petkov in Bulgaria and Iuliu Maniu in Romania.

46. "Dr Dragoljub Jovanović je sprovodio direktive inostrane špijunske službe upravljene protiv narodne vlasti, unutrašnjeg poretka, nezavisnosti i bezbednosti Jugoslavije," *Borba*, Oct. 2, 1947, p. 5.

47. At the Dachau trials, thirty-seven middle-level Communist officials, former internees at the Dachau concentration camp during the war, were accused of having become agents of the Gestapo and later of an "imperialist state." The three main trials were held at Ljubljana (April and August 1948) and Split (July 1949). All but seven of the defendants were Slovenes and at least five were veterans of the international brigades in Spain. In a replay of the Moscow trials, they all confessed their crimes and received harsh sentences. Eleven were executed. They and the other defendants were rehabilitated in 1970 and 1971. The political background of the trials is discussed in chap. 3. Among recent works on the Dachau trials, see Boro Krivokapić, *Dahauski procesi* (Belgrade, 1986). A fictionalized memoir of one of the victims is Igor Torkar [Boris Fakin], *Umiranje na rate: Dachauski procesi* (Zagreb, 1984).

tion" of putting power in the hands of the working people and leaving the means of production in the hands of the bourgeoisie was unworkable.[48] Unlike Czechoslovakia and Poland, which nationalized their industry outright in 1945 and 1946, Yugoslavia first nationalized the property of "collaborators," interpreting "collaboration" very broadly. (The fact that a factory operated at all during the war, even if its products were of no military value, was a sufficient basis for expropriation.) As for foreign properties, Belgrade initially nationalized the property of enemy aliens and then proceeded to "sequester" the property of owners from the Allied countries. This move prompted conflicts with Western and even East European states—particularly Czechoslovakia, whose government now owned the property of Czech capitalists in Yugoslavia. In December 1946, however, the complex legal and diplomatic issues arising from the accumulation of policy became irrelevant with the enactment of summary nationalization.

The political cementing of the state economic sector was a precondition for directed, Soviet-style economic planning. The Yugoslav Five-Year Plan of April 1947 was the first long-term plan in Eastern Europe. With rapid industrialization as its primary goal, it projected annual gross investment of 27 percent of GNP in the Yugoslav economy, the highest rate of state investment in Eastern Europe (followed by 20 percent in Poland, 16 percent in Czechoslovakia, 9 percent in Hungary, and 7 percent in Bulgaria)—higher even than that of the Soviet five-year plans of the 1930s, which ranged between 23.2 percent in 1928 and 25.9 percent in 1937.[49] The large portion of national production withheld from Yugoslav consumers represented a vast increase in human misery, especially when it is noted that only 8 percent of the total investment was slated for agriculture. This was the lowest rate of agricultural investment in all of Eastern Europe with the exception of Czechoslovakia, the region's most industrialized country. The Soviet leaders did not care for the direction of Yugoslav planning, but once again, they were faced with accomplished facts.

48. Petranović, *Politička i ekonomska osnova*, p. 234. Kardelj noted that the KPJ did not wish to burden the USSR—"our ally and leader"—with the consequences of rapid nationalization of Western properties, which would accelerate a confrontation between the Soviets and the imperialist world (p. 239).
49. Fejtö, *Histoire*, p. 170.

The KPJ's agricultural policy reflected the party's clear preference for industrialization. The radical agrarian reform of the postwar period limited private holdings to 25 to 35 hectares of arable land. Among the key changes was the allocation of land taken from the departed German minority among the largely Serb colonists of Lika, Bosnia-Hercegovina, and Montenegro. None of these changes, however, betokened a propeasant course. Tito had proclaimed in 1946 that the "peasants are the strongest pillar of our state," but he was campaigning for his supporters at the time.[50] Though Stalin later seized the opportunity presented by this statement to brand the KPJ's policy as highly supportive of kulak interests, the peasants in Yugoslavia were hardly coddled by the KPJ. The goal of collectivization was advanced by the establishment of compulsory quotas of basic agricultural and livestock products to be delivered at prices below market value. Peasant income taxes were high and little farm machinery was available. In fact, no East European country, except perhaps Bulgaria, stood closer than Yugoslavia to the threshold of total agricultural collectivization. By March 1948, well before the break with the USSR, 347,441 hectares of land in Yugoslavia, largely confiscated German farms in Vojvodina, were under cooperative cultivation. Indeed, when the Soviets decreed the rapid collectivization of agriculture throughout Eastern Europe in 1948, after Stalin's allegation that Yugoslavia's agricultural policy was conciliatory to rural landholders, the Yugoslav peasant work cooperatives were the first to be established and also the most numerous (1,318 by the end of 1948).[51]

Tito emulated the Soviet socialist model in many other respects as well. Soviet instructors actively participated in Yugoslavia's Soviet-style army and security police, and Yugoslav military and security officers were sent to the USSR (480 cadets, almost a third of the first postwar class at the Yugoslav military academy, studied in Shuia, in the Ivanovo district of European Russia, from 1945 to 1947). Education, press, publishing, literature and the arts, theater and film were Sovietized, and, as in the USSR, literature became a tool for the shaping of the popular consciousness. "Writers, for example, must show our peasant in the war, revealing that the less he had for the

50. Tito, *Govori i članci*, 2:369.
51. Seton-Watson, *The East European Revolution*, pp. 269–75. Cf. Josip Defilippis, "The Development of Social Holdings in Yugoslavia," in Vlado Puljiz, ed., *The Yugoslav Village* (Zagreb, 1972), pp. 69–81.

defense of his private patch of land, the more militantly resolute he became."[52] Foreign trade was turned almost exclusively to the east. In the words of a Yugoslav student of the period, "by the end of the war, especially after the liberation of Belgrade, in 1944, multifaceted military, political, cultural, scientific, and other ties were already established [between the USSR and Yugoslavia]. Under the circumstances, the USSR was no longer obliged to hold to the 'fifty-fifty' policy. . . . It was given an opportunity for 100 percent influence."[53]

Stalin did not object to influence. He objected to the terms of intimacy. Despite the absorption of Eastern Europe, which he considered proper for the USSR's security, Stalin's strategy in the immediate postwar period was hardly revolutionary. Hoping to maintain the Anglo-Soviet-American coalition, he sought a firm agreement that would commit the United States and the Soviet Union to control of their respective spheres of influence. In Eastern Europe he intended to establish governments friendly to the USSR, usually with total Communist control but under the elaborate pretense that all the elements of pluralist democracy were maintained, including private ownership. The ideological formula of "people's democracy" thus was meant to point to a new state form that supposedly reconciled the differences between social classes.[54] The undesirable vestiges of bourgeois society would collaborate harmoniously with workers and peasants in a peaceful transition to sociopolitical and ideological unity. On this score, as in the war years, Yugoslavia's position deviated from Stalin's. The insistence of the KPJ leaders on the revolutionary nature of power in Yugoslavia (in 1946 Milovan Djilas paired the Yugoslav "uprising" with the French and Russian revolutions) ensured a severely leftist domestic and foreign policy that was at odds with Stalin's strategy.[55]

52. Radovan Zogović, "O našoj književnosti, njenom položaju i njenim zadacima danas," in *Na poprištu* (Belgrade, 1947), p. 199.

53. Bilandžić, *Historija SFRJ*, p. 97. On the relations between Yugoslavia and the USSR after the war, see Branko Petranović, Čedomir Štrbac, and Stanislav Stojanović, *Jugoslavija u medjunarodnom radničkom pokretu* (Belgrade, 1973); and Čedomir Štrbac, *Jugoslavija i odnosi izmedju socijalističkih zemalja: Sukob KPJ i Informbiroa* (Belgrade, 1975).

54. For an interpretation that regards the formula of "people's democracy" as an implicit "negation of the Yugoslav model of progress toward socialism," see William O. McCagg, Jr., *Stalin Embattled, 1943–1948* (Detroit, 1978), pp. 57–62.

55. On the divergence of Yugoslav Marxist ideology from the Soviet model, especially on the question of "people's democracy," see A. Ross Johnson, *The Transformation of Communist Ideology: The Yugoslav Case, 1945–1953* (Cambridge, Mass., 1972), pp. 24–62.

To be sure, Soviet postwar policy, too, was moving to curtail wartime "liberalism." The new ideological offensive of August 1946,
called the *Zhdanovshchina* after A. A. Zhdanov, the leader of the
militant faction in the Kremlin, was restrictive, xenophobic, and cul-
turally anti-Western. The ideological debates of 1947—in philosophy, biology, and economics—were all meant to demonstrate the
superiority of Russified dialectical and historical materialism and to
free the Soviet intelligentsia of any complexes vis-à-vis "bourgeois
science."[56] Stalin had long, if distantly, admired the United States'
industrial habits and democratic productive processes, and indeed the
mental and physical health of Americans in general, as he made clear
in *Talk with the German Author Emil Ludwig* in 1931. Though
mistrustfulness and the demands of the moment could perhaps reconcile Stalin to the Zhdanovist effort to identify the West as the source
of cultural and ideological corruption, it is far less likely that
Zhdanov received Stalin's leave to prepare for confrontation with the
West in 1946.[57]

The struggle against "kowtowing to the West" has often been seen
as evidence of Stalin's new revolutionary offensive. Stalin is supposed
to have masterminded a "leftist" response to Harry S. Truman's
atomic diplomacy, the doctrine of containment as expressed originally in the Truman Doctrine of March 1947, and the Marshall Plan for
European recovery, which the USSR and its East European allies,
including Yugoslavia, rejected in the summer of 1947. In fact, despite
American attempts to isolate the USSR, Stalin's strategic objectives
remained on course. True, the Soviet leader was determined to force
recognition of Soviet prerogatives in Eastern Europe by a thorough
amalgamation of Moscow's dependencies within a bloc of homogeneous states. But he did not view these states as necessarily "socialist," nor did he regard their acquisition as an incitement to a new

---

56. On this subject see Leszek Kolakowski, *Main Currents of Marxism: Its Origins,
Growth, and Dissolution*, vol. 3, *The Breakdown* (Oxford, 1978), pp. 121–40.

57. Opinions on Zhdanov's role in the ideological and factional struggles of the 1940s
vary widely. Two mutually opposed views are presented in Werner G. Hahn, *Postwar
Soviet Politics: The Fall of Zhdanov and the Defeat of Moderation, 1946–53* (Ithaca,
1982), and Gavriel D. Ra'anan, *International Policy Formation in the USSR: Factional
"Debates" during the Zhdanovshchina* (Hamden, Conn., 1983). Jerry F. Hough's assertion
that Zhdanov most likely was a relative moderate on questions of intellectual freedom but a
hard-liner on the question of the communization of Europe and the diversity of roads to
socialism seems to be closest to the truth. See Jerry F. Hough, "Debates about the Postwar
World," in Susan J. Linz, ed., *The Impact of World War II on the Soviet Union* (Totowa,
N.J., 1985), p. 259.

round in the general crisis of capitalism. Stalin's strategy remained defensive. In early 1947 Stalin had occasion to refer to Lenin's admiration of Clausewitz. Citing Lenin's struggle against "left" Communists (the quotes are Stalin's), the Soviet leader noted that Clausewitz's works confirmed his "position, which is correct from the Marxist standpoint, that under certain unfavorable conditions a retreat is as valid a form of struggle as an offensive."[58]

The views of Zhdanov and his faction may well have been more audacious. But though they harped on the impending American drive for world domination,[59] they effected no immediate change in Stalin's policy. The sole success of the Zhdanov faction on the international scene, at least in the early autumn of 1947, was to soft-pedal the discordant notes between Moscow and Belgrade. The Zhdanovites wished to extend Tito's leftist internal policy throughout Eastern Europe and hence stressed the Yugoslav alliance. Together with the Yugoslavs they pressed for new organizational forms in the Communist movement, the most important of which was the Communist Information Bureau, or Cominform, a sort of European Comintern of mainly ruling parties. The constituent members of the Cominform were, in the telling order of the organization's first official communiqué, the Communist parties of Yugoslavia, Bulgaria, Romania, Hungary, Poland, the USSR, France, Czechoslovakia, and Italy. (Significantly, the Albanian and German parties were not involved.) At the founding meeting of the Cominform at Szklarska Poręba, Poland, in September 1947, Zhdanov's keynote speech expressed the Soviet strategic plan for the ensuing period. Zhdanov spoke of the emergence of "two camps" after the war—the camp of imperialism and the camp of democracy. "The main danger for the working class," Zhdanov emphasized, "lies in underestimating its own forces and overestimating the strength of the enemy. Just as the Munich policy untied the hands of Hitlerite aggression, concessions to the new course of the U.S.A. and the whole imperialist camp, too, might make its inspirers still more insolent and aggressive."[60]

It is quite possible that the Yugoslavs misinterpreted Zhdanov's

58. I. V. Stalin, "Otvet t-shchu Razinu," in *Sochineniia*, 3:30.
59. N. Voznesenskii, *Voennaia ekonomika SSSR v period Otechestvennoi voiny* (Moscow, 1948), pp. 31–32, 189–90.
60. A. Zhdanov, "O mezhdunarodnom polozhenii," *Bol'shevik* 24, no. 20 (1947):20. For another view of developments in international communism during the 1940s, see Fernando Claudín, *The Communist Movement: From Comintern to Cominform*, vol. 2, *The Zenith of Stalinism* (New York, 1975), pp. 455–79.

warmth at Szklarska Poręba as indicating that the mountain had
come to Muhammad. Indeed, Zhdanov cited Yugoslavia as the first
of the "new democracies," in advance of Poland, Czechoslovakia,
and Albania, all of which "played a great role in the liberation war
against fascism," and ahead of "Bulgaria, Romania, Hungary, and to
some extent Finland, which joined the antifascist front."[61] He encouraged Yugoslav leftism by commissioning the criticism leveled by
Edvard Kardelj and Milovan Djilas, the second- and fourth-ranking
leaders of the Yugoslav Politburo, against the "opportunism and
parliamentary illusions" of the French and Italian Communists.[62]
Władysław Gomułka, the Polish party leader, was the only genuine
dissident at the meeting. He openly opposed Zhdanov and the
Yugoslavs, claiming that "peaceful development was at work in Poland. The subject was not the destruction of capitalism, but its bri-
dling."[63] Gomułka also spoke of the "Polish road to socialism," an
idea that Djilas later cited as unthinkable for the Yugoslavs at the
time.[64] Yugoslav support for the Soviet line was rewarded with the
stationing of the Cominform headquarters at Belgrade. The Cominform apparatus was to be strictly Soviet and Yugoslav.

The prominence that the Soviets (the Zhdanov faction alone?) assigned to the KPJ in the fall of 1947 may have been no more than an
elaborate snare.[65] Certainly Stalin as well as the Zhdanovites, whom
he purged in the Leningrad Affair of 1949 after Zhdanov's own
mysterious death, profited by the establishment of the Cominform.
The Zhdanovites wanted to use the Cominform to fuel the general

61. Zhdanov, "O mezhdunarodnom polozhenii," p. 15.
62. For an account of Szklarska Poręba from the point of view of the criticized, by an
Italian delegate, see Eugenio Reale, *Avec Jacques Duclos au banc des accusés à la réunion
constitutive du Kominform à Szklarska Poreba (22–27 septembre 1947)* (Paris, 1958). The
two Yugoslav participants at the Szklarska Poręba meeting remembered their roles quite
differently. Kardelj admitted that the Yugoslavs told Zhdanov that in their view the Italian
and French parties practiced an opportunistic policy, but that the task of criticizing those
parties, as Zhdanov proposed, was for him "extremely unpleasant." See Kardelj, *Sećanja*,
p. 109. Djilas, on the other hand, remembered that "Kardelj and I mentioned to Zhdanov
and Malenkov, as they also suggested to us, the critique of French and Italian parties.
Zhdanov could hardly wait. 'They must be criticized!'" (Milovan Djilas, *Vlast* [London,
1983], p. 111). The report of the two delegates to the KPJ CC, as it emerges in laconic
minutes published by Dedijer, is closer to Djilas's version. See "Zapisnik sjednice CK KPJ
od 30-IX-1947," in Dedijer, *Novi prilozi*, 3:274–76.
63. Dedijer, *Novi prilozi*, 3:276.
64. Djilas, *Vlast*, p. 112.
65. This view is strongly held by most Yugoslav writers. See Dedijer, *Novi prilozi*, 3:272.

crisis of capitalism by separating Western Europe from the United States. (A Yugoslav document of the time noted that the "accession of Western democracies to the Bureau was not excluded.")[66] But the Yugoslav party leaders had failed to diminish the Cominform's power of censure, and Stalin used the organization for the sole purpose of inveighing in public against the KPJ. Kardelj and Djilas did not choose to reach out to the non-Soviet Communists at Szklarska Po- ręba, offended the French and Italians, and let down the Poles and other East Europeans, notably the Czechoslovaks. Moreover, they established a precedent: the Cominform could be used as a forum for ideological operations against member parties. Most important, the KPJ leaders failed to grasp that the new Soviet policy toward the "camp of imperialism" in no sense was prone to incur the risk of war.

As Zhdanov made clear at Szklarska Poręba, "Soviet foreign policy proceeded from the fact of the long-time existence of two systems— capitalism and socialism. From this followed the possibility of coop- eration between the USSR and countries with other systems, provided that the principle of reciprocity and the fulfillment of assumed obliga- tions were respected."[67] The Soviets were parrying the policy of con- tainment with Stalin's favorite tactic of dividing his opponents. The blandishment of agreement was balanced by the Communist policy of resurrecting West European fears of American hegemony. Hence Sta- lin assigned the Western Communist parties the role of peacemakers, militant defenders of national honor, and consistent partisans of de- mocracy, always with no reference to revolution or socialism. Far from contemplating a raid against capitalism, Stalin planned to stir up no local insurrections, regional tests of strength on the fringes of Europe, or any kind of revolutionary offensive. At Szklarska Poręba Zhdanov recognized that the Americans drew their support from the lesser capitalist countries and the colonial and traditional societies: "The imperialist camp is supported by such colonial states as Belgium and Holland, countries with reactionary and antidemocratic regimes such as Turkey and Greece, countries that are politically and eco- nomically dependent on the U.S.A. such as the lands of the Near East, South America, and China."[68] The Chinese Communist Party, then

66. "Zapisnik sjednice CK KPJ od 30-IX-1947," p. 276.
67. Zhdanov, "O mezhdunarodnom polozhenii," p. 16.
68. Ibid., p. 14.

28 Divisions

involved in its bitter civil war against Chiang Kai-shek's Nationalists, was not involved in the Cominform; and, of great importance for Tito's policy, neither was the Greek Communist Party.

On February 23, 1948, at the Red Army Day reception at the Soviet embassy in Tirana, Albania, Soviet chargé Gagarinov lifted his glass before the assembled Albanian leadership and Yugoslav diplomats and proposed an odd toast to "Marshal Tito, insofar as his work strengthens the world democratic front."[69] This first open indication of the Soviet–Yugoslav rift came some two months after Yugoslavia's Balkan policy first posed an obstacle to the new tenor of the Soviets' international strategy. Hence the essence of the conflict is not to be sought in the growing tensions over the unfair economic arrangements that the Soviets imposed on Yugoslavia (especially the establishment of exploitive jointly managed firms that were designed to give the Soviets a monopoly in the Yugoslav market and the benefits of capitalist principles in trade), as Vladimir Dedijer would have it.[70] Nor was the "root cause of the conflict . . . the new line of Communist policy, the conception of people's democracy as a transition stage to socialism," which, according to Doreen Warriner, was supposedly adopted in 1947 when the Cominform presumably decided to undertake the full collectivization of agriculture in Eastern Europe.[71] Certainly many incidents had heightened the Soviets' displeasure: Djilas's vocal protest against the assaults, looting, and rapes committed by Red Army men against Yugoslav civilians in 1944, repeated attempts to stem the willfulness of Soviet personnel in Yugoslavia, heated arguments over the terms of mixed Soviet-Yugoslav enterprises, and the Yugoslavs' public insistence on the distinctiveness of their policy, as when Yugoslav diplomats at the United Nations in 1947 opposed the Soviet-American plan for the

69. Dedijer, *Dokumenti 1948*, 1:170. I am most grateful to John O. Iatrides, of the Department of Political Science at Southern Connecticut State College, and to Ole L. Smith and Lars Bærentzen, both of the Department of Modern Greek and Balkan Studies at the University of Copenhagen, for their valuable comments and suggestions on the following sections on the Greek civil war.
70. Vladimir Dedijer, *Izgubljena bitka J. V. Staljina* (Sarajevo, 1969), pp. 103–41. This thesis was present in rudimentary form in Milentije Popović's famous exposé of Soviet economic exploitation of Eastern Europe. See Milentije Popović, "O ekonomskim odnosima izmedju socijalističkih država," *Komunist* 3, no. 4 (1949):89–146.
71. Doreen Warriner, *Revolution in Eastern Europe* (London, 1950), pp. 53–54.

partition of Palestine in favor of a cantonized Judeo-Arab federation.[72] But such incidents were not the immediate cause of the rift. The dramatic dénouement of 1948 was related most directly to Stalin's fear that Yugoslavia was beginning to see itself as a regional Communist center, with all the possibilities for mischief in relations with the West that such a role implied. The Soviets must have been aware that Belgrade's anti-Western excesses, such as the shooting down of an American military transport plane over Yugoslav territory in August 1946 and the mining of Albanian waters off Corfu in October 1946, with the loss of two British warships, were laid to the charge of Moscow in Western capitals.[73] All the more reason to worry that the West viewed Tito as Stalin's cat's-paw in Balkan affairs, especially in troubled Greece and Albania.

As early as the late spring of 1943, one of the leading Yugoslav Communists—Svetozar Vukmanović-Tempo (b. 1912), the delegate of the KPJ Central Committee (CC) and Tito's Supreme Staff to the Partisans of Macedonia and Kosovo—had proposed the establishment of a Balkan staff through which the Yugoslavs would map out the military (and hence political) behavior of the Communist movement in Albania, Bulgaria, and Greece. The Albanian Communist leaders endorsed the idea of a permanent supreme staff of Balkan

72. Aleš Bebler, *Kako sam hitao: Sećanja* (Belgrade, 1982), pp. 233–34.

73. Yugoslavia's responsibility for the mining of the Corfu Channel—and hence for the incident that cost the lives of 44 British officers and sailors—is documented by accounts of Yugoslav refugees. See Leslie Gardiner, *The Eagle Spreads His Claws: A History of the Corfu Channel Dispute and of Albania's Relations with the West, 1945–1965* (Edinburgh, 1966), pp. 175–93. In his recollections of the incident, the Albanian leader Enver Hoxha (1908–1985) did not credit the Yugoslavs directly with the planting of mines, but he recalled that a Yugoslav general advised a show of strength when the British subsequently violated Albanian waters to clear the mines: "'Open fire on them,' one of Tito's generals told us. But we, being genuine Marxists, took no notice of the 'order' of the Yugoslav general, instead we carried out the advice of the people: 'Measure seven times before you cut'" (*The Anglo-American Threat to Albania: Memoirs of the National Liberation War* [Tirana, 1982], p. 420). Yugoslavia has always denied responsibility for the incident. For a recent statement on this issue, see Danijel Garić, "Dezinformacijske mine protiv Jugoslavije," *Start*, Sept. 21, 1985, pp. 34–36, 61. Michael B. Petrovich, a former member of the American military mission in Yugoslavia, currently a noted historian of the Balkans, remembered that in 1944, 1945, and 1946, "if the Yugoslavs did something that offended us, we assumed that the Soviets approved of it, if they had not in fact instigated it. Yugoslav Communists and Soviet Communists were looked upon as all the same—disagreeable people who destroyed democracy, suppressed freedom, and strove to impose communism upon their neighbors. Thus events in Yugoslavia contributed significantly to the start of the Cold War" ("The View from Yugoslavia," in Thomas T. Hammond, ed., *Witnesses to the Origins of the Cold War* [Seattle, 1982], p. 57).

national liberation armies, made up of the "most respected military and political representatives appointed independently by each Balkan country." The staff was to lead the "struggle of the Balkan peoples for their national liberation and the securing of popular democratic power in all Balkan countries," but its immediate operational scope was restricted to a zone of some fifty miles on both sides of the pre-1941 borders between Albania and Yugoslavia, between Albania and Greece, and between Yugoslavia and Greece.[74]

Though the Albanian party, which was under considerable Yugoslav influence, accepted Tempo's proposal, the Bulgarians and the majority of the Greek Communist leaders procrastinated. Far from the tension between the KPJ and Moscow, they were not at odds with the Soviets over wartime strategies. The Greek Communists, pursuing liberation "under the British flag," kept their party under conspiratorial wraps in the ranks of the British-directed resistance. The Bulgarians held to the Soviet strategy of strikes and sabotage, linking the liberation of Bulgaria to the prowess of Soviet arms. Both feared Yugoslavia's intentions in Macedonia, whose unification within Yugoslavia at the expense of Bulgarian and Greek territorial claims was being popularized, however indirectly, by the Yugoslavs.[75] Both also feared the predominance of Yugoslavia in Balkan affairs. During a meeting with Tempo at the end of August 1943 in a village near Lárisa in Thessaly, Geórgios Siántos, the acting general secretary of the Kommounistikón Kómma Elládas (KKE, Communist Party of Greece), observed that not enough time had elapsed since the dissolu-

74. Svetozar Vukmanović-Tempo, *Borba za Balkan* (Zagreb, 1981), pp. 90, 93. In his memoirs on Albania's relations with Yugoslavia, Enver Hoxha presented himself as being opposed to Tempo's overtures on the Balkan staff. According to Hoxha, his signature with Tempo's on the joint document indicated only a willingness to discuss the matter, though the Albanians hardly suspected that "behind the idea of the Balkan 'staff' hid the megalomaniacal and hegemonistic intentions of the KPJ leadership to rule the Balkans" (*Titistët: Shënime historike* [Tirana, 1982], pp. 47–55).

75. C. M. Woodhouse, *The Struggle for Greece, 1941–1949* (London, 1976), p. 67. In 1943 Tito did indeed favor the unification of the whole of Macedonia within Yugoslavia. He wrote to Tempo on December 6, 1943, "As far as Macedonia is concerned . . . neither you nor the comrades over there [Greeks and Bulgarians] have approached this question correctly. The Macedonian people have the right to self-determination, and even to secession. . . . Sovereign in their rights, the Macedonian people have the right to join the federal community of other peoples. This is what they, in fact, should be doing today by joining the common struggle of the other peoples of Yugoslavia against the German conquerors and Bulgarian occupiers. This is the only guarantee that a genuinely democratic national movement will develop in Macedonia—the guarantee of a better future for the Macedonian people" (Tito, *Sabrana djela*, 18:19).

tion of the Comintern (May 1943) to start thinking of a staff that could be considered a sort of "new Balkan International."[76] But in September 1943, Tito ordered Tempo to abandon all plans for the Balkan staff as "politically incorrect."[77] Quite unlike the other Balkan Communist leaders, Tito evidently believed that Tempo went too far with his Balkan staff, not because it enhanced the Yugoslavs but because it had the potential of actually diminishing the importance of the Yugoslav Partisan movement among the Balkan Communists.[78] In his explanatory note to Tempo, Tito claimed that the abandonment of the Balkan staff underscored Yugoslav primacy in the Balkans: "In every respect Yugoslavia holds the leading role in the Balkans, from the standpoint both of the military might of the [Yugoslav] National Liberation Army and of its experience in the establishment of people's power through national liberation committees and antifascist councils. Therefore, in our opinion, as well as in the opinion of Grandpa, we must be the center of the Balkan countries militarily and politically."[79]

It is more likely, however, that Soviet opinion of Tito's influence in the Balkans was no less guarded then than it was a year later, when Stalin pressed Tito to form a Yugoslav-Bulgarian federation.[80] Stalin's insistence on this step—he also urged it upon Kardelj and Šubašić on November 22, 1944—suggests that he sought to control Tito's policies through the more dependable Bulgaria. The Yugoslavs "wondered why Stalin forced the Yugoslav-Bulgarian federation, because in other circumstances . . . he was very circumspect in all matters that could lead to a sharpening of relations between the Soviet Union and the West."[81] Their mistrust aroused by Stalin's urgency, they offered an alternative that could only strengthen their hand in

76. Vukmanović-Tempo, *Borba*, p. 119.
77. Tito, *Sabrana djela*, 16:225. For the possibility that the Soviets (or Georgi Dimitrov, the Bulgarian Communist leader) had a hand in Tito's decision to end Tempo's action, see Elisabeth Barker, *British Policy in South-East Europe in the Second World War* (London, 1976), p. 191.
78. "The Balkan staff," Tito wrote Tempo on December 6, 1943, "which, as we can see, is nonsense—because it does not and cannot exist (with four commanders and four commissars)—would in fact serve to drive back our national liberation struggle, the Supreme Staff, and AVNOJ with some sort of Pan-Balkan movement, which is not even close to being crystallized in the course of the struggle" (*Sabrana djela*, 18:18).
79. Ibid., 17:36–37.
80. Kardelj, *Sećanja*, p. 103.
81. Ibid., p. 106.

the Balkans. Instead of a dualist union between Sofia and Belgrade, the Yugoslavs proposed a seven-member federation in which Bulgaria would be added to the six emerging Yugoslav republics. Moreover, Pirin Macedonia (the portion of Macedonia that belonged to Bulgaria) was to be united to Vardar (Yugoslav) Macedonia even if the unification with Bulgaria fell through.[82]

Some Bulgarian leaders (notably Trajčo Kostov) opposed any federation, but others (Georgi Dimitrov and Vəlko Červenkov) supported the dualist federation proposed by Stalin. After the failure of Kardelj's mission to Sofia in late December 1944, representatives of the two countries were invited to Moscow in late January 1945 for Soviet arbitration. According to Moša Pijade, the leading Yugoslav delegate, Stalin initially spoke "in the spirit of the Bulgarian proposal, that is, for a dualist federation, explaining his stand with the argument that Bulgaria has been an independent country for a long time." Pijade countered by pointing out that "Serbia and Montenegro were independent a lot longer than Bulgaria; moreover, why should the Croats, who had their state a millennium ago, not be equal to the Bulgars?"[83] In a technical sense Pijade was right, but the prospect of being as independent as Montenegro could not arouse the Bulgarians' fervor. When a day or so later Stalin unexpectedly came around to Pijade's standpoint, he was probably only soothing the Yugoslavs with empty words. By that time he was aware that on January 26 the British government had cautioned the Bulgarians, who had not yet signed a peace treaty with the Allies, against joining a federation with Yugoslavia or ceding Pirin Macedonia to it. For the time being the Yugoslav-Bulgarian federation was as good as dead. "I must admit," recalled Kardelj, "that this did not make us unhappy."[84]

Whereas Stalin's phlegm quenched Tito's parrying of the Bulgarian link, nothing, seemingly, could check the Yugoslavification of Albania, where the Soviets had little say until 1948. In regard to Greece, Stalin aimed to live up to the "percentages agreement" with Churchill, whereby Britain retained a 90 percent political interest in the

---

82. This was certainly the argument that Kardelj used in his negotiations with the Bulgarian leaders at Sofia on December 23, 1944. See Moša Pijade, "Govor o balkanskoj federaciji na Osmom redovnom zasedanju Narodne skupštine FNRJ," in *Izabrani spisi*, tome 1, vol. 5, p. 748.

83. Ibid., pp. 751–52.

84. Kardelj, *Sećanja*, p. 105.

country. Here, too, Tito's policies conflicted with Stalin's. In November 1944 Tito encouraged the KKE's plans to seize Athens, though this course almost certainly implied a clash with the British troops that had already disembarked in Greece to disarm the Communist-led guerrillas and prop up the anticommunist forces.[85] Early in 1945, after the failure of the Communist uprising in December, Georgi Dimitrov (1882–1949), the Bulgarian leader and the Comintern's former general secretary, reflected Stalin's wishes when he informed the KKE that in future the Greeks must take care to avoid confrontation with the British, as such a course could bring little advantage to themselves and a great deal of harm to Yugoslavia and Bulgaria.[86] The Yugoslavs, for their part, were still encouraging the KKE's resistance and promising the Greek Communists military support.[87]

Despite Yugoslav assurances, the Greek party leaders convinced themselves that they could not count on significant support from the north. At a conference between the Communists and Greek nationalists at Várkiza (Attica) in February 1945, the KKE agreed to disarm its powerful guerrilla army in exchange for a limited amnesty and legal status for the party. And at Yalta at the same time, Stalin placed no obstacles in the way of British intervention in Greece, expressing his confidence in British policy. Communist and resistance activists were then hounded by the police and rightist thugs, though the legality of the KKE leadership in Athens was itself never violated.

Níkos Zakhariádēs (1903–1973), who resumed his post as general secretary of the KKE after his return from Nazi captivity in late May 1945, soon developed his "two poles" theory, according to which Greece's foreign policy had to be equidistant from the Soviet Balkans

85. D. George Kousoulas, *Revolution and Defeat: The Story of the Greek Communist Party* (London, 1965), p. 201. I am grateful to Lars Bærentzen for bringing to my attention a very suggestive document from a British War Office file at the Public Record Office (WO 204/8903: Land Forces Greece: General Staff Intelligence Branch, Security Intelligence Middle East: political reports; no. 0747, Dec. 15, 1944). It includes the following intercepted telegram, dated November 30, 1944, from Stérgios Anastasiádes, a member of the KKE leadership on a fact-finding mission to Yugoslavia and Bulgaria, to Siántos: "Saw BULGARIANS and TITO: They advise we must insist on not rpt not being disarmed. No rpt no British interference."

86. Dominique Eudes, *The Kapetanios: Partisans and Civil War in Greece, 1943–1949* (New York, 1972), p. 226.

87. Evangelos Kofos, *Nationalism and Communism in Macedonia* (Salonika, 1964), pp. 146–47.

and the British Mediterranean. His strategy was to pressure the British government and Greek nationalists to restore the balance that had been tipped in favor of London. The combination of legal struggle, subversion, and escalating armed insurgency was meant to produce a general uprising at Stalin's signal.[88] The strategy of armed resistance was clearly favored by the Yugoslavs. Despite advice to the contrary by the Soviets (and by the Italian and French Communists as well), Zakhariádēs ordered the KKE to boycott the parliamentary elections of March 1946. When the elected nationalist majority intensified the persecution of the KKE, Zakhariádēs and the party leadership agreed upon armed resistance.[89]

The KKE's "third round," or third bout of armed struggle since the beginning of the war, received a major boost from the Yugoslavs. Zakhariádēs still pursued limited goals; he would be content to moderate the policies of the Greek cabinet, and he had instructed the guerrillas to wage only defensive operations against nationalist bands, and not to engage the regular Greek army.[90] The militant wing of the KKE, however, had never quite accepted the Várkiza agreement. Under the leadership of the *kapetánioi*, or guerrilla chieftains, the *andártes*, or insurgents, were increasingly organized for the offensive. The leading *kapetánios*, Márkos Vapheiádēs, the former party leader in Salonika, was readying to confront the regular army.[91] Empowered by Zakhariádēs, in October 1946 Márkos united the local insurgent bands from Macedonia to the Gulf of Corinth into the Democratic Army of Greece (DAG), with himself as its supreme commander. The KPJ clearly favored the offensive policy identified with General Márkos.[92]

88. Peter J. Stavrakis, *The Soviet Union and the Greek Civil War* (Ithaca, forthcoming).
89. For Zakhariádēs's main political and strategic concepts in 1945 and 1946, see Heinz Richter, *British Intervention in Greece: From Varkiza to Civil War (February 1945 to August 1946)* (London, 1985), pp. 246–87, 477–517. Richter's interpretation is convincingly challenged by Ole L. Smith in "The Problems of the Second Plenum of the Central Committee of the KKE, 1946," *Journal of the Hellenic Diaspora* 12, no. 2 (1985):43–62.
90. Eudes, *Kapetanios*, p. 269.
91. Dragan Kljakić, *General Markos* (Zagreb, 1979), p. 124.
92. An excellent summary of the Yugoslav role in the Greek civil war is Nicholas Pappas, "The Soviet-Yugoslav conflict and the Greek Civil War," in Wayne S. Vucinich, ed., *At the Brink of War and Peace: The Tito-Stalin Split in a Historic Perspective* (Brooklyn, 1982), pp. 219–37, 324–32. See also John O. Iatrides, "Civil War, 1945–1949: National and International Aspects," in John O. Iatrides, ed., *Greece in the 1940s: A Nation in Crisis* (Hanover, N.H., 1981), pp. 195–219, 385–92; and Woodhouse, *Struggle for Greece*, pp. 169–258 passim.

Yugoslav aid was crucial for the Greek rebellion. The indoctrination camp for KKE cadres at Buljkes, near Bačka Palanka (Vojvodina), became the rear base of the DAG.[93] Transmissions of Radio Free Greece originated in Yugoslavia, as did most of DAG's food and supplies. According to Slobodan Krstić-Uča, who in 1946 was the chief secretary in Serbia of the Yugoslav security police, Uprava državne bezbednosti (UDB-a, Administration of State Security), Márkos was escorted to Greece from Yugoslav territory in September 1946, obviously after consultations with KPJ leaders. The Yugoslavs furnished Márkos with medical supplies and practically all light weapons—rifles, machine guns, and submachine guns—which had to be Wehrmacht issue, so as not to incriminate Greece's northern neighbors. Moreover, the weapons supplied by Albania and Bulgaria were also of Yugoslav origin: "We gave [them] to the Albanians and Bulgarians, and they to the Greeks."[94]

The supply network for Greece was in the firm hands of Aleksandar Ranković (Marko) (1909–1983), the number three man of the Yugoslav Politburo, who was responsible for the security apparatus. Within the UDB-a the Greek line was administered by Generals Jovo Kapičić and Vojislav Biljanović, as well as by Krstić. In the summer of 1947 the Yugoslavs started to send large shipments of arms to Greece, more quickly and more generously than the USSR and its East European allies. All told, according to Krstić, by 1948 the Yugoslavs had sent 35,000 rifles, 3,500 machine guns, 2,000 German bazookas, 7,000 antitank guns, 10,000 field mines, clothing for 12,000 men, and thirty wagons of food. They furnished all the supplies and equipment for the First DAG Division, including five hundred draught horses, and operated three field hospitals, at Mount Osogovo, Katlanovska Banja, and Jasenovo (at the foot of Mount Babuna), all in Macedonia, for the wounded *andártes*.[95] Yugoslavia became a ready sanctuary for DAG fighters as well as for refugees (by early 1948, 8,000 refugees from Greece were settled in the former German villages of Gakovo and Kruševlje, near Sombor, in Vojvodina). Yugoslavia also exercised influence over the DAG through the Slavic Macedonians of northern Greece and their organization, the Narodnoosloboditelniot front (NOF, National Liberation Front).

93. Pappas, "Soviet-Yugoslav Conflict," p. 222.
94. D. Golubović, "Zašto Markos ne kaže sve," *Duga,* July 17, 1982, p. 28.
95. Ibid., pp. 29–30, Cf. Dedijer, *Novi prilozi,* 3:266–67.

The NOF, though it had been formed in April 1945, before the "third round," became a constituent part of the DAG. It commanded the allegiance of almost half of the DAG's fighters (Márkos himself admitted later that 45 percent of the DAG's fighting force consisted of Macedonians).[96] The NOF's founders included Slavic Macedonians from Greece who had been trained in Yugoslavia and had served as officers in the Yugoslav army. The NOF ostensibly fought for the national rights of the Macedonians "within the framework of democratic Greece," but its underlying goal was the unification of Macedonia within the Yugoslav federation. The NOF's autonomy within the DAG was manifested by special units and the running of separate agitprop and educational networks that promoted Macedonian schools, press, and cultural-educational institutions.[97]

Bulgaria's role in the Greek civil war was much more limited than that of Yugoslavia and its client Albania, perhaps because Yugoslavia's Macedonian policy still went against the grain of Bulgarian national aspirations, despite Sofia's official acceptance of Macedonian national individuality.[98] In March 1947, when the Truman Doctrine was promulgated, Washington assumed the burden of British policy against the Greek insurgents, and American military and economic aid was soon flowing to Greece and Turkey. The American containment policy did not at the time differentiate among the Communist parties; all were considered unqualified agencies of Soviet policy. The growing American presence in the Aegean necessarily had a direct effect on Yugoslavia and Bulgaria, as it brought their Communist leaders much more closely together than Stalin wanted them to be.

In late July 1947, at the Yugoslav resort of Bled (Slovenia), Tito and a Bulgarian delegation led by Georgi Dimitrov reached a series of agreements that affected the future of Yugoslav–Bulgarian relations.

96. Jovan Popovski, *General Markos: Zašto me Staljin nije streljao?* (Belgrade, 1982), pp. 9, 76. According to R. V. Burks, 11,000 Macedonian andártes constituted "somewhat less than half the strength of the army" in early 1948 (*The Dynamics of Communism in Eastern Europe* [Princeton, 1961], p. 102).

97. Kofos, *Nationalism and Communism*, pp. 167, 170–71. The most detailed account of the NOF is Risto Kirjazovski, *Narodnoosloboditelniot front i drugite organizacii na Makedoncite od Egejska Makedonija (1945–1949)* (Skopje, 1985). According to Kirjazovski (p. 176), by the end of the civil war, Slavic Macedonians accounted for 14,000 of the 35,000 DAG troops.

98. Kofos, *Nationalism and Communism*, p. 169.

The two sides agreed to conclude a treaty of friendship and detailed a series of measures on economic relations, imposts, and legal arrangements aimed at establishing the closest possible alliance between the two states. Yugoslavia waived its right to the war reparations incurred by Bulgaria, and Dimitrov concurred with Yugoslav demands for a new policy in Pirin Macedonia. Beginning in September 1947, Bulgaria imported some ninety teachers from Yugoslav Macedonia, introduced new, de-Bulgarized textbooks in Pirin schools, started to promote the Macedonian language and culture, and encouraged contacts among Macedonians on both sides of the frontier. Portraits of Tito and Lazar Koliševski (b. 1914), premier and KPJ secretary of Yugoslav Macedonia, were introduced to the Pirin region alongside those of Dimitrov and Stalin. In view of the "provocations of Greek monarchofascists" in the Balkans, the delegations at Bled pointedly recommended close contacts and coordination between the two governments in all important international affairs that concerned the two countries.[99]

From the Western standpoint, the Bled agreements were clearly aimed against Greece; Bulgaria's full accession to Yugoslavia's tenets on Macedonian affairs was seen as linked to the Yugoslav plan to push into Aegean—or Greek—Macedonia.[100] But whereas the worried Turks, for example, believed that the final dissolution of the Yugoslav–Bulgarian dispute over Macedonia prefigured "Slavic expansion" in the Balkans,[101] the KKE leadership breathed a sigh of relief, convinced that Bled was a response to Stalin's signal for an offensive in Greece. Zakhariádēs, who consistently had impeded the growth of the DAG by restraining Márkos from inflicting more than pinpricks, now gave up the privilege of legality and in mid-September ordered the full mobilization of the KKE. Zakhariádēs's military strategy was no better than his sources of information. In the field by late November, he ordered Márkos to drop guerrilla tactics in favor

99. Slobodan Nešović, *Bledski sporazumi: Tito-Dimitrov (1947)* (Zagreb, 1979), pp. 49–73, 126–34, 63.

100. According to a noted Greek conservative (who offers no proofs for his claim), during the same summer Márkos himself negotiated a new agreement with the Yugoslav and Albanian staffs at Bled. These agreements, which significantly increased military aid to the DAG and placed its officers under the supervision of a joint Balkan Communist staff, were underwritten by the Soviets. See Evangelos Averoff-Tossizza, *Le Feu et la hache: Grèce 46–49* (Paris, 1973), pp. 190–91.

101. Nešović, *Bledski sporazumi*, p. 113.

of positional war—just at the moment when the government's military effort was showing the effects of lavish American aid and expert assistance.[102] Also at the end of November, as the Greek authorities stepped up the execution of imprisoned Communists, Tito and Dimitrov met at Evksinograd near Varna to sign the Yugoslav–Bulgarian friendship treaty. One month later Yugoslav-operated Radio Free Greece announced that a Provisional Greek Democratic Government had been formed on Mount Grámmos, in liberated territory close to the Albanian border city of Korçë. The Greek civil war could no longer be turned backward.

Zakhariádēs was laboring under the misapprehension that Stalin backed a Balkan offensive. On the contrary, the Soviet government and press ignored the Bled and Evksinograd agreements.[103] Soviet annoyance was evident on November 29, after the second meeting between Tito and Dimitrov, when Stalin saluted the Yugoslav state holiday in his most stiffly precise manner. The Soviets evidently took umbrage not only at Tito's actions in Greece but especially at the policies he pursued in Albania. On November 20, Nako Spiru, the member of the Albanian Politburo responsible for economic policy, committed suicide. Despite his long association with the Yugoslavs, Spiru had opposed their measures to control the Albanian economy. A nervous and melancholy twenty-eight-year-old, he felt isolated among his comrades, who either supported the Yugoslavs or dared not oppose them openly. In 1946 he had signed a series of unequal economic deals with Yugoslavia. When he spoke among intimates upon his return from Belgrade, he had commented dryly: "So, are the people saying that Nako Spiru sold Albania to Yugoslavia just as [ex-king] Ahmet Zogu sold it to Italy?" Spiru's desperate protest was all the more poignant because he had the ear of Enver Hoxha, the party leader and premier, and had developed close ties with the Soviets, "who did not conceal their sorrow over his loss."[104]

In the months preceding Spiru's suicide, the Albanian Politburo had become a battleground for pro- and anti-Yugoslav forces. The pro-Yugoslavs were Koçi Xoxe (1911–1949), Pandi Kristo, and Kristo Themelko (a Slavic Macedonian), and they had the tacit support of Tuk Jakova and Bedri Spahiu. Through Xoxe, minister of the

102. Eudes, *Kapetanios*, pp. 302–7.
103. Nešović, *Bledski sporazumi*, pp. 120–22, 164–65.
104. Hoxha, *Titistët*, pp. 292, 356.

interior and organizational secretary of the Partia Komuniste e Shqipërisë (PKSH, Communist Party of Albania), the KPJ exercised almost total control over the Albanian party and state administration. Spiru tried to offset the Yugoslav influence by relying on the Soviets and on behind-the-scenes support from Hoxha and two of Hoxha's supporters, Hysni Kapo and Gogo Nushi. Yugoslavia's extensive economic investment and aid in Albania, as well as its oversight of Albanian party, military, and security affairs, proceeded from the premise that Albania was hardly distinguishable from Yugoslavia's own underdeveloped republics. In fact, Albania's unification with Yugoslavia had been taken for granted by the KPJ leaders since the end of the war. Moša Pijade, for example, proposed that the plans for the new federal hall in Belgrade include room for seven cabinets, for Yugoslavia's six republics and Albania.[105] But Belgrade had no hope of bringing this curious assumption to reality against Soviet opposition.

Hints of Soviet displeasure merely hastened Tito's designs. After Spiru's suicide, according to Djilas, "Tito became increasingly nervous and started to hurry the unification with Albania. In his circle of intimates, he did not hide his fears, nor could he, that the 'Russians' will beat us to it and 'grab' Albania."[106] In December his emissaries imposed upon Albania a Yugoslav-controlled joint coordinating commission, which was to oversee the integration of the two economies. A similar mechanism was proposed for the unified command of the Yugoslav, Albanian, and Bulgarian armies, as a first step toward the unification of the Balkan Communist armed forces. When General Mehmet Shehu, chief of the Albanian general staff, opposed this idea, he was dismissed at the instigation of Koçi Xoxe.[107] Moreover, Djilas says, "under the pretext that Albania was threatened by 'Greek reaction' and the 'imperialists' stationed in Greece, Tito ordered that two complete and completely equipped divisions be readied for stationing in Albania."[108] A Yugoslav air regiment was already on its way to Albania.

Stalin's reaction was swift. He undoubtedly linked the Yugoslav moves with the proclamation of a Greek provisional government at

105. Dedijer, *Novi prilozi,* 2:902.
106. Djilas, *Vlast,* p. 121.
107. Hoxha, *Titistët,* pp. 387–403.
108. Djilas, *Vlast,* p. 121.

Grámmos, and at the end of December he summoned a Yugoslav party delegation to Moscow. He specifically requested Djilas's participation in the mission, hoping perhaps to win this key Politburo member away from Tito.[109] Upon his arrival in Moscow in early January 1948, Djilas was stunned by Stalin's provocative show of support for Yugoslavia's "swallowing" of Albania.[110] The point was to hasten an unvarnished avowal of Yugoslavia's plans for Albania while simultaneously lulling the Yugoslavs into a false sense of security.

The effect of the baited snare was to overturn the Yugoslav Balkan policy by enticing it into overdrive. On January 26, Tito formally requested from Hoxha a base for the Yugoslav divisions at Korçë, opposite Grámmos, so that the Yugoslav units would be able to intervene quickly in case of Greek nationalist provocation. Convinced that the Yugoslav occupation of Albania was imminent, Hoxha secretly, on his own authority, appealed to Stalin for protection.[111] At practically the same time, in Bucharest, Dimitrov spoke to the press about the inevitability of a federation that would unite all East European people's democracies, including Greece, whose participation he pointedly stressed.[112] Just as pointedly, *Pravda* disavowed his statement on January 29. While behind the scenes Molotov threatened the Yugoslav leadership with a public rift, Stalin summoned Tito and Dimitrov to Moscow. In an affront to the Soviet leader, Tito sent Kardelj instead.

It is generally agreed nowadays that, as Tito put it, the "first conflict [between Moscow and Belgrade] broke out on account of Albania."[113] Indeed, the sensitivity over the Yugoslav forces in Albania and Belgrade's military aid to the DAG obliged Kardelj, as late as 1953, to forbid any reference to these subjects in Tito's official biography.[114] But it was the larger issue of Yugoslavia's independent and

109. Ibid., p. 123.
110. Djilas, *Conversations with Stalin*, pp. 143–46.
111. Hoxha, *Titistët*, pp. 405–10.
112. Dedijer, *Dokumenti 1948*, 1:167.
113. "Zapisnik sa sednice CK KPJ od 12. i 13. aprila 1948," in Dedijer, *Novi prilozi*, 3:370. Cf. Djilas, *Vlast*, p. 118.
114. Dedijer, *Novi prilozi*, 3:318. As late as 1961, Djilas considered it prudent to say nothing about the fact that Kardelj blamed Tito for the precipitate stationing of two divisions in Albania. Djilas had been in Moscow since mid-January 1948 and welcomed Kardelj's delegation there on February 8. When asked why such a tense period was chosen to press for troops in Albania, "Kardelj responded with resignation, 'The Old Man [Tito] is

combative foreign policy, as well as Belgrade's readiness to assert its militant alternative to the USSR in Eastern Europe, especially among the Balkan Communist parties, that dominated the dramatic meeting with Stalin on February 10. Stalin charged the Bulgarians and Yugoslavs with ignoring the Soviet Union. He insisted, over Kardelj's objections, that when Yugoslavia had signed the Bled agreements without consultation with Moscow, it had been pursuing a policy, not simply committing an error of omission. Dimitrov's federalist schemes and the projected entry of the Yugoslav divisions into Albania, too, were initiated without Soviet approval. The Albanian adventure could still lead to serious international complications, as it "would give the Americans an excuse to attack"—and just at a time when the Soviets wanted "to reach a state of affairs with the Americans that would provide them some sort of peace."[115] When the treaty of Evksinograd committed the Balkan partners to all "initiatives directed against hotbeds of agression," it was calling for preventive war. Stalin, too, believed that the reference was to Greece. In his nervousness about the DAG's general offensive, which commenced on February 5, and the shelling of Salonika by Márkos's forces a day before the Moscow conclave, he was unwilling to excuse such zeal. In Stalin's view, the phrase from Evksinograd was an excess perhaps forgivable in an inexperienced Komsomol activist but never in Tito and Dimitrov.

The Greek uprising had to fold immediately. "What do you think," Stalin lectured Kardelj, "that Great Britain and the United States— the United States, the most powerful state in the world—will permit you to break their line of communication in the Mediterranean Sea! Nonsense. And we have no navy."[116] Stalin insisted that the federa-

pushing this. You know yourself. . . .' " Djilas excluded the "Moscow whisperings with Kardelj from [his] *Conversations with Stalin,* so as not to give arguments to Soviet-Albanian propaganda at a time when the whole matter was still of current interest": Djilas, *Vlast,* p. 131.

115. "Zapisnik sa sednice CK KPJ od 1. marta 1948. godine," in Dedijer, *Novi prilozi,* 3:304.

116. Almost identical accounts of the meeting can be found in Djilas's memoirs; see *Conversations with Stalin,* pp. 173–84, and *Vlast,* pp. 131–36. Kardelj's version differs considerably. Some of its peculiarities, as on the nature of federation with Bulgaria, probably result from confusion between this and earlier meetings, but in some particulars, as on the importance and relevance of the stationing of Yugoslav troops in Albania, Kardelj's account is dissembling and unreliable. Moreover, it is contradicted by the extant minutes of the KPJ CC meeting of March 1, 1948. See Kardelj, *Sećanja,* pp. 111–17.

tion between Bulgaria and Yugoslavia be effected immediately. And
in the early hours of February 12, Molotov summoned Kardelj to the
Kremlin and ordered him to sign a treaty that obliged Yugoslavia to
consult the USSR on all foreign policy matters.

The meeting with Stalin changed nothing. Stalin's insistence on a
Yugoslav-Bulgarian federation, which initially would exclude Albania, was no more than a delaying tactic. Nor, given Dimitrov's
mood, was this the most reliable way of exercising control over
Belgrade. At his dacha near Moscow, Dimitrov tried to convince
Kardelj that the federation would make the South Slavs strong and
independent of Stalin. "Together," Dimitrov argued, "we shall build
a more democratic socialism."[117] On February 22, Moscow rejected
new Yugoslav economic requests. The time for surgery was at hand.

The question of socialism came up again at the meeting of the KPJ
CC on March 1. In a statement that alluded to the Soviet doctrine of
people's democracy, Kardelj noted that the ideological differences
between Moscow and Belgrade had to do with the question of socialist development in Eastern Europe, as the Soviets did not wish to
see "established among these countries a certain formation that
would permit the development of these countries toward socialism."
Tito agreed, noting that Yugoslavia confirmed its path to socialism
despite the limiting Soviet notion of encirclement. He stressed that if
Yugoslavia was to remain independent, it had to withstand Soviet
economic pressure. Under the circumstances, the federation with Bulgaria could only introduce a Trojan horse inside the KPJ. As for
Albania, Kardelj intimated that Moscow wished to edge the
Yugoslavs out of Hoxha's army: "We must maintain a tight grip on
Albania, because we invested a great deal there and the country is
important to us. We should continue our policy on all questions of
political and economic cooperation as before. We should demand
that the Soviet advisers in Albania be within our group. (Their
number according to our appraisal.) Our division is near Ohrid. It
would not go alone, but with still greater forces; let each grab his
own."[118]

And indeed, the KPJ had already engineered a turnabout in Al-

117. Kardelj, *Sećanja*, p. 118.
118. "Zapisnik sa sednice CK KPJ od 1. marta 1948. godine," in Dedijer, *Novi prilozi*,
3:305.

bania. During the marathon Eighth Plenum of the PKSH CC (February 26–March 8), Koçi Xoxe carried out a purge of anti-Yugoslavs, forcing Hoxha into self-critical retreat. On March 18 the Soviets withdrew all of their military advisers from Yugoslavia. And on March 27, the seventh anniversary of the military coup against the Yugoslav government that acceded to the Axis, Stalin sent his famous First Letter to the KPJ CC. Two days earlier, the Communists had staged their coup d'état in Czechoslovakia. Within a month, as the neologism "cold war" rapidly gained currency, five West European countries concluded a treaty of self-defense, the Brussels Treaty, which was the forerunner of NATO.

The violence of Stalin's words was calculated to shake the leadership of the KPJ. Stalin defended the withdrawal of Soviet military and civilian advisers on the grounds that they could not function in an increasingly hostile atmosphere and under the surveillance of Yugoslav security organs—a practice that the Soviets otherwise encountered "only in bourgeois countries, and by no means in all of them." The worsening of Soviet–Yugoslav relations, according to Stalin, was due to several factors. Yugoslav officials, notably such "dubious Marxists" as Milovan Djilas, Svetozar Vukmanović-Tempo, Boris Kidrič (1912–1953), and Aleksandar Ranković, were responsible for the anti-Soviet atmosphere that was gaining ground in Yugoslavia. Stalin clearly wanted to bring down these key officials, who were responsible for, respectively, the party Agitprop (including all media and cultural affairs), the political directorate of the army, the economy, and security and cadre policy. Their "left phrases" about the degeneration of the Soviet party, the prevalence of great-state chauvinism in the USSR, Soviet economic penetration, and the like were strikingly reminiscent of Trotsky. Moreover, the notion that Yugoslavia alone was the true standard-bearer of revolutionary socialism was also a throwback to Trotsky's leftist verbiage about permanent revolution. "We think," Stalin added portentously, "that the political career of Trotsky is sufficiently instructive."

Taking advantage of Tito's penchant for excessive centralism and secretiveness (membership, party hierarchy, and official conclaves were kept under conspiratorial wraps even after the war), Stalin was at his most unctuously sanctimonious as he attacked the lack of democracy in the KPJ, the control of Ranković's UDB-a over the party, and the supposed dissolution of the KPJ within the ranks of the NFJ, the organization of the nonparty masses. And quite ignoring the facts, he charged the KPJ with a lack of class militancy. Hence, in a virtual paraphrase of Kardelj's and Djilas's criticism of the Italian and French parties at Szklarska Poręba, he also attacked the leftist KPJ for its "opportunistic theory of peaceful transition to socialism," manifested above all in its alleged toleration of capitalistic, or kulak, elements in the countryside. Finally, in a classic Stalinist gambit, he charged the Yugoslavs with harboring a known British spy in the person of Vladimir Velebit, the assistant foreign minister.[119]

From the moment he decided to attack Tito, Stalin proceeded with consistency. From the First Letter through the final break of June 1948 and thereafter, the Soviet leader impeached the leadership of the KPJ and argued for an internal turnabout in Yugoslav communism. Supremely confident of his towering stature in all Communist parties, Stalin expected his faithful to push aside all "dubious Marxists": "We do not doubt that the Yugoslav party masses would indignantly disown this anti-Soviet criticism as alien and hostile to them, if only they knew about it. We think that this is precisely the reason why the cited Yugoslav leaders make these criticisms in secret, behind the scenes, behind the backs of the masses."[120] The struggle for the Yugoslav party membership was joined.

119. Dedijer, *Dokumenti 1948*, 1:201–6.
120. Ibid., p. 204.

2

Factions

The struggle we began more than fifty years ago for the resolution of party affairs was very hard, since factionalism was
deeply rooted, and it went on a long time, practically from the
founding of the KPJ. . . .

Tito, 1977

Though Tito retained a lively memory of Stalin's bans, he was
nevertheless astonished at the brutality of the First Letter, which
made clear Stalin's determination, as a start, to make a shambles of
the Yugoslav Politburo. Two of its members, Tito and Kardelj, to
whom the letter was addressed, he sneered at. Two more, Djilas and
Ranković, he dismissed as dubious Marxists. More distressing still,
Stalin's references to whisperings in Yugoslavia about great-state
chauvinism in the USSR alerted Tito to the presence of a Soviet
confidant in his Politburo. Indeed, Sreten Žujović-Crni, the general
secretary of the NFJ, transmitted the details of the KPJ CC meeting of
March 1, 1948, to the Soviet ambassador, A. I. Lavrentiev. And
Andrija Hebrang, the ranking Croat Communist and Žujović's occasional ally, who had been dismissed from the Politburo in April 1946,
had to be restrained from seizing Stalin's letter as justification for a
comeback in the interest of moderation. Stalin's deluge threatened to
inundate the parched banks of Yugoslav communism with fresh factional runoffs.

The history of the KPJ was the history of unremitting internal
struggle. The importance of factional conflict in the Communist
movement has always commanded attention. But contrary to recent
interpretations, which regard Communist factionalism as ka-
leidoscopic, "operating on the basis of personal struggles for power
and influence rather than on any particular, consistent ideological

lines or specific issue-orientations,"[1] Yugoslav Communist factions did not exhibit a succession of shifting phases. They were stable because they expressed the interlaced structure of revolutionary responses to the national question in Yugoslavia.[2] The Communists endeavored to become the leading party among each of Yugoslavia's nationalities—to constitute themselves as *the* nation, as Marx counseled parenthetically—and hence they necessarily expressed many contradictory national viewpoints, sometimes even in the bourgeois sense of the word. As a result, Yugoslav factional victors could not safely adopt the losers' platform. The factional wars seesawed back and forth, each side depending for weight on variations of old programs.

As was normally the case after the Bolshevik revolution, Yugoslav communism had its origins in factional struggle.[3] The Socijalistička radnička partija Jugoslavije (komunista) (SRPJ[k], Socialist Workers' Party of Yugoslavia [Communist]), which was founded in April 1919, was a product of several splits in the socialist movement of the lands that were joined in December 1918 within the Kingdom of the Serbs, Croats, and Slovenes—commonly Yugoslavia. The socialist movement in Slovenia, Croatia-Slavonia, and Dalmatia, and to a lesser extent in the other South Slavic lands that were previously parts of Austria-Hungary, was manifestly unitaristic—that is, it adhered to the ideology of the "national oneness" of Serbs, Croats, and Slovenes and disavowed the national and historical individuality of these peoples as a reactionary idea. The prominent South Slavic socialist leaders of the Habsburg Monarchy—such men as Vitomir Korać, Vilim Bukšeg, and Anton Kristan—took these ideas one step further in the course of World War I. They increasingly favored victory for the Entente and the emergence of a Yugoslav state, which they saw as the progressive outcome of a national revolution that must be supported. After the collapse of Austria-Hungary, these right socialists saw nothing wrong in taking part in efforts to speed up unilateral

1. Gavriel D. Ra'anan, *International Policy Formation in the USSR: Factional "Debates" during the Zhdanovshchina* (Hamden, Conn., 1983), pp. 7–8.
2. The origins and structure of the nationality problem are discussed in Ivo Banac, *The National Question in Yugoslavia: Origins, History, Politics* (Ithaca, 1984).
3. The emergence and early years of communism in Yugoslavia are discussed in Ivo Banac, "The Communist Party of Yugoslavia during the Period of Legality (1919–1921)," in Ivo Banac, ed., *The Effects of World War I: The Class War after the Great War; The Rise of Communist Parties in East Central Europe, 1919–1921* (Brooklyn, 1983), pp. 188–230.

unification with Serbia. After the unification, ostensibly working for the "special interests of the working class," they assumed cabinet posts in the Belgrade royal ministries, thereby furnishing socialist authority for the flawed process that was already being challenged by the movements of disaffected nationalities, notably the Croat peasant movement of Stjepan Radić.[4]

The opponents of "ministerialists" in Slovenia and Croatia were just as unitaristic as Korać and his right socialists but were less firmly rooted in the reformist trade unions, and, being receptive to the non-urban strata, were quite alert to the mass disenchantment with Serbian supremacy in the immediate postunification period. Such men as Djuro Cvijić (1896–1938) and Kamilo Horvatin, among Zagreb's pro-Bolshevik intelligentsia, were graduates of the prewar Nationalist Youth movement, which sired various forms of rebellion, including that of the Sarajevo assassins. To their minds, the ideal of a messianic South Slavic state was betrayed by the bourgeoisie. And since the middle classes had proved incapable of bringing forth an amalgamated Yugoslav nation, that task, too, fell to the proletarian revolution. The left-wing socialists of Croatia and Slovenia viewed the Belgrade authorities as counterrevolutionary, opposed socialist participation in the government, called for a boycott of interim legislative bodies, denounced the government's limited agrarian reform, and— partly under the influence of former Austro-Hungarian prisoners of war, who were returning from Soviet Russia with red allegiances— demanded that the socialists of Yugoslavia adhere to the Third International.[5]

The Serbian socialist movement, by contrast, developed in a small, nationally homogeneous, and predominantly agricultural state. Its leaders were intellectuals and students whose socialism was doctrinaire and remote from the economic struggle of factory workers. Trade unions were relatively weak in Serbia because capitalist productive relations were slow to develop there. Hence their emphasis on "pure" class struggle, a tradition of keeping aloof from "petit bour-

---

4. The right socialist view of participation in royal governments is expressed in Vitomir Korać, *Povjest Radničkog Pokreta u Hrvatskoj i Slavoniji* (Zagreb, 1929), 1:254–55.

5. On the role of the Austro-Hungarian soldiers of South Slavic extraction captured by the Russians in the shaping of Yugoslav communism, see Ivo Banac, "South Slav Prisoners of War in Revolutionary Russia," in Samuel R. Williamson, Jr., and Peter Pastor, eds., *Essays on World War I: Origins and Prisoners of War* (Brooklyn, 1983), pp. 139–44.

geois" peasants, and a tendency to view the national question as of concern only to the bourgeoisie. In their view, bourgeois parties alone—the Radicals of Nikola Pašić, for example—were supposed to fight for Serbian national aspirations, thereby contributing to the development of capitalism, without which, according to the "stage theory" of revolution, socialist development could not proceed. As a result, by a curious dialectic, Serbian socialists (and their Bosnian comrades, who were under the strong influence of the Serbian Social Democratic party) saw nothing irregular in the expansionist and assimilatory program of the Serbian national leadership. By the same token, their unvarnished view of the bourgeoisie made them equally immune to Yugoslavist unitarism and to any temptation to participate in the "national revolution." Initially, too, the Serbian and Bosnian parties marched in step into the Comintern encampment.

Following the split with the "ministerialists" and the Unification Congress (Belgrade, April 20–23, 1919), Yugoslavia's left socialists briefly cohered within the SRPJ(k), which was a combination of, on the one hand, Serbian and Bosnian Marxist orthodoxy (more Kautskyan than Leninist) and, on the other, Croat and Slovene unitaristic (and Russophile) philobolshevism (see figure 1). The precarious bond fell apart one year later at the Second Congress, held at Vukovar (Slavonia) from June 20 to 24, 1920. The leftist majority pushed through a new program, new statute, and new unambiguous name for the party—the Communist Party of Yugoslavia (KPJ). The elections for the leadership demonstrated that the left commanded the votes of 242 (or 240) delegates against 63 (or 65) votes of the so-called centrists (centrumaši).[6]

The split engendered by the friction at Vukovar cut across the old divisions. Croatian centrists, such as Vladimir Bornemissa and Gejza Brudniak, were opposed to the party's new statute, with its provisions

6. Among general studies on the history of the KPJ, see especially Ivan Avakumovic, *History of the Communist Party of Yugoslavia*, vol. 1 (Aberdeen, 1964); Fedor I. Cicak, "The Communist Party of Yugoslavia between 1919–1924: An Analysis of Its Formative Process," Ph.D. dissertation, Indiana University, 1965; Rodoljub Čolaković, Dragoslav Janković, and Pero Morača, eds., *Pregled istorije Saveza komunista Jugoslavije* (Belgrade, 1963); Pero Morača, *Istorija Saveza komunista Jugoslavije: Kratak pregled* (Belgrade, 1966); Pero Morača and Dušan Bilandžić, *Avangarda, 1919–1969* (Belgrade, 1969); Pero Morača, Dušan Bilandžić, and Stanislav Stojanović, *Istorija Saveza komunista Jugoslavije: Kratak pregled* (Belgrade, 1976); and Stanislav Stojanović, ed., *Istorija Saveza komunista Jugoslavije* (Belgrade, 1985).

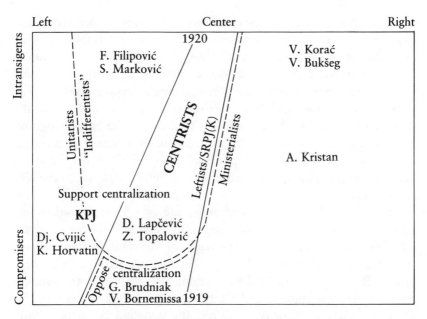

1. From the Unification Congress to post-Vukovar, 1919–1920

for the full centralization of the party, including the abolition of
regional (provincial) committees and top-down leadership ("secretaries [of district party committees] are direct organs of the Central
Party Council").[7] But unlike the Serbian and Bosnian centrists, such
as the veteran Serbian socialists Dragiša Lapčević and Živko Topalović, Croatian centrists were just as unitaristic as Croatian Communists. Hence they did not object to the reference to national oneness in
the lengthy party program: "The KPJ will continue to defend the idea
of national oneness and the equality of all nationalities in the
country."[8]
    The Serbian centrists, by contrast, objected less to centralization
than to the new Bolshevik program of the KPJ, with its declared aim
of immediate struggle for the dictatorship of the proletariat in the

7. "Statut," in Moša Pijade, ed., Istorijski arhiv Komunističke partije Jugoslavije, vol. 2,
Kongresi i zemaljske konferencije KPJ, 1919–1937 (Belgrade, 1949), p. 45.
8. "Politička situacija i zadaci Komunističke partije u Jugoslaviji," in ibid., p. 42. On the
Vukovar Congress, see Zdravko Krnić, ed., Drugi kongres KPJ: Materijali sa simpozija
održanog 22. i 23. VI 1970. povodom 50-godišnjice Drugog (Vukovarskog) kongresa KPJ
1920 (Slavonski Brod, 1972).

form of a Soviet republic, establishment of a popular red army, and
expropriation of the bourgeoisie.[9] On the national question, however, their views were identical to those of such Serbian Communists
as Filip Filipović and Sima Marković (1888–1938), who were indifferent to the issue of nationality. These two secretaries of the KPJ's
Central Party Council, elected at Vukovar, kept nationality out of the
debate, reduced it to the one quoted sentence in the party program,
but also endowed it with a touch of realism by inserting an ambiguous reference to "all the nationalities." "The people who were at the
head of our movement in Croatia," wrote Sima Marković to the KPJ
representative in the Comintern in July 1920, "pursued a purely
centrist policy thanks to the earlier statute by which, instead of one
party, we actually had a loose federation of several regional parties.
The new statute, based on the principle of full centralization, put an
end to this ailing system. Though the regional party princes rose
against centralization more than anything else, the Vukovar Congress
accepted the new statute (and all the other proposed resolutions) by
an overwhelming majority."[10] When the Croatian centrists, in July
1920, refused to yield the party newspaper, archives, and treasury to
the KPJ's Liquidation Executive Committee, they were expelled. By
December, after the publication of the Manifesto of the Opposition,
all other centrists, mainly Serbians and Bosnians, were expelled, too.

The KPJ actually made advances after its consolidation of the leftist
platform, and its showing at the elections for the Constituent Assembly in November 1920 was quite strong. The KPJ gained 198,736
votes, or 59 mandates (as opposed to 46,792 votes, or 10 mandates,
by the "ministerialists" and 360 votes for the centrists—the latter in
Zagreb, the only district where they competed). It was now the fourth
strongest party in Yugoslavia, with 12.34 percent of the ballots cast.
But these advances were deceptive. The KPJ performed below its
national average in the more industrialized Slovenia and Croatia-
Slavonia and in Bosnia-Hercegovina, areas where the parties of the
disaffected nationalities were legal. In fact, the KPJ's most impressive
showing was in utterly undeveloped Montenegro and Macedonia;

9. For the objections of Serbian centrists at Vukovar, see the remarks of one of their
former leaders, Živko Topalović, *Začeci socijalizma i komunizma u Jugoslaviji* (London,
1960), pp. 90–109.
10. Arhiv Instituta za historiju radničkog pokreta Hrvatske (AIHRPH), Fond Kominterne:
I/11: Sima Marković to Ilija Milkić, Zagreb, July 14, 1920.

there the KPJ was the only outlet for the protest votes of the recusant nationalities. Hence the relative electoral vitality of the KPJ obscured the party's isolation, which became manifest with the first tests of strength between the Communists and the established order.

In December 1920 the Communists led a series of strikes that closed the important mines of Slovenia and Bosnia. In response, the government sent the army to suppress the miners and then banned Communist propaganda and the work of party organizations. The KPJ offices and newspapers were seized and shut down. In August 1921, after several assassinations by young extremists acting on their own authority (the group that killed Milorad Drašković, a former minister of the interior, was called Red Justice), the KPJ was formally banned and known Communist leaders were arrested as instigators of terrorist acts. As a result, the party that in May 1920 had claimed some 50,000 members could count no more than 688 members in 1924. The parties of the disaffected nationalities, such as Radić's Croat Peasant Party, which the Communists denounced as an organization of "fat bellies and empty heads . . . existing only on the ignorance and lack of consciousness of peasants and some workers," did nothing to relieve the plight of the KPJ.[11]

The recovery of the Yugoslav Communist movement was a slow and painful process; it could not begin until the KPJ carefully examined the causes and implications of its decline and scrutinized the inherent weaknesses of its stand on the national question.[12] The slow reappraisal occasioned a new round of factional struggle that lasted for the remainder of the 1920s. The broad division between the right and left factions started over the organizational question (see figure 2). The right was led by Sima Marković, Lazar Stefanović (1885–

11. Lupoglavski seljaci i radnici, "Glas sa sela," *Štampa*, Dec. 24, 1921, p. 2.

12. Among the voluminous literature about the KPJ's evolving positions on the national question in Yugoslavia, see Dušan Lukač, *Radnički pokret u Jugoslaviji i nacionalno pitanje, 1918–1941* (Belgrade, 1972); Latinka Perović, *Od centralizma do federalizma: KPJ u nacionalnom pitanju* (Zagreb, 1984); Desanka Pešić, *Jugoslovenski komunisti i nacionalno pitanje, 1919–1935* (Belgrade, 1983); Janko Pleterski, *Komunistička partija Jugoslavije i nacionalno pitanje, 1919–1941* (Belgrade, 1971); Paul Shoup, *Communism and the Yugoslav National Question* (New York, 1968); Wayne S. Vucinich, "Nationalism and Communism," in *Contemporary Yugoslavia: Twenty Years of Socialist Experiment*, ed. Wayne S. Vucinich (Berkeley, 1969), pp. 236–84, 391–402; and three works by Gordana Vlajčić: *KPJ i nacionalno pitanje u Jugoslaviji* (Zagreb, 1974), *Revolucija i nacije: Evolucija stavova vodstava KPJ i Kominterne 1919–1929. godine* (Zagreb, 1978), and *Jugoslavenska revolucija i nacionalno pitanje, 1919–1927* (Zagreb, 1984).

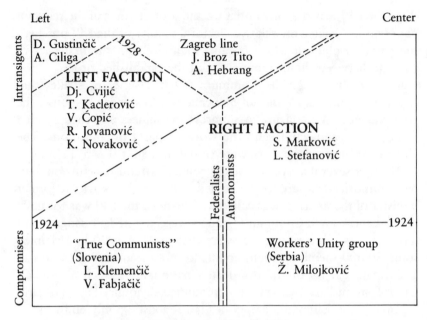

Left   Center

Intransigents	D. Gustinčič *1928* Zagreb line	
	A. Ciliga J. Broz Tito	
	LEFT FACTION A. Hebrang	
	Dj. Cvijić	
	T. Kaclerović	
	V. Ćopić	
	R. Jovanović RIGHT FACTION	
	K. Novaković S. Marković	
	L. Stefanović	

D. Gustinčič ⟋ *1928* ⟍ Zagreb line
A. Ciliga ⟋   J. Broz Tito
   ⟋ LEFT FACTION   A. Hebrang
   Dj. Cvijić
   T. Kaclerović
   V. Ćopić
   R. Jovanović   RIGHT FACTION
   K. Novaković ⟋   S. Marković
                              L. Stefanović

Federalists | Autonomists

1924   1924

Compromisers

"True Communists"   Workers' Unity group
(Slovenia)   (Serbia)
   L. Klemenčič   Ž. Milojković
   V. Fabjačič

2. The left and right in the 1920s

1950), and Života Milojković (1888–1947), all veterans of the Serbian socialist movement and the latter two among Belgrade's leading
trade unionists. Their faction worked through legal channels, notably
the labor movement, to regain the government's approval for a revived KPJ. The left faction favored an underground organization on
the Leninist model and called for an appraisal of Yugoslavia's on-
going political problems in accordance with Communist theory. The
faction's principal figures came from various places: Djuro Cvijić and
Vladimir Ćopić (1891–1939) headed the KPJ's organization in
Zagreb; Triša Kaclerović (1897–1964), Rajko Jovanović (1898–
1942), and Kosta Novaković (1886–1938) were the leading Communist journalists in Belgrade. They were all, however, typical Communist intellectuals. Their following was centered mainly in Croatia and
was thinnest in Serbia, notably in Belgrade.

Though the national question was the key to all the differences
among the factions, the positions of the participants in the debate
over this issue were by no means consistent. Before 1923 both sides
were blind to the real meaning of the national question, refusing to
recognize that the movements of non-Serb nationalities had a mass

base and expressed the interests of the lower classes. The Croat struggle in particular was seen as a creature of native capitalists. *Borba* (Struggle), the organ of the left faction in Zagreb, believed that the national radicalism of Radić's Croat Peasant Party and the Croat Party of Right, an urban nationalist party that stemmed from the pre-1914 Croato-Habsburg movement of Josip Frank, was nothing but a bogey invented by Croat capitalists to put pressure on the Serbian bourgeoisie: "The phraseology and ideology of these intra-strata and their Frankist and Radićist parties are only the outward shell of the so-called Croat problem. The basic content of that problem, however, lies above all in the struggle between the Croat and Serb bourgeoisie."[13]

The leaders of the right faction held identical positions, but adapted them to their factional requirements. At the First Land Conference of the KPJ, held in Vienna in July 1922, Sima Marković noted that the ruling bloc of Serb parties and the oppositional bloc of Croat parties were the two main foci of Yugoslavia's political life, and held that both blocs represented the interests of their respective bourgeoisies, who were attempting to equate their class interests with the interests of their respective nationalities. "That maneuver, unfortunately, has succeeded up to a point, especially in Croatia, where nationalism has not yet disappeared in the working class." Though the struggle of the Croat opposition ran parallel to that of the KPJ, every effort should be made to remove the poor peasant masses, "which by their position belong to us," from under the influence of Radić's party.[14]

Even at that early date, however, voices of dissent were raised within each faction. In the left faction, Kosta Novaković noted at the Vienna conference that the non-Serb national movements were a response to harsh oppression, directed mainly at the peasantry. In Macedonia, to which he devoted special attention, "slogans of autonomy and widest self-government could not satisfy the population. Here, more than in any other region of Yugoslavia, the principle of national

13. "Sitna buržoazija i seljaštvo u hrvatskoj politici," *Borba*, April 29, 1922, p. 4. In an earlier article *Borba* claimed that modern Croat capitalism had no connection with nineteenth-century Croat nationalism: "Its ideology is *the ideology of the modern bourgeoisie*. Its economic aim is *the exploitation of the whole of Yugoslavia*. Its political goal is *the state of the Serbs, Croats, and Slovenes, but without Serbian hegemony*": "Klasni sastav 'Hrv. Bloka' i njegova politika," *Borba*, April 20, 1922, p. 4.

14. AIHRPH, Fond Kominterne: 18/3/I: "REZOLUCIJA o političkoj situaciji i najbližim zadacima Partije" (Vienna, July 10, 1922), pp. 9–10, 14.

self-determination is part of the [political] agenda." In the right faction, Marković's Slovene allies deserted him on the nationality question. Lovro Klemenčič (1891–1928) and Vladislav Fabjančič (1894–1950), two leading Communists in Slovenia, the latter a former Yugoslavist unitarist, also pointed to Serbian misrule as the chief cause of the national resistance of non-Serbs of all classes. Moreover, in the first attack on Yugoslavist unitarism within the KPJ, Klemenčič affirmed the national individuality of Serbs, Croats, and Slovenes, arguing that theories of their national oneness were nothing but a mask for imperialism, reaction, and white terror. The Klemenčič-Fabjančič group of "True Communists," as they styled themselves, seceded from the KPJ on two occasions, in 1923 and 1924, before their final expulsion by the Comintern. But these consistent federalists always directed their hardest blows at the left faction, which, despite its reluctance to abandon unitarism, evidently was considered a greater threat to Slovene and Croat individuality than the Serbian and antifederalist coterie of Sima Marković.[15]

The inconsistencies in factional views on the national question were turned adrift in 1923. In January of that year the KPJ formed a legal party, the Independent Workers' Party of Yugoslavia, whose organizations and press became a public battleground where the factions contended over the national question. At the urging of the Communist International, whose Fourth Congress in November 1922 ruled that the class and national aims of the proletariat of the oppressed nations supplemented each other, Yugoslav Communists commenced a painstaking debate on the national question. In the course of that debate the left faction became identified with the federalist program of state organization, an antiunitarist stand on the links among the South Slavic nationalities, and support for the non-

15. Lukač, Radnički pokret, pp. 83–85. According to Klemenčič, the "linguistic, religious, and ethno-historical differences between the Serbs and Bulgars were far fewer than those between the Serbs and Slovenes. Hence, if Serbs and Slovenes are considered one people, it is . . . more [logical] that the Serbs and Bulgars in fact are one people." In Klemenčič's skewed scheme, the adventurist "liquidators" of the "Kaclerović-Novaković-Cvijić Serbian Left group" consistently were undoing the constructive legal work of Marković's "Communist faction." One of their acts of sabotage was the defense of the "thesis of the so-called national oneness and centralism—the slogan that cloaked white terror!": AIHRPH, Fond Kominterne: 50/II-1, 2: "Komunistička partija u S.H.S." (March 2, 1924), p. 5.

Serb national movements. The right faction was antifederalist (opting for autonomism, that is, a localized and limited form of self-government that was not based on nationality), technically antiunitarist (Marković continued to maintain that the individuality of each South Slavic people was as inconsequential as their supposed oneness, though he ultimately went along with individuality), and hostile to the non-Serb national movements.

It is important to note that these opposing views stemmed in part from contrary assessments of the Yugoslav state and of Communist prospects for revolution in Yugoslavia. The left faction, counting among its principals many disenchanted Yugoslavist unitarists, adapted itself to the national movements, which plainly were opposed to the centralist Yugoslav state. This was not, as contemporary Serbian historians frequently assert, a policy of senseless obedience to the Comintern line, according to which the destruction of the "offspring of Versailles" among the East European successor states would weaken the imperialist front against the first socialist state. True, both the Comintern and the left faction used Yugoslavia's national question, but they did not invent it; the breakup of Yugoslavia was facilitated less by the Comintern line than by national inequality. The promotion of the centralist Yugoslav state, which the Yugoslav Communists favored in 1919, was not simply bad from the standpoint of the Soviets' state interest; it was harmful to the prospects of Communist revolution in Yugoslavia—even among the Serbs, who were inured to the arguments of various proponents of centralism.

When Djuro Cvijić and the left faction in general called for the federalization of Yugoslavia, they were already convinced that the national question could not be solved within the Yugoslav parliamentary order; the goal of federalism was a part of the revolutionary process throughout the Balkans. This view was deepened by Rajko Jovanović, who denounced the autonomism of Sima Marković as a tactic that isolated the Communists from the national movements while contributing to their alliance with the autonomist bourgeoisie.[16] As for Marković, he did not deny that the national question could be solved only by socialism. But precisely because he did not envision a speedy socialist revolution in Yugoslavia, he saw the task

---

16. Rajko Jovanović, "Nacionalno pitanje," *Radnik-Delavec,* Nov. 4, 1923, p. 4.

of the Communists as consisting of finding ways to "reduce national struggles to a minimum within the framework of capitalist society." He firmly held that the national question was really a constitutional question. The Communists had to work for the autonomist organization of capitalist—but fully democratic—Yugoslavia. Political autonomy would establish capitalist equality, restrict hegemony, and secure national peace in Yugoslavia; "political groupings along national lines would become superfluous and class struggle would be given free reign."[17]

Sima Marković was indifferent to the national question but not to alliances with the national movements, which in his view were always bourgeois to the core. He would have no truck with the peasant masses of Croatia and Slovenia, whose alleged "national-bourgeois revolutionism" he dismissed as "fairy tales for children."[18] The left faction, too, was not enamored of Stjepan Radić, but its leaders clearly perceived that Radić's party "became the representative of the whole Croat people in the full sense of the word, because it expressed pronounced and sharp resistance to the policy of Serb centralism."[19] Outside of the left faction but close to its new positions stood nonfactional independents who pressed for a harsher judgment on Sima Marković. Dragotin Gustinčič (1882–1974), a leading Slovene Communist, argued that the differences between the Balkans and Central Europe were so grave that the Central European areas of Yugoslavia (Slovenia, Croatia, Vojvodina) did not fit well within any Balkan federal scheme.[20] And Ante Ciliga (b. 1898), a member of the Croatian Communist directorate, repudiated the old national program of the KPJ as nothing but a "Marxist-economic *defense* of Serbian hegemony." Marković's claim that the Serbian bourgeoisie practiced hegemony because of its backwardness and weakness was, according to Ciliga, nothing but a justification of hegemonism. Rather than imagining that they were opposing underdog capitalists, the Commu-

17. Sima Marković, *Nacionalno pitanje u svetlosti marksizma* (Belgrade, 1923), pp. 122–23.
18. Cited in Lukač, *Radnički pokret*, p. 163.
19. Kosta Novaković, "Nacionalno pitanje u Jugoslaviji: Autonomija ili federacija," *Radnik-Delavec*, Oct. 28, 1923, p. 3.
20. Momčilo Zečević, *Na istorijskoj prekretnici: Slovenci u politici jugoslovenske države, 1918–1929* (Belgrade, 1985), pp. 230–31. Gustinčič also believed that the Slovenes and Croats "in a proletarian federation would be . . . victims [of Serbian Communists], just as we are today the victims of [Pašić's] Yugoslavia" (ibid., p. 233).

nists should fight for national federal states with their own national armies and enter into direct negotiations with Radić for the establishment of a united front of workers and peasants.[21]

The Third Land Conference of the KPJ, held in Belgrade in early January 1924, marked the decisive victory of the left faction over the right. The resolutions that emerged from the conference, notably on the national question, were elaborations on the earlier proposals by Cvijić and others. The KPJ, donning its legal cloak, proclaimed the right of each nation "to free secession and the formation of its separate state, or rather [in the case of any minority] of accession to its national state." Nevertheless, the party really preferred "voluntary federative (allied) state unification, as the most suitable form for the economic and cultural development of the whole as well as the parts."[22]

Without changing his stand on the national question, Sima Marković offered no resistance to the victory of the left faction. But some of his old factional allies, notably Života Milojković, resisted the decisions of the Third Conference even after they were passed by an overwhelming majority in a referendum of party organizations.[23] The line of the Third Conference, however, hardly fulfilled the Comintern's requirements: the Fifth World Congress of the Comintern, held in Moscow June 17–22, 1924, had instructed the KPJ that the "general slogan of the right of nations to self-determination must be expressed in the form of separating Croatia, Slovenia, and Macedonia from the Yugoslav composite and in their establishment as independent republics."[24]

21. Mbt. [Ante Ciliga], "Za jasnoću i odlučnost u nacionalnom pitanju," *Borba*, Oct. 18, 1923, p. 5. Expelled from the KPJ in 1929 as a Trotskyist, Ciliga later claimed that his federalism was the opposite of what he held to be cynical Soviet support for every sort of anti-Serbianism in the 1920s: "Though a Croat and a theoretician in the Yugoslav party that opposed Serbian hegemonism in 1923–1925, I openly confronted this chauvinist Stalinist Machiavellianism, knowing full well that in the end the non-Serbs would be as victimized by this game as the Serbs": Ante Ciliga, *La Yougoslavie sous la menace intérieure et extérieure* (Paris, 1951), pp. 48–49.

22. "Rezolucija o nacionalnom pitanju," in Pijade, ed., *Istorijski arhiv*, 2:70–71.

23. Of the members of the Independent Workers' Party who participated in the referendum, 1,625 supported the resolution on the national question, 84 were against, and 3 abstained. The oppositional votes came from Serbia (81), Vojvodina (2), and Slovenia (1). But even in Serbia, the majority (577) was for the left faction. The right faction was centered on the organizations of Belgrade, Kruševac, Niš, and Pirot. See Lukač, *Radnički pokret*, pp. 191–92.

24. Cited in Pijade, ed.. *Istorijski arhiv*, 2:421.

Moscow's decision was prompted by Stjepan Radić's visit there in
June and July 1924, when the Croat leader, still seeking international
allies in his struggle for a Croat republic, enrolled his party in the
Peasant International (Krestintern), an agency of the Comintern.[25]
Some months after his return to Yugoslavia, the Pašić government
had Radić arrested and extended the anticommunist laws to the
Croat Peasant Party. Threatened with the dissolution of his movement, Radić agreed to recognize the dynastic order, state unity, and
the centralist constitution. In a devastating blow to the opposition, he
further agreed to a coalition government with Pašić's Radical Party,
the chief pillar of Serbian supremacy. Radić was freed from prison on
July 18, 1925, the day four of his deputies joined Pašić's cabinet. In
November he himself became minister of education.

The right faction was given no time to savor the wreck of the
Comintern strategy. In the midst of the electoral wrangling with Radić in November 1924, a KPJ referendum repudiated the right faction. Seventy-nine organizations supported the party leadership, by
then firmly in the hands of the left faction; only one—that of
Belgrade—supported the remnants of the right opposition led by
Života Milojković. The plenum of the KPJ CC denounced the opposition on November 25, 1924, noting that the "national question cannot be identified with the constitutional question, since that is tanta-
mount to maintaining the integrity of imperialist states." The Balkan
peasant movements "objectively have a revolutionary character even
when they are under the dominant influence of the bourgeoisie." The
stand of the right opposition, in particular, "meant the extension of
unconscious concessions to the great-state prejudices of the Serb proletariat and peasantry."[26] Života Milojković was expelled from the
KPJ at this point. He and his followers immediately formed the
Workers' Unity (or Unification) group. Their publications openly inveighed against the "Communist Frankists" of the left faction, who
taught Croat workers how to serve their national bourgeoisie in the
name of communism.[27] Marković, who still maintained his ties with

25. Mira Kolar-Dimitrijević, "Put Stjepana Radića u Moskvu i pristup Hrvatske republikanske seljačke stranke u Seljačku internacionalu," Časopis za suvremenu povijest 4,
no. 3 (1972): 7–29.
26. AIHRPH, Fond Kominterne: KI 66/II: "ODLUKA C.P. VEĆA O SPORU U PARTIJI," Nov.
25, 1924, p. 10.
27. S. N., "Hrvatski 'levičari,'" Radničko jedinstvo, Nov. 29, 1925, p. 1.

the opposition, continued in the leadership, though his views were repudiated by Stalin himself in a speech of March 30, 1925, before the Yugoslav commission of the Comintern's executive committee.

Stalin would not allow Marković—and the Yugoslav Communists in general—to underestimate the revolutionary potential of the national movement. Radić's maneuvers made no difference in the context. If Radić had "betrayed" the national cause, the Communists had to seek cooperation with those leaders who did not give up in the struggle against Serbian hegemony. In Dalmatia especially, such Croat Communist leaders as Vicko Jelaska (1897–1968), Ivo Baljkas (1892–1977), and Ivo Marić (1894–1968) sought electoral alliances with the dissident Radićists and other Croat nationalists who challenged Radić,[28] but this strategy proved bankrupt. Radić's popularity among the Croats diminished somewhat, but the Croat opposition did not give up on Radić, as they assessed his concessions to Belgrade as unavoidable. And indeed, Radić's coalition with the Radicals was fraught with contradictions that foreshadowed its ultimate demise.

Radić's new round of opposition, which began in January 1927, sharpened Yugoslavia's state crisis. Within the Communist movement, which was steadily moving leftward, calls for direct action revived the old skirmishes between the left and right factions. In February 1928, however, two noted militants, Josip Broz (Tito) and Andrija Hebrang (1899–1949?), persuaded the delegates to the Eighth Conference of Zagreb's KPJ organization to adopt an antifactional resolution and appeal to the Comintern to end the factional struggle in the party. The originators of the "Zagreb line" belonged to the left faction, but they were as eager to upset the left's scholastic and passive leadership as they were to thwart the rightists.[29] Their desire for action coincided with tremors in Yugoslavia and a sharp leftward turn in the Comintern.

28. In the campaign for district elections in Dalmatia in January 1927, Jelaska, Baljkas, and Marić signed an electoral agreement with the Radićist dissidents. The resulting Croat Peasant-Worker Bloc condemned the government's policy of "weakening the position of the non-Serb peoples in the state, aimed in the first place at parceling Croatia out of existence and weakening the compactness of the Croat people": "Deklaracija Hrvatskog Seljačko-Radničkog Bloka," in *Poruka Hrvatskom seljačkom narodu pred izbore za Oblasnu Skupštinu* (Split, 1926), p. 14. Among the signatories of this manifesto was a Catholic priest.

29. On the Eighth Conference, see Gordana Vlajčić, *Osma konferencija zagrebačkih komunista* (Zagreb, 1976).

In June, Radić and several other deputies were shot at by a Serb Radical deputy during a debate on the floor of the National Assembly. Two Radićist deputies were killed outright; Radić himself, wounded, lingered on till August. Massive protest demonstrations in Croatia against this political crime were led in part by the KPJ. In July and August the Comintern's Sixth World Congress adopted the new leftist line and called for an upsurge in revolutionary struggle, since the temporary stabilization of capitalism was deemed to be at an end. In October, the KPJ's Fourth Congress, convened in Dresden, adopted the line of the Communist International. But in addition to affirming the breakup of Yugoslavia, the KPJ asserted a need for Communist leadership in the armed struggle of the oppressed nationalities. This was no longer a matter of supporting national movements. Despite Radić's tragic death, the Communists held that the non-Serb nationalities were led by the parties of "national reformism." The illusions about Radić's party had to be overcome and the "hegemony of the national bourgeoisies in the movements of oppressed nationalities had to pass to the working class under the leadership of the Communist party."[30]

The Fourth Congress spelled the end of the old factions. The new party leadership excluded such old stalwarts as Sima Marković and Djuro Cvijić, though the prospective new leaders, such as Tito and Hebrang, were not advanced on account of their recent imprisonment. The new leadership (Djuro Djaković, Žika Pecarski, and Djuro Salaj) on the whole represented the Comintern-trained activists. They soon expelled Sima Marković from the party and downgraded his allies (Lazar Stefanović) in a campaign against the "right danger." But they also accused the old left faction of "relegating the KPJ to the role of an accomplice of the Croat bourgeoisie."[31]

On January 6, 1929, King Aleksandar, proclaiming his determination to guard the national oneness of the Serbs, Croats, and Slovenes and the state's integrity with no intermediaries, abolished the constitution, the parliament, and political parties. The KPJ took the royal dictatorship and the paralysis it engendered in the opposition parties as a signal for action. The KPJ Politburo announced that the regime's

30. "Rezolucija o privrednom i političkom položaju Jugoslavije i o zadacima KPJ," in Pijade, ed., *Istorijski arhiv*, 2:164.

31. AIHRPH, Fond Kominterne: KI/146/III: "Rezolucija o borbi protiv desne opasnosti u KPJ" (1929), p. 6.

general crisis could be met only by combat: "The only way out of this crisis for the working class and the peasantry is armed struggle—civil war against the rule of the hegemonistic Serbian bourgeoisie. No parliamentary and democratic combinations, no governments, elections, and pacifist expectations are capable of meeting a single demand of the working class, the peasantry, and the oppressed nationalities. For the working people there is no solution but armed struggle."[32]

The Third Period (1928–1935) was as ravaging for the KPJ as for the other Comintern sections. Though the dictatorial regime of King Aleksandar increased national tensions to a level unprecedented in the brief history of the Yugoslav state, the minuscule Communist party lacked the resources to lead the non-Serb nationalities in any confrontations with the dictatorship, least of all in armed struggle. Not for want of trying, however; the KPJ's cadres were decimated during the Third Period. Most active party members were arrested and sentenced to long prison terms by special antisubversive tribunals. Several major leaders, including Djuro Djaković, the party's former political secretary, were killed in armed clashes with the police. As a result, the party's command structure became impaired, and the KPJ had at least two centers during most of the 1930s. One center was in exile, notably in the USSR, Vienna, Prague, and Paris, with considerable influence among the migrant Croat miners in Belgium and later with a significant contingent in the international brigades in Spain. The other was in Yugoslav jails, notably in Srijemska Mitrovica, which became a kind of the Communist training school under a relatively liberal regime that permitted the grouping of political prisoners.

If the KPJ overestimated its ability to mobilize under the harsh conditions of the dictatorship, the party's larger fault was its inability to influence the movements of non-Serb nationalities, which were the principal source of opposition to the regime. True, after July 1932, when the Comintern directed the Yugoslav Communists to aid the Croat, Slovenian, Macedonian, and Montenegrin "national revolutionaries," the KPJ started to court these incipient underground movements, notably the Ustaša movement of Ante Pavelić, an exiled Croat nationalist who hoped to establish an independent Croat state

32. Ibid., KI/148/III: "Svima pokrajinskim Sekretarijatima" (January 1929), p. 1.

with the aid of Mussolini and (later) Hitler. The KPJ leaders spoke approvingly of the pockets of armed insurgency that the Ustašas stirred up in Lika in 1932, but in their determination "to participate most actively" in the Ustaša movement, with the aim of steering it to the left,[33] they overlooked Pavelić's irreversible profascist orientation, which precluded both the growth of a genuine (mass) nationalist movement and a lasting alliance with the Communists.

More important, the KPJ remained isolated from the Croat Peasant Party, which, though outlawed, still claimed the loyalty of most Croats and increasingly the support of all groups opposed to the dictatorship, including the democratic forces in Serbia. Vladko Maček, Radić's successor at the helm of the Croat Peasant Party, shunned the KPJ. The Communists actually believed they could wrest the leadership of the "bourgeois-democratic revolutionary movement" from Maček's moderates by denouncing them as the "main social base of Serbian imperialism among the oppressed nations" and by branding their policy as "treason against the struggle for self-determination, including secession, of the Croat and other peoples of Yugoslavia."[34] Though Maček and other "capitulationist leaders of national reformism" resisted armed struggle on principle, their influence over the nationality movements was immeasurably deeper than the momentary enthusiasm elicited by either Communist or Ustaša adventures, including the sensational assassination of King Aleksandar by the Ustašas in 1934. The ensuing regime of Prince Pavle (Paul) represented a slow movement away from the dictatorship, whose failures weakened the country at a time of growing fascist threat in Central Europe.

The dramatic rise of Hitler's Germany in the mid-1930s also presented a problem for the Communist movement. The Third Period, with its fire against the moderate left (the Social Democrats in West-

33. Lukač, Radnički pokret, p. 256. To be sure, the KPJ did not fail to note early on that Pavelić's Ustašas were "national fascists" and that they "were waiting for the 'liberation' of the Croats and the establishment of Great Croatia with the help of Italian fascism." But during the Third Period fascism was not viewed as the main enemy. Hence Pavelić, too was merely *"waiting* for the victory of Italian imperialism, thereby objectively enabling the Croat bourgeoisie to launch a 'new' period of 'realistic politics'—the policy of agreement with Belgrade and bondage to Serbian and French imperialism": Jadranski [Rajko Jovanović], "Nacionalreformističke punktacije i borba za hegemoniju nad revolucionarnim pokretima masa u Jugoslaviji," *Klasna borba* 8, nos. 19–20 (1933): 36.

34. Ibid., p. 45.

ern Europe and the peasant parties in Central and Southeastern Europe), precluded any common effort against the fascist forces, and that policy had to be reversed. The shift in gear was amply demonstrated by the Soviets' resolve to strengthen the enfeebled system of French East European alliances, since France's friends (especially the Little Entente of Czechoslovakia, Romania, and Yugoslavia) were no longer perceived as the principal danger to Moscow. On the contrary, in the new Communist strategy, the Little Entente "played a decisive role in Central and Eastern Europe and, should it remain faithful to the democratic bloc of pacifist countries, would be the main barrier against an invasion by Hitler. . . . The destruction of the Little Entente or its entanglement in the web of Hitler's intrigues would in good part end the first phase of a German invasion of the East."[35]

With the shift toward the new Popular Front strategy, the KPJ had to moderate its hostility toward the leaders of the Croat Peasant Party and the other oppositional forces. The Communists now freely admitted that the two streams of antidictatorial sentiment (national-peasant-democratic and Communist) had not cooperated or cohered during the previous period. Far from reclaiming leadership of the opposition on the new basis, the KPJ lowered its sights: "The introduction of communism in Croatia is today out of the question. . . . Therefore, the duty of Communists is to . . . win the whole [Croat peasant] movement for the Popular Front. That means no splitting of the Croat Peasant Party, no setting up of some separate left wing in opposition to the Croat Peasant Party."[36] But it also meant that the Communists no longer insisted on dismantling Yugoslavia; they increasingly favored its federalization.[37] "The present situation," according to a leading Croat Communist, "directs [the Croats] toward

35. Milan Nikolić [Milan Gorkić], "Prodiranje Hitlerizma u Jugoslaviju," *Klasna borba* 10, nos. 1–2 (1937): 22.

36. Milan Gorkić, "Problemi i zadaće Narodne Fronte u Jugoslaviji," ibid., pp. 58, 74.

37. The party shifted away from independence for Yugoslavia's constituent nationalities in the summer of 1935 at the plenum of the KPJ CC (Split, June 9–10) and the meeting of the KPJ Politburo (Moscow, August 1). For details see Lukač, *Radnički pokret*, pp. 290–98. On the significance of the Split plenum in the context of the party's nationality policy, see Tonči Šitin, "Borba KPJ za primjenu marksističkog stava u nacionalnom pitanju s posebnim osvrtom na ulogu Splitskog plenuma CK KPJ 1933. [1935] godine," *Naše teme* 19, nos. 10–11 (1975): 1605–41. It should be noted that the KPJ CC admitted in the plenum's resolution that it was wrong "to fill the heads of the masses with claims that their [national] leaders are traitors and compromisers. Such claims, however correct historically, today drive the masses away from us": "Rezolucija Plenuma CK KPJ," in Pijade, ed., *Istorijski arhiv*, 2:360.

an alliance and agreement with the Serb *people* and the other peoples
of Yugoslavia" on the basis of a democratic constituent assembly.[38]

The KPJ's shift toward the Popular Front strategy coincided with
the rise of Josip Čižinski (1904–1939), better known under his
pseudonym, Milan Gorkić. A Bosnian Communist of Czech origin,
Gorkić is still occasionally cited as a typical Comintern bureaucrat,
with no trace of national allegiance or independent initiative. But
despite his relative youth and long residence in the USSR (he left
Yugoslavia in 1923 and worked in various Comintern agencies in
Moscow until 1932, when he was reintroduced to the Yugoslav sector), Gorkić was not always an obedient underling: his impatience
with discipline and with Moscow's supremacy was an issue in several
party rows during the mid-1930s.[39] Most important, though his discipline did not falter during the Third Period, Gorkić was by disposition a man of the Popular Front. Rather than sabotage the new
Moscow line, as the KPJ tended to do, Gorkić pursued the Popular
Front to the extent of advocating an "alliance of the toilers with the
middle strata."[40] Moreover, he worked for Communist ties with the
Social Democrats, Croatian and Serbian peasant parties, Montenegrin federalists, and Slovene Christian Socialists—even, apparently, with the traditionally pro-Russian Serbian nationalist right.[41]

Indeed, the logic of the Popular Front in Yugoslavia determined a
revision of the KPJ's negative stand toward the Yugoslav state.
Gorkić himself wrote in 1937:

The objection to the Communists as "antistate" elements was long
justified by the claim that the Communists inflame nationality conflicts
and that they oppose the state of Yugoslavia as such. These claims today

38. Stjepan Livadić [Stjepan Cvijić], *Politički eseji* (Zagreb, 1937), pp. 29, 64–65.
39. The best, most complete, and most sympathetic account of Gorkić's life can be found
in Nadežda Jovanović, "Milan Gorkić (prilog za biografiju)," *Istorija 20. veka* 1, no. 1
(1983): 25–57. Note especially the reference to Gorkić's determination to halt the Comintern's arrogant treatment of the KPJ leadership (p. 39) and his defiance of the Comintern in
calling CC plenums without Moscow's approval (p. 50).
40. *Proleter* 13, no. 9 (1937): 12. Stjepan Cvijić explicitly stated in his essay on the Croat
question that "everybody knows that a popular front without bourgeois parties is pure
nonsense": Livadić [Cvijić], *Politički eseji*, p. 78.
41. Gorkić's ties with Slobodan Jovanović, the leading Serbian historian and head of the
nationalist Serb Cultural Club, are explored in the context of the "synodal line" among the
Serbian elite in Vladimir Dedijer, *Novi prilozi za biografiju Josipa Broza Tita*, vol. 3
(Belgrade, 1984), pp. 149–53. The "synodal line," according to Dedijer, refers to the
supporters of Eastern Orthodox reciprocity centered on the Moscow synod.

lack all serious foundation. Communists are against national oppression and Great Serbian supremacy. But though we remain faithful to the principle of full national self-determination, we Communists are against the tearing apart of the present-day state territory of Yugoslavia and support the free agreement of all free and equal peoples of Yugoslavia for the establishment of a new, free, and happy Yugoslavia. The manifesto of our party's CC of January 1937 explicitly states, "Every effort to break up the present-day state territory or to threaten its survival means, under the current international circumstances, to aid fascism and its preparations for war. Every effort along these lines is contrary to the vital interests of all peoples of Yugoslavia"[42]

Gorkić personally—at least until the KPJ consultation in Moscow in August 1936—apparently believed that, the KPJ's support of Yugoslavia's state unity ought to be conditioned on reform of the regency regime; but the Comintern insisted on unconditional support of Yugoslav unity, and Gorkić then agreed.[43] Small wonder that when Gorkić became the KPJ's general secretary in the fall of 1936, his central committee included two of his young Serb followers, Sreten Žujović and Rodoljub Čolaković.[44]

The consolidation of the party on the basis of Gorkić's version of the Popular Front did not affect developments in Yugoslavia, where the underground remained weak and most of its cadre in prison (see figure 3). A struggle for a more flexible Communist party was waged behind the walls of Srijemska Mitrovica and other major prisons. The focus of this struggle was Mitrovica's prison committee (*kaznionički*

42. M. Gorkić, *Novim Putevima (Pouke iz provala)* (Brussels, 1937), p. 89.

43. Nadežda Jovanović, "Je li u razdoblju 1934–1937. M. Gorkić bio protiv jedinstvene jugoslovenske države?" *Časopis za suvremenu povijest* 15, no. 1 (1983): 85–86.

44. Žujović joined the KPJ in 1924 and worked as an organizer in Belgrade. Arrested on numerous occasions, he served briefly as secretary of the party organization in the Vračar section, on Belgrade's south side. In 1933 he emigrated to the USSR and enrolled in a Comintern school. As the "Serbian member of the leadership," he was regarded (with Rodoljub Čolaković) as one of Gorkić's men at the KPJ summit, which also—but at greater distance—included Tito. See Rodoljub Čolaković, *Kazivanja o jednom pokoljenju,* 3 vols. (Sarajevo, 1964–1972), 3:348–54. Žujović's enthusiasm for the Popular Front is evident in one of his articles on the example of the Popular Front in France: "The striving for full unity of the working class is being increasingly expressed in a demand for a single workers' party. The slogan of the Communist party [of France]—'one class, one trade union, one party'—has been accepted with great enthusiasm. The established common Coordinating Committee of both parties [Communist and Socialist] is working on this . . .": M. Životić [Sreten Žujović], "Ugledajmo se na Francusku Narodnog Fronta," *Klasna borba* 10, nos. 1–2 (1937): 92–93.

Ultraleft   Left   Center

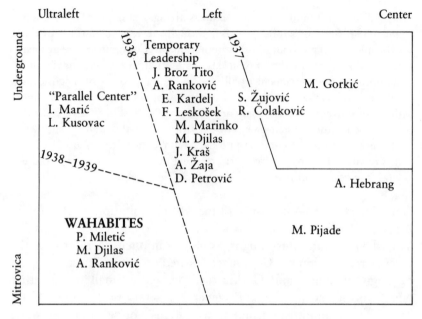

3. From Gorkić to Tito, 1933–1939

komitet) of the KPJ, popularly known as Kakić. From 1934 the committee was dominated by Petko Miletić-Šepo (1897–1939?), a noted
Montenegrin Communist, whose fundamentalist radicalism, preach-
ing of self-mortification, and crude anti-intellectualism earned his
followers the name of Wahabites, after the fanatical movement in the
Arabian peninsula.

    Though he opposed the new Popular Front policy, Miletić's
Wahabism was more a cult of his own austere personality than a
genuine political line. His methods of terror and intimidation were
directed against the older Communists, such as Andrija Hebrang,
Moša Pijade, Josip Kraš, and Djuro Pucar, who opposed Miletić's
constant and costly confrontations with prison authorities in favor of
taking advantage of imprisonment to cultivate political and cultural
allies.[45] Miletić's followers—such men as Milovan Djilas and Alek-

45. Moša Pijade's mischievous humor is probably at the source of the Wahabite label. In
the early phase of the conflict, when the controversy was still relatively civil, Pijade wrote a
satirical canto, "Martovska revolucija" (The March revolution). It begins with the following verses: *"Dragi moji Vahabiti / Divlji kao trogloditi"* (My dear Wahabites / As wild as
troglodytes). See France Filipič, "Moša Pijade: Martovska revolucija," in *Poglavja iz revolucionarnega boja jugoslovanskih komunistov 1919–1939*, 2 vols. (Ljubljana, 1981),
2:44–97.

sandar Ranković—"were younger men who had become politically active under the dictatorship." And Miletić "understood clearly," Djilas has written, "that he had to rely on the young aggressive generation that developed under the dictatorship if he was to succeed in prison, or outside of it, for that matter. It was obvious that soon the left wingers would constitute the backbone of the party."[46] With the young militants in hand, Miletić started to organize physical attacks against the "right opposition." On August 6, 1937, an attempt was made on the life of Hebrang, but failed. The metal stick aimed at Hebrang's skull left the veteran conciliator in convalescence for months. Hebrang and some seventeen of his followers received permission to spend those months in solitary confinement, apart from Miletić's majority.

The scandal of the prison war in Mitrovica broke out at the worst possible moment for the KPJ. In July 1937 Milan Gorkić was summoned to Moscow from Paris, then the headquarters of the KPJ CC, and upon his arrival was deposed and arrested. The Stalinist purges soon made a shambles of the KPJ's apparatus in the Soviet Union. Of some 900 Communists and sympathizers of Yugoslav origin in the USSR in 1936–1937, including some 50 KPJ officials, at least 800 were arrested during the Great Purge. Of that number only about 40 survived the Soviet gulags. Among the victims were the topmost leaders of the KPJ, including, besides Gorkić, Djuro Cvijić, Vladimir Ćopić, Filip Filipović, Kamilo Horvatin, Sima Marković, and Kosta Novaković. The purge created a leadership vacuum in the KPJ, whose officers were shunned by the Comintern. The KPJ no longer received subsidies from Moscow and its very future was in doubt. In Paris, Gorkić's followers in the KPJ Politburo (Rodoljub Čolaković and Sreten Žujović) were under boycott. Moreover, two of the Paris leaders, Ivo Marić and Labud Kusovac, started to position themselves to succeed Gorkić. Marić and Kusovac, the first a Croat from Dalmatia, the second a Montenegrin, represented themselves as the real leaders of the KPJ. Their "Parallel Center" had the support of some Comintern officials, including Ivan Srebrenjak (Antonov), a Croat Communist and long-time Soviet operative, who later led the Soviet military intelligence center in wartime Zagreb.[47] Most important, Marić and

46. Milovan Djilas, *Memoir of a Revolutionary* (New York, 1973), p. 181.
47. Kusovac, too, had long-time associations with the Soviet intelligence service. Together with Mustafa Golubić and Pavle Bastajić, both high Soviet operatives of Yugoslav origin, Kusovac worked in the Vienna center of La Fédération Balkanique, an agency for

Kusovac were supported by Miletić and maintained a private channel to the Kakić. In the middle stood Tito, the party's organizational secretary, who had his own vision of the party's reconstruction.

In the fall of 1937 Tito intervened in the Mitrovica affair, first by persuading Hebrang and his followers to quit their solitary cells. By December 1937 Tito had deposed Miletić and conferred a mandate to form a new Kakić upon Moša Pijade, Hebrang's sometime ally against Miletić's Wahabites. Though Miletić still had supporters in the Comintern, his deposition weakened the "Parallel Center." By May 1938 Tito had established the Temporary Leadership, predict-ably a compromise body, which included Moscow-educated Slovenes (Edvard Kardelj and Miha Marinko), moderate Croat Popular Front-ers (Josip Kraš and Andrija Žaja), former Wahabites (Milovan Djilas and Aleksandar Ranković), and others. In the fall of 1939, when Tito finally received the Comintern's mandate to form a new KPJ summit, the Temporary Leadership became the new CC, minus all the Croat moderates except Kraš. Two additional hard-liners, Ivan Milutinović, a former Wahabite from Montenegro, and Rade Končar, a Serb from Croatia, were added to this body in 1940.

The political aspect of the struggle between Hebrang and Miletić did not directly concern the national question.[48] Like Gorkić, Hebrang argued for cooperation between the Communists and all democratic and patriotic forces, which the extreme left opposed. Hence Hebrang's openness to the Croat Peasant Party, many of

---

revolutionary work among the national minorities of the Balkans, under direct Soviet security control. See Milomir Marić, "Ponoćni vrisak Mustafe Golubića: Kazačok u Beču," *Duga*, Nov. 18, 1985, p. 75.

48. Vladimir Dedijer and his informant X-601 misrepresent the facts when they claim that Hebrang held "that the national question in Yugoslavia can be solved only by the breakup of Yugoslavia and the establishment of independent states," whereas the other prisoners (Miletić's followers) "stood by the other thesis, that is, that the right of nations to self-determination and secession is not an obligatory and automatic demand for secession but only one of the possible roads toward the solution of the national question, the breakup of Yugoslavia not being obligatory for the Communists": Dedijer, *Novi prilozi*, 3:341–42. First, the sources give no hint of such a dichotomy. On the contrary, Miletić had the support of Juco Rukavina, a leader of the imprisoned Ustašas, in his struggles against the prison authorities, which would have been impossible had he supported a conditional Yugoslav union. Miletić's reputation among the imprisoned Ustašas was built on his stature as a Montenegrin "national militant." Second, the logic of Miletić's opposition to the Popular Front argued against any readiness to defend the country's integrity in the face of German and other revisionist pressures, one of the corollaries of the Popular Front in Yugoslavia.

whose militants he introduced to the KPJ. Hence, too, the antagonism of the Wahabites to Radićist reformism, which, in their view, was only a peasant version of Social Democracy. Indirectly, therefore, this struggle, too, concerned the national question, as the political potential of various South Slavic nationalities was often indistinguishable from that of their national parties. In a sense, the legitimacy of the non-Serb national movements within the KPJ depended on the Popular Front, as the alternative was a purist withdrawal from the whole area of nationality relations, which could only weaken opposition to the regime in Belgrade. As Tito put it in 1943, "Gorkić wanted to dissolve the party organizations and lower them to the level of a mass—broad—organization."[49] For that reason, the fall of Gorkić was a loss for the Popular Front which could not be balanced by the diminution of Miletić's role in the party. After all, Miletić's chief fault in Tito's eyes was lack of discipline. Writing to the Kakić in November 1937, Tito censured Miletić for "undertaking public actions in the country independently of us via various private connections . . . which can harm the prestige of our firm [party]."[50]

Not surprisingly, the kind of popular front that Tito envisioned was really a compromise with the various modes of leftism, including Wahabism without Miletić. When the Executive Committee of the Comintern confirmed Tito's mandate in January 1939, officially conferring upon him the leadership of the KPJ, it also, in Tito's words, made the new leadership "duty bound to continue decisively to purge the party of all alien, vacillating elements."[51] Not even this action resolved the question of Miletić. According to Josip Kopinič, a Slovene Communist in Soviet service and Tito's ally in the conclusive struggles of 1938–1939, the cadre commission of the Comintern included a group, mainly Bulgars and Germans, who opposed Dimitrov's option for Tito and preferred Miletić.[52] They continued to work against Tito even after January 1939, accusing him of

49. Josip Broz Tito, *Sabrana djela*, 20 vols. (Belgrade, 1977–1984), 17:134.

50. Ibid., 3:126. Later on, in 1943, Tito cited Miletić's political errors, but only as secondary considerations: "Errors of Petko Miletić: Unprincipled desire to mount the leadership, then ultraleftism. His left sectarian stand on the Popular Front question in France is well known" (ibid., 17:134).

51. Josip Broz Tito, "Izvještaj o organizacionom pitanju na V konferenciji KPJ 1940. god.," in Pero Damjanović, Milovan Bosić, and Dragica Lazarević, eds., *Peta zemaljska konferencija KPJ (19–23. oktobar 1940)* (Belgrade, 1980), p. 16.

52. Vjenceslav Cenčić, *Enigma Kopinič* (Belgrade, 1983), 1:89.

Trotskyism and a variety of other sins. Miletić's release from prison
in June 1939 and his swift journey to Moscow tightened the ring
around the KPJ's new general secretary. But Tito's allies prevailed.
Instead of replacing Tito, Miletić was quickly arrested by the NKVD
and disappeared into the labyrinthine Soviet camps.

    The fall of Petko Miletić was neither the beginning nor the end of
Tito's purge of the KPJ. Since 1937 Tito had wielded his broom in an
effort to establish a fully bolshevized party. In contrast to the later
identification of Tito with a more open type of Communist movement (typical of the 1950s and thereafter), his principal goal in the
late 1930s was to form the KPJ in the Soviet mold of a monolithic
party, one that would stand firm against any alternative versions of
Marxism. The conflict over strategy in the KPJ from 1938 to 1940
(see figure 4) thus meant more than the removal of the remnants of
various political factions, though that was a primary task. Tito got rid
of diverse leaders who were tied to Miletić, expressed loyalty to other
purged factions, or simply acted independently in their local party
organizations, as was only natural under the conditions of illegality.
In a series of moves from 1937 to 1940, as part of his effort against
the "Parallel Center," Tito purged the regional committee for
Dalmatia (Vicko Jelaska and Ivo Baljkas), which had long established
regional-national ties with Ivo Marić, also a Dalmatian Croat. In
1939 Tito expelled Ljuba Radovanović, a lone adherent of Sima
Marković's right faction, whom Tito accused of "preparing, together
with a few other diehard followers of Sima Marković, to establish
some sort of party of old 'Bolsheviks,' in other words, to create a split
within our party in Serbia."[53] There were purges of Wahabites in
Montenegro (Jovan Marinović, the secretary of the regional committee for Montenegro, and the Ćufka brothers, Kosta and Aleksa, leaders of the KPJ organization at Cetinje). And, among various similar
cases, the Slovene leadership purged Mirko Košir and Dušan Kermavner.[54] But by far the most important of Tito's purges was di-

53. Josip Broz Tito, "Za čistotu i boljševizaciju partije," in *Sabrana djela*, 5:82.
54. Mirko Košir (1905–1951) was the secretary of the KPJ's regional committee for
Slovenia in 1936. An opponent of Gorkić, he opposed any contacts with Gorkić's leadership in Vienna and with the KPJ in general. He argued that Slovene Communists ought to
have a four-member commission in Moscow that would adapt the Comintern's directives to
Slovene conditions—directly, without consulting the KPJ. (This was not the only case of
"Slovene separatism" in the KPJ. In 1936, the Slovenian branch of SKOJ withdrew from
the statewide organization.) In 1948, Košir was one of the Slovenian Communists sen-

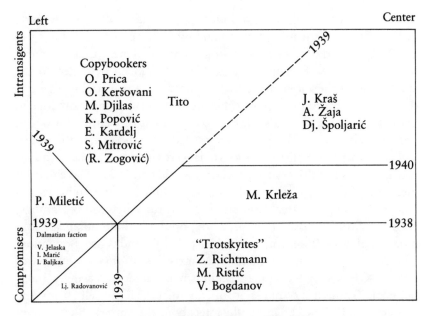

Left ——————————————————————— Center

Intransigents

Copybookers
O. Prica
O. Keršovani
M. Djilas   Tito
K. Popović
E. Kardelj
S. Mitrović
(R. Zogović)

1939

J. Kraš
A. Žaja
Dj. Špoljarić

1939

1940

P. Miletić

M. Krleža

1939 ———————————————————————— 1938

Compromisers

Dalmatian faction
V. Jelaska
I. Marić
I. Baljkas

"Trotskyites"
Z. Richtmann
M. Ristić
V. Bogdanov

Lj. Radovanović   *1939*

4. The conflict over strategy, 1938–1940

rected against the dissident Communist intelligentsia and various party tendencies that argued for a real popular front in which the KPJ would leave behind its underground habits, play the role of a loyal partner to the democratic and nationality-based opposition, and deemphasize its ties with Stalinism.

Tito's most decisive battle against the left intelligentsia was fought against the group gathered around Miroslav Krleža (1893–1981), the foremost Croat author of the twentieth century. Krleža's versatility—he wrote plays, novels, poetry, and literary and political essays—was one of the principal means by which Marxism acquired intellectual weight, not just in Croatia but in all Yugoslavia. A party member since 1919, Krleža almost singlehandedly brought all traditional val-

---

tenced in the rigged Dachau trials as a "Gestapo agent." He died at the Goli Otok concentration camp. For a tendentious account of the Košir case, see Miha Marinko, *Moji spomini* (Ljubljana, 1974), pp. 169–73. Dušan Kermavner's conflict with the party also involved the national question. According to his son, "The conflict between Dušan Kermavner and Kardelj . . . concerned the stand toward Central Europe and Yugoslavism. They tagged father with the label of Austro-Marxism, of Central European orientation; Kardelj criticized him for an insufficiently positive stand toward Yugoslavia." See Taras Kermauner, "Dijalog o razlikovanju (VI)," *Književnost* 44, nos. 1–2 (1988): 56.

ues and ways of thinking into doubt. According to Vladimir Bakarić (1912–1983), the leading Croat Communist after 1944, in the early 1920s Krleža "did more for the progressive movement than the party in its entirety."[55] Perhaps because his communism belonged to the springtime of the movement, Krleža harbored a private but still evident distaste for Stalin's policy. His opposition was most obvious in aesthetic matters. Krleža's Marxism, a product of Central European critical tradition, could not be channeled into the pragmatic straitjacket of socialist realism. His journals were open to leading Communist-leaning surrealists, such as Marko Ristić and Oskar Davičo, both members of the Serbian surrealist circle. In time he came to be associated with younger critical Communists of various heterodox leanings, such as Zvonimir Richtmann, who popularized Freudianism and modern physics (Einstein, Bohr, Heisenberg), and Vaso Bogdanov, who challenged many postulates of Marxist historiography and party policy. Krleža's opposition to Stalinism became increasingly more political. Though he did not openly distance himself from the Moscow trials, Krleža had no illusions about the purges and privately denounced them. His closest personal and party friends, Djuro Cvijić and Kamilo Horvatin disappeared in the Great Purge, and Krleža frequently alluded to them as "our tombs in Siberia." In a conversation with a literary historian in 1975, Vladimir Bakarić "stressed that Krleža feared 'totalitarianism,' and that there were strong allusions about the party's 'totalitarianism' in [Krleža's] novels *Na rubu pameti* [At the edge of reason, 1938] and *Bankvet u Blitvi* [Banquet in Blithuania, 1938–1939]."[56] Moreover, Krleža would accept no narrowing of the Popular Front; in an internal party debate in 1935 he argued forcefully for broad cooperation with the nationality opposition.[57]

The conflict with Krleža reached its climax in 1939, after the inauguration of Krleža's journal *Pečat* (Seal). Three of the journal's leading contributors, Richtmann, Ristić, and Bogdanov, were by that time under the party's boycott, having been denounced by Tito himself as "Trotskyites." It was a common pejorative at the time, though there

55. Vasilije Kalezić, "Partijska linija u sećanju Vladimira Bakarića," *Književna reč*, Dec. 25, 1983, p. 8.
56. Ibid.
57. For the best account of the literary side of the KPJ's conflict with Krleža, see Stanko Lasić, *Sukob na književnoj ljevici, 1928–1952* (Zagreb, 1970). For a chronology of Krleža's activities at the time of the "conflict," see Stanko Lasić, *Krleža: Kronologija života i rada* (Zagreb, 1982), pp. 201–91.

were hardly any real Trotskyists in Yugoslavia. Krleža continued to defend his associates. The high point of his defense was his essay *Dijalektički antibarbarus* (The dialectical antibarbarus), which filled the whole issue of *Pečat* in December 1939. The chief targets of this salvo were the anti-Krležian Communist writers and critics, notably Ognjen Prica, Milovan Djilas, Radovan Zogović, and Jovan Popović, whose creative effort Krleža ridiculed; hence, he argued, their animus: "This is the way things stand in our dialectical Parnassus: Every well-intentioned literary criticism to the effect that a particular legally published piece of writing—a novel or a poem, for example—is worthless because it is laughably dilettantish and illiterate receives the following response nowadays: 'Excuse me, sir, you are denying dialectics, you are a Trotskyite, and you are promulgating nothing short of political banditism.'"[58] Though Stalin and his politics were never mentioned, *The Dialectical Antibarbarus* disected the Stalinist mentality with a precision that was bound to cause a stir.

In response, the party leadership, notably Kardelj and Djilas, prepared the so-called *Književne sveske* (Literary copybooks), setting forth the ideological disqualification of Krleža's circle. The principal articles in the collection were written by Ognjen Prica, Otokar Keršovani, Milovan Djilas, Koča Popović, and "Josip Šestak," actually Stefan Mitrović as edited by Kardelj. Todor Pavlov, the sole non-Yugoslav contributor, was a leading Bulgarian Communist, who developed the "theory of reflection," the theoretical foundation for Stalinist aesthetics.[59] An article on Krleža's theory of art by Radovan Zogović (1907–1986), who as Djilas's aide and the most consistent exponent of socialist realism in the KPJ was logically at home among the Copybookers, was not finished in time to be included in the collection.[60] Tito, who was in the USSR from September 1939 to

58. Miroslav Krleža, "Dijalektički antibarbarus," *Pečat* 1, nos. 8–9 (1939): 176.
59. *Književne sveske* 1, no. 1 (1940): 1–313.
60. Despite the close political and personal association between Zogović and Djilas (their mothers were cousins), the first political conflict in which they both participated found them on opposite sides. In 1932, when Djilas's concerns were still mainly literary, Zogović joined Savić Marković-Štedimlija, Milivoje Matović-Zatarac, and Vuk M. Kukalj in attacking Djilas and several other young Montenegrin writers. They accused Djilas of advancing the interests of the bourgeoisie in his literary work. In his self-criticism Djilas agreed that "until yesterday" his "stand on and conception of art and the artist's duty were at bottom erroneous. . . . Today I want an uncompromising struggle with everything and everybody that deviates from the principles of collective—and above all collectivistic—duty and tasks in art. The writer is only an expression of the aspirations of that class whose cause he espouses either consciously or unconsciously": Milovan Djilas, "Moj odgovor," *Zeta*, April 3, 1932, p. 3.

March 1940, was not directly involved in the preparation of the *Književne sveske,* but he approved the collection before its publication in the summer of 1940. In October 1940, at the Fifth Land Conference of the KPJ, the purge of the *pečatovci* was confirmed. Tito stated in his report that, "thanks to the mobilization of the whole party against [those who were taken in by Krleža], we succeeded in the main in thwarting this attempt by the revisionists and enemies of the working class."[61]

The purge of Krleža's group was closely connected with attempts to bolshevize the Communist movement in Croatia. The Popular Front policy won such a strong base there that it became the linchpin of Communist activities in Yugoslavia. The Comintern had conferred some dignity on the Communist movement in Croatia and in Slovenia in 1937 by forcing the establishment of the nominally independent Communist parties of Croatia and Slovenia within the KPJ. This inexpensive gesture, which Tito carried out, did not grant genuine autonomy to the Communists in these lands, but was designed to show the Croats and Slovenes how highly Moscow valued the revolutionary potential of their national movements in the struggle against

---

61. Tito, "Izvještaj o organizacionom pitanju," *Peta zemaljska,* p. 41. The KPJ was simultaneously waging a similar campaign against Krleža's friends outside Croatia. In Macedonia, the KPJ expelled Kočo Racin, the founder of Macedonian literature. "They asked me," Racin told a comrade, "to attack Krleža. They said: It is important that you as a Macedonian publicly take a stand, because this way it seems that only we Montenegrins are chasing him! I distanced myself from the *Pečat* and the whole of Krleža's group, but I cannot—kill me if you want—I cannot go against my teacher. Because of him, because of his *Plamen* and *Književna republika* [*Flame* and *Republic of letters,* Krleža's journals in the 1920s], I became a Communist, which for me means: I became a man! . . . Zogović attacked him as a compromiser and waverer": Antun Kolendić, "Racin na robiji (I)," *Književnost* 41, nos. 1–2 (1986): 236. The principal casualty in Slovenia was Bratko Kreft, a noted playwright and critic, who was expelled from the KPJ in 1940. See Marko Jenšterle, *Skeptična levica* (Maribor, 1985), pp. 78–93. In December 1939 the KPJ clashed with and isolated a group of students (Albert Kos, Lev Modic, Drago Šega, Vlado Vodopivec), members of the leftist Slovenian Club at the University of Ljubljana, who openly attacked Stalinism. In a letter to a group of leftist Slovene intellectuals, they noted that "all that we have and the only thing in which we can see meaning for our generation is faith in the work for a new world from which will grow a new life for man—including Slovene man. This faith in the ideal can be justified only by a sincere honest endeavor, which does not kill fellow workers and fighters as heretics only because they do not link the cause in which they believe to individual, temporary leaders. Or are we going back some hundred years, to a time when the only measure of truth or untruth was authority? The need for discipline and organization, which at this moment is more dominant than ever, surely cannot be equated with medieval scholastic authority": cited in Ivan Kreft, *Spori in spopadi v spominih in dokumentih,* 3 vols. (Maribor, 1981), 1:421–22. Cf. Slavko Kremenšek, *Slovensko študentovsko gibanje, 1919–1941* (Ljubljana, 1972), pp. 328–31.

the dictatorial regime of Prince Pavle. The Komunistička partija Hrvatske (KPH, Communist Party of Croatia), established in August 1937, did not bridge the widening gap between the Communists and the Croat national movement, certainly not along the lines envisaged by the still imprisoned Hebrang, but its symbolic importance nevertheless should not be underestimated. When elections for Yugoslavia's National Assembly were announced for December 11, 1938, the KPH refused to participate through the legal party established by the KPJ for the purpose (Party of the Working People) and opted instead to support the ticket of Maček's Croat Peasant Party.

The 1938 elections, the last in Yugoslavia before the war, were a key event in the slow process of restoring parliamentary democracy in Yugoslavia and closing the breach between Serbs and Croats after a decade of dictatorship. The United Opposition, headed by Maček and his party, was a coalition of all forces, Serbs included, hostile to the pseudoparliamentary and Great Serbian regime of Prime Minister Milan Stojadinović, who was slowly steering the Yugoslav ship of state toward the fascist flotilla. Under the circumstances, the KPH leadership believed that the victory of the opposition, also called the Bloc of National Agreement, was a prerequisite for the full victory of democracy in Yugoslavia. The stakes were too high to permit absenteeism in the form of a Communist-led Party of the Working People. And indeed, though the elections were rigged, Maček's ticket won 44.9 percent of all votes. Despite Stojadinović's technical victory, his position was so weakened that Prince Pavle dismissed him in February 1939. From Tito's standpoint, however, the decision of the KPH CC to vote for Maček was an indication that the Croat party leadership "fell under bourgeois-national influence, rode on the tail of the Croat Peasant Party, and thus worked in the interest of the enemies of the working class." Moreover, when the Comintern changed its line after the USSR signed a nonaggression pact with Germany—the war between the Western democracies and Hitler in the wake of the invasion of Poland was to be seen as the Second Imperialist War—the KPH leaders dug in their heels and took "a stand in favor of the defensist [pro-Western] position of Maček, the [Serb] Independent Democrats, and other bourgeois parties."[62] As a result, Tito removed Josip Kraš, the KPH secretary, and two other Croat Communist lead-

62. Tito, "Izvještaj o organizacionom pitanju," in *Peta zemaljska,* p. 17.

ers (Andrija Žaja and Djuro Špoljarić) from the KPH CC. The whole affair was directly connected to the fall of Krleža, because he, too, supported the line of the KPH leadership in the 1938 elections and later expressed dismay at Soviet policy in Poland and at the Finnish war.

The struggle against the Croat "revisionists" was intensified after the success of Prince Pavle's policy of compromise with the Croat Peasant Party. After Stojadinović was dismissed, the prince regent appointed a new prime minister, Dragiša Cvetković, and charged him with finding a way to appease the Croat opposition. This was also a demand of the Western powers, which wanted a stable Yugoslavia in the event of a confrontation with Hitler. The decade-long struggle against the Croat and other nationality oppositions was hence conceded to have failed. The Cvetković-Maček Agreement (*Sporazum*) was promulgated on August 26, 1939, three days after Ribbentrop concluded the nonaggression pact with Stalin in Moscow. The agreement created an autonomous Croat banate (*Banovina*), whose territory encompassed Croatia-Slavonia (without portions of eastern Srijem), Dalmatia, and those counties of Bosnia-Hercegovina where the Catholic Croats outnumbered the Orthodox Serbs. Maček became vice-president in the Cvetković cabinet and the Croat Peasant Party took over the regional and local administration in the Banovina. All areas of public policy other than the military, foreign affairs, and joint finances were turned over to the autonomous Croat administration headed by Ban Ivan Šubašić.

The agreement satisfied most of the demands of the Croat national movement, isolating the separatist Ustaša fringe. But whereas the Cvetković-Maček regime represented the high point of civil and national liberties among the Croats, these benefits still were largely denied to the other non-Serb national movements, the exact political status of Slovenia and Serbia was undefined, and the Communists remained illegal. Moreover, though Cvetković represented the interests of a segment of the Serbian political elite, many nationalist circles in Serbia—in the Orthodox church, in the army, in political parties, and among the intellectuals—opposed the agreement as detrimental to Serb interests.

The agreement divided the Communists. Croat Communists could not deny its positive effects, and their liberal stand complemented the pro-agreement feelings of most Croats. In Serbia, however, Communist opposition to the agreement strengthened the leftist stand that coincided with both the sectarian Comintern line of the Second Imperialist War and Serb national sentiment. As for Tito, he characterized the agreement as a compact in which the Serb bourgeoisie made concessions in order to turn the Croat bourgeoisie into "a partner in the struggle against the working class."[63] His position was consistent with his strategic struggle for a Communist offensive, in which he found few partners in the KPH leadership. At a meeting with the KPH CC in Zagreb in the spring of 1940, he appointed a new KPH leadership headed by Rade Končar, a Serb from Croatia. At the same time, Vladimir Bakarić, consistently a Tito loyalist in the KPH summit, was coopted by the KPH Bureau.

The Fifth Land Conference of the KPJ (really a sort of minicongress) took place in deep conspiracy on October 19–23, 1940, at Zagreb. This was the culmination of Tito's strategic victory within the KPJ. The political line of the Fifth Conference was strictly leftist, but so was the overall Comintern position from 1939 to 1941, when the Communist parties were instructed to terminate all Popular Front alliances with the democratic forces. The KPJ, too, was no longer interested in building Popular Front coalitions, such as the Party of the Working People, which the Communists initiated in 1936–1937. As Tito noted in his organizational report to the Fifth Conference, "in view of the newly created political situation and the growing strength of reaction, it was decided not to create any Party of the Working People; we must instead devote all our energies to the establishment of a unified and strong KPJ, which will be capable of executing its tasks in the present period."[64] He went on:

> When the Second Imperialist War broke out, the KPJ CC immediately took the correct stand in appraising the war. In its manifesto and theses the KPJ CC accurately characterized the war as imperialistic. It underscored the position that the peoples of Yugoslavia have no stake in the war. And since the danger existed that the rulers of Yugoslavia would want to push Yugoslavia into the war on the side of the English and French warmongers, the CC was decidedly against the mobilization that the regime wanted to undertake at that time—but failed to carry out, thanks especially to the party's directive and the resistance of the masses. Hence, after the outbreak of this Second Imperialist War,

63. Josip Broz Tito, "Jedinstvo reakcije protiv radnog naroda," in *Sabrana djela*, 5:78.
64. Tito, "Izvještaj o organizacionom pitanju," p. 21.

important new tasks faced our party because of the newly created situation. The whole struggle and work of the party had to be placed on strictly class foundations. We had to terminate plans for—or any actual agreements with—the summits of various bourgeois, so-called democratic parties, which were becoming increasingly reactionary and were agencies of the English and French imperialistic warmongers. Our party and all sections of the Communist International were faced with the following tasks: to struggle for the working masses by fashioning the Popular Front from below . . . , to struggle against the high cost of living, against war, for the freedom and democratic-national rights of the working and nationally oppressed masses of Yugoslavia.

It was found necessary, in the directives of the Communist International and the documents of the CC of our party, to try tirelessly to unmask the role of the imperialistic warmongers. We had to explain to the masses the causes of the war and the pseudodemocracy of the English and French imperialists. We had to unmask and lead a tireless struggle against various agents of the imperialist powers—England and France—which tried with all their might to push Yugoslavia into the war on their side.[65]

Tito's victory in the conflict over strategy created for the first time a tightly knit and fully bolshevized Communist organization in Yugoslavia. All the old factions were pushed aside, their principal spokesmen either outside the KPJ or on its fringes. But the advantages of centralization and discipline were gained at a high cost. The KPJ was organizationally stronger but politically more isolated. Many of its members, especially in Croatia and Slovenia, were waiting for better times and the return to the Popular Front. As it happened, the one-sided hostility to the democracies in World War II proved impossible to maintain even before the Axis aggression against Yugoslavia in April 1941. And though the USSR did not become involved in the war until June, Stalin tried to offset Germany's plans for Yugoslavia. Armed resistance against the invaders—the course favored by the KPJ—was set in motion soon after the military defeat of the Yugoslav army, but under dramatic new circumstances: Yugoslavia had been partitioned out of existence by Germany, Italy, and their allies.

The unity of the KPJ was tested in two ways during the war. First, the partition of the Yugoslav state and the emergence of a satellite

65. Ibid., pp. 23–24.

regime in Croatia (the Italians planned to set up a similar satellite regime in Montenegro) created local conditions that varied widely. Under the circumstances, coordinated action encountered numerous new obstacles. Moreover, the Axis strategy was at first directed specifically against the Serbs; whenever they could, the occupiers appealed to the other nationalities in terms of liberation from the Serb yoke. This strategy created enormous problems for the KPJ in those areas where the Yugoslav state had been least stable. Hardly any Albanians, for example, could be rallied to the cause of Yugoslavia's restoration. And in Macedonia, the KPJ organization under Metodi Šatorov went over to the Bulgarian Communist party, effectively recognizing Bulgaria's acquisition of Macedonia. Clearly, since the utility of the KPJ was predicated on the restoration of Yugoslavia, the only goal the Communists could espouse was a qualitatively different Yugoslav state, which inevitably brought them into conflict with the exponents of the old regime—the government in exile and its Chetnik guerrillas at home.

The struggle for the federalist position on the national question, which could appeal to all of Yugoslavia's national groups, was complicated by the second obstacle to the unity of the KPJ—really a new round of conflict over strategy (see figure 5). Though the factions that Tito pushed out of the KPJ in the late 1930s took no effective part in the armed struggle, the Partisan camp under Tito was not always monolithic. As we have seen, after 1941 Tito was in continuous conflict with Stalin over the leftist policies of the KPJ. Equally important, a strategic conflict was brewing in the KPJ's own ranks.

After Germany attacked the USSR, Tito genuinely sought to change the party line from the Communist class struggle to a war for national liberation against the occupiers and their domestic accomplices. One can argue that the effectiveness of this change was severely limited by the fact that most of the prewar parties staked Yugoslavia's future on an Allied victory rather than on insurgency. Still, when the prewar parties clearly opposed insurrection (and the Communists), one cannot blame the KPJ for seizing an opportunity that the others missed. The terror of the occupiers and of various domestic factions notably the Ustaša terror against the Serbs in Croatia and Bosnia-Hercegovina, the harsh German measures in Slovenia and Serbia, the unpopularity of the Italians in Dalmatia and Montenegro, and the Chetnik terror against the Muslims and Croats—created a spon-

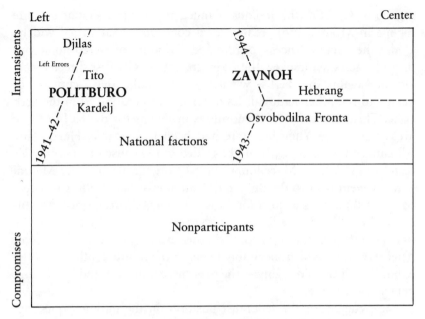

5. The conflict over strategy, 1941–1944

taneous insurgent base, to which the militarized KPJ cheerfully offered its organizational structure. In time it absorbed the amorphous mass movement in most areas of Yugoslavia and infused it with its own ideology. The problem was that the KPJ leaders were not always certain what to do with their success. What was the aim of the Partisan movement and how did it interact, if at all, with the final Communist goal of class revolution?

The ultraleft in the party's Politburo never doubted that the aim was to seize power and sovietize Yugoslavia. The relative ease with which the outlawed KPJ operated in the new circumstances, winning followers where it once reaped indignation, strengthened the general trend toward the left in the leadership. In August 1941, Milovan Djilas, the leftmost member of the Politburo and the KPJ CC's delegate in his native Montenegro, introduced to the Montenegrin party organization the notion of the "forthcoming antifascist revolution, which is nothing other than a necessary stage in the proletarian revolution."[66] This ultraleftist position was repudiated in Montenegro,

66. Cited in Djuro Vujović, "O lijevim greškama KPJ u Crnoj Gori u prvoj godini narodnooslobodilačkog rata," *Istorijski zapisi* 20, no. 1 (1967): 52.

but Tito and his supporters adopted it in the winter and spring of 1941–1942.

In December 1941 the Partisans in Serbia were overcome by a joint German-Chetnik offensive. This defeat stemmed in good part from the leftist policy pursued by Tito in the liberated territory centered on Užice, in southwestern Serbia, as the social radicalism of the Communists helped the Chetnik cause. The Serbian peasants, according to one uncritical account, were attracted to Chetnik slogans "because they saw [in them] the possibility of safeguarding their property."[67] After the collapse of the Užice Partisan republic, the remnants of Tito's forces were obliged to withdraw into the Sandžak and then to eastern Bosnia. This humiliating reversal foreclosed the likelihood of rapprochement with the London Yugoslavs and their local supporters. The Partisans' loss of Serbia encouraged the pro-Chetnik forces, which had not dared to oppose the Communist leadership there when it was an insurgent stronghold. A series of anticommunist putsches took place within the staffs of various insurgent units and several Communist activists were assassinated. Moreover, the British government's continued support of Draža Mihailović, despite the tactical links between the Chetniks and the occupiers, led the KPJ Politburo to suspect that the alliance between the USSR and Great Britain was weakening. The Soviet victory over the Germans at Moscow in December 1941 strengthened the leftist tendencies in the KPJ. Tito's leadership now held that the end of Hitler was at hand. Hence, they thought, the growing fear of the USSR in the West and the corresponding attempts to stem the red tide. In short, according to the KPJ Politburo, the wartime struggle was entering the "second—proletarian—stage," in which the war against the Axis was secondary to the task of class struggle against the domestic counterrevolution, which would lead to the seizure of all power by the Communists.

The leftist line of the KPJ Politburo, which is nowadays generally referred to as the period of Left Errors, lasted until the spring of 1942.

67. Milan M. Miladinović, "Marksističko obrazovanje i vaspitanje u Užičkoj Republici," in Života Marković, ed., Užička Republika, 2 vols. (Belgrade, 1978), 2:299. The most radical measures taken by the KPJ in the Užice region were the sequestration or nationalization of four firms at Čačak (an electric plant, a paper factory, a steam mill, and a trading company) and the seizure of thirty hectares of land from an Orthodox monastery at Trnava for the purposes of agrarian reform. In addition, the KPJ exercised a variety of controls over the economy in the liberated territory. See Jaroslav Dašić, "Privredna delatnost u oslobodjenom Čačku 1941. godine," in ibid., pp. 55–68.

Its effects were felt most strongly in eastern Hercegovina and Montenegro, and to a lesser extent in Vojvodina and Slovenia. In practice, loyalty to the party was measured by one's severity toward the "fifth column" and the "class enemy." These terms were applied to anyone of above-average means or prominence, including members of prominent Communist families. Among the victims was Petar Kovačević of Grahovo (Montenegro), father of seven sons (all Communists, three of them holders of the Order of People's Hero), whose sentence of execution was underwritten by one of his sons.

The burning of "enemy" villages and the confiscation of "enemy" property were commonplace during the Left Errors. Partisan units were given quotas of "fifth columnists" to be shot. Perhaps as many as 500 were executed in Hercegovina alone. Partisan newspapers printed the names of executed "kulaks," occasionally ending with the menacing phrase "to be continued." Plans were laid for the building of soviets and kolkhozes. Churches were desecrated and such anti-Western jingles as "Partisans, prepare your machine guns to greet the king and Englishmen" were quite popular. In addition to the Partisan slogan, "Death to fascism—liberty to the people," a new slogan was gaining currency: "The Red Army is with us—victory is ours." Idleness in the villages was treated as military desertion, and peasants were fined or sentenced to forced labor if their houses were untidy or if they were infested by lice.[68]

In the end, the red terror of 1941–1942 turned out to be a serious mistake. The "second stage" not only was completely out of tune with the Soviet position but, more important, weakened the base of the Politburo's control to the point of virtual collapse. Terrorized peasants who were anything but kulaks or collaborators swelled the Chetnik ranks in Montenegro and eastern Hercegovina. Buoyed by the self-inflicted propaganda defeat of the KPJ, the Chetniks and the occupiers inflicted several military defeats on the Partisans in the spring of 1942. The Politburo then repudiated the Left Errors, "ignoring the fact that the [wrong line] in fact was formulated by the KPJ CC."[69] The principal exponents of the Left Errors (Milovan

68. For an analysis of the Left Errors, see Branko Petranović, "O levim skretanjima KPJ krajem 1941. i u prvoj polovini 1942. godine," *Matica srpska: Zbornik za istoriju*, no. 4 (1971), pp. 39–80; and Rasim Hurem, *Kriza narodnooslobodilačkog pokreta u Bosni i Hercegovini krajem 1941. i početkom 1942. godine* (Sarajevo, 1972), pp. 140–184.
69. Petranović, "O levim skretanjima," p. 67.

Djilas and Ivan Milutinović in Montenegro and Boris Kidrič in Slovenia) were not punished, but some local leaders were (Miro Popara
and Petar Drapšin in Hercegovina and several members of the party
leadership in Montenegro). Curiously, Božo Ljumović, political secretary of the KPJ regional committee for Montenegro and a future
Cominformist, whom Djilas considered an opportunist and a rightist,
was also removed from the Montenegrin party leadership, at least for
the time being. But in rejecting the excesses of the Left Errors, the KPJ
leadership did not reject the leftist goals of class revolution and Communist control; they merely transferred them to the framework of a
struggle for national liberation from the occupiers.

The vanguardist program of the KPJ Politburo could not be applied
to all parts of Yugoslavia with equal vigor. National factions within
the party (Macedonians, whose party organization under Šatorov
defected to the Bulgarian Communist party, and Kosovar Albanians)
had to be won to the discipline of a party that continued to uphold
the uncertain integrity of the dissolved Yugoslav state. More important, in those parts of divided Yugoslavia where the KPJ developed its
most extensive base, the party depended on a stable partnership with
its allies. Hence the respect for the semblance of coalitionist political
structures in the Partisan movements of Slovenia and Croatia, where
the Communists stressed the national struggle against the occupiers
and eschewed any mention of class revolution.

Despite the military reversals that Tito's staff continued to experience, the political line of the Politburo steadily gained ground at
the expense of the broader popular front that originally prevailed in
the northwest. In Slovenia, for example, the political leadership of the
Partisan movement was vested from the beginning in the Osvobodilna fronta (Liberation Front), which was organized at the
Communists' initiative in April 1941 as an apparent coalition of four
groups: the Communist party, the Christian Socialists (a leftist Catholic faction that addressed the concerns of most of Slovenia's solidly
Catholic common people), the left Sokols (Falcons—a nationalist
sports and social society), and a group of independent leftist intellectuals. But in the spring of 1943, after the growing strength of the
Christian Socialists became evident among the Slovene peasants, the
Communists forced their partners to sign the secret Dolomite statement (named for the mountain range where the Osvobodilna fronta

had its headquarters), whereby the noncommunists abrogated their separate group organizations and recognized the leading role of the Communist Party in the Slovene liberation movement.[70]

A far more complicated situation obtained in Croatia. In establishing the Independent State of Croatia, the occupiers were attempting to tap the strong sentiment for independence among the Croats. The Ustaša dictatorship, really a thinly veiled Italo-German condominium, soon disappointed Croat expectations. The isolation of the Ustašas underscored especially the unpopularity of their persecution of the Serbs and of their territorial concessions to the Italians in Dalmatia. Hence the original base of the Partisan movement among Croatia's Serbs (in Lika, Kordun, Banija, and Slavonia) and among the Croats of Dalmatia. Still, resistance against the Ustašas and the occupiers could be turned into a general uprising only with the participation of the Croat Peasant Party. But it was in the area of insurgent activity that Maček's party demonstrated all of its weaknesses. The mass party of passive opposition was organizationally incapable of leading the Croat resistance. In fact, it can fairly be said that the Croat Peasant Party fell apart in 1941; whereas Maček and the bulk of the party followed a wait-and-see policy, the right wing accepted Pavelić and the left wing gravitated toward the Partisans.[71]

The KPH could profit by the paralysis of the Croat Peasant Party only by seizing the patriotic ground conceded by Maček. This was the platform of Andrija Hebrang. After more than a decade in prison, the KPJ's leading exponent of the Popular Front became the natural leader of the national-minded Croat Communists. Arrested by the Ustašas in February 1942, Hebrang was exchanged for two captured Ustaša officials after six months and then became the political secretary of the KPH and a member of the KPJ Politburo.

By the summer of 1943 the Partisan movement in Croatia had scored some dramatic gains, in part because the KPH avoided many

70. As one Slovene Christian Socialist noted in his group's Partisan organ, the Communists' political maturity was the reason they often "incorrectly belittled other groups, something that perhaps stems from faith in their doctrinal infallibility and from the slighting of human qualities. This tendency goes hand in glove with sectarianism, that is, a priori mistrust of and impatience with other founding groups [of the Liberation Front], which is the greatest danger for the Liberation Front": [Stanko?] Kociper, "Pomembnost in plodovitost sodelovanja osnovnih skupin v O.F.," *Slovenska revolucija* 1, no. 4 (1942): 36.

71. The most complete history of the Croat Peasant Party during the war is Fikreta Jelić-Butić, *Hrvatska seljačka stranka* (Zagreb, 1983).

of the errors of Tito's supreme staff.[72] The Croatian Partisans, well away from the Politburo's eye, followed their own dictates and imposed no rigid ideological restraints on the noncommunists in the movement. The organizational vehicle for their policy was the Zemaljsko antifašističko vijeće narodnog oslobodjenja Hrvatske (ZAVNOH, Land Antifascist Council of People's Liberation of Croatia), Croatia's equivalent of AVNOJ—that is, the highest representative body in the land, intended to evolve into the Croatian parliament (*Sabor*). From the beginning the members of ZAVNOH were plainly identified as adherents of separate parties—the Croat Peasant Party, the Independent Democratic Party (the main Serb party in Croatia), KPH, various popular associations and trade unions—or as independents. Though the Communists stressed that their party was the "leading force in the national liberation struggle," the KPH increasingly used the language of Croat patriotism in its "mass line." The goal and the meaning of the Partisan struggle, according to the Hebrang nucleus of the KPH, was the resolution of the national question. "The struggle that the Croat people are today waging for their national liberation, though this struggle contains a series of new developments and changes, is nevertheless a natural, logical continuation and the highest expression of the centuries-old national struggle—to determine their own fate freely in their own home."[73]

The Croat struggle for national liberation, the KPH argued, was always frustrated by the treason of its leaders. The KPH was free of this stain precisely because its course of struggle alone could save Croatia from the two calamitous paths prepared for the Croats by Pavelić and Maček.

> If the national liberation army did not exist in Croatia, if Croatia did not have ZAVNOH, if thousands upon thousands of Croats, despite Maček's invitation to "wait," did not rise with arms in hands against the enslavers of the Croat people, the freedom-loving peoples would today look upon Croatia as a hostile country and upon the Croats as the allies of the greatest enemy of human society. . . . On the one hand, Pavelić's "Independent" Croatia is waging war on the Allies. On the other hand, Yugoslavia is formally being represented abroad by Great Serbian

72. The best available account of the wartime KPH is Ivan Jelić, *Komunistička partija Hrvatske, 1937–1945*, vol. 2 (Zagreb, 1981).
73. "Tragom stoljetne borbe hrvatskog naroda za oslobodjenje," *Naprijed*, May 26, 1943, p. 1.

hegemonist elements—the exiles in the London government, Draža Mihailović, etc.—who are supported by certain reactionary imperialist circles abroad. These Great Serbian and anti-Croat elements have only one goal: despite the single-minded wish of Yugoslavia's popular masses, who want the Yugoslavia of the future to be a homeland of free and equal peoples, these gentlemen wish to revive Great Serbian hegemony in Yugoslavia, to subjugate the Croat, Slovene, and other peoples of Yugoslavia, and once again to crack the whip of exploitation and oppression over them.[74]

Insofar as Maček did not distance himself from the London Yugoslavs or encourage armed struggle against Pavelić, he was strengthening the position of the Great Serbs. The solution was a free Croat state. A free Croatia was a precondition for a Yugoslavia strong enough to protect all the peoples of the Slavic South, because "to the Croats, the idea of a single state community of South Slavs never meant giving up their aspirations to unite and organize themselves, in accordance with their right as a people, within their own national Croat state—to administer and rule themselves."[75]

Hebrang's support for the Croats' national aspirations did not prejudice the KPH's standing among the Serbs of Croatia, who were still the principal base of the Partisan movement in Croatia proper and in Slavonia. The Serbs continued to flock to the "forest" not only because the Partisans were the only real refuge from Ustaša misrule but because, more important, they understood that the existence of Yugoslavia depended on the federalist program of the KPJ. They were therefore increasingly won over to Hebrang's view that the ideas of a federal Yugoslavia and a free Croatia were essentially interdependent: "The full equality of the Serbs of Croatia is a basic precondition for and a living need of free Croatia. And a free Croatia is a condition for and a requirement of free Yugoslavia; and vice versa."[76]

Hebrang's national communism—his urging of the party to embrace the "swelling mass movement" of the people—was incompatible with any variant of leftist exclusivism. Hence his battle against the "sectarianism" in the ranks of the KPH, which eventually brought

---

74. Bc., "Jedini pravilni put," *Naprijed*, Aug. 11, 1943, p. 1.
75. "Sabor ujedinjene Hrvatske izrazio je nepokolebivu volju hrvatskog i srpskog naroda da žive u Demokratskoj Federativnoj Jugoslaviji," *Naprijed*, June 26, 1944, p. 2.
76. "Za slobodnu Hrvatsku u slobodnoj Jugoslaviji," *Naprijed*, Nov. 17, 1943, p. 1.

him into conflict with the KPJ Politburo. "One has only to look at the 'ultraleftist' sectarian slogans on the walls of houses and on fences throughout the liberated territory, in the press, etc.," said one of the KPH's editorials, "to see how sectarianism—and phrasemongering, too, which is its complement—is blooming." Many Communists not only allowed various "ignorant fanatics to fly only red flags and to show 'leftist' sectarian slogans, but did the same themselves, though our audience is the masses of the people and our rallies [must be] national-militant and antifascist in character." Moreover, the ultra-left underestimated the firmness of the Soviet coalition with the Western Allies: "These comrades are falling for fascist slanders and carefully contrived fancies, which are designed to force a wedge between the Allies, weaken the coalition, and isolate the USSR, which would mean the weakening and isolation of the whole consistent antifascist movement throughout the world."[77]

The social policy of the KPH was as moderate as its overall Popular Front approach. The KPH repeatedly stressed that economic life on Partisan territory was being conducted "on the basis of private ownership, private initiative, and freedom of trade."[78] Croatian Partisans encouraged the free exchange of goods, except when shortages of such staple commodities as grain encouraged speculation and hindered military supply. Moreover, ZAVNOH and the Croatian headquarters staff declared in 1943 that the "national liberation movement is introducing no radical changes in regard to social life" and that it "recognizes the inviolability of private ownership as well as the broadest possibilities for the expression of initiative in industry and in other economic activities."[79] Hebrang himself tried to answer questions about the social order after the war in his rousing report to the Second Session of ZAVNOH (Plaški, October 14, 1943):

> The first problem is the question of land for the peasants, because the land must belong to those who cultivate it without respite or compensation. Workers, too, have their demands and their rights. They must be guaranteed better work conditions, a better livelihood, and greater influence in public life. The middle strata, those small people who were

77. "Udarimo po sektaštvu," *Naprijed,* Aug. 11, 1943, p. 2.
78. Branko Zlatarić, "Naša gospodarska politika i njezini problemi," cited in Hodimir Sirotković, ed., *Zemaljsko antifašističko vijeće narodnog oslobodjenja Hrvatske: Zbornik dokumenata 1943* (Zagreb, 1964), p. 96.
79. "Izjava o ciljevima i načelima Narodno-Oslobodilačke Borbe," in ibid., p. 133.

totally exploited and oppressed by capital, also have their demands, which we shall take into consideration so that they can live in a more human way. In short, the position of the working masses must be thoroughly improved. . . . The Democratic Republic of Yugoslavia will clip the wings of capital, which will be supervised and will serve its people.[80]

In his famous speech at the Third Session of zavnoh, at Topusko on May 8, 1944, Hebrang declared that the "national liberation movement has been and is leading the struggle not for communism but . . . for common popular aims—for national liberation and democracy."[81] The Topusko session also adopted a declaration that guaranteed to the peoples and citizens of Democratic Croatia the rights of ownership and property, of private initiative, of freedom of religion and conscience, and of speech, press, assembly, consultation, and association (the latter four within the framework of the Partisan movement for the duration of the war).[82] Small wonder that Kardelj faulted the Slovene party leadership for publishing the "decisions of the Third Session of zavnoh, because we [the KPJ Politburo] do not agree with them in everything."[83]

Hebrang's call for a "true war against sectarianism" was meant to

80. "Drugo zasjedanje zavnoh-a," in ibid., p. 459. Dr. Ivan Ribar, one of the leaders of the prewar Democratic party and the president of avnoj, who attended the second session of zavnoh, was enthusiastic about Hebrang's speech, which he clearly regarded as a new departure for the Partisan movement—the inauguration of an original social model: "As the president of avnoj I rejoice that such a political report as the one delivered by Comrade Andrija was brought forth at this very spot within zavnoh. . . . This political report inaugurates our new policy, which has no connection with politics outside Yugoslavia" (ibid., p. 468).
81. "Treće zasjedanje zavnoh-a," in Hodimir Sirotković, ed., Zemaljsko antifašističko vijeće narodnog oslobodjenja Hrvatske: Zbornik dokumenata 1944 (Zagreb, 1970), 1:607. Marko Belinić, one of the KPH leaders who increasingly fell out with Hebrang, credited the KPH secretary with sole responsibility for the Topusko political report: "At the Third Session of zavnoh, Hebrang read the main political report. . . . Hebrang worked on the report, but informed neither Stevo [Ivan Krajačić] nor me about its contents, although the three of us made up the secretariat of the [KPH] Politburo." Belinić privately objected to Hebrang's denial that the aim of the Partisan struggle was communism: " 'The aim of the national-liberation struggle and of our revolution was the liberation of the country, but also the elimination of wage labor and class exploitation. True national liberation is unthinkable,' I said [to Hebrang], 'without social liberation.' He got mad and burst out at me, 'You are a hardened sectarian' ": Marko Belinić, Put kroz život (Zagreb, 1985), pp. 77–78.
82. "Deklaracija o osnovnim pravima naroda i gradjana demokratske Hrvatske," in Sirotković, ZAVNOH: 1944, 1:666.
83. Zbornik dokumenata i podataka o narodnooslobodilačkom ratu naroda Jugoslavije, vol. 2, pt. 13, Dokumenta CK KPJ i VŠ NOV i POJ 1. maj—31. avgust 1944 (Belgrade, 1982), p. 582.

break the resistance of those KPH forces that were opposed to any appeal to the members of the Croat Peasant Party. He rightly suspected that such sectarian tendencies thrived in Dalmatia, where the influence of the KPJ Politburo was much stronger than in his Partisan "republic," the vast liberated territory "from the Kupa to the sea"— that is, in Banija, Kordun, Lika, Gorski Kotar, and Hrvatsko Primorje. Hebrang claimed that "fear of cooperation with the Croat Peasant Party and its adherents (which is evident in some comrades) only reveals their own political weakness and insecurity."[84] In short, his line was far closer to the coalitionist Soviet positions during the war than to the leftist stance of the KPJ. Small wonder that as early as November 1943 the KPH called for a "free, popular democratic, federative community in Yugoslavia and the Balkans."[85] Small wonder, too, that Stalin and not Tito was cited as the only authority in the main organ of the KPH until September 1943, and that even Partisan poets associated with the Croat Peasant Party, such as Ivan Goran Kovačić, wrote poems in honor of the coalitionist KPH, linking it with the classics of communism by a sort of intuitive populism:

Tvoj silan jezik dade moćna usta Sinu
  (Ko pobuna su strašna, ko Pobjeda krasna)
Markse i Engelse, stijeg Lenjinu, Staljinu
  (Vi, četiri ognja Osvještenja klasna!)

Your forceful tongue gave mighty lips to the Son
  (They are as terrible as rebellion, as beautiful as Victory),
Marx and Engels, the banner to Lenin, Stalin
  (You, four flames of class Awakening!)[86]

By the summer of 1943 Hebrang's line was a source of much displeasure in the KPJ leadership. Not only were the Croat Communists behaving like independent combatants[87]—perhaps inescapably

84. A-a [Andrija Hebrang], "Slomimo otpor sektaša koji spriječavaju uklapanje pristaša HSS-a u NOF," *Naprijed,* Sept. 8, 1943, p. 2.
85. "Tekovine Velikog Oktobra—spas čovječanstva," *Naprijed,* Nov. 3, 1943, p. 1.
86. Ivan Goran Kovačić, "Komunističkoj Partiji," *Naprijed,* Sept. 22, 1943, p. 2.
87. During the first half of 1943 Tito's supreme staff and the Partisan units attached to it were fighting for their lives against two massive enemy encirclement efforts—"Operation Weiss" (the Fourth Offensive in official Yugoslav periodization) and "Operation Schwartz" (the Fifth Offensive)—and there was no time to devote to the political situation in Croatia. Though the Croatian Partisans were fighting battles of their own during this

so under the conditions of guerrilla war—but they were becoming an independent political factor. The point at issue in the growing conflict was Hebrang's Croatocentrism. In the propaganda of the Croat Partisans, Djilas complained, "one detected an inadequate stress on Yugoslavia, and rather too great an emphasis on Croatia."[88] The KPJ Politburo was much against Hebrang's plan to give the Croat Peasant Party a new lease on life, though the conflict over this issue was much more subtle than is often claimed.[89]

It is possible, though not likely, that Hebrang wanted to revive the Croat Peasant Party as an independent political entity in coalition with the KPH. Still, there was no mention of such a full-fledged revival in the proposals that Božidar Magovac, the leader of the pro-Partisan wing of the Croat Peasant Party, laid out before ZAVNOH in June 1943. Magovac's point of departure was that the "spirit of the [peasant] movement was completely preserved and even somewhat strengthened," despite all wartime obstacles. Nevertheless, there were impediments to the "linking of the self-sacrificing endeavors of the national liberation struggle and those of the peasantry organized in

period, the Supreme Staff was distressed that they were not relieving the enemy pressure, and in August Tito quietly replaced the commander of the Croatian headquarters staff, Ivan Rukavina, with Ivan Gošnjak. Velimir Terzić, a Montenegrin Communist and deputy chief of staff at Tito's headquarters, simultaneously became Croatia's chief of staff. See Tito, *Sabrana djela*, 16:269, n. 70.

88. This complaint was at the heart of an inspection report that Djilas wrote for Tito's supreme staff in 1943. See Milovan Djilas, *Wartime* (New York, 1977), p. 315.

89. Hebrang's attitude toward the Croat Peasant Party and its role in the Partisan movement is a subject of much controversy. One school of thought holds that the Croat Peasant Party was revived in Hebrang's Croat Partisan republic and at the ZAVNOH session at Plaški became an equal partner of the KPH. The Politburo faulted Hebrang especially for the revival of the Peasant Party. See Ivan Supek, *Krunski svjedok protiv Hebranga* (Chicago, 1983), pp. 96, 105. This is also the position of Hebrang's adversaries, who claim that Hebrang overestimated the importance of the Croat Peasant Party and wanted to make it a partner of the KPH. For a typical example of this view, see Dragan Kljakić, *Dosije Hebrang* (Belgrade, 1983), p. 155. The second school of thought holds that the policy of the KPH in regard to the Croat Peasant Party—and therefore that of Hebrang—was part of a long-term strategy aimed at terminating party pluralism in the national liberation movement. See Vojislav Koštunica and Kosta Čavoški, *Stranački pluralizam ili monizam: Društveni pokreti i politički sistem u Jugoslaviji, 1944–1949* (Belgrade, 1983), pp. 53–54. This position has been shared in the 1980s by the Zagreb political establishment (minus the bias against party monism). According to this view, Hebrang was in no position to influence the Titoist line of the KPH. "The uprising [in Croatia] developed so broadly that no individual, even at the most responsible levels at that time, could change its course in any essential way": Milutin Baltić, "KPH je pokrenula mase u oslobodilačku borbu," *Vjesnik*, July 22, 1985, p. 3.

the peasant movement." Without identifying those impediments, Magovac went on to list his proposals. He asked for the revival of *Slobodni dom* (Free home), the chief organ of the Croat Peasant Party, which Magovac had edited before the war, but which would now be published as a Partisan newspaper, though "entirely freely and independently in the spirit of the Croat peasant movement's program." Magovac proposed the establishment of an "Executive Committee of the Croat Peasant Movement" which would have sole authority to recognize the authentic "members" of the "movement (or the Croat Peasant Party)." He also called for mutual political respect among the "members" of the national liberation struggle and for Partisan support of Magovac's aides.[90] Clearly the impediments to which Magovac alluded earlier included fear of Communist hegemony in the "forest." But the avoidance of the term "party" and the idiosyncratic use of "members" suggests that the remedy was not—as it could not be in 1943—the restoration of the Croat Peasant Party's prewar status. The party suited for peacetime could not reverse two years of wartime decomposition.

The KPH CC accepted all of Magovac's demands and *Slobodni dom* resumed publication on Partisan territory in July 1943. The main point of Hebrang's letter to the KPH committees on this matter was that the Partisans thereby gained an "important weapon in the struggle against the chief danger in Croatia—the traitorous portion of the Croat Peasant Party's leadership," that is, the Maček loyalists. Hebrang also stressed that *Slobodni dom* was targeted for the "unliberated areas of Croatia," presumably to explain its slightly different tone, which was tailored to appeal to the unconvinced.[91] If Hebrang meant his policy toward Magovac's group to go further, he was deterred by Tito's directive of August 14, 1944, in which the KPJ leader noted that "we [the Politburo] consider it a mistake to aid the creation of some new Croat Peasant Party as a basis for cooperation in the nat[ional] li[beration] struggle. Agreements must be made on the basis of ZAVNOH. . . . The creation of a new Croat Peasant Party is a purely internal affair of those who wish that."[92]

Tito was inclined to suspect Hebrang. But as Kardelj quickly in-

90. Božidar Magovac, "Zemaljskom antifašističkom vijeću narodnog oslobodjenja Hrvatske," in Sirotković, *ZAVNOH: 1943*, pp. 235–36.

91. CK KPH, July 13, 1943, in ibid., pp. 272–73.

92. Tito, *Sabrana djela*, 16:106.

formed Tito from Hebrang's headquarters, the "political representation [of Magovac's Croat Peasant Party] is within the ZAVNOH framework . . . so we can control them [Magovac's group]. We agreed that
they will not establish independent Croat Peasant Party organizations
in the field, but will work for a single all-national liberation movement under the leadership of the committees of national liberation, in
which they will have people chosen by themselves, so long as [their]
adherents decide to cooperate with the committees. . . . [Magovac's]
leadership [will approach the peasant] movement only through ZAV-
NOH. Their 'Executive Committee' will have the general political
function of the Croat Peasant Party's representative," but not that of
an organizational or recruiting center.[93] Clearly the Magovac group
was no more than a "mass organization" under the leadership of the
KPH, and that is precisely how the KPH leaders—Hebrang included—treated the "Croat Peasant Party groups and individuals,"
or the "adherents of the Croat Peasant Party"; they always soft-
pedaled the organization's party character when they referred to the
Peasant Party among the components of the national liberation
front.[94] In fact, from the KPH's point of view, the "Croat Peasant
Party [did] not exist as a party; it ha[d] disintegrated." Hence the
warnings to KPH activists not to protect the good name of the old
Croat Peasant Party and not to print articles that "create an impression that the Croat Peasant Party men are the representatives of the
Croat people—especially of the peasantry . . . [or] that we are working for the salvation of the Croat Peasant Party."[95]

For all that, there was an aspect of "saving the Radićists" in
Hebrang's policy. Hebrang kept assuring the KPH committees that
"our cooperation with the mass of the Croat Peasant Party's adherents is no maneuver."[96] Indeed, in many areas, as in Karlovac
county, the Communists "took the path of organizing the Croat
Peasant Party as a party with special organizations."[97] Hebrang

93. *Zbornik dokumenata i podataka o narodnooslobodilačkom ratu naroda Jugoslavije*,
vol. 2, pt. 10. *Dokumenta CK KPJ i VŠ NOV i POJ, juli–oktobar 1943* (Belgrade, 1962), p.
206.
94. Sirotković, *ZAVNOH: 1943*, pp. 341, 349.
95. Mladen Iveković, "O našoj štampi," in Sirotković, *ZAVNOH: 1944*, 1:106–7.
96. CK KPH, Aug. 19, 1943, in Sirotković, *ZAVNOH: 1943*, p. 351.
97. "Referat dr Save Zlatića-Miće, sekretara OK KPH za Karlovac o radu partijskih
organizacija u karlovačkom okrugu u vremenu izmedju Druge i Treće okružne partijske
konferencije (mart 1942–novembar 1943)," in Djuro Zatezalo, ed. *Treća konferencija
KPH za okrug Karlovac, 1943* (Karlovac, 1979), p. 87.

wanted to spark an uprising among the old followers of Radić and
Maček without arousing suspicions about Communist intentions. Despite his attacks against Maček, it has been claimed that he believed
Maček to be a neutral in Croatia's wartime maze.[98] And it is characteristic that "at all meetings of the [KPH] CC Politburo, Hebrang
always strongly stressed the strength of the Croat Peasant Party and
the authority of Maček, claiming that [the KPH] should be very
careful in its actions and 'not rush headlong.' "[99] Hebrang was well
aware of the strength of the Radić-Maček legend and, unlike the
younger and more self-assertive generation of Croat Communists,
represented by such men as Bakarić, he was probably sentimentally
attached to it himself.

Tito shared no such sentiments. He had no objection to captive
parties within the Partisan movement, but he feared their potential
for independent action. "Do not establish the Croat Peasant Party
organization from below," he wrote to Djuro Pucar in July 1944.[100]
He was less worried by the committees of notables "from above,"
such as the Magovac group. But even Tito could be flexible when the
occasion arose. In September 1943 he cautioned the headquarters
staff for Croatia not to resist demands by the Croat Peasant Party
people for their own commissars in Partisan units: "The explanation
that you gave to the Radićists about the role of the politcommissars is
correct, but we cannot reject [their] demand to appoint their own
commissars in units here and there—not double commissars, but by
parity, in agreement with them, so that they trust us."[101] Less flexible
were the Serb members of the Politburo, such as Hebrang's old opponent Djilas, who concluded that "by placing the primary emphasis on
attracting the Croatian masses, Hebrang gave the party a predominantly Croatian tone,"[102] and thereby aroused anxiety among the
Serbs of Croatia.

It is difficult to take the measure of all the fears that possessed the
Serbs of Croatia. The Ustaša terror left a residue of suspicion about
all Croats, though perhaps less than is usually imagined. The Serbs

98. Jakov Blažević, *Tražio sam crvenu nit* (Zagreb, 1976), p. 77. This claim is dropped in
the updated version of Blažević's memoirs. See Jakov Blažević, *Suprotstavljanja . . . i ljudi:
Za novu Jugoslaviju po svijetu* (Zagreb, 1980), p. 139.
99. Belinić, *Put*, p. 130.
100. *Zbornik dokumenata*, vol. 2, pt. 13, p. 494.
101. Ibid., pt. 10, p. 247.
102. Djilas, *Wartime*, p. 315.

certainly felt safer when Croats were recruited to the Partisan movement in large numbers. Many Serbs, however, were susceptible to
Chetnik propaganda, which scored a considerable success in the Kordun in May 1944, when four Partisan commanders, all Serbs, deserted to the Germans, tricking some ninety Serb Partisans into going
with them. Though all but the ringleaders and fourteen others returned, the KPH district committee for Karlovac took stern measures
after this incident. Sixteen deserters were tried and sentenced; five
were executed. The party cells in the Plaški Partisan detachment were
dissolved. Of the 116 party members in the detachment, 25 remained
in the KPH, 34 were returned to candidacy and 14 to SKOJ, and 43
were expelled. The deserters were clearly unhappy about the status of
Serbs in Partisan Croatia. They felt that the Cyrillic script was being
discouraged, that discussion of the Ustaša massacres against the Serbs
was frowned upon, and that the Serbs were not sufficiently represented in ZAVNOH and in the KPH CC.[103]

These resentments were typical of the time and cannot be traced to
actual wrongs. Moreover, Hebrang personally tried to mitigate the
Serbs' mistrust by having the presidency of ZAVNOH adopt the "obligatory introduction of Roman and Cyrillic script in all schools of
Croatia, so that where the Croat children were in the majority, instruction would begin in Roman script, and where Serb children were
in the majority, instruction would begin in Cyrillic script."[104] And,
most likely at his request, ZAVNOH tried to get a font of Cyrillic type
from Allied sources for the benefit of *Srpska riječ* (Serb word), a
ZAVNOH newspaper aimed at the Serbs of Croatia.[105] Still, Hebrang's
emphasis on the overriding loyalty of Croatia's Serbs to their Croatian homeland probably was difficult for some Serbs to swallow. But
that line alone had a chance to break the circle of Serbian hegemony
and Croat revanchism. Rade Pribićević, the head of ZAVNOH's Serb
Club, declared, "We shall do our duty to Croatia, as would every
good son of Croatia, and we shall defend her state and federal rights
within our common Yugoslavia. . . . There are three Croats for every

103. Djuro Zatezalo, ed., *Četvrta konferencija KPH za okrug Karlovac 1945* (Karlovac, 1985), pp. 52–55.
104. Hodimir Sirotković, ed., *Zemaljsko antifašističko vijeće narodnog oslobodjenja Hrvatske: Zbornik dokumenata 1944* (Zagreb, 1975), 2:101.
105. Ibid., p. 116.

Serb in Croatia. What right, then, has that one Serb to ask the three Croats to join him in harnessing themselves to the Great Serbian cart, so that in the name of that one Serb both Serbs and Croats may be oppressed?"[106] Hebrang certainly believed that the reality of the Serb position in Croatia required the Serbs to accept a minority position; they had equal rights, but in a Croat entity.

One might conclude that it was the Croat Communists' insistence on "setting up shop on their own," rather than Hebrang's supposed political pluralism, that led to several more confrontations with Tito.[107] On September 20, 1943, ZAVNOH proclaimed the unification of the formerly Italian-held territories (Istria, Rijeka, Zadar, etc.) with the "matrix land of Croatia." Tito criticized the Croats for "assuming a sovereignty that belonged to Yugoslavia alone."[108] He continued to veto Hebrang's initiatives. In February 1944 he over-ruled Hebrang's attempt to create a Croat Partisan government on the model of Tito's National Committee for Liberation, and in March he stopped what he took to be Hebrang's attempt to establish a system of regular courts in Croatian liberated territory. During the same month the KPJ CC objected to one of Hebrang's dispatches as having a "tone that is not customary in communication with higher party forums." And then in April 1944 there was a clash over a slogan that appeared in a Croat Partisan journal: "Long live a free and united Croatia in fraternal federative community with free Serbia and free Slovenia." "It is simply unbelievable," wrote Tito to Hebrang, "that you could let this slip by, ignoring the other peoples and excluding the word Yugoslavia. In our considered opinion this is no accident. This is consistent with your line. . . ."[109] After this inci-dent Tito summoned Hebrang to the supreme staff at Drvar (Bosnia),

106. Rade Pribićević, "Srpska misao i velikosrpska sila," *Srpska riječ,* July 22, 1944, p. 1.
107. Djilas, *Wartime,* p. 407. As Bakarić put it, Hebrang "never mentioned Yugoslavia. In that sense, he was not merely a federalist but a confederalist": "Titove kritike Hebranga: Intervju sa drom Vladimirom Bakarićem," *Vjesnik,* Oct. 25, 1976, p. 4.
108. Djilas, *Wartime,* p. 317. Djilas's formulation closely follows Tito's own words on the matter: "It is incorrect for ZAVNOH alone to proclaim the nullification of all agreements [that formed the basis of Italy's sovereignty over the territories in question], and solely by its own signature. The proclamation should also have been signed by AVNOJ, with the accom-panying signature of the presidency of ZAVNOH. Otherwise, it will not be valid in the eyes of foreign powers and signifies the separatism that all the allies oppose" (*Sabrana djela,* 17:3).
109. Tito, *Sabrana djela,* 19:8, 122, 280, 214.

sternly rebuked him, and ordered the members of the KPH CC to
repudiate Hebrang's ideas.[110] It was only a matter of time before
Hebrang would be forced out of the KPH leadership.

Matters came to a head in September 1944. In early September the
KPJ CC tried to soften the criticisms that the KPH leadership directed
against the district committee for Dalmatia.[111] In mid-September
Tito denounced a ZAVNOH regulation making the catechism a required school subject in Croatian Partisan territory. He expressed
enormous surprise at this "very crude error," which he termed a
"rotten concession" that introduced an "element of obscurantism
among the achievements of our struggle."[112] Two days later he bris-
tled at Hebrang's decision to form a news agency for Croatia: "Immediately discontinue work on your so-called telegraphic agency
TAH [Croatian Telegraphic Agency]. What is the meaning of this?
You are being swept along at full steam into separatism. Can't you
see that federal states, too, have only one official telegraphic agency?
If no one else will do, let the Soviet Union be your example."[113] On
September 18, Tito ordered Kardelj to go to Croatia and investigate
Hebrang's separatist tendencies: "Should Andrija hold to such views,
we shall have to remove him as secretary of the KPH."[114] Kardelj,
Djilas, Ranković, and Milutinović then made the case for Hebrang's
dismissal. Sreten Žujović-Crni and Franc Leskošek were the only
members of the Politburo who were not involved in Hebrang's removal from Croatia.

Writing for the group, Kardelj indicted Hebrang in a letter to Tito

110. For the substance of the discussion at Drvar, see Marko Belinić, *Do naših dana*
(Zagreb, 1966), pp. 122–25. Belinić "was trying to prove that the party's influence surpassed all previous influence of the Croat Peasant Party among the masses, that the [KPH]
dominates with its actions, its ideational and political positions. This was at odds with
Hebrang's estimates" (ibid., p. 124).

111. *Zbornik dokumenata i podataka o narodnooslobodilačkom ratu naroda
Jugoslavije*, vol. 2, pt. 14, *Dokumenta CK KPJ i VŠ NOV i POJ 1. septembar–31. decem-
bar 1944* (Belgrade, 1981), pp. 21–23. The conflict over Dalmatia had been brewing ever
since December 1943, when Hebrang effectively accused Tito of treating Dalmatia as if it
were not part of Croatia. See Tito, *Sabrana djela*, 18:293–94, n. 244.

112. *Zbornik dokumenata*, vol. 2, pt. 14, p. 113. A little earlier, in August 1944, the
presidency of ZAVNOH had ordered its judicial commission to draft a proposal prohibiting
divorce and not even permitting married partners to live apart unless they had first made
material provisions for the custody and support of their children: Sirotković, *ZAVNOH:
1944*, 2:259.

113. Sirotković, *ZAVNOH: 1944*, 2:124.

114. Dušan Živković, ed., *Hronologija radničkog pokreta i SKJ, 1919–1979* (Belgrade,
1980), 2:300.

6. The Yugoslav Communist leadership at Jajce, November 1943 (from left to right): Ivo Lolo Ribar, secretary of the League of Communist Youth of Yugoslavia (killed in a German attack shortly after this photo was taken); Aleksandar Ranković, the party's organizational secretary; Milovan Djilas; Josip Broz Tito; Sreten Žujović-Crni; Andrija Hebrang; Moša Pijade; Edvard Kardelj. Missing: Franc Leskošek and Ivan Milutinović. All but Pijade were members of the Politburo.

dated September 30, 1944. The KPH leader's principal offense was nationalism. "Andrija at every daily step exudes some nationalist *uklon* [Russian for "deviation"]. True, in their newspapers and propaganda [the Croats] talk a great deal about Yugoslavia. In reality, this obscures a tendency toward aversion to Yugoslavia. I do not claim that this tendency is conscious with Andrija, but it is clearly seen in a series of everyday little things. I doubt that I would be exaggerating if I said that Andrija does not like the Serbs and Slovenes, and that he considers Yugoslavia a 'necessary evil.'" Kardelj harped on Hebrang's bad attitude toward the Serbs, which Kardelj cited in support of a special "national liberation front of Serbs in Croatia," something that Hebrang clearly resisted and Tito never approved. A further point was the way the Croat party leadership ignored the KPJ CC. He also accused Hebrang of autocratic tendencies, commandism, and individualistic personal habits, and of promoting reactionary customs, specifically obligatory church weddings. "For all of these reasons," concluded Kardelj, "we consider it indispensable to remove Andrija from the position of secretary of the KPH CC and to send [Vladimir] Bakarić over there to fill that post." The group also proposed that the KPH Bureau coopt Vicko Krstulović and that Dušan Brkić become the KPH's organizational secretary. Bakarić and Krstulović were Hebrang's enemies ("he really hates Bakarić and Vicko Krstulović"). Krstulović, secretary of the district committee for Dalmatia, was rewarded for his loyalty to the Politburo ("Andrija and the whole KPH CC in fact have fallen down on Dalmatia because, in the first place, Dalmatia shows far closer links with Yugoslavia than does the rest of Croatia").[115] Brkić was the leader of the pro-Hebrang Serbs.[116] His proposed promotion was probably meant to bring his group along.

Hebrang was genuinely popular in Croatia, and it was no easy task to remove him. A public attack on his views was out of the question, especially since Croat public opinion was still by no means securely pro-Partisan. On October 5, 1944, Tito ordered Ranković to send Kardelj, Djilas, and Bakarić to KPH headquarters, remove Hebrang, install Bakarić in the KPH leadership, and bring Hebrang to Belgrade. Two weeks later, on October 20, Belgrade fell to the Soviets and Partisans.[117] Still in the Politburo, Hebrang became the virtual economic tsar of Yugoslavia in liberated Belgrade. He was appointed minister of industry and head of the planning commission and the economic council in the emerging federal government. But, like ancient King Antaeus, he lost much of his power after he was removed from his native ground.

It has been said that the "charge of 'nationalism' often hinted at the multiparty democracy that appeared in the national liberation movement," the aim being to discredit political pluralism in the eyes of other nations.[118] Since multiparty democracy was not, as we have

115. "Značajan istorijski dokumenat iz ratne arhive K.P.J.," in *Naša reč* 33, no. 313 (1980): 10–12.
116. Among the Serb Communists in Croatia, Hebrang was in conflict with Mile Počuča. Kardelj's letter suggests that Stanko Opačić-Ćanica and Rade Pribićević had reservations about Hebrang. Dušan Brkić and Rade Žigić were Hebrang's men.
117. *Zbornik dokumenata*, vol. 2, pt. 14, p. 210.
118. Ivan Supek, "Obnovljeni humanizam: Povodom obljetnice Kongresa kulturnih radnika Hrvatske, Topusko, 25–27. [lipnja] 1944" (unpublished article, Zagreb, 1984), p. 21.

seen, a prominent bone of contention in the KPJ, the charge of "nationalism" more likely was meant to undermine or discredit the national groupings in the party which feared a new centralist Yugoslavia. And indeed, "the development of federalism after the Second Session of AVNOJ [at Jajce in 1943] tended strongly to give national (land) identifications to the institutions of the members of the federation, which was still under construction." The consolidation of the federation during 1944, which was "completed with the liberation of the whole country and the adoption of the constitution [in 1946], especially with the building up of the armed forces, provoked a reaction in some national party leaderships."[119] Before 1944 the KPJ Politburo took care to appeal to each nationality of Yugoslavia in terms of its individual aspirations. In the course of 1944 and in the immediate postwar period the focus shifted to the new state and its aspirations. Tito set the mood in January 1944 when he called for avoidance of leftist sectarianism, but at the same time for greater centralism and control: "We should change the tone of our press and agitation altogether in the sense that all questions must be approached from the standpoint of a new, independent state entity, which is nobody's offshoot, but the creation of our peoples' struggle. . . . We must do away with all sorts of little district newspapers, which publish without much control and usually sow confusion. The problems of these districts must be brought into the central land press, which ought to pay more attention to concrete questions than to 'high' politics."[120] High politics were not for the lands (future republics) but only for the inmost center.

Despite the new mood at the center, the Partisan federation was too centralist for most non-Serbs and too diffuse for the Serbs. Its membership was slimmer than had been envisioned and more prone to pragmatic border solutions. The land assemblies or their equivalents, originally all-purpose political bodies, were established after the First AVNOJ (at Bihać in November 1942), except for the Main National Liberation Committee for Serbia, which was established in November 1941 and vegetated for three years, from the fall of the Užice Partisan republic to the liberation of Serbia in October 1944. Besides the Serbian committee, they were the Slovenian National Liberation

119. Branko Petranović, "KPJ i društveno-političke promene u Jugoslaviji od AVNOJ-a do Ustavotvorne skupštine," *Institut za izučavanje istorije Vojvodine: Istraživanja* 1 (1971): 389.
120. Tito, *Sabrana djela*, 18:231.

Committee (October 1943); the land assemblies for Croatia (ZAV-NOH), Montenegro and the Bay of Kotor (ZAVNOCGiB), the Sandžak (ZAVNOS), and Bosnia-Hercegovina (ZAVNOBiH), and the Main National Liberation Committee for Vojvodina (all in November 1943); and the land assembly for Macedonia (ASNOM, August 1944). After the Second AVNOJ at Jajce, these political bodies became representative, legislative, and executive bodies—the supreme civil authorities in a states-system. The transformation took place in Slovenia with the establishment of the Slovenian National Liberation Assembly (SNOS, Črnomelj, February 1944), in Croatia at the Third ZAVNOH (Topusko, May 1944), in Bosnia-Hercegovina at the Second ZAVNOBiH (Sanski Most, June–July 1944), in Montenegro and the Bay of Kotor with the establishment of the Montenegrin Antifascist Assembly of People's Liberation (CASNO, Kolašin, July 1944), in Macedonia at the First ASNOM (Prohor Pčinjski, August 1944), and in Serbia with the establishment of the Great Antifascist Assembly of People's Liberation (VASNOS, Belgrade, November 1944). In April and early May 1945, "people's governments" were established in the six federal units (the term "republic" was still eschewed) of Serbia, Croatia, Slovenia, Macedonia, Montenegro, and Bosnia-Hercegovina, in the hierarchical and nonalphabetical order that had been in use since the AVNOJ meeting at Jajce.

The simple citing of these facts reveals all manner of untidiness. What happened to the Sandžak, which was on an equal footing with Serbia and Croatia in 1943? How did Montenegro and the Bay of Kotor come to be Montenegro alone? Why did Vojvodina fail to become a federal unit and what was meant by Vojvodina to begin with? And where was Kosovo (or Kosovo-Metohia—Kosmet for short) in these combinations?

The answers point to a pragmatic state of federalism. The land assembly for the Sandžak (ZASNOS) was established as a concession to the Muslims, who constituted 43.09 percent of the region's population in 1931 and were generally anti-Partisan.[121] From the Muslim

121. The total population of the Sandžak (the counties of Bijelo Polje, Dežava, Mileševa, Nova Varoš, Pljevlja, Priboj, Sjenica, and Štavica) was 204,068 in 1931 (the year of the last prewar census). Of that number 87,939 (43.09%) were overwhelmingly Bosnian Muslims, with a sprinkling of Albanians. The majority of 115,260 (56.48%) were Orthodox Serbs or Montenegrins; the negligible remainder were Catholics and others. On the rise and fall of the Sandžak's autonomy in Partisan Yugoslavia, see Zoran Lakić, "Zemaljsko antifašističko vijeće narodnog oslobodjenja Sandžaka," in Nikola Babić, ed., AVNOJ i narod-

point of view, the best solution was unification of the Sandžak with Bosnia-Hercegovina, to which it had belonged within the Ottoman Empire before the Congress of Berlin (1878). The Sandžak would then have become an autonomous province within Bosnia-Hercegovina. If that solution failed, the Muslims preferred to see it unattached, or attached to Serbia or Montenegro. The worst solution, in the Muslim view, was to divide the Sandžak between Serbia and Montenegro, as had been done after the Balkan wars of 1912–1913. This idea was also opposed by not a few Serbs and Montenegrins, who wanted the whole region for their respective federal units.

In January 1944 the land assembly of Montenegro and the Bay of Kotor cited the Sandžak as part of the emerging Montenegrin federal unit, provoking disapproval among the "Orthodox" (Serbs) and fear among the Muslims.[122] The KPJ CC denounced the Montenegrin initiative in a letter of March 31, 1944, to the district committee for the Sandžak: "We not only dispute such a thoughtless step, we condemn it. AVNOJ and the National Committee are not defining borders today, because that is premature—AVNOJ's decisions were offered only in principle. As far as the Sandžak is concerned, it will have the status that its freely elected representatives decide. In this respect, what Comrade Tito wrote about Vojvodina in the first issue of *Nova Jugoslavija* [New Yugoslavia] goes also for the Sandžak."[123] Not that Tito supplied a clear clue to guide his readers through the maze of the party's federal policy. "Vojvodina," he wrote in the cited article, "will receive the widest autonomy, but the questions of autonomy and of the federal unit to which this province will belong depend on the people themselves, or rather on their representatives, when the definitive state organization is determined after the war."[124] Still, a careful reader of Tito's article could see that (1) Vojvodina would not

---

nooslobodilačka borba u Bosni i Hercegovini (1942–1943) (Belgrade, 1974), pp. 678–94; Branko Petranović, "Položaj Sandžaka u svetlosti odluke Drugog zasedanja AVNOJ-a o izgradnji Jugoslavije na federativnom principu," *Istorijski zapisi* 24, nos. 3–4 (1971): 567–75.

122. Petranović, "Položaj Sandžaka," p. 571.

123. "Oblasnom komitetu KPJ za Sandžak," in Tito, *Sabrana djela,* 19:284.

124. Tito, *Sabrana djela,* 19:88. This citation is incomplete in Tito's collected works. For the full citation see Ranko Končar, "Problem autonomije Vojvodine u kontekstu odluka Drugog zasedanja AVNOJ-a," in Babić, ed., *AVNOJ,* p. 629. According to Josip Smodlaka, in the entry of December 30, 1944, in his unpublished diary, even at that late date Tito agreed with Smodlaka (but how unflinchingly?) that the best solution for Vojvodina would be to grant it the status of a federal unit (*AVNOJ,* p. 629, n. 20).

be a federal unit (republic); (2) no referendum would be held to determine whether it should be a federal unit; and (3) the extent of Vojvodina's autonomy within another federal unit was still not clear. The same, then, applied to the Sandžak.

In February 1945 the presidency of AVNOJ held that the Sandžak had no "national basis" for autonomy. An autonomous Sandžak would constitute an "uncalled-for and irrational crumbling of the Serbian and Montenegrin totality and of Yugoslavia in general."[125] Once decided at the top, the "liquidation of the Sandžak's current status" soon followed. On March 29, 1945, ZAVNOS decided to divide the region between Serbia and Montenegro along the demarcation line of 1912 and then dissolved itself.[126]

Vojvodina's prospects were not so bleak. The party, military, and representative institutions of Serbia and Vojvodina (the regional party committee, the headquarters staff, the main national liberation committee) were of equal rank during the war. For all that, there was no mention of Vojvodina at Jajce. Worse still, the KPJ Politburo did not approve the request of the KPJ regional committee for Vojvodina that "we form a land assembly for Vojvodina."[127] Jovan Veselinov-Žarko, the wartime secretary of Vojvodina's regional committee, remembered some years later that "after the liberation of Belgrade we learned that at the Second Session of AVNOJ, in the absence of Vojvodina's representatives, the opinion already prevailed that because of its national composition, autonomous Vojvodina ought to enter into the framework of federal Serbia."[128] All that was needed was the

125. From the letter of the presidency of AVNOJ to the Executive Committee of ZAVNOS, cited in Petranović, "KPJ i društveno-političke promene," p. 389.
126. Sreten Vukosavljević, a former deputy of the Democratic party from Prijepolje, sociologist, professor at the University of Belgrade, and the president of ZAVNOS, failed to sign this decision, which gave two of Sandžak's counties (Pljevlja and Bijelo Polje) to Montenegro and the rest to Serbia.
127. Cited in Končar, "Problem autonomije Vojvodine," p. 627.
128. Jovan Veselinov-Žarko, *Svi smo mi jedna partija* (Novi Sad, 1971), p. 35. The Serb population of the Banate of Danube (1931) north of the Sava and Danube rivers, without Baranja but including the cities of Pančevo and Zemun, which were within the Belgrade administrative area—an area only slightly larger than postwar Vojvodina—was 715,735, or 45.11% of the area's total population. Veselinov, acutely aware of the area's peculiarities, was removed from Vojvodina because of his insistence on genuine autonomy. According to Dušan Popović, a party leader from Vojvodina, "after the war it was urgently demanded that Vojvodina sever direct ties with the federation, submit itself to Serbia, and lose its identity. By way of illustration, a conflict arose in 1944–45 over the position of the province. As a result, the political and organizational secretaries of the regional committee (Jovan Veselinov-Žarko and Isa Jovanović) had to go": "Moraju se reći sve istine," *NIN*, Oct. 16, 1983, p. 27.

agreement of Vojvodina's main national liberation committee, which dutifully went along on April 6, 1945.

Unlike Vojvodina, which became an autonomous province (*pokrajina*) of Serbia, Kosovo and Metohia (Kosmet) were accorded the lesser dignity of an autonomous district (*oblast*) of Serbia. The KPJ Politburo evidently never intended to treat Kosmet as a federal unit. The region was not mentioned at Jajce, nor was its leadership authorized to form a land assembly. When, in 1944, the KPJ district committee for Kosovo and Metohia unilaterally promoted itself to the status of a regional committee, simultaneously changing the Serbo-Hellenic term Metohia into Albanian Dukagjin, the KPJ CC reversed this decision.[129] Sreten Žujović-Crni, apparently alone among the topmost Yugoslav Communists, wished to divide Kosmet between Serbia and Albania, provided Albania joined the Yugoslav federation.[130] As minority areas, but under vastly different circumstances, Vojvodina and Kosmet were under martial law after the war.

There remained the question of the borders of the six federal units. On February 24, 1945, the presidency of AVNOJ discussed the proportional representation of the federal units in AVNOJ. Mile Peruničić, the secretary of AVNOJ, at that point brought out a highly revealing document in which the then frontiers of the federal units were explained as follows: "SLOVENIA was included in the frontiers of the former Drava banate; CROATIA in the frontiers of the former Sava banate with the thirteen counties of the former Primorje [Littoral] banate and the county of Dubrovnik from the former Zeta banate: BOSNIA-HERCEGOVINA in the frontiers defined by the Congress of Berlin [1878]; SERBIA in the frontiers before the Balkan wars with the counties taken from Bulgaria [Caribrod and Bosiljgrad] by the Peace of Versailles;

---

129. *Zbornik dokumenata*, vol. 1, pt. 19, *Borbe na Kosovu, 1941–1944* (Belgrade, 1979), p. 462.

130. Dedijer, *Novi prilozi*, vol. 2 (Rijeka, 1981), pp. 903–4. According to a recent interpretation by Kosta Čavoški, a dissident Serbian scholar, Kosovo and Metohia, oddly, were not mentioned in the documents of the First and Second AVNOJ or the later directorates of that body. "And, strangest of all, unlike the Sandžak and Vojvodina, Kosovo and Metohia were not represented at all in AVNOJ throughout the war. This can lead to the conclusion that the then status of these districts was not only an internal Yugoslav matter but an international question, and that the KPJ leadership waited until the end of the war to solve that question definitively": "Iz istorije stvaranja nove Jugoslavije," *Književna reč*, Dec. 25, 1986, p. 7. If Čavoški means to suggest that Tito at any time toyed with the idea of turning Kosmet over to Albania, his interpretation is farfetched. For the KPJ leadership, and Tito especially, the only alternative to the ultimate disposition of Kosmet was a variant of the Žujović solution; that is, partial or complete inclusion of Kosmet within the Yugoslav republic of Albania.

MACEDONIA—Yugoslav territory south of the Kačanik Range and Ristovac; MONTENEGRO in the frontiers before the Balkan wars together with the counties of Berane [Ivangrad] and Kotor, as well as Plav and Gusinje."[131] Outside the federal units were the districts (*oblasti*) of Vojvodina, Kosovo and Metohia, Sandžak, and Pančevo and Zemun, the last being two counties of Vojvodina directly north of Belgrade, which evidently were being considered for a new federal capital.

A comparison of the official borders of February 1945 and Yugoslavia's final internal lines reveals significant changes. Besides the incorporation of territory regained from Italy in Slovenia and Croatia, the division of the Sandžak between Serbia and Montenegro, and the special status of Vojvodina and Kosmet within Serbia, the borders of the federal units were adjusted in the following way: (1) Croatia lost the counties of Šid and much of Ilok in Srijem (Srem) to Serbian Vojvodina, but gained from it the counties of Darda and Batina in Yugoslav Baranja. (2) Croatia also gained the county of Dvor, which was not in the Sava banate, but was also not included in the Bosnia-Hercegovina of the Congress of Berlin. (3) The district of Pančevo and Zemun disappeared, much of it given outright to Serbia proper. (4) Bosnia-Hercegovina lost the salient of Sutorina to Montenegro, and with it a corridor to the Bay of Kotor. (5) Macedonia lost the counties of Preševo and Trgovište to Serbia, including the monastery of Prohor Pčinjski, the site of the First ASNOM. Clearly the contest over frontiers among the national KPJ leaderships had winners and losers, and some who fell in between.

The Montenegrin leadership was especially aggressive in its quest for a larger unit. At the third session of the land assembly for Montenegro and the Bay of Kotor, which convened at the Morača Monastery in July 1944, the leadership demanded "that separate mention of the Bay of Kotor be excluded."[132] The Bay of Kotor had 38,989 inhabitants in 1931: 63.39 percent Orthodox and 35.14 percent Catholic; that is, roughly, an almost 2:1 ratio of Serbs to Croats. Those Kotor Communists who favored autonomous status within

---

131. *Zakonodavni rad Pretsedništva Antifašističkog veća narodnog oslobodjenja Jugoslavije i Pretsedništva Privremene narodne skupštine DFJ (19 novembra 1944–27 oktobra 1945)* (Belgrade, n.d.), p. 58.

132. Obren Blagojević, "Neki momenti iz rada Izvršnog odbora ZAVNO Crne Gore i Boke," *Istorijski zapisi* 24, nos. 3–4 (1971): 566, n. 6.

Factions 105

Montenegro were obliged to leave their posts.[133] Still, the extension of Montenegro's name to the Bay of Kotor and the acquisition of two southern Sandžak counties were the limit of Montenegro's territorial increase. Except for the pivotal Hercegovinian Sutorina, Montenegro did not get the Metohia, Hercegovina, or Dubrovnik—three demands that were a source of conflict with its neighbors.[134] But it kept Plav, Gusinje, and Rožaj, which had long been coveted by the Kosovar Albanians.

The whole question of Montenegrin nationality permeated the issue of Montenegro's borders. Milovan Djilas, the chief Communist theorist of Montenegrin nationhood, advanced a most limited agenda. Together with the majority of the KPJ Politburo, he stood in between Montenegrin Serbophiles and nativists, asserting that "Montenegrins belong to the Serb branch of the South Slavic tribes" and allowing for the possibility of a future Serbo-Montenegrin amalgamation.[135] His rival Žujović supported the immediate unification of Serbia and Montenegro.[136] In a similar vein, federal Bosnia-Hercegovina, whose status was most uncertain as late as 1943, was for a while considered a potential autonomous partner of either Serbia or Croatia. The reason was the notion that federal units had to be national homelands of Yugoslavia's constituent South Slavic nationalities. Since at that time the KPJ encouraged the Bosnian Muslims to declare themselves to be either Serbs or Croats, it followed that multinational Bosnia-Hercegovina was only a Serbo-Croat condominium. Despite this obstacle, Bosnia-Hercegovina soon graduated to become an autonomous province of the federation itself, and then

133. Dedijer, *Novi prilozi*, 3:172.
134. Zoran Lakić, "Neke karakteristike konstituisanja i rada CASNO-a," *Istorijski zapisi* 24, nos. 3–4 (1971): 602–3.
135. Milovan Djilas, *Članci, 1941–1946* (Zagreb, 1947), pp. 199, 201. *Demokratija*, the organ of Milan Grol's non-NFJ Democratic party, which was barely tolerated in the early fall of 1945, expressed the views of the Serbian anticommunist opposition on the Montenegrin question when on September 27, 1945, it challenged the national criterion that was invoked in the shaping of the Montenegrin federal unit: "If the people of Montenegro are happy with the borders of their federal unit and the conditions of life that are being secured in this unit, fine. But it is clear that the arguments for the separation of Montenegro, which is not only self-administered but federal, can be neither economic nor national—expressed in terms of an imagined nationality. In general, the discussion of nationality is pointless. Every part of our people will be what it feels that it is": cited in Slobodan Nešović and Branko Petranović, eds., *AVNOJ i revolucija: Tematska zbirka dokumenata, 1941–1945* (Belgrade, 1983), p. 850.
136. "Plenarna sednica CK KPJ od 12. IV 1948," in Dedijer, *Novi prilozi*, 3:384.

a full-fledged federal unit.[137] As a result, its borders became firmer. A resolution of the First ZAVNOH (Hebrang was one of its authors) recognized a "free Bosnia-Hercegovina." In time the Croat Communists gave up the county of Livno, in southwestern Bosnia (71 percent Croat), whose local party committee and Partisan units had been within the KPH since 1941. In turn, Bosnia-Hercegovina gave up the county of Dvor (88 percent Serb)—a historical part of Croatia-Slavonia but outside the autonomous Croatia of 1939—and the south Dalmatian operational zone (from the Neretva River to the Bay of Kotor), which had been under the command of the Hercegovinian operational staff since 1942.[138]

In late 1942 Moša Pijade proposed the establishment of a Serb autonomous province in Croatia, an idea that Tito immediately vetoed.[139] Later on, in the course of discussions over the constitution in 1945, a group of Dalmatian unitarists argued for a separate federal unit of Dalmatia.[140] Croat and Slovene Communists were at odds over the disposition of Istria. But by far the most nettlesome border dispute during the war involved the question of Srijem, a historical area of Croatia-Slavonia. Five of Srijem's counties (Ilok, Šid, Vinkovci, Vukovar, and Županja, with a Serb population of 53,479, or 31 percent, in 1931) had belonged to autonomous Croatia in 1939; the remaining counties (Irig, Ruma, Sr. Mitrovica, Stara Pazova, and Zemun) and the city of Zemun (with a total Serb population of 149,190, or 64 percent) were outside.

---

137. Petranović, "KPJ i društveno-političke promene," pp. 380–81.

138. Veseljko Huljić, "Medjupovezanost razvitka NOP-a u Dalmaciji i Bosni i Hercegovini do kapitulacije Italije," in Babić, *AVNOJ,* pp. 213–15.

139. Vladimir Dedijer recalled that Pijade, with whom he lodged at the time, came up with this scheme in Drinići, ten kilometers from Tito's headquarters at Bosanski Petrovac, in northwestern Bosnia. Pijade "had one volume of the official census of 1931 and was attempting to establish the borders of the Serb autonomous region. But he simply could not confirm that the Serbs were a majority. He poured kerosene into his lamp for the second time, but still had no solution. I wanted to sleep and in the wee hours suggested that he take two counties from northwestern Bosnia, which border on Croatia, and thus get his Serb majority. When I woke up at dawn, Moša already had a finely drawn map and the statute, in his beautiful handwriting, of the Serb autonomous province in Croatia. He saddled his bay horse and rode off to Josip Broz at Petrovac. He returned faster than he went" (*Novi prilozi,* 2:903). In 1931 the population of Lika, Kordun, and Banija (minus six coastal communes and the county of Dvor) was 460,083. Of that number, Serbs constituted 269,098, or 58.5%.

140. Boro Krivokapić, "Jovan Djordjević: Život s državom," *NIN,* March 30, 1980, p. 9.

The German and Hungarian occupiers destroyed the Partisan movement in the lowlands of the Banat and Bačka by the end of 1941, even before the Partisans of Vojvodina managed to stand on their own feet. Only in the Fruška Gora range of eastern Srijem did the predominantly Serb Partisans manage to organize themselves against Ustaša misrule. But precisely because they were cut off from Vojvodina, where the regional party committee no longer existed, as well as from Serbia, where the uprising was in decline, the KPJ CC felt that Srijem ought to be linked with Slavonia in party and military affairs. As a result, from 1942, the area committee for (effectively eastern) Srijem was attached to the KPH Commission for Slavonia, and in military affairs Srijem entered into the third operational zone of Croatia. The nature of these links was an immediate source of controversy. Henceforth, the Croat Communists assumed that Srijem was a part of Croatia. This assumption was evident in the behavior of the KPH CC, which in August 1942 brought Josip Hrnčević, then among the Partisans at Fruška Gora, into its four-member commission for Slavonia as the representative of Srijem.[141] Likewise, in 1942 ZAVNOH included the veteran Serb Communist Nikola Grulović in the eight-member Initiative Committee of ZAVNOH as "a man of Srijem." And in June 1943, Srijem was listed among the regions of Croatia in the ZAVNOH-approved temporary geography curriculum for elementary schools on Partisan territory.[142] As for the Communists of Srijem, they interpreted the links with the KPH far more loosely. Convinced that they were the nucleus of the party in the whole of Vojvodina—which in their opinion consisted of Srijem (or at least its eastern part), Bačka, Banat, and Baranja—they remonstrated with the KPJ Politburo over the Croat attempts to subjoin them.

At the beginning of 1943 the KPJ regional committee for Vojvodina was reestablished under the auspices of Srijem Communists. Their leader, Jovan Veselinov-Žarko, assumed the post of Vojvodina's regional secretary. Almost immediately the KPJ CC divided Srijem, transferring the territory to the east of the Vukovar-Vinkovci-Županja line from Croatia to the regional committee and headquarters staff for Vojvodina. This was a considerable diminution of

141. Pavle Gregorić, *NOB u sjeveroistočnoj Hrvatskoj 1942. godine* (Zagreb, 1978), p. 175.
142. Sirotković, *ZAVNOH: 1943*, pp. 37, 259.

Croatia's territory, which was now divested of the counties of Šid and Ilok and the eastern portions of the counties of Vukovar, Vinkovci, and Županja, all parts of autonomous Croatia in 1939 and the last two counties with absolute Croat majorities. Small wonder that the KPJ CC felt that the discussion of border issues ought to be muted out of fear that it "might alienate the Croat elements from the national liberation struggle."[143]

Not that there was much discussion after the war. The plenary session of the Main National Liberation Committee for Vojvodina which underwrote the accession of Vojvodina to federal Serbia in April 1945 also gave up Baranja, because that part of prewar Vojvodina "gravitated toward Croatia economically, geographically, and nationally."[144] All that remained was to fix the border between Croatia and Serbia's Vojvodina. The demarcation commission, chaired by Milovan Djilas, held by the

> ethnic principle—to leave little "alien" population in Serbia or Croatia. . . . The only disputed areas were Ilok and the Bunjevci [Croats of northwestern Bačka]. The first—at my [Djilas's] proposal—went to Croatia, because the Croats were the majority there, though it entered the Vojvodina Serb terrain like a blind gut. As for the Bunjevci—a significant Croat group—they remained in Vojvodina by the decision of the Politburo, as a result of the commission's proposal, because their accession to Croatia would have meant the transfer of a considerable Serb group and the disruption of [Vojvodina's] ethnic composition in favor of the Hungarian minority.[145]

Indeed, the Hungarians were very much a despised minority after the war. They were exposed to harsh repression and there were calls for their expulsion from Yugoslavia, along with the Germans.[146]

The muted conflict over the structure and composition of the emerging Partisan federation revealed all the contradictions of Tito's

---

143. Končar, "Problem autonomije Vojvodine," p. 627.
144. Nešović and Petranović, *AVNOJ i revolucija*, p. 731.
145. Milovan Djilas, *Vlast* (London, 1983), pp. 84–85. For an alternative view of the commission's proceedings by one of its Croat members, see Jerko Zlatarić, "Kako se krojila hrvatska istočna granica," *Nova Hrvatska* 15, no. 6 (1973): 10–13.
146. Veselinov, *Svi smo*, pp. 171–72.

nationality policy.[147] In principle, Tito's federalism was the negation of prewar hegemonism and wartime chauvinisms. Yet Tito operated in accordance with the Soviet federal model, which not only was more apparent than real but actually put a premium on the power of the center. As we have seen, Tito used the Soviet model to justify centralism. ("If no one else will do," he wrote to the KPH leaders in denouncing their news agency, "let the Soviet Union be your example.") Small wonder that Tito failed to see the sense in many of his comrades' attempts to solve Yugoslavia's national question by means of formal axiomatic constructions (national parties, regional committees, land assemblies, federal units, borders). The building of national institutions might carry weight with the noncommunists, but the running of Yugoslavia would in no way differ from the running of the KPJ.

Still, if national sensitivities had to be stroked, they had to be Serbian sensitivities in the last phases of the war. Partisan support was thinnest in Serbia, which was quite won over to the Chetnik idea that the Partisan movement was not just an aggressive Communist organization but a Croat nationalist one at that.[148] Indeed, Serbian public opinion shunned the Communists less for their illiberality than out of fear "that Serbdom [would] perish in a federal Yugoslavia."[149] From 1944, therefore, Tito increasingly restrained the federalist expectations raised by the Second AVNOJ.[150] In time he learned the Yugoslav variant of Hegelian *Aufhebung*. Federalism could be ordered in such a way as to preserve the substance of centralism. Tito

147. On the principal aspects of the federalist discourse within Partisan Yugoslavia after the Second AVNOJ, see Janko Pleterski, *Nacije—Jugoslavija—revolucija* (Belgrade, 1985), pp. 477–531.

148. This point was being driven home to the Western Allies by—among others— Colonel S. W. Bailey, a British liaison officer at Mihailović's headquarters. See Tito, *Sabrana djela*, 20:210–11.

149. Josip Smodlaka, *Partizanski dnevnik* (Belgrade, 1972), p. 232.

150. Branko Petranović accurately described this change in his analysis of how Serbia gained Vojvodina and Kosmet at the end of the war: "The development of Vojvodina and Kosovo-Metohija in the course of the war, accompanied as it was by the institutionalization of the party, army, and administrative organs, turned in the opposite direction in the last phases of the war and after the liberation: these districts were included within Serbia, which became a complex unit. These processes, in fact, were directed by the party leaderships headed by the KPJ CC, whose starting point was the state of affairs established in the course of the war and the nature of internationality relations in Yugoslavia": "Osnivački kongres Komunističke partije Srbije," *Medjunarodni radnički pokret* 16, no. 4 (1973): 114.

put the matter succinctly at the founding congress of the Communist Party of Serbia in May 1945: "Various elements . . . are saying that Tito and the Communists split up Serbia. Serbia is within Yugoslavia, and it is not our intention to create states within Yugoslavia which will make war on one another. . . . It is only a matter of administrative division."[151]

Tito's unstudied way of handling the national question—indeed, his apparently long-held belief that the "nationalities of Yugoslavia would ultimately merge into one true nation"[152]—was bound to provoke resistance in KPJ circles for whom the struggle for national liberation, especially from the vestiges of Serbian supremacy, still had great resonance. Hebrang became the natural focus of this resistance. From the beginning of his stay in Belgrade, Hebrang fought for Croat interests publicly and behind the scenes. He opposed the new borders of Croatia, especially as they affected Srijem.[153] He opposed the proposed rate of exchange of Croatia's wartime kunas for the new Yugoslav dinars, a rate far more unfavorable than that applied to the Serbian occupationist dinar: "The masses in Croatia will not accept [this rate of exchange]. They will say over there that this is a new conspiracy against the Croats. . . . I am convinced that this is not right and against the interests of the Croat people."[154] He tried to mitigate the political damage of the show trials being orchestrated by Jakov Blažević, Croatia's prosecutor general and Hebrang's old enemy from wartime Lika. Specifically, Hebrang opposed the trial of fourteen directors of the First Croatian Savings Bank, who were tried in November 1946 as collaborators.[155] Finally, as head of the plan-

151. Milan Borković and Venceslav Glišić, eds., *Osnivački kongres KP Srbije (8–12. maj 1945)* (Belgrade, 1972), p. 213. It is ironic that Tito's remarks were addressed to the founding congress of the Communist Party of Serbia, not because the establishment of the separate Serbian branch of the KPJ came late (the Slovenian and Croatian organizations were founded in 1937 and the Macedonian in 1943) but because, as Branko Petranović has pointed out, before 1945 the lack of a separate Serbian Communist party simply mirrored the Soviet model: among the Soviet republics, Russia alone has no separate party within the VKP(b)/KPSS(CPSU). See M. Lučić and S. Dautović, "Korak u razvoju Partije," *Politika,* June 12, 1985, p. 11.

152. Milovan Djilas, *Tito: The Story from Inside* (New York, 1980), p. 134.

153. Djilas claims that Hebrang wanted the whole of Srijem, including Zemun, for Croatia (*Vlast,* p. 84). Since Djilas always displayed a special animus toward Hebrang, this claim, too, probably should be abridged to include only those portions of Srijem that were in the autonomous Croatia of 1939.

154. *Zakonodavni rad Pretsedništva AVNOJ-a,* pp. 106–7. Cf. Aleksandar Petković, *Gospodo i drugovi* (Belgrade, 1981), pp. 29–32.

155. Blažević, *Tražio sam,* pp. 77, 169–71.

ning commission, Hebrang was accused of favoring Croatia in his investment policy.[156] One of his old political opponents had recently publicized Hebrang's supposed decision to have Slovenia's aluminum plants stripped and installed at Šibenik, in Croatia's bauxite-rich Adriatic region.[157]

Hebrang's stand on the national question was reflected in an economic policy that did not fit Tito's radical socialist model. At the Fifth Party Congress in July 1948, Boris Kidrič accused Hebrang and Žujović (retroactively linked by their fates, though their ideological orientations were hardly identical) of "Trotskyite-Bukharinite anti-Marxist" economic policies. Both men, Kidrič argued, were minimalists, and they had obstructed and denigrated the ambitious development policy set forth by the Politburo.

> This is proven most clearly by their stand on the question of state capitalism. First, they questioned whether we were capable of completing [postwar] reconstruction without the strong economic influence of capitalists [presumably foreign, but perhaps also domestic] and whether we could begin to institute and broaden the socialist arrangement of our economy simultaneously with reconstruction. Then came the absurd "theory" that the purely state sector of our economy was of a state capitalist type and that it lacked the conditions for direct development into a purely socialist type. [This was] the course of passive waiting for the "second stage" and at the same time a dryly practical and unprincipled use of capitalist methods and forms of economic work on our whole economic front, even in the state and cooperative sectors.[158]

Kidrič's words defined the economic policy of the KPJ Politburo rather than that of Hebrang. It is clear that Hebrang was being tarred with the supposed errors of E. S. Varga, the Soviet economist of Hungarian origin who bore the brunt of Zhdanovite ire in the economic debate of 1947. Like Varga, who put no faith in the "people's democracies," Hebrang was accused of underestimating the significance of the "economic uplifting of [Yugoslavia] and the widening of the socialist offensive" and of failure to recognize the arrival of the

156. Ivan Supek, *Krivovjernik na ljevici* (Bristol, 1980), p. 123.

157. Dedijer, *Novi prilozi*, 3:209.

158. Boris Kidrič, "O izgradnji socijalističke ekonomike Federativne Narodne Republike Jugoslavije," in *Peti Kongres Komunističke partije Jugoslavije: Izveštaji i referati* (Belgrade, 1948), p. 462.

"second stage in the general crisis of capitalism."[159] But unlike Varga, who was quietly restored to his offices after Stalin purged the Zhdanov faction, Hebrang was beyond the reach of Stalin's help, as much as he probably counted on it. Moreover, Hebrang's alleged pursuit of a Soviet—but not Zhdanovist—economic model is far from proven. His go-slow attitude was perhaps as much a reflection of his economic realism (and of advice from such prewar liberal economists as Mijo Mirković) as of dependence on Stalin's regional strategy. In July 1945, when he opposed demands by the Communist trade unions that the production of state and private firms be controlled through so-called workers' commissioners,[160] was he fighting against party meddling in the economy or was he being a Stalinist enemy of premature workers' self-management? And in May 1946, when he said that Yugoslavia had not yet reached the socialist level of development,[161] was Hebrang playing the role of a Yugoslav Varga or of Stalin's fireman?

Hebrang's ties to the Soviets are difficult to reconstruct. His detractors see him as the Politburo member who regularly informed the Soviet leadership about internal party matters.[162] They cite his behavior during his sole visit with Stalin, at the head of the Yugoslav military and state delegation in January 1945, as an exercise in obsequiousness when Stalin charged that Djilas slandered the Red Army by referring to its outrages against Yugoslav civilians and that the Yugoslav army was inferior to the Bulgarian armed forces: "Comrades, tonight we have also heard some admonitions from Comrade Stalin. We have no right to be angry, because Comrade Stalin is always right. As Communists, we must admit that we committed errors in both foreign and domestic policy, and I shall make a report

159. Ibid., p. 461.

160. *Rad zakonodavnih odbora Pretsedništva Antifašističkog veća narodnog oslobodjenja Jugoslavije i Privremene narodne skupštine DFJ (3 aprila–25 oktobra 1945): Po stenografskim beleškama i drugim izvorima* (Belgrade, n.d.), pp. 151–53.

161. *Prvo redovno zasedanje Saveznog veća i Veća naroda: Stenografske beleške 15 maj–20 jul 1946* (Belgrade, n.d.), p. 877. Less than a year later, however, in a debate over the First Five-Year Plan in the National Assembly, Tito used formulas that were perhaps more moderate than Hebrang's. Whereas Tito differentiated between the Soviet "socialist economy" and the Yugoslav "all-popular economy," Hebrang claimed that the Yugoslav state, the "state of a new type," had created a "primary economic sector of socialist character as the material foundation of the people's power": *Treće redovno zasedanje Saveznog veća i Veća naroda: Stenografske beleške 26. III–26. IV 1947* (Belgrade, n.d.), pp. 327, 332, 336.

162. Dedijer, *Novi prilozi,* 3:197.

about this to the Politburo."[163] His adherents cite the same meeting with Stalin as the point of Hebrang's final disenchantment with the USSR. According to Olga Kohn-Hebrang, his wife since 1942, Hebrang told her upon his return from Moscow: "Don't be sorry you missed our plane to Moscow. You'd have been disillusioned. We're better off not going there."[164] Nor are his ties to Žujović any more evident. Hebrang opposed Žujović on the issue of the exchange rate for kunas and he opposed Žujović's draft for the state tax law in May 1945.[165] It is not likely that he shared Žujović's desire to narrow the Popular Front and it is inconceivable that he could have agreed with Žujović that Montenegro must be united with Serbia and that state finances should be completely centralized.[166] When all is said and done, Hebrang's chief characteristic was national communism, which came to be translated into moderation in theory and in practice.[167] Nevertheless, because of his isolation in the Politburo, he sought Stalin's intervention in order to "change the party line in Yugoslavia, and perhaps, too, to change the leadership."[168]

The silent dénouement—unknown to the public—took place in April 1946. At the time Hebrang expected to lead the government delegation at the economic negotiations with the Soviets. Instead, Tito excluded him from the proceedings. Hebrang wrote a letter of protest to Kardelj, accusing Tito of personal animosity.[169] On April 19, 1946, the Politburo accused Hebrang of trying to revive the old factional struggles and ruled in favor of Tito. "Hebrang's letter," noted the report of the special KPJ CC commission, "or better, Hebrang's attack, both in the way it was written and in the problems it poses, is a unique event in the history of the [Polit]Bureau of the KPJ CC since its formation in 1937. In this letter Hebrang used an

163. Gojko Nikoliš, *Korijen, stablo, pavetina: Memoari* (Zagreb, 1981), p. 639.

164. Supek, *Krunski svjedok*, p. 199.

165. *Zakonodavni rad Pretsedništva AVNOJ-a*, pp. 111, 195.

166. "Plenarna sednica CK KPJ od 12. IV 1948. godine," in Dedijer, *Novi prilozi*, 3:380, 384.

167. Alone among the KPJ leaders, Hebrang encouraged legal opposition. Dragoljub Jovanović, a Serbian agrarian deputy who was briefly permitted to voice his views in the national assembly, recalled that his three-hour speech in December 1945 on the official draft constitutional proposal provoked bitter resentment among Communist leaders, except for Andrija Hebrang, "who stated that I brought out many correct things about the economic part of the constitution": *Ljudi, ljudi* (Belgrade, 1975), 2:240.

168. Supek, *Krivovjernik*, p. 123.

169. Djilas, *Vlast*, pp. 85–86.

unhealthy approach, and one that is not permissible within the party, to cast suspicions of personal intolerance on Comrade Tito. The alleged reason is the fact that a dispatch from Moscow was addressed to him [Hebrang], and hence Comrade Tito's lack of confidence in Comrade Hebrang's economic policy in fact stems from that circumstance."[170] The head of the commission was Hebrang's old Wahabite enemy Aleksandar Ranković. The penalty was Hebrang's expulsion from the Politburo. (Žujović's reluctance to criticize Hebrang invited a party reprimand.) By 1947 Hebrang had lost his posts as minister of industry and president of the economic council, both to Boris Kidrič. Isolated and disgraced, he was still head of the federal planning commission when, in March 1948, Stalin's First Letter caught up with him.[171] He was under house arrest by early April.

At the plenary session of the KPJ CC which Tito convened on April 12 to answer Stalin's First Letter, the sense of impending calamity was rendered more ominous by the prospect of a new round of factional struggle. Spasenija Cana Babović attributed Stalin's charges to vestiges of the old factional divisions. And Miha Marinko, a senior Slovene Communist, noted that "it must be assumed that all the information on which [the Soviet leadership] relied refers to the old factional remnants." He specifically referred to Dragotin Gustinčič as a person who was bent on wrecking party unity, and Tito added the names of Hebrang and Žujović: "Revolution does not devour its children. The children of this revolution are honest. We must do everything to render harmless those who would seek to destroy the unity of our party."[172] Given the history of factional struggle within the KPJ, it was only natural for Tito to suspect that Stalin would seek to untune the strings of Tito's discipline.

The factional struggles within the KPJ, from the struggle against the "ministerialists" of 1919 to the wartime and postwar conflict over strategy, demonstrate the continuity of the internal strife that

170. Cited in Kljakić, *Dosije Hebrang*, p. 191.
171. At the plenum of the KPJ CC of April 13, 1948, Ranković read Hebrang's letter to the Politburo. This letter has never been released. According to Kardelj, in it Hebrang accounted for "his stand and sharply criticized our party's policy in all areas, of course in harmony with Stalin's letters. That was some sort of dissertation by the future head of the Communist party of Yugoslavia": *Borba za priznanje i nezavisnost nove Jugoslavije: Sećanja* (Belgrade, 1980), pp. 128–29.
172. "Plenarna sednica CK KPJ," in Dedijer, *Novi prilozi*, 3:376, 382.

shaped the history of Yugoslav communism. Any typology of these cases would also demonstrate that they all concerned nationality relations. The national question in Yugoslavia was the most important political problem for the Communists, too, although it was not always considered to be the strategic problem for the revolutionary movement. The KPJ overcame Yugoslavist unitarism in the left–right struggle of the 1920s, and unitarist ideology never again reasserted its primacy within the party. The KPJ also overcame the dilemma posed by the apparent need either to maintain centralism (which it espoused in the early 1920s) or to propose the breakup of Yugoslavia (which it espoused from 1928 to 1935). The federalist option of 1935 laid to rest the issue of state organization, on a platform of maintaining the historical provinces within a united Yugoslavia.

The question of who won and who lost these factional struggles cannot be answered automatically. All but one of these clashes were won by the left; the sole exception was the reversal suffered by Miletić's Wahabites. But there was a vast difference—in method and in form—between the left of Djuro Cvijić and the left of Miletić and Djilas. Moreover, the rise of Djilas and Ranković in Tito's reconstructed leadership shows that the only Wahabite of stature who succumbed to the party pruning was Miletić himself. Most interesting, the principal losers of the old factions—provided they had survived and of course with exceptions—were swept away in the purge of the Cominformists: Sima Marković's man Ljuba Radovanović and Sima's widow, Brana; Dragotin Gustinčič; Gorkić's man Sreten Žujović and his opponents from the Parisian Parallel Center and its friends in Dalmatia (Ivo Marić, Ivo Baljkas, Vicko Jelaska); the Croat Popular Fronters Djuro Špoljarić and Šime Balen; Hebrang himself and some of his Serb followers, such as Dušan Brkić.[173] These were

173. Among the other ranking notables who were arrested after the Resolution, some KPJ leaders, all with close ties to Russia, ought to be singled out. Nikola Kovačević, alias Nikita Chudnovskii (b. 1890), was one of the founders of the KPJ. As a prisoner of war in Russia he joined the Bolsheviks and became one of the party secretaries for the Bolshevik South Slavic group. A Bosnian Croat, he served briefly as a Communist deputy in Yugoslavia's Constituent Assembly (1920–1921) and as the KPJ secretary for Vojvodina. He was the KPJ's delegate at the Sixth Congress of the Comintern. Kovačević graduated from the International Lenin School (ILS) in Moscow, served in the Comintern apparatus, and fought in the Spanish Civil War. Antun Franović (b. 1899), a graduate of Moscow's Communist University of Western National Minorities (KUNMZ), spent eight years (1927–1935) in the USSR. He was a member of the KPJ regional committee for Dalmatia and an instructor of the KPJ CC in 1935–1936. Franović was arrested by the Yugoslav police in

perhaps not the most representative members of the Cominformist
camp—if such it was. But it is important to note that these old KPJ
leaders were generally all to the right of Tito and that Stalin's four
"dubious Marxists" (Djilas, Vukmanović-Tempo, Kidrič, Ranković)
represented the KPJ's ultraleft.

1937 and was expelled from the party for "treasonous conduct before the class enemy." In
the Mitrovica penitentiary he sided with Petko Miletić, and he continued to do so even after
the CC condemned Miletić. Dimitrije Stanisavljević-Krka (1899–1969), a former member
of Sima Marković's faction, was briefly a secretary of the KPJ's regional committee for
Bosnia-Hercegovina and commissar of the Dimitrov Battalion in Spain. He spent most of
the 1930s and the war years in the USSR and was a functionary of the NKVD. Živojin
Pecarski (b. 1894), a party leader in southern Serbia (Niš), was one of the KPJ Politburo
secretaries in 1928–1929. From 1929 to 1945 he was in the USSR. Mita Despotović
(1904–1951) spent fifteen years (1929–1944) in the USSR, where he attended ILS and
KUNMZ. He was the KPJ's representative in the Comintern in 1938 and the secretary of the
party organization in Subotica after the war. Mirko Marković (b. 1907), a 1929 graduate
of KUNMZ, was the leading Communist among the South Slavic immigrants in the United
States, especially during the war. He was a commander of the Washington Battalion in
Spain and the dean of the economic faculty in postwar Belgrade. He stood for the Resolu-
tion publicly at the party meeting of the whole University of Belgrade in September 1949.
Jeered by a majority that included mere novices, he left the meeting shouting, "You can
expel me, because you are an expelled party!" (Milomir Marić, Deca komunizma
[Belgrade, 1987], p. 285; the biographical information is taken from the indexes in Tito's
collected works). On Nikola Kovačević, see Ivan Očak, U borbi za ideje Oktobra:
Jugoslavenski povratnici iz Sovjetske Rusije, 1918–1921 (Zagreb, 1976). These cases are
also mentioned in Sofokli Lazri and Javer Malo, Dans les prisons et les camps de concentration de la Yougoslavie (Tirana, 1960), pp. 21–22, 24–26, 29, 30. The same source also
mentions the following old party members who were imprisoned in Yugoslavia after the
Resolution: Vladislav Žerjavić, Vjekoslav Smoljan, Drezdić, Majcen (?), Ljubomir Kragu-
jević, Ilija Vujović, and Pavković, all veterans of the Russian revolution; Andrija Milić,
Marko Spahić, Lože Lončarić, and Silvester Furlan, all of whom fought in Spain; and
Nikola Petrović, Kristina Kusovac (the wife of Labud Kusovac), Ante Zorić, Ivan Korda,
Kartovcev (?), Mustafa Begić, Adolf Štumf, Marija Preželj, Mustafa Trbonja, Vilim (?),
Brana Marković, Vidak Arsenijević, and István Dobos.

3

Leap Year

I recall the first days when the conflict between the Soviet Union and Yugoslavia began artificially to be blown up. Once when I came from Kiev to Moscow, I was invited to visit Stalin, who, pointing to the copy of a letter lately sent to Tito, asked me, "Have you read this?" Not waiting for my reply, he answered, "I will shake my little finger—and there will be no more Tito. He will fall."

N. S. Khrushchev in his Secret Speech, at the
Twentieth Congress of the CPSU

Nineteen hundred and forty eight, a dangerous year it was. The FIFTH OFFENSIVE has again entered us. It is a matter of survival, I thought. We shall divide. Sutjeska is a swift and narrow river. I expressed my thoughts to no one.

The Russian is facing you, not a goldfinch . . . .

The Narrator in Antonije Isaković's novel *Tren 2*

Tito convened the first meeting of the KPJ CC since 1940 at the Old Palace in Belgrade's Dedinje section on April 12, 1948. The first and main item on the agenda was Stalin's First Letter and the KPJ response. Tito's draft reply was calm but determined. Tito repudiated all Soviet accusations at length, attributing them to slander and "suspicious information." He reminded the Soviet leadership of the KPJ's achievements and past loyalty, protested against the insulting tone of Stalin's letter, and even indulged in a bit of a counterattack by citing the Yugoslavs' displeasure at the recruitment and spying activities of Soviet intelligence agencies in Yugoslavia. The strategy of Tito's defense was set in an early sentence in which the Yugoslav leader, eschewing Stalin's ductile ideological baits, took his stand on the firm ground of national independence and equality: "No matter how much some of us love the land of socialism, the USSR, he can, in no

case, love his own country less, which also is building socialism—in
this concrete case the Federative People's Republic of Yugoslavia, for
which hundreds of thousands of its most progressive people fell [in
the war]. And since the Yugoslav experience had many "unique features," it was indeed true that the KPJ was "building socialism in our
country in somewhat different forms."[1] Or, as Kardelj put it in the
course of discussion, "our party contributed quite a few new elements
to the treasury of Marx[ism]-Len[inism]. [We made a] contribution to
the struggle against imp[erialism] in the international arena. We supported the USSR in a creative way."[2]

The stand of the party leadership was no mere rub on the green of
more pliant Communists. Sreten Žujović, the only member of the KPJ
CC who openly opposed Tito at the plenum, was necessarily unable
to abandon positions that implied dependence upon, inequality with,
and imitation of the Soviet Union. "In assessing the correctness of
each differing view," said Žujović, "we are making ourselves equal to
the [Soviet Communist party]." He added, "I am not afraid of dependence upon the Soviet Union. I think that our aim is that our country
become a part of the USSR." He also raised the ultimate argument
that had not been questioned by a whole generation of Communists:
"What can come of our stand in international relations? Where is our
place, in which camp? Between the USSR and the imper[ialist]
camp?"[3] Right or wrong, there was no communism without the Soviet Union.

1. Vladimir Dedijer, ed., *Dokumenti 1948* (Belgrade, 1980), 1:239–40, 246.
2. "Zapisnik sa sednice CK KPJ od 12. i 13. aprila 1948.," in Vladimir Dedijer, *Novi prilozi za biografiju Josipa Broza Tita* (Belgrade, 1984), 3:374.
3. Ibid., pp. 377, 372. Why did Žujović side with Moscow in 1948? He was, after all, a supporter of Gorkić, and so was removed from the Paris-based Politburo in 1937 at Moscow's instigation. His demotion certainly hurt the KPJ's moderate forces; it was pre-cisely Žujović's tolerance toward the ostracized victims of the old party purges in Serbia, whom he attempted to draw into the KPJ's "legal" work during his clandestine visits to Yugoslavia in the mid-1930s, that aroused the suspicions of Belgrade's ultraleftist young revolutionaries, among them Djilas: Milovan Djilas, *Memoir of a Revolutionary* (New York, 1973), pp. 262–64. On instructions from the Comintern, Tito "completely re-moved" Žujović from the leadership, on the grounds that Žujović was not yet ready for such responsibility: Josip Broz Tito, *Sabrana djela,* 20 vols. (Belgrade, 1977–1984), 4:41.
Tito was less distrustful of Žujović than of the other former leaders. He reintroduced Žujović to the KPJ CC in 1940 over the objections of Djilas and Ranković, who by then outranked the older *massovik.* As the wartime commander of the headquarters staff for Serbia, Žujović strengthened his influence in his native region and kept his thoughts to himself. He was pleased by the Soviet pressure in 1948. His quiet estrangement from Tito's leftist leadership went back to the terrors of total isolation in a Parisian hostel on the rue

Žujović's intransigence prompted Tito's decision to call for the plenum's collective stand against the dissenting member, as further cooperation with him "would be impossible." Tito linked the case of Žujović with that of Hebrang, who, Tito said, was "under investigation for his behavior in the [Ustaša] concentration camp, for which reason he was not invited to the meeting." Tito went further and denounced Hebrang as the "main culprit in the [Soviet] mistrust of our CC." He cited the time in 1946 when the Soviets were sending dispatches directly to Hebrang, and claimed that in economic policy Hebrang "pursued a line contrary to the stand of the CC."[4] Although Žujović dissociated himself from Hebrang's economic policy, with which he truly had little connection ("I did not agree with Hebrang on economic questions"), he was expelled from the KPJ CC and a special commission consisting of Ivan Gošnjak, Blagoje Nešković, and Vida Tomšič was appointed to investigate the "case of Hebrang and Žujović." The point was to establish a firm link between these two quite separate cases. By the third week of April, Hebrang and Žujović were apprehended (Hebrang was taken by an armed guard commanded personally by Ivan Gošnjak, his former friend and the head of the KPJ CC commission investigating his case) and escorted to a safe house in Srijemska Kamenica (on the south bank of the Danube, opposite Novi Sad), because the leadership feared that the Soviets aimed to have Hebrang and Žujović spirited away to Moscow.[5]

The case of Andrija Hebrang was then given a new twist. In an attempt to cast irrevocable discredit on Hebrang, perhaps especially with those Serbs that were likely to sympathize with Soviet views, Ranković was given leave to concoct an indictment that would reveal Hebrang as an Ustaša mole in the KPJ leadership. According to this convenient fiction, Hebrang capitulated to the Ustašas during his six months of captivity in 1942 and agreed to work for them after his release in the prisoner exchange of September 1942. As the leading

Sablière in 1938. Soon after Stalin's First Letter was delivered to the KPJ leadership in April 1948, Vukmanović-Tempo asked Žujović about his health: " 'By God, I'm well,' he replied in a rather caustic tone, 'happy, satisfied, not like some others.' " In the same conversation, he requested a new general's uniform: Svetozar Vukmanović-Tempo, *Revolucija koja teče* (Belgrade, 1971), 2:64.

4. Dedijer, *Novi prilozi*, 3:382–83.

5. Ivan Supek, *Krunski svjedok protiv Hebranga* (Chicago, 1983), p. 201; "Razgovor s Vladom Popovićem o Staljinu, Molotovu i Ždanovu," in Dedijer, *Novi prilozi*, 3:331.

Communist in Croatia, the charge went, Hebrang had opportunity and motive to introduce various Ustaša agents into the sensitive areas of party and military apparatuses, compromise the movement's secrets and strategic plans, and do serious damage to the Croatian Partisan movement. The Soviets, it was said, knew of his betrayal and blackmailed him into submission. This theory fitted neatly with the official thesis that Croat "national deviationism" was always connected with the Ustašas.[6] The charges against Hebrang were no more convincing than the Stalinist charge that Bukharin was an agent of the Gestapo and the Japanese. The dragnet for Hebrang was cast wide to suggest a vast conspiracy that included real Ustašas, various noncommunist Croats (among them Božidar Magovac of the pro-Partisan Croat Peasant Party), and Communists of Hebrang's circle.[7] Rather

6. All the elements in the case against Hebrang can be found in Mile Milatović, *Slučaj Andrije Hebranga* (Belgrade, 1952). Major General Milatović, later deputy minister of the interior for Serbia—that is, the real head of the UDB-a for Serbia—was the chief investigator in the Hebrang case, as the military courts had jurisdiction over espionage cases. For years, however, it was rumored that the real author of this official version of the Hebrang case was Dobrica Ćosić, the leading Serbian novelist and a prominent Communist (until his conflict with the party over the national question in May 1968). On June 24, 1985, at the plenum of the Croatian Writers' Association (DKH) in Zagreb, Dunja Hebrang, a poet and essayist and the daughter of Andrija Hebrang, accused Ćosić, by then a leading Serbian dissident, of hypocrisy. Thirty-three years earlier, she said, Ćosić, a latter-day fighter for human rights and artistic freedoms, was involved in a slightly different literary production, the book *Slučaj Andrije Hebranga* (The case of Andrija Hebrang), "an apocryphal political biography of Andrija Hebrang, whose literary author was Dobrica Ćosić, with police author Mile Milatović. When Dobrica Ćosić shaped his apocryphal political novel with such appropriate assistance, Andrija Hebrang had been dead for *three* years and could not rise to his own defense. In that book Hebrang was *posthumously* indicted without legal procedure, without sentence, without proof, and without any fault on his part": "Plenum Društva književnika Hrvatske (24. lipnja 1985)," *Republika* 41, no. 6 (1985): 35. Ćosić responded three weeks later, on July 16, by stating that he "had no reason to deny this insinuation, because it was simply absurd." Still, in an allusion that shifted blame to Tito, Ćosić added that he himself was in no position to affect the outcome of the Hebrang case: "The daughter of Andrija Hebrang . . . should know who alone could decide the fate of Andrija Hebrang, a member of Yugoslavia's topmost political leadership. There should be no lack of information and ignorance on that score in this [country]. Therefore, what we are faced with here must be lack of courage to direct the anger accumulated subsequently to the proper quarters, where everything was decided autonomously and decisions were issued without recourse on the fate of men and peoples, politics and books": Dobrica Ćosić, "Društvu književnika Hrvatske," *Književne novine*, September 1, 1985, p. 2.

7. Among the persons implicated in the case of Andrija Hebrang were (1) Olga Kohn-Hebrang, Hebrang's wife; (2) Francka Klinc, a veteran Slovene Communist, the widow of both Pera Popović-Aga (1905–1930), one of the renowned seven secretaries of SKOJ, and Ivan Srebrenjak (Antonov, d. 1942), head of the Soviet military intelligence network in Zagreb who was executed by the Ustašas; (3) Bogdanka (Seka) Podunavac, a friend of Olga Hebrang and a wireless telegraph operator for Josip Kopinič, head of the Soviet (Comintern) civilian intelligence network in Zagreb; (4) Lujo Čačić, a former wireless telegraph operator for the Agitprop of the KPH CC; (5) Josip Šaban, a member of the prewar SKOJ

like Trajčo Kostov, whom the Bulgarian Stalinists tried and executed in 1949 as a Titoist and an agent of the Bulgarian royal police (because he survived his wartime imprisonment), Hebrang had to account for the relatively decent treatment he had received from his political enemies.[8] But unlike Kostov, Hebrang was neither tried nor

---

leadership in Croatia, expelled from the KPJ before the war, and a personal friend of Vladimir Bakarić—hence someone who could be used, should it prove necessary, to link Bakarić, Hebrang's successor in the KPH leadership to the Hebrang case; (6) Vladimir Frajtić, a prewar Croat political prisoner who drew close to the Communists, including Hebrang, in Srijemska Mitrovica, and later ran a safe house for the KPH CC in Zagreb, until his arrest by the Ustašas in 1942; and (7) Tibor Vaško, an Ustaša police official.

Ranković's plan was to connect these prisoners, all of them intimates, associates, or at least acquaintances of Hebrang, in an alleged Ustaša and Gestapo intelligence ring within the KPJ. Physical and mental torture was applied to force these men and women to confess to the charges, thereby opening the way for a choreographed show trial. A particularly sinister aspect of these procedures was an attempt to link the victims of fascism with service to the Nazi and Ustaša cause. Olga Hebrang, who was Jewish, lost her former husband, infant son, and other members of her immediate family in the Holocaust. And Bogdanka Podunavac, daughter of a Serb Orthodox priest from Pakrac (Slavonia) who had been a defendant in Ban Rauch's anti-Serb high treason trial of 1909, lost several members of her family in Ustaša massacres. Of those arrested, Klinc, Podunavac, Čačić, and Šaban died in prison. Podunavac, pregnant at the time of her arrest, aborted under torture and then "hanged herself." Šaban, too, "committed suicide." Čačić was killed "while attempting to escape." Frajtić was sentenced to death in 1952. The sentence was never carried out. Though it was never commuted, it was set aside and he was released in 1960. Vaško, already sentenced in 1946 to twenty years in prison as a collaborationist, was released in 1962. Olga Hebrang was sentenced to twelve years in prison in 1951. Among the absurdities in her case was the charge that she betrayed the location of the Partisan headquarters for Croatia to the Ustašas, and so was responsible for the enemy bombing in which Elias (Ilija) Engel, a deputy chief of staff, lost his life. In fact, Engel was shot from an enemy plane in Moslavina in May 1944, far from the headquarters and in an incident unrelated to the bombing. She was released in 1960, her surname officially changed to Markovac. A Serb war orphan whom she and her husband had adopted was permanently taken from the family and raised to hate his adoptive parents. Despite continuing interest in this cause célèbre, which has received considerable publicity since 1983, none of the principals have yet been rehabilitated, either judicially or politically. For more information see Supek, *Krunski svjedok,* pp. 201–53; Milomir Marić, "Špijun ili žrtva," *Duga,* Dec. 16, 1984, pp. 21–23, and "Strasti će nam doći glave," *Duga,* Jan. 25, 1986, pp. 13–14.

Although the Yugoslav Cominformists generally ignored the Hebrang case, one of their newspapers, published in Moscow, carried an early article on the plans against Hebrang. According to this report, "in connection with the arrest of Comrade Hebrang, the Titoists have collected 400 Ustašas in Lepoglava and other prisons and brought them to Zagreb, where they wish to prepare them to testify that Comrade Hebrang supposedly cooperated with them and was an Ustaša spy. All of these Ustašas were functionaries. Ranković's Janissaries are now attempting in various perfidious ways—by bribes and special favors—to win over these criminals for their shameful slanders against Comrade Hebrang": V., "Ustaški zločinci kao svjedoci protiv druga Hebranga," *Za socijalističku Jugoslaviju,* Nov. 5, 1949, p. 5.

8. The accusations against Trajčo Kostov were almost identical to those against Hebrang. Kostov was accused of betraying party secrets to Nikola Gašev, head of the anticommunist section of the Bulgarian police, in April 1942, and of signing an agreement

rehabilitated.[9] He died in prison under highly ambiguous circumstances, probably in 1949.[10]

As soon as Moscow learned of the arrest of Hebrang and Žujović,
Stalin instructed Ambassador A. I. Lavrentiev to make an oral request
that representatives of the Soviet party be permitted to participate in

---

to work for Gašev. Moreover, Kostov was said to have used his reputation as a "tough"
Communist who withstood all tortures to enhance his position in the Bulgarian party, in
which he served as secretary of the CC after the war. See *Sudebnyi protsess Traicho
Kostova i ego gruppy* (Sofia, 1949), pp. 6–7.

Adam Ulam was the first scholar to notice the odd parallel between the uses made of the
lenient treatment of Kostov and Hebrang by, respectively, the Bulgarian and Croatian
authorities during the war. The extent to which Ulam, writing in 1951, fathomed the
obscure purposes of the Cominformist purge is remarkable. Nothing about the case of
either Kostov or Hebrang, Ulam pointed out, aroused the suspicion of his Communist
colleagues until he had been charged with other crimes. See Adam Ulam, *Titoism and the
Cominform* (Cambridge, Mass., 1952), p. 37, n. 57. And indeed, Vladimir Dedijer approvingly recorded Hebrang's account of his arrest and wounding by the Ustašas in the
edition of his diary published in 1945: the Ustašas "stomped [Hebrang] with their feet,
kicked him in the ribs, and then took him to a hospital. He was lying with hands and feet
bound. After a few days they took him to the jail on Savska Cesta [Sava Road], because they
heard that our shock brigaders planned to storm the hospital. One day Pavelić himself came
to the jail on Savska Cesta to see Hebrang. He came with his entourage, all puffed up, and
while his attendants whispered among themselves, Pavelić took a look at Comrade
Hebrang, one of whose eyes was covered by a bandage. He walked out at once. Hebrang
spent a long time in Ustaša prisons. He was later transferred to [the concentration camp at]
Nova Gradiška and held in solitary confinement": Vladimir Dedijer, *Dnevnik,* pt. 1
(Belgrade, 1945), p. 301. This and other passages favorable to Hebrang were expunged in
all subsequent editions of Dedijer's diary.

According to one source, based on the private testimony of a high-level Ustaša police
official, Hebrang survived his captivity because of the calm courage of his political stance.
He said to his Ustaša interrogators, "You are fascists, I am a Communist. I am no less a
Croat patriot than you. The difference between us is that you want a fascist Croat state and
I am fighting for a Communist one": Jere Jareb, *Pola stoljeća hrvatske politike* (Buenos
Aires, 1960), p. 121.

9. There is some evidence that the deposed Croat party leadership of 1970–1971
worked to have Hebrang rehabilitated. They tried, for example, to have Milatović's book
withdrawn from libraries. In recent years, the official Croat party position is that Hebrang
did not serve the Gestapo or the Ustašas but that he was indeed a nationalist. Though their
approaches differ, several recent books published in Zagreb have totally discredited the case
against Hebrang. See Milenko Doder, *Kopinič bez enigme* (Zagreb, 1986), pp. 96–113.

10. Hebrang supposedly committed suicide. When discovered by Milatović, "Hebrang
was lying on the floor. One end of the rope was hanging from the radiator, the other around
his neck" (Milatović, *Slučaj,* p. 266). The date is not certain, although Milatović's account
suggests that it was probably in May or June 1949. Curiously, in biographic notices about
Hebrang in the first four volumes of Tito's *Sabrana djela,* the date is given successively as
"1948?," "1949," no date, and "1948." The last date is cited in every succeeding volume.
In one of his last conversations with Milatović, Hebrang supposedly said: "I am sorry . . . that I am dying at Serb Communist hands" (Milatović, *Slučaj,* p. 231).

In a recent book based wholly on Milatović, Dragan Kljakić offers a new twist to the tale
of Hebrang's suicide. According to this version, Hebrang "ran toward the radiator and hit

the investigation of this case. The Yugoslavs rejected the request. Stalin then dispatched his searing Second Letter to the KPJ CC, on May 4. He denied that Žujović and Hebrang (always in that order in Soviet materials) or anybody else had misinformed the Soviet leadership about the situation in Yugoslavia. The differences between Moscow and Belgrade involved matters of principle, not just misreadings of scattered incidents. Stalin also denied that Hebrang was his source in the KPJ leadership: "We state that the Soviet side received no information from Comrade Hebrang. We state that the talk between Comrade Žujović and the Soviet ambassador in Yugoslavia, Comrade Lavrentiev, did not reveal a tenth of what was contained in the erroneous and anti-Soviet speeches of Yugoslav leaders."[11] Stalin went on to denounce the reprisals against Žujović and Hebrang as evidence of an anti-Soviet attitude in the Yugoslav leadership.

Stalin repeatedly accused the Yugoslavs, and Tito personally, of equating the Soviet Union with the imperialist great powers. Yugoslav errors could be traced primarily to the "unbounded arrogance" of Yugoslav leaders, which might yet be their downfall. In fact, the Yugoslavs' achievements were not so very great. They could be compared with those of the Communist parties of Poland, Czechoslovakia, Hungary, Romania, Bulgaria, and Albania, and were inferior to those of the French and Italian parties. The only reason the French and Italian parties were not in power was that the Soviet army could not come to their aid, as it had done in the case of Yugoslavia when it liberated Belgrade after the Germans destroyed Tito's headquarters at Drvar.[12] No party, Stalin was intimating, could come to power without Soviet military aid. Or presumably stay in power.

Stalin's Second Letter concluded with the suggestion that the Yugoslavs take their case to the Cominform. Instead, at the plenum of the KPJ CC of May 9, 1948, the Yugoslav leadership expelled Hebrang and Žujović from the CC and the party, thereby opening the door for their formal arrest under charges of treason and espionage. The Soviets were quick to warn Belgrade that the Yugoslavs would be

---

the ribbed metal with the top of his head at full force. A trace of blood in the middle of the room suggested that the suicide probably returned again to strike his head against the radiator. The second attempt was fatal": Dragan Kljakić, *Dosije Hebrang* (Belgrade, 1983), p. 310.

11. Dedijer, *Dokumenti 1948,* 1:262–63, 279.
12. Ibid., pp. 280–81.

pilloried as "criminal murderers" should any harm come to Hebrang and Žujović. The Yugoslavs rejected this warning, and in an official response to Stalin's Second Letter, Tito and Kardelj rejected any Cominform arbitration. They accused the Soviets of disloyally predicting the outcome of the conflict by lobbying the other ruling parties and then reaffirmed their loyalty to socialism, the Soviet Union, and Marxism-Leninism. Their letter ended on a stoical note: since Moscow would be appeased by no arguments or proofs, the future would decide who was right.[13]

On May 19 a messenger from the Soviet party apparatus brought Tito an invitation (signed by M. A. Suslov) for KPJ representatives to attend a special Cominform meeting on the Yugoslav question. Attendance at this meeting, subsequently scheduled for late June in Bucharest, Romania, became a highly controversial issue in the KPJ. In the end the plenum of the KPJ CC unanimously rejected the invitation on May 20. Stalin then dispatched his Third Letter, which, according to Kardelj, "was no longer addressed to Tito and Kardelj, but to Tito and Hebrang."[14] This letter was less harsh than the previous one; apparently Stalin was buoyed by Tito's unwillingness to face his critics. He reminded the Yugoslavs that they had not hesitated to level "stern Bolshevik criticism" at the French and Italian Communists at Szklarska Poręba. Should Tito and Kardelj refuse to attend the meeting of the Cominform, "then it means that they have nothing to say to the Cominform in their defense, and thus that they tacitly admit their guilt and are afraid to face the fraternal Communist parties." That was a different road from that of "the united socialist front of the people's democracies with the Soviet Union"; that was the road of "nationalism."[15]

In the lull that followed the Third Letter, the KPJ CC issued a public call for the party's Fifth Congress, to be held in Belgrade on July 21. Stalin, for his part, continued his attempts to persuade the Yugoslavs to go to the Cominform meeting. Gomułka and several German Communist leaders urged Tito to attend. Only Dimitrov

13. Ibid., pp. 285–86.
14. Edvard Kardelj, *Borba za priznanje i nezavisnost nove Jugoslavije: Sećanja* (Belgrade, 1980), p. 128. The published versions of the Third Letter contains no evidence to corroborate Kardelj's intriguing claim.
15. Dedijer, *Dokumenti 1948*, 1:290.

showed signs of sympathy for the Yugoslavs.[16] Still, when the official invitation arrived on June 19, specifying the agenda, date, and place of the meeting—"on the situation in the KPJ" on June 21 at Bucharest—the KPJ leadership quickly informed the Cominform that it would send no delegation, since the meeting was likely "to deepen rather than to resolve the differences."[17] Representatives of the other Cominform parties then met without the Yugoslavs and, eschewing the secrecy of the previous phases of the dispute, publicly issued the famous Cominform Resolution of June 28, 1948, which immediately caused a sensation around the world. It was almost certainly not an accident that the resolution was promulgated on St. Vitus's Day (Vidovdan), the date of the Serbian national defeat by the Turks at the Field of Kosovo in 1389 and of the Sarajevo assassination that precipitated World War I in 1914.

The Cominform Resolution initiated the public phase of the conflict between Belgrade and the Moscow-dominated Communist movement. The KPJ was accused of anti-Sovietism, of such practical and ideological errors as an incorrect agrarian policy and departures from Leninist theory of the party, of a lack of intraparty democracy, and of repeated refusals to accept criticism. The most serious charge, as detailed in point 8, held that the KPJ leaders "have placed themselves in opposition to the Communist parties within the Information Bureau, have taken the road of seceding from the united socialist front against imperialism, betraying the cause of international solidarity of the working people, and have taken a nationalist position." There followed a blanket condemnation of the KPJ's antiparty policy and attitude: "The Information Bureau considers that, in view of all

16. Dimitrov had already expressed his private support for the Yugoslavs on April 19, when, during an official trip, his train passed through Belgrade on the way to Prague. Speaking with Djilas alone in his compartment, Dimitrov urged him, "Stand firm! Stand firm!" When Djilas replied that the Yugoslavs were more likely to be excessively firm than irresolute, Dimitrov said warmly, "The most important thing is that you stand firm and everything else will come by itself." When Dimitrov's wife, Rosa, joined the two, she told Djilas that "we have been afraid for you [Yugoslavs] lately." The atmosphere changed when Červenkov and the other Bulgarian leaders joined the group: Milovan Djilas, *Vlast* (London, 1983), pp. 150–51. Dimitrov sent Tito "fraternal greetings and best wishes" on his birthday, May 25, and as late as June 25 responded with "heartfelt thanks" to Tito's greetings on his own birthday: Dedijer, *Dokumenti 1948*, 1:293, 298. Later on, Dimitrov, too, joined the Cominform campaign against Yugoslavia, but never as enthusiastically as the other Bulgarian leaders.

17. Dedijer, *Dokumenti 1948*, 1:297.

this, the KPJ CC has excluded itself and the KPJ from the family of
fraternal Communist parties, the united Communist front, and conse-
quently is outside the ranks of the Information Bureau." The concluding section revealed Stalin's immediate intentions:

> The Information Bureau does not doubt that in the bosom of the KPJ
> there is a sufficient number of healthy elements, faithful to Marxism-
> Leninism, faithful to the internationalist traditions of the KPJ, faithful to
> the united socialist front.
> The task of these healthy members of the KPJ is to compel their
> present leaders to admit their errors openly and honestly and to correct
> them, to abandon nationalism and to return to internationalism, and to
> strengthen the united socialist front against imperialism with all of their
> might, or—if the present leaders of the KPJ prove incapable of this—to
> remove them and to raise high a new internationalist leadership of the
> KPJ.
> The Information Bureau does not doubt that the KPJ will be able to
> fulfill this honorable task.[18]

In short, the "health" of the KPJ members would be judged by their
willingness to overthrow Tito's leadership. Having had similar experiences in the past, Stalin was confident that censure would be enough
to bring the recusants back in line. He rightly counted on the effects
of his immense charisma among the Yugoslav Communists and expected that the KPJ leaders would beat a hasty retreat, sacrifice the
"dubious Marxists," throw themselves on Stalin's mercy, and initiate
a purge that would ultimately swallow Tito and Kardelj. Beyond
those expectations Stalin really had no strategy. The Soviet leadership
offered little besides the slogans of "internationalism" and the
"building of socialism with the support of the Soviet Union." Other
than the mobilization of the national minorities, especially the Albanians and Hungarians, the Soviets and their Cominform allies had
nothing to say on Yugoslavia's national question, the overriding issue
in Yugoslav politics. Nor did the Soviets ever threaten to destroy the
Yugoslav federation. As Stalin explained to Enver Hoxha in
November 1949, "We must not leave any way for the Titoite enemy
to accuse us later of allegedly waging our fight to break up the
Yugoslav Federation. This is a delicate moment and needs very care-

---

18. Ibid., p. 305–6.

ful handling, because by saying, 'See, they want to break up Yugoslavia,' Tito not only gathers reaction around him, but also tries to win the patriotic elements to his side."[19]

He did so in any case. For Tito, the confrontation with the Soviets was only secondarily over ideology. From the beginning the Yugoslav leadership emphasized that the Soviet attack was an attack on the Yugoslav state, not just an ideological dispute among Communists. The response to the Cominform Resolution, which the Yugoslavs— much to the Soviets' surprise—printed in the party organ *Borba* on June 30, stated that "party and state organs in certain countries of people's democracy have committed a whole series of unprovoked acts that offend the peoples of Yugoslavia, their state, and state representatives."[20] And at the Fifth Congress of the KPJ (July 21–28, 1948), the gathering that disappointed Stalin's hope for a quick turnabout in the Yugoslav party, Tito stressed that the Cominform Resolution "was not just an attack on the leadership of our party. This is an attack on the unity of our party, an attack on the unity that our peoples won with their blood, this is an invitation to all the destructive elements to wreck what we have been building for the happiness of our peoples up to now; this is a call to civil war, a call to destroy our country."[21]

Though Stalin personally never inveighed against Tito after the split, at least not publicly (he left that to the lesser Soviet and allied leaders and their mammoth propaganda machine), his most glaring error was to insult the self-esteem of Yugoslav Communists by deriding the Partisan struggle and belittling its importance. Tito and the Partisans, after all, had their own powerful charisma. The early Cominformists were no less confused than loyal Titoists by the rewriting of the Partisan story. Tito could easily strengthen his position by appealing to their sense of common experience. In an emotional speech to army commanders, reserve officers, and party leaders after the completion of military maneuvers in Šumadija (Serbia), Tito summoned up the history of Partisan struggle:

19. Enver Hoxha, *With Stalin: Memoirs* (Tirana, 1979), p. 143.
20. Plenum Centralnog komiteta Komunisticke partje Jugoslavije, "Izjava Centralnog komiteta Komunističke partije Jugoslavije povodom rezolucije Informacionog biroa komunističkih partija o stanju u Komunističkoj partiji Jugoslavije," *Borba*, June 30, 1949, p. 4.
21. *Peti kongres Komunističke partije Jugoslavije: Izveštaji i referati* (Belgrade, 1948), p. 156.

There are no longer any journalists and foreigners here. I said what I had to say for public consumption, but these hours we have spent together and your vows brought me to think about everything that is behind us and that lies ahead of us. All of this provoked within me an irresistible need to confess to you. Yes, comrades, do not be surprised. For the first time in my life, just as the Christian believer senses the need to confess, I want to tell you my whole life, so that you may judge whether I could have chosen any other road than this road of ours. . . . I am not a believer, and I did not feel obliged to settle accounts before anybody outside our country, not even in Bucharest, when the Information Bureau demanded that of me. For the work in our country, among our people, we are responsible only to ourselves. Together with me at Užice and across the Lim, through eastern Bosnia and the Krajina, under the Grmeč and on the Neretva, you experienced the first Chetnik stab in the back, the white death of Mount Igman, the starving columns of children from Banija and the Kordun, the ravage of typhus and the carnage of thousands of our comrades on the Sutjeska. . . . I know that you who cleared the paths of revolution with me, who defended the litters of typhus patients with me, who fed with hope the survivors in burned and ravaged villages with me, best understand and will convince yourselves still further that we could have chosen no other road.[22]

By drawing attention to the history of common struggle and the plight of the Yugoslav state, Tito was also defending the integral nature of Communist ideology. He evidently felt that any ideological challenge to Stalin—a call for a different model of socialism—carried dangers for the Yugoslavs, too. Maintaining momentum under conditions of total isolation, Tito started to reproduce Stalin's program of "socialism in one country," against both East and West. Again and again he displayed a robust self-confidence that must have been irritating to the Russians, drawing as it did on their own historical experience. They counterattacked by completing a historical circle: Yugoslav "socialism in one country" was invalid in the absence of Soviet participation. In the words of an émigré Yugoslav Cominformist leader:

The revisionists in the leadership of our party have recently started to claim that we realized a revolution in the course of the war. . . . It must be stressed that the fable about the "realization of revolution" is con-

22. Dedijer, *Novi prilozi*, 3:366.

nected with the claim that the "peoples of Yugoslavia liberated themselves with their own forces." The basic aim of these claims is the wish
to "prove" that the revolution in individual countries and the liberation
of colonial peoples from the imperialist yoke can be realized not on the
basis of unified forces of the international working class, all the exploited masses and colonial peoples, but in isolated struggle by the
peoples of individual countries and colonies, which has nothing in common with the united struggle of the international proletariat against
imperialism.[23]

Homemade revolution had become counterrevolutionary.

The ideological split would come later. In 1948 and well into 1949
the KPJ repeatedly vowed its loyalty to Stalin and the Soviet Union.
Still, in January 1949, at the Second Congress of the Communist
Party of Serbia, Tito adopted a new tone when he spoke of the
domestic Cominformists. Never forgiving in battle, Tito now declared that the Cominformist opposition was no less dangerous than
the party's more familiar enemies: "Do not permit anyone to wreck
the ranks of our party, no matter who he is. Be aware that this is
enemy activity, not only toward our party but also toward our peoples. [Expressions of approval.] Be vigilant and merciless toward anyone who would attempt such a thing."[24]

Not that the Cominformists had been coddled before 1949. Supporters of the Resolution had been subject to arrest since the summer
of 1948. In early August, however, Colonel General Arso Jovanović,
Tito's wartime chief of the Supreme Staff and later of the General
Staff of the Yugoslav army, together with Major General Branko
Petričević-Kadja and Colonel Vladimir Dapčević, both on the staff of
the army's main political directorate, the former its deputy chief in
charge of organizational-instructional affairs, attempted to flee to
Romania after failing in an attempt to organize a military coup d'état.
Their decision to flee came after five meetings between Dapčević and
General G. S. Sidorovich, the Soviet military attaché in Belgrade.
According to one view, the flight of Jovanović and his accomplices
was connected with a Soviet plan to organize a Cominformist govern-

23. Radonja Golubović, "Buržoaski nacionalizam Titove klike pod maskom socijalizma," Nova borba, Dec. 29, 1948, p. 1.
24. "Govor druga Tita na Drugom kongresu Komunističke partije Srbije," Borba, Jan.
22, 1949, p. 1.

ment in exile that would have legitimized all forms of pressure against Yugoslavia, possibly even an invasion in the guise of "liberation."[25] General Jovanović was killed by a Yugoslav frontier guard at the Romanian border near Vršac. General Petričević made his way back to Belgrade, where he was arrested. Colonel Dapčević, brother of the renowned Partisan commander Peko Dapčević, was arrested in early September while trying to cross the Hungarian frontier.[26] Their mutiny hardened the Yugoslav stand against internal pro-Soviet forces.

The "conspiracy of generals" was a harbinger of Soviet military pressure against Belgrade. The Soviet Union and its East European allies first imposed a total military blockade on Yugoslavia. While the conflict lasted they provoked as many as 7,877 border incidents, in which seventeen Yugoslav border guards lost their lives. In addition, the Soviets and their allies infiltrated various Cominformist saboteurs across the frontiers, causing the deaths of perhaps a hundred more Yugoslavs. Most ominous, there is evidence that the Soviets planned to invade Yugoslavia from 1949 to perhaps 1951.

On August 18, 1949, the Soviet government warned Belgrade that arrests of minority Russians in Yugoslavia, most of them White émigrés who had been recruited by Soviet intelligence after the war and whom Moscow regarded as Soviet citizens, would not be tolerated. The Yugoslavs were told that the Soviet side would be compelled to resort to other, more effective means should the "fascist tyrants" continue to molest "Soviet citizens." This warning provoked the first of the recurring war scares that troubled Yugoslavia until well into 1952. As the Soviets and their allies nullified their treaties of friendship with Yugoslavia and massed their troops on the Yugoslav frontiers, the Yugoslav authorities prepared for attack. According to Svetozar Vukmanović-Tempo, whom Tito appointed supreme commander of Partisan detachments—that is, the irregular troops that were to remain on the territory that the government and the army planned to evacuate—the Yugoslavs were prepared to "destroy bridges, factories, railways—everything that could be of use to the enemy. The decision was taken to lay mines on roads, organize ambushes, destroy the enemy's manpower, disable his equipment and

25. Miodrag Marović, "Općenarodni plebiscit za Tita," *Danas*, July 5, 1983, p. 72.
26. For more on the "conspiracy of generals," see Djordje Ličina, *Izdaja* (Zagreb, 1985), passim. See also Dragan Marković and Savo Kržavac, *Zavera Informbiroa* (Belgrade, 1987), pp. 241–47.

armaments. The aggressors were to feel as if they were sitting on a volcano."[27] The Yugoslavs started to evacuate food reserves and state archives.

The Soviets actually did have a military plan for the invasion of Yugoslavia. Its details are outlined by Béla K. Király, commander of Hungarian infantry in 1949, who emigrated to the United States after 1956. As the designated commander of the Hungarian contingent of the invading armies and later head of the Hungarian General Staff Academy, Király was privy to Soviet strategic plans, which included a first-echelon attack by Soviet forces against Belgrade, supported by the Hungarians and the Romanians.[28] Király believes that an attack against Yugoslavia was linked in Soviet eyes with the Korean issue.[29] Once the Americans and the United Nations decided to intervene in Korea, the Soviets thought better of their plan to invade Yugoslavia and quietly abandoned it after 1951.[30] All the same, the Cominformist émigrés expected Soviet intervention in Yugoslavia as late as 1952.[31] As for Stalin, he may have been less sanguine about an invasion of Yugoslavia than his military plans suggest. According to Enver Hoxha, the Soviet leader repudiated the attack as early as November 1949.[32]

For Belgrade, the Soviet military threat was very costly, part of the enormous economic pressure that the Soviets and their allies exerted against Yugoslavia. From 1949 to 1956 Yugoslavia invested an extremely large percentage of its national income in the military, as much as 21.4 percent in 1952.[33] Moreover, Yugoslavia's First Five-Year Plan depended on long-term Soviet loans amounting to $400 million and undisturbed trade with the Soviet Union and the East European countries. All of these expectations disappeared as the Soviets and their allies broke off all economic treaties and trade agreements with Yugoslavia. Whether these actions were taken unilaterally

27. Vukmanović, Revolucija, 2:106.
28. Béla K. Király, "The Aborted Soviet Military Plans against Tito's Yugoslavia," in Wayne S. Vucinich, ed., At the Brink of War and Peace: The Tito-Stalin Split in a Historic Perspective (New York, 1982), pp. 284–85; and map, p. xii.
29. Walter Ulbricht, the East German leader, seems to have been the most determined advocate of armed intervention. See Dedijer, Novi prilozi, 3:443, 445–46.
30. Királyi, "Aborted Plans," pp. 286–88.
31. Slobodan Pauljević, Strašno budjenje (Rijeka, 1982), p. 133.
32. Hoxha, With Stalin, pp. 26, 142–43.
33. Jozo Tomasevich, "Immediate Effects of the Cominform Resolution on the Yugoslav Economy," in Vucinich, At the Brink, pp. 102–4.

(as by Albania and Hungary) or informally and by circumvention and evasion (as by the others), the effect was the same. The Soviet bloc meant to wreck Yugoslavia's economy. Yugoslavia's only recourse was to reorient its trade toward the West—the first step in the country's diplomatic revolution.

The Soviet campaign against Yugoslavia signaled the real beginning of the Sovietization of Eastern Europe. The program of this very radical and intolerant new period, which was marked by excesses of cold-war rhetoric and a redefinition of the "popular democratic" interim model in the direction of the "dictatorship of the proletariat," was outlined at a meeting of the Cominform member parties in Hungary's Mátra Mountains on November 27, 1949. After listening to a report by Gheorghe Gheorghiu-Dej, general secretary of the Romanian Workers' (Communist) Party, titled "The Yugoslav Communist Party in the Power of Murderers and Spies," the participants promulgated the so-called Second Cominform Resolution, which stated explicitly that "whereas the meeting of the Information Bureau of the Communist parties in June 1948 noted the "transition of the Tito-Ranković clique from democracy and socialism to bourgeois nationalism, in the time that has elapsed since that meeting of the Informburo the clique has completed its transition from bourgeois nationalism to fascism and outright betrayal of Yugoslavia's national interests."[34]

The application of the term "fascist" to the Yugoslavs justified a call for a great purge in Eastern Europe. As Gheorghiu-Dej noted in his report to the Cominform meeting, the watchword of the day was state vigilance—the vigilance of the state of the dictatorship of the proletariat: "It is well known that in the countries of people's democracy the old state apparatus was not removed all at once, as happened at the time of the Great October Socialist Revolution [in Russia]. This means that the vigilance of Communists must be strengthened in the extreme. . . . The most important lesson that flows from the experience of the great Bolshevik party is that the introduction of Bolshevik order in our own party house is indispensable for an increase in vigilance. The basic means in that regard is a reexamination of party members." Gheorghiu-Dej called for a purification of ideology and greater vigilance in science, literature, art, and music—in all aspects

34. Dedijer, *Dokumenti 1948*, 2:535.

of culture. He announced the good results of the purge in Romania. The time had come to throw out all the "hostile and alien" elements that had wormed their way into the party at the "time when we accepted members through the big door."[35]

The purge in Eastern Europe was not, however, concerned with obscure figures. At the time of the Second Cominform Resolution the Albanian leadership had already tried, condemned, and executed Koçi Xoxe (May–June 1949); the Hungarian leadership had done the same with László Rajk, former minister of the interior (September 1949). Trajčo Kostov, a member of the Bulgarian Politburo, was arrested in June 1949 and was tried and executed in December. In Poland, Gomułka was put under house arrest in July 1951. The Romanians purged (but never tried) Ana Pauker, Vasile Luca, and Teohari Georgescu. And in the most fearsome purge trial, the Czechoslovak Stalinists condemned and executed Rudolf Slanský, Bedřich Geminder, Vladimír Clementis, and nine other party leaders in November 1952.[36] In addition to the purges in the ruling parties, the anti-Tito spy mania engulfed militants on distant battlefields. As early as January 1949, at the Fifth Plenum of the KKE, Márkos Vapheiádēs was expelled from the Greek party's central committee, then confined in Albania, and finally exiled to Penza, in the Volga region of the USSR.[37] And in February 1949 the American leftist correspondent

---

35. Ibid., pp. 551–52.

36. Trajčo Kostov's views on the nature of postwar power in the people's democracies were incompatible with Yugoslav radicalism. For Kostov, state power in Bulgaria was the rule of the "democratic portion of the bourgeoisie in alliance with the working class and peasants, and not a revolutionary dictatorship of workers and peasants" (cited in Mito Isusov, *Komunističeskata partija i revoljucionnijat proces v Bəlgarija 1944/1948* [Sofia, 1983], pp. 88–89). Small wonder that Tito had no sympathy for the demoted Kostov. Speaking at the Third Congress of the NFJ on April 9, 1949, Tito noted that the KPJ leadership "for years suspected that Trajčo Kostov was somebody's agent." See "Politički referat druga Tita na Trećem kongresu Narodnog fronta Jugoslavije," *Borba,* April 10, 1949, p. 3. For more on Kostov's relations with the Yugoslavs, see Arso Milatović, *Pet diplomatskih misija* (Ljubljana, 1985), 1:118–29. As for Slanský, though his views were far closer to the Yugoslavs', he, too, was an object of Yugoslav derision for his part in the Cominform campaign against Yugoslavia, even after his arrest in November 1951. For a typical example of how the Yugoslavs ridiculed this "Galician rabbi," see Marijan Stilinović, *Sumrak u Pragu* (Zagreb, 1952), pp. 10–11.

37. Jovan Popovski, *General Markos: Zašto me Staljin nije streljao?* (Belgrade, 1982), pp. 112–20. Márkos had a better time of it than ten leaders of the Greek Macedonian NOF, headed by Paskal Mitrevski, who were transported to the USSR and sentenced to imprisonment at hard labor in Vorkuta for "crimes against the international workers' movement." For more on this bizarre case, see Dragan Kljakić, *General Markos* (Zagreb, 1979), pp. 207–10.

Anna Louise Strong, propagator of Mao Zedong's rigid views on atomic weapons as "paper tigers," was arrested in Moscow as an "imperialist spy" and immediately linked with the Yugoslavs.[38]

Of the purge victims, Xoxe alone had special links with the Yugoslavs, so the Soviets had to manufacture such links for the others by suborning Yugoslav Cominformist émigrés to testify against them. Nevertheless, with the notable exception of Kostov and Gomułka (both moderate exponents of the Popular Front) and the Romanian leaders (who were the victims of a leftist and nativist campaign by Gheorghiu-Dej), most of the purge victims were leftists and, like the Yugoslavs, uneasy about Stalin's coalition politics in the immediate postwar period. Now that Stalin had turned to the left, they (like the Yugoslavs) could not be permitted the unholy joy of having been more revolutionary than Stalin.

By a curious reversal of roles, Tito was cast in the rightist mold that long had fitted Stalin. By predictable reflex, the Yugoslav defense was appropriately leftist. In foreign affairs this initially meant a harsh anti-Western stance. It was such "Western agents" as Kostov who were responsible for the poisoning of Soviet–Yugoslav relations. After the demotion of Kostov, *Borba* carried a comment from the official Yugoslav news agency which said that the "uncovering of the spy network in Bulgaria, involving high party and state functionaries, shows that the leaders of new Yugoslavia were correct in claiming that the slanderous campaign against the KPJ was most closely connected with the spying activities of imperialist countries and their aggressive plans."[39]

Since the Soviet critique of Yugoslavia's economic policy was harshest in regard to agriculture, the KPJ's leftist defense in domestic affairs was not notable in the speedy drive for the collectivization of agriculture. The Yugoslav leaders were acutely aware that the Soviets accused them of pursuing a non-Marxist course in the countryside— of protecting a private peasant economy and the concentration of land in the hands of rich peasants—or kulaks. (After the Resolution,

38. D. L., "Hapšenje Ane Lujze Strong i podmetanja Radio Praga," *Borba*, Feb. 19, 1949, p. 3. In 1949, the year of Mao Zedong's victory in China, the KPJ repeatedly expressed their solidarity with the Chinese Communists, in whom they recognized kindred spirits and potential allies against Stalin. For a typical statement see Peko Dapčević, "Kina na pragu pobjede," *Borba*, May 1, 1949, p. 2.

39. "Uhapšen je niz visokih bugarskih državnih i partiskih rukovodilaca," *Borba*, April 2, 1949, p. 4.

Dušan Petrović-Šane, one of the KPJ leaders in Serbia, shouted at the peasants during a rally, "——your kulak mother, Stalin attacked us on account of you!")[40] The KPJ's solution to this problem was to authorize the "creation of peasant working cooperatives more boldly and more quickly." This decision, taken at the Second Plenum of the KPJ CC in January 1949, was to be carried out on a voluntary basis. In fact, the means used to force the peasants into cooperatives amounted to administrative, economic, and political pressure. Coupled with enforcement of the very unpopular compulsory deliveries of grain and produce, the KPJ's agrarian policy prompted mass resistance. At the Third Plenum of the KPJ CC, in December 1949, Vladimir Bakarić reported that in Slavonia alone as many as fifty peasants were killed during attempts to extract grain from them after the harvest. Peasants held rallies at cemeteries with the slogan "Arise, ye dead, change your places with the living." At the same plenum Jovan Veselinov described some aspects of "dekulakization" in Vojvodina: "A peasant would say that he had 140 cubic meters of grain, but he had to deliver 220 meters, meaning that he was 80 meters short. We would then measure and confiscate all of his grain, although we knew that he really did not have what was expected of him. We did this in order to fulfill the plan. . . . But there were other errors, too; our people lost their tempers, slapped faces, pulled mustaches. (Comrade Tito: 'On occasion put pistols in people's mouths.') All sorts of things were happening."[41]

The cost in peasant suffering was enormous. Veselinov admitted that resistance was strong, especially among the Hungarian peasants in Vojvodina, "where defunct merchants and kulaks carried out Cominformist propaganda."[42] Considering the great importance of peasants in the Yugoslav Partisan war and their strong showing in the party (49.4 percent of all KPJ members were active peasants in July 1948), the cost was all the greater; the vast peasant exodus from the party began in 1949. Nor did collectivization bring any economic benefits. By 1951, 60.99 percent of the land in Macedonia and 44.77 percent in Montenegro, both food-import areas, was collectivized, but only 14.13 percent in Croatia. The exception to the greater accep-

40. Dedijer, *Novi prilozi,* 3:358.
41. Branko Petranović, Ranko Končar, and Radovan Radonjić, comps., *Sednice Centralnog komiteta KPJ (1948–1952)* (Belgrade, 1985), pp. 275, 413, 423–24.
42. Ibid., p. 424.

tance of collectivization in the passive areas was grain-rich Vojvodina, where 41.09 percent of the land was collectivized by 1951,
largely because the colonist population on former German farms was
politically more pliable. Even so, by 1953 the KPJ was obliged to
terminate its detrimental policy in the countryside, and found a face-
saving formula for the dissolution of collective farms.[43]

The conflict with the Cominform fostered rigid administrative
measures in every aspect of Yugoslavia's public life. Just as in the
Soviet Union during Stalin's revolution from above after 1928, the
party and police apparatuses of Yugoslavia were vastly strengthened
after the Cominform Resolution. The split that emancipated the KPJ
from the Soviet Union promoted home-grown Stalinism. Besides
strengthening the system of repression, especially by building camps
for arrested *ibeovci,* the KPJ leadership introduced new centralizing
measures in the party. The system of control was consolidated in
1949 by the introduction of districts (*oblasti*) within the republics (in
both party and state organizations), which thus reduced the status of
"national leaderships," that is, the republics.[44] As these measures
hardly made for a distinctive socialism, they undermined the
Yugoslav cause in European and world leftist circles and even among
some South Slavic left-wingers overseas.[45]

43. The best and most succinct account of the collectivization campaign in Yugoslavia is
Tomasevich, "Immediate Effects," pp. 120–26.
44. Petranović et al., *Sednice,* pp. 204–6.
45. In the aftermath of the Yugoslav split there were a few exceptions to Stalinist loyalty
among the Communists of the nonruling parties, notably in Italy. Valdo Magnani, secretary
of the Italian Communist party's Reggio Emilia federation, and Aldo Cucchi, Magnani's
deputy in Bologna, resigned from the party in 1951 and soon formed the Movimento
Lavoratori Italiani (later the Unione Socialisti Indipendenti), which showed some strength
in the Veneto, the Marche, and to a lesser extent Emilia. The *magnacucchi,* as the Italian
Communists derisively referred to this small group of dissidents, were primarily critical of
the party's dependence on the Soviet Union. Though critical of Tito's dictatorial methods
and of Yugoslavia's policy in Trieste, Magnani and Cucchi anticipated that Yugoslavia
would evolve toward a more democratic socialism. Relations between the KPJ and these
premature Eurocommunists (Magnani was restored to the Italian Communist Party in
1961) developed slowly and mirrored the sentiments of other Italian anti-Cominformists,
notably the Morelli-David-Mazzini group in Rome and Elio Petri. On Italian Titoism see
Eric R. Terzuolo, *Red Adriatic: The Communist Parties of Italy and Yugoslavia* (Boulder,
Colo., 1985), pp. 139–44. Other pro-Yugoslav groups and individuals worth noting include the Unabhängige Arbeiterpartei Deutschlands in West Germany; Jésus Hernández, a
former member of the Spanish Communist Party's Politburo; the French leftist writer Jean
Cassou; and the British Labourite Konni Zilliacus. In the South Slavic emigration the pro-
Tito torch was carried by Luj Adamič, the noted American leftist author of Slovene origin
known as Louis Adamic. He gives his impressions of Yugoslavia's conflict with the Cominform in *The Eagle and the Roots* (Garden City, N.Y., 1952).

Yugoslavia's total isolation after 1948 was the cause of minute stocktaking in the KPJ leadership. The disillusionment with the Soviets and the KPJ's inability to make inroads in the world Communist movement encouraged the Yugoslavs to see international tensions in terms of unequal relations between strong and weak states—not in class terms. This position, expressed by Kardelj on the floor of the United Nations in September 1949, was but a step from a search for a partnership with the new, emerging, and neutral states of the former colonial world. The Yugoslav diplomat Josip Djerdja encouraged this course after his visit to India in 1951.[46] Having ruled out the possibility of building a new International, the KPJ leaders also encouraged contacts with "all the progressive democratic movements in the world," that is, the noncommunist left, especially in Western Europe. Nevertheless, Yugoslavia's isolation could be breached—and its need for economic and military assistance fulfilled—only by Western governments.

At the beginning of the Soviet–Yugoslav conflict the KPJ leaders showed no signs of wavering in their hostility to the West. In fact, the early stages of conflict between Belgrade and Moscow were accompanied by a worsening of Yugoslavia's relations with the West. On March 20, 1948, only one day after the Soviets withdrew their specialists from Yugoslavia, the Western powers proposed that both zones of the disputed territory of Trieste (including the Yugoslav-held Zone B) be assigned to Italy. At the Fifth Congress Kardelj reaffirmed that Yugoslavia belonged to the "camp of anti-imperialist forces headed by the Soviet Union."[47] But during that same summer Tito confided to Djilas his secret hope that the Americans would come to his aid: "The Americans are not fools. They won't let the Russians reach the Adriatic."[48] And by October the British foreign minister, Ernest Bevin, reacting to a report on Yugoslavia's predicament, proved Tito's astuteness by writing a concise directive on how to behave toward the Yugoslav leader: "Keep him afloat."[49] By 1949 Tito reciprocated with concessions in Trieste and Austria, and, most

46. Dedijer, *Novi prilozi*, 3:554.
47. *Peti kongres*, p. 327.
48. Milovan Djilas, *Tito: The Story from Inside* (New York, 1980), p. 125.
49. Cited in Jože Pirjevec, *Tito, Stalin e l'Occidente* (Trieste, 1985), p. 285. This book, based in good part on recently released Western diplomatic documents, offers keen insights into early Western reactions to the Soviet–Yugoslav split. See esp. pp. 182–95, 232–34, 239–43, 274–76, 282–87, 304–6.

important, by closing the frontier with Greece and withdrawing all support from the Greek insurgents, because the KKE sided with the Cominform against Belgrade.

These were the first steps in an emerging commensal association between Yugoslavia and the West. At the Third Plenum of the KPJ CC in December 1949, in words that were not made public at the time, Kardelj noted a "tendency among the imperialists to exploit the contradictions between the socialist states, very much in the same way as we wish to exploit the internal contradictions of the imperialist system." Yugoslavia, Kardelj believed, was especially useful to the West in the area of propaganda. The Soviets had once attacked the Western countries as warmongers, aggressors, and opponents of equality among states; now these charges were flung back at them as the West pointed to the concrete example of Yugoslavia.[50] When Kardelj presented Yugoslavia's case against the Soviets at the United Nations General Assembly in September 1949, he effectively internationalized an internal Communist dispute. Small wonder that the Western countries immediately rewarded Yugoslavia by supporting its election to the UN Security Council, despite Soviet opposition.[51] These steps were followed by Yugoslavia's neutral (effectively pro-Western) stand on the Korean question and the extension of economic and military aid to Yugoslavia by the United States and other Western countries.[52] By 1955 the United States had given $598.5 million in economic aid and $588.5 million in military aid to Yugoslavia.[53] A further $420 million was distributed through

50. Petranović et al., *Sednice*, pp. 470–71.

51. On Yugoslavia's use of the United Nations in its political confrontation with the Soviet Union see Jadranka Jovanović, "Borba Jugoslavije protiv pritiska SSSR-a i istočnoevropskih država u Organizaciji ujedinjenih nacija (1949–1953): Glavni momenti," *Istorija 20. veka* 2, nos. 1–2 (1984): 85–111.

52. When the UN Security Council voted on June 25, 1950, to condemn the North Korean attack against South Korea, Yugoslavia abstained. Yugoslavia's official stand on the Korean question, as expressed by Kardelj in September 1950, focused on the nefarious Soviet role. The Yugoslavs held that the "military action of the North Korean government did not serve the genuine liberation of the Korean people." In Korea, as elsewhere, "the hopes of the popular masses for liberation . . . were being misused for the aims of an alien hegemonistic policy." See "Izjava druga Edvarda Kardelja o stavu FNRJ prema ratu u Koreji," *Borba*, Sept. 6, 1950, p. 1. On American economic and military aid to Yugoslavia, see Tomasevich, "Immediate Effects," pp. 108–13.

53. John C. Campbell, *Tito's Separate Road: America and Yugoslavia in World Politics* (New York, 1967), p. 29.

UNRRA. Other Western countries and the World Bank extended loans that amounted to over $400 million.[54]

Acceptance of military aid from the West was a very delicate matter for the Yugoslavs. The Soviets accused Yugoslavia of receiving Western arms two years before Belgrade actually did so. Speaking at a closed session of the Fourth Plenum of the KPJ CC (June 1951), Tito noted that Western military aid was "in our interest and we, comrades, will pay no heed to what the Informburo will say about this. They said that two years ago and so have nothing further to say. Now we are going to take what they accused us of taking."[55]

The rapprochement with the West altered the whole system of Yugoslav radicalism. Despite Tito's warnings that the KPJ must be "on guard, especially among the younger members of the party, that we do not forget that we are a socialist country, in view of our [new] stand toward the imperialist world,"[56] the party's leftist rigidity of the first two years after the Cominform Resolution was followed by three years of heady ideological revisionism in an attempt to find a Yugoslav alternative to Soviet ideological postulates within the thesaurus of Marxism. As a result, the certainty of doctrine was challenged in every conceivable area, from the dethroning of socialist realism which culminated in Miroslav Krleža's speech at the Third Congress of Yugoslavian Writers (October 1952) to tremors in philosophy and the social sciences. The most important area of inquiry, however, was the definition of the Soviet social system. Only by finding the social basis of "Cominformist revisionism" could Yugoslavia hope to avoid repeating Soviet mistakes and develop a truly socialist model of postrevolutionary society. As A. Ross Johnson has convincingly demonstrated, the search for the roots of Soviet degeneration led to escalating claims that the Soviet system was (1) merely a bureaucratically distorted socialist system (Boris Ziherl); (2) a unique system midway between capitalism and socialism, with an economic base that exhibited socialist tendencies but was dominated

54. Thomas T. Hammond, "Foreign Relations since 1945," in Robert F. Byrnes, ed., *Yugoslavia* (New York, 1957), p. 27. Cf. Vaclav L. Benes, Robert F. Byrnes, and Nicolas Spulber, eds., *The Second Soviet-Yugoslav Dispute* (Bloomington, Ind., 1959), p. xiii.
55. Petranović et al., *Sednice,* pp. 614–15.
56. Ibid., p. 478.

by a bureaucratic-despotic caste (Kardelj and the majority of the KPJ leadership); (3) a new type of class society in which the ruling bureaucratic caste restored capitalism in a special—state-capitalist—form, without (hence the contradictory nature of view) changing the socialist economic base (Djilas); (4) a state-capitalist society in which socialism never existed, dominated by a new bureaucratic ruling class (Zvonimir Kristl and Janez Stanovnik).[57]

If we except the last view, which counted the socialist period in Yugoslavia from 1948, thereby undermining the historical legitimacy of the KPJ in the interwar and wartime periods, the classic formulations of Kardelj and Djilas left the door open to the possibility of a political-ideological (but not social) revolution in the Soviet Union, rather along the lines advocated by the Yugoslavs. Specifically, the chief source of bureaucratic counterrevolution was the fetishism of the state. The building of socialism could not advance without the steady withering of the state's political functions, which were to be exercised directly by the producers via assemblies of voters, councils of citizens, and—in industry—workers' councils. The new anti-etatist socialist state had to be devoid of excessive administrative organs and serviced by a relatively small state bureaucracy. These were the chief ingredients in the new Yugoslav doctrine of workers' self-management. The first workers' councils were formed in 1950, and the state increasingly transferred the administration of factories and other enterprises to such elective bodies.

These measures did not yet signify the full abandonment of planning. Nor did the greater autonomy of enterprises and local government significantly reduce the power of the state. In comparison with the parched earth of Soviet practice, however, the Yugoslav innovations were a flood tide. This is especially the case with the new role of the party, which was being redefined as an ideological conscience-raiser. Having increased its membership by 63 percent from mid-1948 to mid-1952, the KPJ was clearly no longer a conspiratorial cadre party. The leadership wanted to highlight the necessity of severing the link between the party and the state by removing this in-

---

57. A. Ross Johnson, *The Transformation of Communist Ideology: The Yugoslav Case, 1945–1953* (Cambridge, Mass., 1972), pp. 98–112. Some Yugoslav Communists, including briefly Tito at the Sixth Congress, expressed the view that the Soviet system was really a form of bourgeois dictatorship that surpassed Hitlerism in its excesses. See Andro Gabelić, *Tragovima izdaje* (Zagreb, 1951), p. 274.

creasingly mass organization from the running of state affairs. As unlikely as this divorce was in practice, the Sixth Congress of the KPJ, in November 1952, adopted a resolution to the effect that the party would no longer be a "direct operational leader and taskmaster in economic, state, or social life, but would act by means of its political and ideological pursuits, and principally by persuasion, in all organizations, organs, and institutions, so that its line, or that of its individual members, would be accepted."[58] To underline its new function, the KPJ changed its name to Savez komunista Jugoslavije (SKJ, League of Communists of Yugoslavia).

The Sixth Congress was indeed the high point of the KPJ's attempts to reconcile socialism and democracy. The death of Stalin in 1953, the resulting curtailment of Soviet pressures, and suspicions about Western intentions in the wake of the Trieste crisis were the first developments that moved the SKJ from its peculiar middle ground between the Soviet and Western systems. Tito was becoming increasingly mistrustful of further democratization, and at the Second Plenum of the SKJ CC, in June 1953, he engineered a halt in party reform.[59] The principal opponent of Tito's reversal in policy was Milovan Djilas, who traveled the road from the extreme left of the Yugoslav party (until approximately 1950) to the limit of "right liquidationism" (after the Sixth Congress). At the end of 1953 Djilas published a series of articles in Borba in which he effectively called for a multiparty system.[60] Djilas's expulsion from the SKJ leadership at the Third Plenum, in January 1954, was a precondition for an improvement in relations with the USSR.[61] By March, Yugoslav commentators were expressing favorable views of G. M. Malenkov's New Course, which was seen as "relief" from state pressure for the beleaguered East European countries.[62] And over a year later, in May 1955, N. S. Khrushchev and N. A. Bulganin made their famous visit

58. Šesti kongres KPJ (Saveza komunista Jugoslavije) (Belgrade, 1952), p. 268.
59. Djilas, Vlast, pp. 251–53.
60. The most important of these articles are found in Abraham Rothberg, ed., Anatomy of a Moral: The Political Essays of Milovan Djilas (New York, 1959).
61. Kardelj, Sećanja, p. 145. The émigré Cominformist press commented on the fall of Djilas in somewhat moderate tones, leaving open the possibility that Yugoslavia would restore its "premordial ties with the fraternal peoples of the countries of people's democracy": "Djilasov 'slučaj' i jugoslovenska stvarnost," Za socijalističku Jugoslaviju, Feb. 6, 1954, p. 6.
62. Ivo Pelicon, "Sovjetski blok godinu dana bez Staljina," Naša stvarnost 8, no. 3 (1954): 104.

to Belgrade, expressed regrets over the "disturbance" in the relations between the USSR and Yugoslavia, and promised to place those relations on new foundations.[63]

Both sides stood to gain from the rapprochement. For the Yugoslav leadership, no less than for the Soviets, the end of violent polemics meant an end to dangerous uncertainty about the socialist system itself. According to one Yugoslav view, to which Kardelj subscribed after Stalin's death, several key Yugoslav leaders felt that a "change took place in the relation of world forces, that the USSR got weaker and the USA got stronger, and that every significant weakening of the USSR would weaken our [Yugoslav] positions, too."[64] Socialism was an object of theoretical inquiry, but also a system of power.

63. Dedijer, *Dokumenti 1948*, 3:536–38.
64. Dedijer, *Novi prilozi*, 3:620.

PART II

THE HEALTHY FORCES

4

Numbers and Footholds

In late 1948 and early 1949 the KPJ leaders could look forward only to further confrontation with the Soviet Union. Their chief political obstacle was the widespread belief among the party's rank and file that the conflict with the Cominform would in time be overcome. This "most dangerous illusion," as Djilas termed it, obstructed Yugoslav self-defense, for the Cominformists were not yet so alienated from the leadership that they were incapable of functioning within the party.[1] Ranković's private observation aptly described the fluidity of the fronts: "The worst part is that you can't know who the enemy is! Up to now the enemy was outside the party, on the opposite side, and now he can be yesterday's closest comrade."[2]

The scope of the Cominformist challenge was one more issue in the split. From the beginning, the Cominformist parties set their propaganda apparatus in motion to build up the internationalist and revolutionary image of the "healthy forces." Tito and his adherents responded with measures of their own: Stalin's "internationalists" became the official KPJ's "handful of renegades, ambitious and demoralized elements" (Djuro Pucar); "vacillators and careerists" (May Day slogan, 1949); "speculators, cold and soulless intellectuals who never had any understanding of the struggle of our working masses, . . . old opportunists, liquidators, and cowards . . . antiparty elements . . . Trotskyites . . . spineless characters who aspire to a com-

---

1. Branko Petranović, Ranko Končar, and Radovan Radonjić, comps., *Sednice Centralnog komiteta KPJ (1948–1952)* (Belgrade, 1985), p. 180; Milovan Djilas, *Vlast* (London, 1983), p. 71.
2. Djilas, *Vlast,* p. 158.

fortable life" (*Borba*); "spies enlisted by who-knows-whom" (Petar Stambolić); and even "nonhumans" (*neljudi,* Djilas).[3] The vilification of those who sided with the Cominform Resolution followed the established Soviet pattern. Not only were the *ibeovci* in error, but their past contributions had to be expunged. Arso Jovanović became "a poor military leader, who lost a whole series of battles."[4] It followed that the number of Cominformists was insignificant.

Attempts to assess the exact number of Cominformists were long frustrated by contradictory figures. The early KPJ estimates regularly minimized the number of *ibeovci.* In his New Year's message of 1949 Tito said that "only a few tens of despised traitors" fell out of the party in 1948.[5] And Djilas characterized the Cominformist opposition as "null" in November 1949. He added that this was the "weakest opposition that to date had stood in the path of progress of the new Yugoslavia."[6] Andrija Mugoša, the party's organizational secretary in Montenegro, claimed in October 1948 that there were "only 32 renegades from the line of our Central Committee among the 16,245 members of the Communist party in Montenegro."[7] And according to the Croat party leadership, by the end of 1952 the KPJ organization in Croatia had expelled 4,140 Cominformists.[8] In 1952, however, only about 18 percent of all KPJ members were from Croatia, which was in any case one of the republics least affected by Cominformism. One Yugoslav anticommunist source claimed that during one nineteen-month period following the height of the expulsions (January 1, 1950–August 1, 1951) the KPJ expelled 7,700

3. See Djuro Pucar, "Politički izveštaj o radu Pokrajinskog komiteta KPJ za Bosnu i Hercegovinu," *Borba,* Nov. 3, 1948, p. 2, and May 3, 1949, p. 2; "Pravo lice jednog izdajnika i špijuna," *Borba,* Dec. 9, 1948, p. 2; Petar Stambolić, "Politički izveštaj Centralnog komiteta KP Srbije," *Borba,* Jan. 19, 1949, p. 2; Milovan Djilas, "Borba za socijalizam u Jugoslaviji i Peti kongres KPJ: Govor druga Milovana Djilasa održan 1 septembra na sastanku partijskog aktiva Druge proleterske divizije," *Borba,* Sept. 4, 1948, p. 1.

4. Peko Dapčević, "Govor druga Peka Dapčevića na sastanku partiskog aktiva Ministarstva narodne odbrane," *Borba,* Sept. 19, 1948, p. 2.

5. "Govor maršala Tita: Neka je srećna 1949. godina svim našim trudbenicima, svim gradjanima nove Jugoslavije," *Borba,* Jan. 1, 1949, p. 1.

6. "Odgovori druga Milovana Djilasa na pitanja pretstavnika 'Njujork tajmsa' i Agencije Frans pres," *Borba,* Nov. 5, 1949, p. 1.

7. Andrija Mugoša, "Izveštaj o organizacionom radu Pokrajinskog komiteta KPJ za Crnu Goru," *Borba,* Oct. 6, 1948, p. 2.

8. "Izvještaj Centralnog komiteta SK Hrvatske o radu Saveza komunista Hrvatske od II. do III. kongresa," *Treći kongres Saveza komunista Hrvatske (26.–28.V.1954.)* (Zagreb, 1956), p. 65.

Table 1. A Yugoslav anticommunist estimate of numbers of members expelled from KPJ for Cominformism, January 1, 1950–August 1, 1951, by republic

Republic	Members expelled
Serbia	2,000
Montenegro	2,100
Bosnia-Hercegovina	2,000
Slovenia	350
Macedonia	750
Croatia	500

Source: Hoover Institution Archives, Dinko A. Tomašić Collection, J., "Ciscenje u KPJ [sic]," p. [1].

Cominformists (see Table 1). Albanian sources claimed a much higher number: "Over 200,000 Communists, half of the total membership, were expelled from the Yugoslav Communist Party during the period 1948–1952."[9] The discrepancy is marked, but even 4,140 is not a small number; in April 1941 the KPJ organization in Croatia had between 3,600 and 4,000 members.[10]

One hint that the losses in membership were higher than has been acknowledged was the mass campaign to enroll new party members which was initiated in 1948. A report on one exiled ex-Communist, who was expelled from the KPJ in 1947 for siding with his peasant father in a dispute over food deliveries, explains that "he got along as best he could until the summer of 1948, after the Cominform Resolution, when he was readmitted during the mass enrollment. Before that there were equally massive expulsions and purges . . . of Cominformists."[11]

The number of Cominformists arrested is also uncertain. As it

9. Sofokli Lazri and Javer Malo, Dans les prisons et les camps de concentration de la Yougoslavie (Tirana, 1960), p. 14. The authors of this narrative cite Yugoslavia's recently released political émigrés as their sources. They were almost certainly Vladimir Dapčević and Mileta Perović, both former Cominformist prisoners at Goli Otok, who fled to Albania and wrote a report on their experiences at Berat in July 1958. The Cominformist émigrés stuck to this figure. See, for example, Centralni komitet Komunističke partije Jugoslavije, Program Komunističke partije Jugoslavije (n.p., 1976), p. 7. By contrast, in Gheorghiu-Dej's report on the Cominform meeting of November 27, 1949, the Cominformist side originally claimed only vague "thousands" of "Yugoslav patriots" who were expelled from the KPJ and imprisoned for their loyalty to the Soviet side. See Vladimir Dedijer, ed., Dokumenti 1948 (Belgrade, 1980), 1:546.
10. Ivan Jelić, Komunistička partija Hrvatske, 1937–1941 (Zagreb, 1972), p. 321.
11. Hoover Institution Archives, Dinko A. Tomašić Collection (hereafter HIA-TC), interview no. 11, p. 2.

cannot be assumed that those identified as Cominformists were always imprisoned, one cannot equate the expelled KPJ members with those confined for Cominformism. In June 1951 Ranković admitted to only 8,403 Cominformist arrests during the three years after the Resolution (June 1948–June 1951), and in the autumn of 1952 he stated that 11,128 *ibeovci* were sentenced in an "administrative manner" (that is, without trial) and that the regular civil and military courts sentenced an additional 2,572.[12] That would mean that at least 13,700 persons were arrested as Cominformists. This is a large number, though it represents only 4.08 percent of all party members at the beginning of 1948. In contrast, the claim made by an Albanian source that no fewer than 5,000 were arrested among the officer corps is equivalent to 10.6 percent of the entire officer corps—an exceptionally heavy numerical and qualitative loss.[13]

The old estimates were largely a product of the split. We now know that they were either wrong or misleading. At a seminar for journalists in 1975 Jure Bilić, then secretary of the KPJ CC executive committee, noted that in the course of the conflict there were 54,000 registered Cominformists.[14] And in August 1983, Radovan Radonjić, professor of political science at the University of Titograd and a leading Montenegrin Communist, released the first of completely new

12. Aleksandar Ranković, *Izabrani govori i članci: 1941–1951* (Belgrade, 1951), p. 387; and "O predlogu novog Statuta Komunističke partije Jugoslavije i nekim organizacionim pitanjima Partije," *Šesti kongres KPJ (Saveza komunista Jugoslavije)* (Belgrade, 1952), p. 123. Ranković's figures were accepted by a number of Western scholars. See D. A. Tomasic, *National Communism and Soviet Strategy* (Washington, D.C., 1957), pp. 142–43; Fred Warner Neal, *Titoism in Action* (Berkeley, Calif., 1958), p. 37; George W. Hoffman and Fred W. Neal, *Yugoslavia and the New Communism* (New York, 1962), p. 142; Woodford McClellan, "Postwar Political Evolution," in Wayne S. Vucinich, ed., *Contemporary Yugoslavia: Twenty Years of Socialist Experiment* (Berkeley, Calif., 1969), p. 130; and Dennison Rusinow, *The Yugoslav Experiment, 1948–1974* (Berkeley, Calif., 1977), p. 30. Other writers, too, credited only a small number of Cominformists. See Jan Yindrich, *Tito v. Stalin: The Battle of the Marshals* (London, 1950), p. 113; Hamilton Fish Armstrong, *Tito and Goliath* (New York, 1951), p. 292; Leigh White, *Balkan Caesar: Tito versus Stalin* (New York, 1951), p. 126; and Adam B. Ulam, *Titoism and the Cominform* (Cambridge, Mass., 1952), p. 125. A few assessments, however, advanced the high figures currently credited. See Josef Korbel, *Tito's Communism* (Denver, 1951), p. 316; Ernst Halperin, *The Triumphant Heretic: Tito's Struggle against Stalin* (London, 1958), p. 93; and Andrew Borowiec, *Yugoslavia after Tito* (New York, 1977), p. 54.
13. Lazri and Malo, *Dans les prisons*, p. 20.
14. Jure Bilić, "Otvoreno i kritički—ne samo o 'kriznim' situacijama," in Ante Gavranović et al., eds., *Jugoslavija, samoupravljanje, svijet—danas* (Zagreb, 1976), p. 95. The term "registered Cominformists" refers to those individuals who were regarded as such by the Yugoslav authorities and whose movements accordingly were monitored.

Cominformist statistics, which were incorporated in Radonjić's portions of the new official party history (1985) and his simultaneous monograph on the Cominformist phenomenon. Radonjić's findings, which cite 55,663 registered and 16,288 arrested or sentenced Cominformists, are presented in Tables 2 and 3. According to his sample, 5,081 Cominformists were workers, 5,626 peasants, 4,008 students or middle school pupils; 4,153 were Yugoslav Army officers and soldiers, 1,722 belonged to the security forces, and 2,616 belonged to various party leadership groups.[15]

If it is assumed that the 55,663 Cominformists were party members, which need not necessarily be the case, they would constitute 54.48 percent of the 102,168 KPJ members who were expelled from the beginning of 1948 to the end of 1951.[16] If we proceed from the same assumption, they would constitute 19.52 percent of all party members in 1948, or almost a fifth of the membership. From 1948 to 1951, however, party membership was extremely fluid. During that period 534,262 new members were introduced to the party. On the

15. See Jelena Lovrić, "Staljinizam ne miruje: Dr Radovan Radonjić o sukobu sa Staljinom, Rezoluciji Informbiroa, Golom otoku, novim pojavnim oblicima staljinizma i sadašnjem trenutku Saveza komunista Jugoslavije," *Danas*, Aug. 16, 1983, p. 12; Stanislav Stojanović et al., eds., *Istorija Saveza komunista Jugoslavije* (Belgrade, 1985), p. 364; and Radovan Radonjić, *Izgubljena orijentacija* (Belgrade, 1985), pp. 74–77. As Radonjić's figures do not always accord with his internal evidence, I have been obliged to renegotiate his results, in part on the basis of official Yugoslav censuses. The results of these modifications, however, do not differ markedly from Radonjić's figures.

16. This calculation is based on KPJ membership during the years of the conflict, as shown in the following table compiled by Gojko Stanič, a professor in the Faculty of Political Sciences in Ljubljana. See "Broj i kretanje članova SK Jugoslavije od 1945. do 1947. godine," *Politika*, June 24, 1982, p. 7. Although Stanič's totals apparently account for deaths, resignations, and reinstatements not separately specified, they clearly indicate the KPJ base against which the Cominformist base must be seen.

Year	KPJ members at beginning of year	Admitted into KPJ during year	Expelled from KPJ	KPJ members at end of year
1948	285,147	215,987	13,521	482,938
1949	482,938	78,889	27,654	530,812
1950	530,812	105,836	26,636	607,443
1951	607,443	133,550	34,357	704,617
1952	704,617	119,941	43,744	772,920
1953	772,920	25,096	72,467	700,030
1954	700,030	20,666	56,179	654,669
1955	654,669	24,889	34,181	624,806

Table 2. Number and percent of known Cominformists, 1948–1955, by region of origin

Republic or autonomous region	Number	Percent of all Cominformists	Percent of republic's or region's population[a]
Montenegro	5,007	9.00%	1.32%
Serbia proper	28,661	51.49	0.69
Vojvodina	5,389	9.68	0.32
Macedonia	2,662	4.78	0.23
Kosmet	1,514	2.72	0.21
Croatia	6,953	12.49	0.19
Bosnia-Hercegovina	4,543	8.16	0.18
Slovenia	934	1.68	0.07
Total	55,663	100.00%	0.35

[a]1948 census.
Reconstructed from Radovan Radonjić, *Izgubljena orijentacija* (Belgrade, 1985), p. 75.

Table 3. Number and percent of arrested and convicted Cominformists, 1948–1963, by nationality

Nationality	Number of arrested and convicted Cominformists	Percent of all arrested or convicted Cominformists	Percent of nationality's total population[a]
Serbs	7,235	44.42%	0.10%
Croats	2,588	15.89	0.07
Slovenes	566	3.47	0.04
Macedonians	883	5.42	0.10
Montenegrins	3,439	21.13	0.74
Muslims[b]	—	—	—
Albanians	436	2.68	0.06
Hungarians	244	1.50	0.05
Turks	7	0.04	0.003
Slovaks	—	—	—
Italians	87	0.53	0.24
Romanians	22	0.14	0.04
Bulgars	251	1.54	0.41
Czechs	63	0.37	0.18
Other or unknown	202	1.24	0.14
Unaccounted for	265	1.63	—
Total	16,288	100.00%	0.10

[a]1953 census.
[b]Yugoslavia's census of 1953 did not list Muslims as a national category, but allowed for "Yugoslavs—nationality undeclared." Neither category appears in the statistics on arrested Cominformists.
Source: Radovan Radonjić, *Izgubljena orijentacija* (Belgrade, 1985), p. 77.

average, the KPJ had 476,585 members during those years. The 55,663 Cominformists constitute 11.68 percent of that number. Hence one cannot agree with Radonjić and other Yugoslav analysts in their confidence that the number of *ibeovci* was insignificant.

Professor Radonjić's statistics also tell us a great deal about the social, regional, and national backgrounds of the Cominformists. The *ibeovci* were clearly an elite group: almost 40 percent of their number were veterans of the Partisan war. But, as Radonjić has shrewdly observed, what at first glance seems like Cominformism's strength is an indication of its limitations and powerlessness.[17] The Cominformist problem was an elite problem, not a problem of the larger society. It was also a regional problem. True, the Cominformists came from all republics and national groups, but they were not equally represented in them. Their concentration was above the Yugoslav average in Montenegro and Serbia proper. The numbers of arrested *ibeovci* suggest that they were overrepresented among the Montenegrins, Bulgars, Italians, and Czechs (in that order). Of the more significant groups, they were underrepresented among the Slovenes, Hungarians, Albanians, and Croats (in that order). The Muslims of Bosnia-Hercegovina were not counted as a separate category in the statistics on arrested Cominformists, but it appears that they, like the Slovenes, were not very susceptible to Cominformism. Serbs and Macedonians maintained the Yugoslav average, with above-average representation of Serbs only in Serbia proper.

The national incidence of Cominformism cannot be entirely accidental. The break with Stalin caused immense moral and psychological dilemmas among the patriarchal and Russophile Serbs and Montenegrins, especially in the war-ravaged Dinaric Mountain chain. In renouncing Stalin, these peasant (or ex-peasant) Communists would be repudiating a part of themselves, turning their backs not only on their own inspiration but also on their relatives and kinsmen who battled and died with Stalin's name on their lips. Many could not bring themselves to take this step, and in many instances blood ties committed others who might have stuck with the KPJ. As one Serb army lieutenant who fled to Trieste noted, "among the people a patriarchal spirit exists and kinship ties are strong, even though [the

---

17. Radonjić, *Izgubljena orijentacija*, p. 74.

authorities] are trying to break them." In many families competing allegiances were stronger than blood and close relatives denounced one another and even persecuted their relatives, but more often the Cominformist orientation of one member was enough to sway his kinsmen.[18] In this way the KPJ inadvertently reinforced the patriarchal traditions of the Dinaric mountaineers—so strongly that tradition-bound and clannish Montenegro became the Cominformist bastion. Thus at least one regional variant of Cominformism seems to have been quite distinct from the ideological variants based on old party factions.

National and factional allegiances were not the only factors in Cominformism. Another consisted of invidious comparisons between the failings, inequalities, and terrors of Yugoslavia's postwar society and the legendary—not the real—achievements of the Soviet Union. The last vestiges of the KPJ's intraparty democracy were so radically curtailed during the postwar period that the Communist movement of Yugoslavia was "faced with the danger of transforming revolutionary etatism into total autocracy."[19] Radovan Radonjić has described all the negative by-products of this period. The emergence of a privileged stratum at the party summit as a consequence of centralization threatened the KPJ's organizational autonomy and exacerbated difficulties among the nationalities, always the most important issue in multinational Yugoslavia. "As early as 1949 [various economic problems] manifested themselves through a slowdown in the tempo of economic development, unevenness in the development of various regions, and the passivity of the working masses."[20]

Not surprisingly, these developments caused a good deal of disillusionment, especially among veteran Communists, who had grown up in a party dominated by the legend of new socialist man. In Dragan Kalajdžić's documentary novel *Otok gole istine* (The island of naked truth) the author's Cominformist alter ego, Augustin, started "to think differently" because he was disgusted by the arrogance and greed of the Yugoslave elite.[21] One defector, a former major of military counterintelligence (Kontraobaveštajna služba, KOS), explained:

18. HIA-TC, interviews no. 56, pp. 14–15; no. 8, pp. 2–3; no. 29, pp. 5, 11.

19. Dušan Bilandžić, *Društveni razvoj socijalističke Jugoslavije*, 2d ed. (Zagreb, 1976), pp. 93–107.

20. See Radovan Radonjić, *Sukob KPJ sa Kominformom i društveni razvoj Jugoslavije (1948–1950)*, 2d ed. (Zagreb, 1976), pp. 114–49.

21. Dragan Kalajdžić, *Otok gole istine* (Zagreb, 1985), pp. 42–43.

"All those who became disillusioned are today overwhelmingly Cominformists. Because of their ideals—they are the so-called leftists—they cannot go over to the side of reaction. These men have no real knowledge of life in the Soviet Union; they know only what they have read in Soviet propaganda."[22]

To be sure, there were not a few reckoners and waverers among the Cominformists. The same defector had his own distinctive terms to classify KPJ members: "crystal-clears," 30 percent; "Salonika veterans" (*solunaši*), after the privileged stratum of Serbian veterans of World War I, 30 percent; and "purchased souls," 40 percent. The second group, he thought, was especially susceptible to Cominformism. The "Salonika veterans" performed well during the war and expected to be rewarded for their services. But "since at the end of the war they demonstrated no abilities that were needed in peacetime, naturally they did not get what they wanted, and as a result they joined the Cominform."[23]

There were also the ones who weighed the strengths of the opposing sides and decided that a power as great as the Soviet Union could not lose in a conflict with little Yugoslavia. This type is well described in the growing corpus of imaginative literature on the Cominformist theme. Aleksandar Popović's Cominformist, Vasa Vučurović, a captain of the UDB-a, is obsessed by the power of his rank. Pavle Ugrinov's KPJ loyalist Nastas says of his comrades that "for many the strongest argument will be that we are alone and small." Jozo Laušić's opportunistic village party boss Ivan Vatavuk, known as Zulum (from Turkish *zulüm*, injustice, violence, terror), lost his position in 1948 for inventing the "Marxist-Leninist sign of the cross": "Partija, SKOJ, Staljin je moj. Zdravo!" (Party, SKOJ, Stalin is mine. Hail!). "How could I know for sure," recalled Zulum, "that Mustachio [Stalin] would go all the way? And how could I know for sure that our Old Man [Tito] would clip him . . . ?" According to Slobodan Selenić's Maksimilijan, the *ibeovci* were "schoolteachers

22. HIA-TC, interview no. 29, p. 118.
23. Ibid., p. 164. The *solunaši* were the Serbian veterans of the 1915–1918 Salonika front, much praised and occasionally helped by Yugoslavia's interwar regimes. As is often the case with veterans, the *solunaši* frequently behaved as if their sole purpose were to make sure that everyone became more than familiar with their exploits—hence the term *solunaš* as a synonym for "bore." One exiled medical student recalled a colleague who declared his support for the Resolution in the hope of being expelled from the party so he could avoid the time-consuming meetings. This risky enterprise misfired. See ibid., no. 31, p. 4.

and prefects who wanted to be ministers and ministers who wanted to be above ministers." And Mirko Kovač's Tomislav K. says, "The outcome is clear. . . . We must yield. They are stronger, and Stalin is unique."[24]

That was also the reasoning of real-life Communist leaders. After the patching of the split, when Veljko Vlahović rebuked Gian Carlo Pajetta for all the injuries that the Yugoslavs sustained from the pro-Moscow parties, the Italian Communist leader cut him short: "Dear comrade," said Pajetta, "we behaved toward you exactly as you would have behaved toward us if our roles were reversed."[25] And when Dolores Ibarruri ("La Passionaria") later told Tito of her shame for her part in the attacks on the KPJ, the Yugoslav leader was understanding: "There's no need to blame yourself on that account, Dolores. Don't worry. . . . Besides, believe me, if I'd found myself in [your] situation, I'd probably have behaved as you did."[26] Nor was there any lack of support of the KPJ for opportunistic reasons. In the words of the Hercegovinian village leader Dimitrije V. in Mirko Kovač's novel *Vrata od utrobe* (The gate of the womb), "I'm not against Soviet communism over there, among them, but we don't need it here. The one we have is good enough for us. Besides, even if it were no good, it's in power."[27]

The anti-Cominformist purge was a unique opportunity for the KPJ leadership to cleanse the land of all potential troublemakers. As the purge widened, denunciations against real and imaginary *ibeovci* accelerated. The society's overdose of cathartic strained all its organ systems and Cominformania claimed many unintended victims. In a Rijeka factory, for example, party members who complained of low wages were regarded as Cominform sympathizers; in the same plant in 1952, "directives were given to report anybody who spoke against U.S. military aid [to Yugoslavia], because [such opposition] would indicate that the speaker was a Cominformist." A Bačka Ukrainian

24. Aleksandar Popović, *Mreščenje šarana i druge drame* (Belgrade, 1986), p. 203; Pavle Ugrinov, *Zadat život* (Belgrade, 1979), p. 340; Jozo Laušić, *Bogumil* (Zagreb, 1982), p. 130; Slobodan Selenić, *Pismo/glava* (Belgrade, 1982), p. 176; Mirko Kovač, *Vrata od utrobe* (Belgrade, 1971), p. 276.

25. Gian Carlo Pajetta, *Le crisi che ho vissuto: Budapest Praga Varsavia* (Rome, 1982), p. 46.

26. Dolores Ibarruri, "Moja sećanja: Tito mi je oprostio," *Intervju,* July 6, 1984, p. 45.

27. Kovač, *Vrata,* p. 293.

reported that "if somebody sang Russian songs, he would automatically land in jail." Indeed, in the army "if somebody complained about something, he was immediately looked upon as an *ibeovac* or an enemy of the regime." The official KPJ attitude was close to the sentiment that Slavko Komar reportedly hoped to instill in the Zagreb University party organization: "With every ten expulsions from the university organization, it is better to kick out a few innocent ones than to allow even one enemy to remain hidden."[28]

According to this same report, the university party organization purged a fifth of its members between 1948 and 1950, but of those purged, only a quarter agreed with all points in the Resolution, even the absurd ones: "These were mainly the more serious and older Communists, but among those who left the university party organization there were a few who were just recruited from SKOJ." The rest agreed with one or two points. The most common criticism was that Tito acted against Communist discipline when he refused to send a KPJ delegation to the Cominform meeting in Bucharest. Some charged Tito with violations of intraparty democracy, and KPJ students from rural areas agreed with the Resolution's sections about Yugoslavia's agricultural policy. There were also a few random cases of simple disciplinary infractions. Most significant, those who were becoming disillusioned with communism in general "nevertheless thought that not everything in our country was going well and that Stalin, despite some false accusations, put his finger on much that was wrong with the KPJ."[29]

The doubts of many Communists about the issues raised by the Resolution are a promising literary theme. Ferdo Godina's Andrej Tratnik is the prototype of an earnest Communist torn by dual loyalties, to his party and to the international movement as it then was. The KPJ's insistence that party members denounce the Resolution was a change in direction much too radical for many Communists. Dušan Jovanović's Montenegrin Cominformist Svetozar Milić, in the play *Karamazovi* (The Karamazovs), confronts the secretary of his party organization with the words "Something that has always been white can't all of a sudden become black! The Madonna can't become a whore without a reason! God cannot become the devil. The Earth is

28. HIA-TC, interviews b.b. [ZS], pp. 1–2; b.b. [PM], p. 4; no. 56, p. 3a; ibid., "Zagrebacko sveuciliste u eri komunistickog rezima [sic]," p. 19.

29. "Zagrebacko sveuciliste [sic]," pp. 20–21.

a planet and revolves around its axis, and also around the Sun. That's how we learned! That's what we believed in." Branko Hofman's Peter imprudently shares similar thoughts with his comrades: "I don't know whether they were lying before or they're lying now. If they were lying before, it's even worse." And Mladen Markov's Maksin is surprised that he is questioned about Stalin's popularity during the war: "If I hadn't believed in that, I wouldn't have joined the struggle."[30] Such doubts are often combined with an irrational arrest for the offense of Cominformism. Mahmut Zolj, the father in Abdulah Sidran's screenplay for the prize-winning film *Otac na službenom putu* (*When Father Was Away on Business*), is denounced to the police by his faithless mistress for saying, "Who loves whom . . . in this madhouse," which is interpreted as an antistate statement. When Pavle Ugrinov's "Comrade Well" is asked by his cell secretary for his views on the Resolution, he can manage to say only "Well . . ." and is subsequently arrested.[31]

Imaginative literature has been instrumental in shaping the perceptions of Cominformism.[32] Though historical novelists and playwrights vary in their approaches, they still find it easiest to paint the dogmatist fanatic as the commonest Cominformist type. He could be Žarko Komanin's "mad-headed" Ilija Radjević in the novel *Prestupna godina* (Leap year), or Slobodan Selenić's peasant-hating Svetozar Slišković, or Ivan Ivanović's peasant-hated militiaman Stojanča.[33] These are seldom the "men of the great furnace of the Comintern," as Antonije Isaković calls the fanatical old Soviet faithful in his novel *Tren 2* (Moment 2), but it is frequently intimated that the intellectual elite of the group, such as Ugrinov's Professor Karadžić (modeled on Mirko Marković), were veteran Communists with ties to the old party factions.[34] In that sense, too, imaginative literature anticipated historical research.

30. Ferdo Godina, *Molčeči orkester* (Maribor, 1981), pp. 37–38; Dušan Jovanović, *Karamazovi* (Belgrade, 1984), pp. 25–26; Branko Hofman, *Noč do jutra* (Ljubljana, 1981), p. 95; Mladen Markov, *Isterivanje boga: Seljačka tragedija* (Belgrade, 1984), 2:86–87.
31. Abdulah Sidran, *Otac na službenom putu* (Belgrade, 1985), pp. 51, 133; Pavle Ugrinov, *Carstvo zemaljsko* (Belgrade, 1982), p. 36.
32. To what extent can be seen in Milivoje Marković, *Preispitivanja: Informbiro i Goli otok u jugoslovenskom romanu* (Belgrade, 1986).
33. Stojanča's fate is described in Ivan Ivanović, *Arizani* (Belgrade, 1982), pp. 113, 227–28.
34. Ugrinov, *Zadat život*, p. 369.

If Cominformism reshaped a variety of oppositional tendencies, its adherents also varied widely in function, territory, and nationality. And since services and national footholds were not of equal strategic importance, it mattered a great deal where the *ibeovci* managed to extend their influence. Although no party or state institution was entirely immune to Cominformism, pro-Resolution sentiments were especially dangerous in the police and the army, which were entrusted with the defense of the political system and on whose reliability the KPJ depended for preventive measures against the Cominformists. "They can say whatever they want now," recalls Radiša Prokić, the former secret policeman in Slobodan Selenić's novel *Pismo/glava* (Heads/tails), "but patriotism was at the highest level in the UDB-a at that time. I'm speaking for the Serbs, 'cause I know 'em best, but the other Yugoslavs think the same. . . . They say we made arrests and gave beatings. Sure enough, we beat up and beat back, we revealed and accused falsely, we did even worse things, perhaps we made mistakes, perhaps we went overboard, but I'd like to see what song these fancy pants would be singing if in '48 we'd failed to send to the camps all those who wanted to sell out the country for ideas and positions."[35]

Not that there were no *ibeovci* among secret policemen; recent official Yugoslav sources cite as many as 1,722. The security apparatus in Bosnia-Hercegovina was thoroughly purged after all state security personnel in the second district of Sarajevo declared themselves for the Resolution.[36] Things were not much better in the other districts of Bosnia's capital or in the rest of the republic. Pro-Resolution sentiment won among the UDB-a chiefs in Mostar and Banja Luka. In Serbia, too, there were *ibeovci* in the security forces. At least eleven security officers with the rank of lieutenant colonel were arrested: Dušan Čolaković and Veljko Stefanović were with the Ministry of the Interior; Veljko Tomić was in the federal headquarters of the UDB-a; Petar Banovac and Radomir Djurić were in the UDB-a for Serbia; Remzo Duranović and Djoko Strocki were in the ministry of the Interior of Bosnia-Hercegovina; Nenad Vasić was head of the first section of the UDB-a for Bosnia-Hercegovina; Božo Ivanović and

35. Selenić, *Pismo/glava*, pp. 274–75.
36. Jelena Lovrić, "Staljinizam ne miruje," *Danas*, Aug. 16, 1983, p. 12. Lazri and Malo. *Dans les prisons*, p. 20. Jovo Stupar, head of the republic's UDB-a, was one of those arrested. See HIA-TC, interview no. 54, p. 15.

Veljko Krstajić were, respectively, head and commander of the militia in Montenegro; and Vukosav Bošković was head of the UDB-a in Bijelo Polje (Montenegro). Ante Zorić, a high-ranking UDB-a official at the Belgrade headquarters and a long-time resident of the USSR, was also arrested.[37] Several officers of the UDB-a at the Belgrade headquarters and in Vojvodina escaped to Romania.[38]

These were exceptions, however, for the UDB-a had been specifically created to keep an eye on known opponents of the regime and to uncover hidden or potential "class enemies." Aleksandar Ranković, the member of the Politburo in charge of the security apparatus, staked his extraordinary prestige in the UDB-a on a policy of treating the *ibeovci* no differently from all other enemies of the state. His special anti-Cominform staff included Svetislav Stefanović-Ćeća, deputy minister of the interior, nominal head of the federal UDB-a, and an old comrade from the Wahabite days in Mitrovica; Veljko Mićunović, a future ambassador to Moscow and Washington, Stefanović's assistant; Jovo Kapičić, state councilor in the Ministry of Foreign Affairs; Vojislav Biljanović, a high UDB-a operative in Montenegro; Mile Milatović, Hebrang's examiner, later ambassador to Poland and Canada and assistant to Serbia's minister of the interior; and Jefto Šašić, head of the KOS.[39]

Ranković was unswervingly loyal to Tito. Before the Resolution Stalin had singled him out, along with Djilas, Kidrič, and Vukmanović-Tempo, as one of four "dubious Marxists" in the KPJ leadership, and his name (sometimes the term *palach,* executioner, was substituted) appeared frequently in the Soviet press.[40] Ranković and his staff did not set the UDB-a on its anti-Cominform course solely by the force of their arguments: Mićunović allegedly summoned the UDB-a chiefs one by one and, pistol on the table, told them, "Either you rally to the political road of the Central Committee and carry out all the tasks assigned to you or you will certainly be placed before a firing squad."[41] But pro-Cominform inclinations could hardly sur-

37. Lazri and Malo, *Dans les prisons,* pp. 46–47, 26–27.
38. Slobodan Pauljević, *Strašno budjenje* (Rijeka, 1982), pp. 10–21, 78, 193.
39. Lazri and Malo, *Dans les prisons,* pp. 11–12. The national composition of this body (four Serbs, three Montenegrins) was a conspicuous indication of, among other things, the relative strength of the *ibeovci* among Serbs and Montenegrins.
40. Vladimir Dedijer, *Izgubljena bitka J. V. Staljina* (Sarajevo, 1969), p. 149; see, e.g., *Izvestiia,* Sept. 9, 1948, p. 2.
41. Lazri and Malo, *Dans les prisons,* p. 16.

vive within the UDB-a in any case. In the daily skirmishes with the *ibeovci,* the secret policemen "carried out investigations against the Cominformists and thus compromised themselves [with the pro-Soviet forces]."[42] In time the UDB-a became so indispensable that high political appointments frequently went to its officers, a development that was not lost on Cominform propagandists.[43]

The military was an altogether different matter. By all accounts, Cominformism reached epidemic proportions in the Jugoslovenska armija (JA, Yugoslav Army; renamed the Yugoslav People's Army in December 1951). Although insiders, such as a former lieutenant who was stationed in Sarajevo, claimed a moderate 10 to 15 percent for the Soviet side, outsiders placed the number much higher.[44] One former KOS officer, who said that he personally arrested some ninety Cominformist army men (he acted as an agent provocateur in a Zagreb jail where a number of suspected Cominformists were temporarily detained), felt that *ibeovci* predominated in the JA, and that only the vigilance of military counterintelligence kept them from being more successful. In support of his claim he cited a survey of JA officers on the question of the Korean war: some 80 percent favored sending JA units to aid the North. The KPJ political command interpreted this result as a clear sign of clandestine Cominformism.[45]

As in the case of other Cominformist arrests, the number of pro-Resolution officers imprisoned is uncertain. An early Albanian estimate of 5,000 is close enough to a recent official Yugoslav figure of 4,153 *ibeovci* in the JA, apparently including ordinary soldiers, but is surpassed by Milovan Djilas's estimate of 7,000 imprisoned officers.[46] One Western appraisal, typically conservative, reports five

42. HIA-TC, interview no. 29, p. 23.

43. For example, Lazar Koliševski, the KPJ leader in Macedonia, felt obliged to defend the appointment of a former UDB-a lieutenant colonel to the top post in the trade union organization in Macedonia: "[The Cominformists] are annoyed that the UDB-a is vigilantly guarding the fruits of the people's revolution, that it is mercilessly purging all types of imperialist spies, wreckers, and all sworn enemies . . . of socialism who are today hiding behind the Cominform Resolution": Lazar Koliševski, "Idući smelo putem kojim nas vodi CK KPJ na čelu s drugom Titom, mi ćemo bez obzira na sve prepreke izgraditi socijalizam u našoj zemlji," *Borba,* May 12, 1949, p. 2.

44. HIA-TC, interview no. 56, p. 6a. One university student thought that as many as 75–80 percent of all Communist army men were *ibeovci* (ibid., interview no. 66, p. 149).

45. Ibid., interview no. 29, pp. 105 and 7.

46. Lazri and Malo, *Dans les prisons,* p. 20. The official Yugoslav estimate appears in Lovrić, "Staljinizam ne miruje," p. 12. Milovan Djilas gives his estimate in *Tito: The Story from Inside* (New York, 1980), p. 87.

graduates of the Soviet K. E. Voroshilov Military Academy (two of them generals), twenty-eight graduates of the equally prestigious M. V. Frunze Military Academy, and sixteen graduates of other Soviet military schools.[47] Of the officers who were not trained in the USSR, the Albanian source names four arrested generals, three reserve generals, seventeen colonels, and forty-seven lieutenant colonels, from various army commands and services. Among them were the chief military prosecutor, General Veljko Žižić, officers of the Military Council of Yugoslavia's Supreme Court (including General Mirko Krdžić, the senior officer on the court, who refused to participate in proceedings against the *ibeovci,* and Milija Laković and Radomir Ilić, both members of the tribunal that sentenced the Chetnik leader Draža Mihailović), commanders of various divisions and lesser units, political commissars, members of the JA's Agitprop (including its head, Vladimir Dapčević), commanders and instructors in various military schools, and the editor of the army newspaper. All but eight (of the total of seventy-one) were Montenegrins or Serbs.[48]

Even in the presidential guard units, responsible directly to Tito, dissent was remarkably high. At least twenty-two officers of the guard's ten regiments were arrested, including Colonel Momčilo Djurić, the senior officer and commander of the Partisan supreme staff's escort battalion, who spent the war at Tito's side. At least two junior officers were sentenced to death for alleged attempts on Tito's life.[49] As in the case of other Cominformists, the death sentences were later commuted to long terms of imprisonment, but the units were subjected to the strictest security measures.[50]

Even when units were regarded as potentially unreliable, however,

47. HIA-TC, "Jugoslovenski kominformisti," p. 6.
48. Lazri and Malo, *Dans les prisons,* pp. 36–48. The exceptions were four Macedonians, one Albanian, one Croat, one Bosnian Muslim, and one Slovene. Yugoslav propaganda went to great lengths to deny defections in the army. In June 1949 *Borba* published a denial of a Cominformist report of the arrest of four officers (Milija Laković, Radovan Ilić, Veljko Žižić, and Jovo Šćepanović) in the division of military justice, under their signatures: "Izjava Milije Lakovića i drugih," *Borba,* June 25, 1949, p. 3. In fact, the four were indeed under arrest. The sister of Šćepanović had unsuccessfully sought the intervention of Djilas, Šćepanović's school friend. See Milovan Djilas, *Vlast* (London, 1983), p. 185.
49. Under arrest, Djurić confessed to having been recruited by Soviet intelligence and revealed the names of his accomplices: Vladimir Dedijer, *Novi prilozi za biografiju Josipa Broza Tita* (Belgrade, 1984), 3:350.
50. Lazri and Malo, *Dans les prisons,* pp. 51–53.

arrests did not always follow. The CC Military Commission is said to have listed some 4,500 officers and 1,500 noncoms as politically unreliable in case of an armed conflict with the Soviet bloc.[51] Cominformist claims that most of the 12,000 officers who were retired between 1948 and 1955 were regarded as security risks by KPJ loyalists are perhaps exaggerated, but it is certain that the morale of the JA plummeted after the Cominform Resolution.[52]

Pro-Soviet sentiments in the army's higher echelons were both of long standing and of recent origin. The JA, no longer a guerrilla army, was initiating a modernization program that seemed particularly urgent in light of Yugoslavia's shaky relations with the West. The USSR was the logical power to help Belgrade in this defense effort. Veljko Mićunović has written:

> Our ties with the Russians were actually strongest in military affairs. Our armies bore the brunt of our common struggle and were symbols of the brotherhood of arms and the strong ties that were created in the past and most affectingly during the last war. Such ties cannot easily be forgotten; they enter a people's history and remain there; they cannot be removed easily, either from the memory of contemporaries or from the consciousness of coming generations.[53]

A larger number of self-taught Partisan officers had been sent to Soviet military academies to acquire Russian military expertise, and there they also learned something of the Muscovite political style. Not a few were enlisted by Soviet intelligence agencies. But even their colleagues, whose loyalties were hardly so divided, could not help losing heart after the June clash.

Links to the Soviet military were crucial for the development of Cominformism in the JA ranks. A former student at Yugoslavia's military academy noted that "all the cadets who returned from Russia were regarded as possible Soviet agents. They [were] subjected to permanent surveillance."[54] To be sure, many JA trainees in the USSR resisted the intense Soviet pressure to come out in favor of the Resolu-

---

51. IIIA-TC, "Povjerljive vijesti iz Jugoslavije," p. 1.
52. Lazri and Malo, Dans les prisons, pp. 54–55; HIA-TC, interview no. 56, p. 10.
53. Veljko Mićunović, Moskovske godine, 1956–1958 (Zagreb, 1977), pp. 278–79.
54. HIA-TC, interview b.b. [DM].

tion. (Yugoslavia's press claimed that this was the response of the overwhelming majority.)[55] Nevertheless, officers who were trained in the Soviet Union and had opportunities to defect frequently did so. Many of those who were in Russia during the spring and summer of 1948 never returned home. The KPJ understandably viewed them as turncoats.

Although the largest number of *ibeovci* officers belonged to the infantry, Cominformist infiltration was most dramatic in the air force. Nearly all the air force officers were Soviet-trained, and some of those whose disaffection was strong simply took air force planes and flew out (though not all went to bloc countries: of the seventeen successful air force defectors during the first ten months of 1951, eleven flew to the West).[56] Major General Pero Popivoda, head of the air force operational service, future leader of the Cominformist emigration, and brother of the KPJ Central Committee member Krsto Popivoda, escaped to Bucharest in 1948; in 1951 he was joined by another brother, Colonel Vlado Popivoda, who flew to Romania with three other airmen.[57]

Military airports at Batajnica, Zemun, and Pančevo, all close to Belgrade (as well as to the Romanian and Hungarian borders), were the sites of repeated Cominformist actions. According to a former pilot, in 1951 alone Batajnica was attacked on three occasions by small groups of Cominformist saboteurs. The commander of the Zemun airport and his assistant fled to Romania in 1949.[58] And in 1948, Berislav Supek, a prewar officer whom the JA later accused of working for an incredible array of foreign intelligence services, made his way to Romania.[59]

As we have seen, prewar military officers, especially those who

55. See, e.g., "Činjenice u vezi s objavljivanjem radio Moskve da se neki gradjani FNRJ izjašnjavaju za rezoluciju Informbiroa," *Borba*, July 26, 1948, p. 6. For a Yugoslav report on Soviet recruitment methods among the JA men in the Soviet military schools, see "Metode ubedjivanja i pritisak na jugoslovenske oficire u Sovjetskom Savezu," *Borba*, May 30, 1949, p. 2.

56. HIA-TC, interview b.b. [DR], p. 1.

57. Savo Kržavac and Dragan Marković, *Informbiro—šta je to: Jugoslavija je rekla ne* (Belgrade, 1976), pp. 168–69; HIA-TC, interview b.b. [DR], p. 1.

58. Ibid., interview b.b. [PV], p. 14; no. 10, p. 1.

59. Supek was accused of working for the Ustašas, the Gestapo, and the NKVD. See "Gestapovski agent u ulozi 'revolucionara' i 'patriote,'" *Borba*, July 12, 1949, p. 3. To these organizations Kržavac and Marković have added OVRA (the Italian secret police) and the Intelligence Service! See Kržavac and Marković, *Informbiro*, p. 167.

were not Partisan veterans, had good reason to be dissatisfied with their standing in the JA.[60] But even former royal officers and non-coms who had served in the Partisan army were not permitted to forget their prewar status. Both Berislav Supek and Pero Popivoda had held positions of authority in the prewar army, as had Colonel General Branko Poljanac, chief of the Partisan Supreme Staff during the first phase of the uprising, in 1941 at Užice, and later deputy chief of staff of the Partisan units in Serbia, and Colonel General Arso Jovanović, a former captain in the royal Yugoslav army. Jovanović was the most famous and the highest ranking of the Cominformist officers. His attempted flight to Romania in August 1948 with Major General Branko Petričević and Colonel Vlado Dapčević, both Montenegrins (as was Jovanović), ended in disaster, terminating the major military conspiracy that the Soviets launched against Tito.

Three other generals—Slavko Rodić, Sredoje Urošević and Radovan Vukanović—displayed pro-Cominform inclinations.[61] With their removal or isolation, overt Cominformist influence apparently stopped in the army top command. Nevertheless, the Cominformist crisis induced the party leadership to rely on various material incentives to foster loyalty in the officer corps. Privilege and differences in rank had already emerged in the Partisan army by the time the war ended, and the Resolution effectively ended any semblence of egalitarianism. The lavishing of wartime ribbons and honors in return for party loyalty showed a new kind of army to old Partisan fighters who were unschooled in the politics of merit.

It is highly significant that most of the notable *ibeovci* discussed so far (including Jovanović, Petričević, Popivoda, and Dapčević), as well as General Djoko Mirašević, were in the army and from Montenegro. Regional and national differences played an important role in the Cominformist ranks. And all statistics agree that Montenegro, the

60. Captain Vaso Parežanin, operational head of his air force division, was a rather typical case. A non-Partisan prewar officer, Parežanin was arrested in 1948 as an accomplice in the attempted defection of Colonel General Arso Jovanović. See HIA-TC, interview no. 79, pp. 198–200.

61. Branko Lazitch, "Cominformists in Yugoslavia," *Eastern Quarterly* 6, nos. 3–4 (1953): 25–26. According to the official Yugoslav version, Slavko Rodić, JA deputy chief of staff, died of meningitis and was buried with highest military and state honors. See Boško Šiljegović, "General-lajtnant Slavko Rodić," *Borba*, April 30, 1949. The Cominformist sources always insisted that he supported the Resolution and hence was liquidated.

smallest of Yugoslavia's republics both in population (377,189 in 1948) and in area, had proportionally the largest number of Cominformists, almost four times the Yugoslav average.

Montenegro, backward and impoverished, was hardly ideal terrain for the urban ideology of Marx and Lenin. Nevertheless, this land became one of Yugoslavia's reddest areas. The hegemonistic policies of interwar Belgrade governments, which abolished all vestiges of pre-1914 Montenegrin statehood and independence, dampened the people's pro-Serbian sentiments. More and more Montenegrins started to think of themselves as a separate nation. And even those who did not contemplate the restoration of the old Montenegrin state headed by the Petrović dynasty became increasingly disappointed and restless. Disaffection swelled Communist ranks. In the 1920 elections for the Constituent Assembly, the KPJ won 37.99 percent of all Montenegrin votes.

Montenegrins' Russophile sentiments date from the time of Metropolitan Vasilije Petrović's first visitations to Russia in the 1750s. The great Slavic empire was viewed as the maternal guardian of the people's faith and liberty, an ally against the ever-present Ottoman menace.[62] These values survived and were enhanced in the Soviet period. As one Montenegrin Communist put it:

62. On Metropolitan Vasilije Petrović's relations with Russia and his contribution to the shaping of the cult of Russia in Montenegro, see Gligor Stojanović, "Stvaranje kulta Rusije u Crnoj Gori," in Istorija Crne Gore, bk. 3: Od početka XVI do kraja XVIII veka, ed. Milinko Djurović et al. (Titograd, 1975), 1:325–71. At the end of his second journey to Russia in 1758, Vasilije wrote: "Montenegrins recognize nobody except God and the great All-Russian ruler" (ibid., p. 352). Similarly, some seven score years later, in a poetic address to King Petar I of Serbia during the Russo-Japanese war, Prince Nikola of Montenegro wrote the following lines:

Tužni glasi od sjevera	Sad voices from the north
što nam stižu sustopice	which we continue to receive
od Rusije i od cara	from Russia and from the tsar
i njegove prestonice—	and from the seat of his throne—
podložni su svakoj brizi	subject us to many worries
i uzdanje da ohlade:	and dampen our trust:
naš narod je na Rusiju	our people are accustomed
vičan snovat' svoje nade . . .	to pin their hopes on Russia . . .
Pa je nešto sad streknuo—	And if we are now awestruck—
čudit' mu se za to nije;	this should also not surprise;
narod srpski i mi oba	the Serb people and the two of us
siraci smo bez Rusije.	are orphans without Russia.

Nikola I Petrović Njegoš, "Poslanica Njegovom veličanstvu kralju Srbije, Petru I," in Pjesme (Cetinje, 1969), p. 155.

The generation to which I belonged could only be—as it was—Russophile twice over. We were reared in the strong and centuries-old pro-Russian traditions of Montenegro, which for centuries was tied to her "protectress Russia." These ties received new content and force . . . in the ideas and the victory of October. . . . The intelligentsia and the student youth were the bearers of this movement. . . . We then had almost no working class.[63]

The identification of communism with Russia contributed to the growth of a vibrant movement in Montenegro. As Montenegro's history was dominated by special regional characteristics, however, communism was harsher and more sectarian there than elsewhere in Yugoslavia. The faction of Petko Miletić, himself a Montenegrin, had a large following in the area, and many Montenegrin Wahabites never fully accepted Tito's leadership. Radonja Golubović, Montenegro's first postwar minister of the interior, Yugoslavia's envoy to Bucharest, and later one of the leaders of the Cominformist emigration, belonged to Miletić's faction in Berane (Ivangrad).[64] Labud Kusovac, one of the leaders of the Parisian "Parallel Center," was another veteran Montenegrin Communist who sided with the Resolution.[65] Among the leaders of local factions, the Resolution claimed the allegiance of Blažo Raičević and Kosta Ćufka, ousted by Tito in 1940 from the leadership of the KPJ's Cetinje organization and the party, who after the war became, respectively, director of the state silo monopoly and mayor of the Cetinje.[66] But even Montenegrin Communists who had no history of factional activity tended toward uncritical emulation of Soviet models. The Left Errors that engulfed the area in 1941–1942 reflected uneasiness with "united front" tactics. Such extremists as Djilas and Milutinović wanted to liquidate the "kulaks," collectivize the pasturelands, and build Montenegrin "soviets" in the midst of the war. Small wonder that even those Montenegrin leaders who ultimately sided with Tito wavered in 1948. Djilas, who rejected Stalin's blandishments and became a fanatical anti-Stalinist, has cited the vacillation of such major Montenegrin

63. Mićunović, Moskovske godine, pp. 19–20.
64. Golubović's association with Miletić is noted in Blažo Jovanović, "Izveštaj o političkom radu Pokrajinskog komiteta KPJ za Crnu Goru," Borba, Oct. 6, 1948, p. 1.
65. Yindrich, Tito v. Stalin, p. 113.
66. Jovanović denounced them as prewar "opportunists, united factionalists, and wreckers of party unity" in his political report to the Founding Congress of the Communist Party of Montenegro in October 1948: Jovanović, "Izveštaj o političkom radu," p. 1.

figures as Blažo Jovanović (1907–1976), secretary of the KPJ's regional committee for Montenegro and president of the republic's
executive council; Veljko Vlahović (1914–1975), deputy foreign
minister and director of *Borba;* and Mihailo Lalić (b. 1914), the
leading Montenegrin novelist.[67]

The authorities made every effort to obscure the large number of
Montenegrin *ibeovci.*[68] Only a few officials were ever publicly announced as having been removed from the party. On August 3, 1948,
it was announced that four ministers of the Montenegrin republic,
Božo Ljumović, Vuko Tmušić, Niko Pavić, and Blažo Borovinić, had
been replaced. Not long after that the four were attacked as *ibeovci.*
Together with Radivoje Vukićević, another ranking Montenegrin
Cominformist, the group constituted the bulk of the highest Montenegrin party leadership. The most important was Božo Ljumović (b.
1895), who had been a KPJ member since 1919 and had served as
secretary of the KPJ regional committee for Montenegro and on the
KPJ CC. He was Yugoslavia's ambassador to Poland, vice-president
of the Montenegrin government (1946–1948), and chairman of the
republic's control commission.[69]

In Montenegro, however, Cominformism was not confined to a
few leaders. The total of 5,007 Montenegrin *ibeovci* reported by
current Yugoslav sources represents only slightly less than a third of
the KPJ membership in the republic in 1948. With only insignificant
exceptions, whole KPJ organizations opted for the Resolution—Bijelo Polje, Kolašin, Berane (Ivangrad), Cetinje, and apparently also
the committees of Nikšić, Bar, and Danilovgrad.[70] During the sum-

67. Djilas, *Vlast,* pp. 143, 156, 165–67, 187.

68. The most detailed information on the numerical strength of the Montenegrin Cominformists and the official measures against them is found in Branislav Kovačević,
Komunistička partija Crne Gore 1945–1952. godine (Titograd, 1986), pp. 416–50.

69. Ljumović, Borovinić, Pavić, and Tmušić were delegates to the Fifth Congress of the
KPJ, after the Resolution. Their biographies appear in "Delegati za Peti kongres KPJ
izabrani na partiskim konferencijama u Crnoj Gori," *Borba,* July 8, 1948, p. 3. The last
three were ministers of, respectively, industry and communal affairs, education, and trade
and supply in the Montenegrin republican government. Their Cominformism was noted in
Blažo Jovanović, "Govor pretsednika vlade Crne Gore Blaža Jovanovića na zasedanju
plenuma Zemaljskog odbora Narodnog fronta Crne Gore," *Borba,* Aug. 15, 1948, p. 3.

70. HIA-TC, "Jugoslovenski kominformisti," p. 5; Lazri and Malo, *Dans les prisons,* p.
9. For a detailed account of the situation in Andrijevica, where the majority of the KPJ
county committee apparently also sided with the Resolution, see Sveto Arsenijević and
Dimitrije Jojić, "Na fašistički teror narod Crne Gore odgovara pojačanom borbom," *Nova
Borba,* Dec. 5, 1949, pp. 5–6.

mer and autumn of 1948 an entire UDB-a division was on duty in Montenegro to suppress the growing Cominformist guerrilla forces and prevent the flight of *ibeovci* to Albania.[71] A special pursuit section was attached to the reconstituted Montenegrin government. Komnen Cerović, a member of the executive committee of the KPJ CC for Montenegro, who headed this task force in 1949, managed to track down and kill the guerrilla leaders—Ilija Bulatović, former secretary of the Bijelo Polje KPJ committee; his deputy, Miloš Radonjić; and Milan Čebelica.[72] The authorities used provocateurs, mass arrests, and intimidation.[73] Some anti-Resolution propaganda apparently verged on the absurd. The chronicler-narrator in Žarko Komanin's novel *Prestupna godina* made the following observation about developments in his village in July 1948: "For a week now nobody has been allowed to utter the words 'Russian potato' [*ruska krtola*], which the people of Crnjiš have eaten since time immemorial and which has been grown under that name from the time of Saint Petar of Cetinje [Petar I Petrović-Njegoš, the metropolitan and ruler of Montenegro from 1782 to 1830] throughout the *nahiye* of Katuni and the whole of Montenegro."[74]

Even those Communists who originally opted for the KPJ leadership were offended by the harshness of the repression in Montenegro. The cases of Stefan Mitrović and Radovan Zogović, both active in the apparatus of the KPJ CC Agitprop under Milovan Djilas and Djilas's old personal friends, are good examples. Mitrović, originally from Sveti Stefan (not a renowned resort then), was one of the pleiad of literature students and part-time poets who were matriculated into the community of revolution at the University of Belgrade. In time he became the secretary of the university's SKOJ. Mitrović belonged to a Communist family that lost three sons and two daughters in the war. Djilas's friend since the early 1930s (in 1932

71. HIA-TC, "Jugoslovenski kominformisti," p. 5.

72. Ibid., Biographies: Komnen Cerović, p. 1. For the biographies of Bulatović and Radonjić, see *Borba*, July 8, 1948, p. 3. For Djilas's account of Bulatović's road to Cominformist insurgency, see *Vlast*, pp. 153, 166; and *Tito*, pp. 80–81.

73. For accounts of anti-Cominformist repression in Montenegro by Cominformist sources, see Jole Marković. "Zverska mučenja neće slomiti najbolje sinove našeg naroda," *Nova Borba*, Jan. 15, 1950, p. 3; D. P., "Čuvajmo se provokatora!" ibid., and "Sve bešnji teror u Crnoj Gori," ibid., Feb. 1, 1950, p. 3; "Crnogorac," "Masovni gestapovski teror protiv učesnika Narodno-oslobodilačke borbe," ibid., Sept. 1, 1950, p. 5; Dj. M., "Masovna hapšenja u Barskom srezu," ibid., Nov. 1, 1950, p. 5.

74. Žarko Komanin, *Prestupna godina* (Belgrade, 1982), p. 109.

Cetinje's literary journal *Zapisi* published a short story by Djilas dedicated "to brother Stevo Mitrović" and in the same issue a poem by Mitrović dedicated "to brother Milovan Djilas"), Mitrović was briefly expelled from the KPJ in 1936 for cowardice during police interrogation. Restored to the party soon thereafter, he remained one of Djilas's closest associates and authored one of the broadsides against Krleža which was revised by Kardelj and published under the pseudonym Josip Šestak in *Književne sveske*. One of the organizers of Communist demonstrations after the military coup d'état of March 27, 1941, Mitrović spent the war in various political capacities and served as Vukmanović-Tempo's deputy in the political directorate of the JA after the war. Most important, he was the secretary of the KPJ CC Agitprop.[75] Zogović, a noted Montenegrin poet and literary critic, was one of the most consistent advocates of Soviet "socialist realism" during the KPJ's confrontation with Krleža. One of his most famous works, *Poem on the Biography of Comrade Tito,* written during the war, echoed Maiakovskii's *Vladimir Il'ich Lenin* in its laudatory style. After the war, Zogović became a much-feared cultural arbiter, though always in the shadow of Djilas. He was the commissioner for culture in the KPJ CC Agitprop, edited *Borba,* and served as vice-president of the Yugoslav Writers' Union.[76]

Mitrović and Zogović were active in the KPJ even after the Resolution. They wrote Djilas's report on the work of the Agitprop for the Fifth Congress, but were increasingly alienated from Djilas and the party.[77] Still, Zogović was elected a candidate member of the KPJ CC at the Fifth Congress and both were members of the KPJ CC for Montenegro in October 1948.[78] Soon thereafter Mitrović was arrested and forcefully urged to confess to having served the Gestapo. In jail—and later at the camp of Goli Otok—he went mad. Zogović, too, broke with the KPJ. In March 1949 he sent a statement to

75. Milomir Marić, *Deca komunizma* (Belgrade, 1987), pp. 221–26.
76. The most extreme example of Zogović's castigation of "decadent" modernist writers can be found in his "Primjer kako ne treba praviti 'Primjere književnosti,'" *Borba,* Aug. 4, 1947, p. 4.
77. Djilas's intolerance and literary pretensions, as well as his Serbian orientation, which Mitrović and Zogović did not share, have been cited as reasons for their slide into Cominformism. For the former view see Dedijer, *Novi prilozi,* 3:452–53; for the latter, see Ivan Supek, *Krunski svjedok protiv Hebranga* (Chicago, 1983), pp. 161–69. Djilas's explanation is found in *Vlast,* pp. 154–55, 157, 177–79.
78. See "Kandidati za članove CK KPJ," *Borba,* July 30, 1948, p. 2; "Izabran je Centralni komitet Komunističke partije Crne Gore," *Borba,* Oct. 9, 1948, p. 1.

Osman Karabegović, president of the KPJ CC's control commission, explaining why he did not wish to participate in the KPJ's struggle against Stalinism. He noted among other things that he "did not agree with the theory of socialist countries' independent development."[79] Zogović's ties to Soviet literary figures were uninterrupted, but his open letter to Tito, addressed "to the Falsifier of History," brought him removal from office and a brief period of arrest.[80] For the next decade or so, until the mid-1960s, he lived in extreme poverty, but at last he was permitted to publish his literary works. His first new poems appeared in *Forum,* a leading Zagreb literary journal edited by his erstwhile foes of the Krleža circle.[81] Unlike the repentant

79. Sava Dautović and Milorad Vučelić, "Obeleženi i zaboravljeni," *NIN,* Dec. 14, 1986, p. 23.

80. HIA-TC, Biographies: Radovan Zogović, p. 1. Cf. Djilas, *Vlast,* pp. 177–79. One of the Soviet bloc's campaigns on behalf of Zogović was organized by Todor Pavlov. See "Vo zaštita na Radovan Zogovič," *Napred,* Nov. 21, 1952, p. 4.

81. Radovan Zogović, "Devet pjesama," *Forum* 4, no. 3 (1965): 391–403. These poems caused a good deal of controversy. One of them ("Zvezdara—That Terrace with Its Feet in the Danube") was interpreted as an attack on modern, alienated Belgrade. Ten years before his death, Zogović published a new cycle of poetry, which is on the whole a thinly veiled allusion to the continuity of a certain style of rule in Serbia and Yugoslavia. Zogović's antihero is Miloš Obrenović, prince of Serbia from 1815 to 1839 (and again from 1858 to 1860). Drawing on documents from Miloš's chancery, Zogović paints a dark picture of a vain, cunning, and ruthless tyrant, a former rebel who has become the scourge of malcontents, a Turkish vassal who maintains himself by a cynical conciliation of the Porte while at the same time reassuring St. Petersburg of loyalty based on the common faith. In one poem, Miloš explains why he had to order the murder of a Russian agent who was investigating Miloš's policies and popular sentiment in Serbia. The prince notes:

> Ako su, borbom prerazvikanom, načeli turski jaram,
> ako se, u muci, i njima obraćam svojom mukom—
> ja sam svoj na svome. Ja za sve što činim—odgovaram
> bogu, Sultanu i narodu. Nikom drugom!

> Kakva prava njima donosi to što Srbija od njih traži?
> Srbija ono traži što joj traktata bukreškog jamči sila.
> A njoj je to plata—jer je na sebe privukla tabor vražji,
> jer se s Portom nije potajno pogodila.

> Though they [the Russians] began to break the
>   Turkish yoke in their much-talked-of struggle,
> and I, sorely troubled, in turn entreat their help—
> I am still my own man on my own land. And whatever
>   I do—I am responsible
> to God, to the Sultan, and to the people. To no one else!

> What right should they have if Serbia entreats them?
> Serbia only wants what the power of the Bucharest
>   Treaty guarantees her.

Mitrović, who died in 1985, Zogović never recanted and continued to describe himself as a "socialist realist" until his death in 1986.[82]

"For Montenegro, the Cominform was not only a revisionist ideological option or a great-state policy but also a deep drama." When asked to comment on this statement by a Belgrade journalist, one contemporary Montenegrin politician answered matter-of-factly, "The roots [of Montenegrin Cominformism] are in the material and social base."[83] This answer seems inadequate. Can material factors—that is, the low level of productive forces in Montenegro—explain the determined statements of Montenegrin colonists in Bačka, who in 1948 vowed never to fight the USSR: "A Communist gun will never fire on Communists"?[84] As Cominformist sources always stressed, Montenegro was indeed slighted after the war: "Montenegro today is in every respect once again one of the most neglected areas of Yugoslavia. The means that supposedly were allocated for the development of Montenegro's national economy were (and are) really spent on military needs. That, of course, has led to a decline in the

---

And that is her reward—because she brought upon
    herself the enemy camp,
and because she struck no secret bargains with the Porte.

Radovan Zogović, *Knjaževska kancelarija* (Titograd, 1976), p. 68. In another poem in the same volume, "Montenegrins Write a Letter to Prince Miloš" (p. 53), Zogović defends Montenegro's militant devotion to Russia in the struggle against common enemies, a quality that Miloš reputedly disparaged as savagery and madness:

Što s Rusijom drže, a Nijemci uzalud zvekću pletom
da ih kakogod odvrlje od Rusije.
Zato smo hajduci i ludaci. O sveto, triput sveto
hajduštvo slabijih na moćne hajduke i na Jude!
O sveto ludilo junaštva—jer kako drugačije
da ono što biti ne može, ipak *bude*?!

Because they [the Montenegrins] stand by Russia,
    and the Germans vainly jingle their coins
in hopes of turning them away from Russia.
That is why we are brigands and madmen. O holy, thrice holy
the brigandage of the weaker against the powerful
    brigands and Judases!
O holy the madness of heroism—for how else
will that which cannot be, nevertheless *become*?!

82. David Binder, "A Yugoslav Poet Ends His Silence," *New York Times*, May 20, 1965, p. 5. Cominformist sources say that Zogović was released from prison only after he signed a letter of repentance: Lazri and Malo, *Dans les prisons*, p. 15.
83. Veljko Milatović, "U sudaru prošlog i budućeg," *NIN*, Feb. 15, 1976, p. 53.
84. HIA-TC, interview no. 64, p. [58].

national economy and to the contraction of an already weakly developed civilian industry."[85] Most official Yugoslav sources now concede the truth of this charge, but they rightly place far greater emphasis on the psychological impact of this neglect.[86]

Montenegro was one of Yugoslavia's prime Partisan zones. It overproduced military and political cadres, many of whom did not get the positions they believed rightfully belonged to them. Even so, Montenegrins were all too conspicuous in the army, the security agencies, and the administration. (In Slobodan Selenić's novel *Pismo/glava*, a young Communist from an old Belgrade bourgeois family found it useful to learn the Montenegrin "dialectal accent"—*pârtija* instead of *pàrtija*—in his attempt to adapt himself to the vocabulary of the new socialist world.)[87] But obviously not all Montenegrins could be at the top. And in an attempt to heal the wounds of war the KPJ was lenient to Chetnik families, at least by the stern standards of Montenegro. Their property was not handed over to the war-ravaged kin of Partisans. But most of all, Montenegro was seen as only a subordinate area, "the whole work of the so-called Montenegrin government," according to a Montenegrin Cominformist, was "reduced to the blind execution of criminal orders from Belgrade."[88] Stalin and the Cominform could set everything right. The ancient belief in Russia found receptive soil: "I do not know what this is all about, but I know that Russia is great and Stalin is mighty."[89]

Then, too, there were specific Montengrin issues. Clan rivalries played a significant role in the political life of Montenegro: the Piperi tribe of the Morača valley was almost exclusively for the Partisans, while the Vasojevići clan of the Lim valley was on the whole on the Chetnik side. In 1948 the lines were blurred. Arso Jovanović belonged to the Piperi, but so did his kinsman Blažo Jovanović, the head of the party in Montenegro. It was against the clan codes to take measures against comrades and clansmen. As Blažo Jovanović confessed to Djilas, "I was deeply affected by the desertion of loyal,

---

85. Dj. Roganović, "Težak položaj crnogorskog naroda," *Pod zastavom interna cionalizma,* Nov. 7, 1953, p. 4.

86. Dedijer, *Novi prilozi,* 3:450–51.

87. Selenić, *Pismo/glava,* p. 195.

88. K. P., "Titovski satrapi surovo eksploatišu radni narod Crne Gore," *Za socijalističku Jugoslaviju,* July 15, 1950, p. 5.

89. Komanin, *Prestupna godina,* p. 111.

tempered comrades, especially since I personally educated many of them and firmly believed in them."[90]

Montenegrin *ibeovci* are a worthy subject for a social historian. The variety of sources that may one day become available will call for interdisciplinary tools. If the leaders of the Cominformist states counted on a real fight in Yugoslavia after the Resolution, there were special reasons why, as Ranković noted, "they had great hopes especially for Serbia and Montenegro."[91]

Dušan Bilandžić, a noted Croat political theorist and historian of Yugoslav socialism, has offered a perceptive explanation of the Cominform phenomenon in terms of Yugoslavia's internal cleavages. As he sees it, Cominformism was always consonant with centralistic unitarism, that is, an ideology that regards the South Slavs as amalgamable (Yugoslavist unitarism), usually on a Serb basis, and advances a program of governance from a single pivot (centralism), always dangerous in multinational states:

> Cominformism, Stalinism as a preoccupation can be traced back long before 1948 and will continue to live in the future. It remains to be seen for how long. . . . In our Yugoslav situation, [Cominformism], in addition to some of its other features, disguises itself as a bureaucratic centralist concept that is characteristically unitarist. This is to say that . . . it actually negates national individuality [of Yugoslavia's constituent nationalities] and tends toward great-state centralism. This is, as it were, its Yugoslav form, and therefore when we speak of this concept, we must look for it . . . precisely in that somewhat concealed form. This concept will continue to change in the future, but it will always be at war with the autonomy of subjective social factors in our society. As a very complex state in all respects, and above all in her national composition, Yugoslavia wants the maximum amount of self-administration and the maximum autonomy of all subjective factors, collectives, organizations of associated labor, institutions, etc., whereas the Cominformist concept attacks this autonomy and seeks a bureaucratic centralist system.[92]

Though Bilandžić's explanation fails to clarify the appeal of Cominformism in Montenegro, it is certainly applicable to the Serbian set-

90. Djilas, *Vlast*, p. 167.

91. Aleksandar Ranković, "Govor druga Aleksandra Rankovića na Drugom kongresu KP Srbije," *Borba*, Jan. 20, 1949, p. 2.

92. Dušan Bilandžić, interview in *Start*, Jan. 14, 1976, p. 11.

ting. Some continuity surely existed between Belgrade's prewar hegemonist policies and the form of centralism that the KPJ adopted as soon as it consolidated its power after the war. The problem is to distinguish between Cominformist centralism and the variant that prevailed in Yugoslavia after 1945. The situation in Serbia and particularly the response of the Serbs in Bosnia-Hercegovina and Croatia to the Cominform Resolution, as well as the drift of Cominformist propaganda emanating from the bloc countries, provide some clues.

Although Cominformism was not widespread in the higher echelons of the KPJ organization in Serbia—perhaps because the party Central Committee had its headquarters in Belgrade, where it was under the watchful eye of the KPJ's federal center—a few old-line Serbian party leaders either sided with the Resolution or wavered on the question.[93] Some Serbian *ibeovci* certainly had ties with Žujović, who had a base in Serbia. And through Rodoljub Čolaković, his old factional ally from Gorkić's leadership of 1936 and a waverer in 1948, Žujović exercised considerable influence in Bosnia-Hercegovina. Most important, the foremost Serbian *ibeovac* was long considered a Serbian nationalist. At a KPJ CC meeting on April 13, 1948, Blažo Jovanović revealed that Žujović had once told him that "Montenegro had to be united with Serbia"; clearly, then, Žujović disagreed with the party's nationality policy.[94] And as early as 1946 Tito made himself sardonically merry over the leadership potential of Hebrang and Žujović: "What leaders of Yugoslavia they would make! One an Ustaša, the other a Chetnik!"[95] Žujović's Serbianism probably played a role in the government's decision to pair him with Hebrang in 1948. The standing of any Serbian political leader could not be enhanced on his home ground through association with an "Ustaša agent," however counterfeit.[96]

Žujović's Serbian nationalism, exaggerated or not, was not a political defect in the Soviet scheme of things. Even before the split Soviet

93. HIA-TC, "Centralni komitet komunisticke [*sic*] partije Srbije," p. 3.
94. "Plenarna sednica CK KPJ od 12. IV 1948. godine," in Dedijer, *Novi prilozi*, 3:384.
95. Quoted in Djilas, *Tito*, p. 124.
96. In his fictionalized account of the fall of Hebrang, Ivan Supek puts the following explanation of the charges against Žujović in the mouth of Stefan Mitrović: "Clear! If a change in leadership was required, who was more qualified than Sreten Žujović? Of all the members of the Politburo, Crni worked the longest in the Comintern and was best known among the European Communist leaders. The gang of four [Tito, Kardelj, Ranković, Djilas] had him arrested to prevent his enthronement. Having connected him with Hebrang, who is accused of collaboration with the Ustašas and Germans, they deprived the Serbs here and in the Cominform of a great deal of gunpowder": Supek, *Krunski svejdok*, pp. 167–68.

representatives in Belgrade encouraged the Serbs to play in Yugoslavia the role held by the Russians in the Soviet Union. According to Djilas, Soviet ambassador Lavrentiev goaded the "Serb functionaries, as if in jest, with their neglect of the Serb nation's 'leading role.' . . . Lavrentiev pointed to our underestimation of the Orthodox church and sought to revive the relations between the [Russian] and Serbian Orthodox churches."[97] And since the Soviet strategy after the split was to return Yugoslavia as a whole to the Soviet camp, Cominformist propaganda was not directed against manifestations of Serbian supremacy. The tactic of stirring up the national minorities (Hungarians, Romanians, Albanians) was not extended to the building of an anti-Serbian front; the point always was to abstract instances of oppression from any national source. Hence the Cominformist press was circumspect in its references to Serbian hegemony. It was admitted that the "domestic bourgeoisie, primarily the Great Serbian bourgeoisie, as well as foreign capitalists" oppressed the peoples of Yugoslavia during the interwar period.[98] But this was not the way the Soviets or Cominformists appraised the situation under Tito. The "new national oppression and national inequality" were an aspect of the degeneration of the Yugoslav system as a whole. Wholesale "bourgeois nationalism," which supposedly obtained in Yugoslavia, began with the Titoist claim that socialism could be built independently of the Soviet Union and ended with the restoration of capitalism in its fascist form. As a result, national inequality, too, was restored, but this feature of "Titoite fascism" sprang from no particular efforts of one nation to exploit another. National inequality in Yugoslavia was transnational, businesslike, passionless, and above all unfocused. It was the work of the new bourgeoisie, not of any particular nationality.

Predictably, capitalism was "restored" most quickly in areas where it had predominated before the war. Hence the "Serbian, Croatian, and Slovenian bourgeoisie" exploited the economically backward republics of Bosnia-Hercegovina, Montenegro, and Macedonia. Whereas the textile industry of Croatia worked at 62 percent of its capacity, textile mills operated at only 41 percent of capacity in Bosnia-Hercegovina and at 36 percent in Macedonia. The "average 'rate of

97. Djilas, *Vlast*, p. 116.
98. M. Ješić, "Titovci—najljući neprijatelji bratstva i prijateljstva jugoslovenskih naroda," *Za socijalističku Jugoslaviju*, Nov. 13, 1950, p. 6.

accumulation' in industry and mining was 489 percent in Serbia and 458 percent in Croatia. In Macedonia, however, it was 674 percent, and in Montenegro 1,300 percent!"[99] And, too, the "Tito clique" inflamed chauvinism by its cadre policy, "sending Montenegrin fascists to Serbia and Serbian fascists to Macedonia, Bosnia-Hercegovina, etc. . . . Croat fascists carried out a purge of the state apparatus [in Croatia in 1950] and arrested 200 Serbs from Croatia."[100] National minorities, notably the Albanians, were oppressed. Serb and Croat "chauvinists, kulaks, and bourgeoisie" were oppressing the Hungarian and Romanian minorities in Vojvodina.[101]

The point was not to see these developments as benefiting any particular group, still less to promote national self-rule. The Cominformist propaganda apparatus in exile, largely Serbian and Montenegrin, was not anticentralist. Its solutions, like those of Slobodan Selenić's Cominformist antihero, Champion Slišković, were centralistically Stalinist. In Slišković's utopia there was only one newspaper in all of Yugoslavia, "but it was printed in many millions of copies and distributed free of charge, under the strictest control of the most responsible people. Order was faultless. Planning was perfect. Peasant smallholding had disappeared and with it the peasantry. The whole of Vojvodina, Mačva [northwestern Serbia], and Semberija [northeastern Bosnia] was a single great kolkhoz, which, according to previously determined computations, produced exactly the right amount of food. There was no waste. Everybody lived modestly and soundly."[102] Presumably national differences, too, had been overcome.

In fact, the whole cultural orientation of émigré Cominformist propaganda was largely Serb. Apart from rare references to the Croat Illyrianists and Ivan Cankar, the leading Slovene realist, the main Cominformist newspapers in exile reserved their cultural-historical columns exclusively for Serb heroes and their ties with Russia; any rift between Serbia and Russia was considered unnatural. "Especially after the glorious victories of the Russians over the Turks, Russia and

99. A. Šalavardić, "Titovska politika nacionalnog ugnjetavanja," ibid., June 6, 1953, p. 4.

100. Ješić, "Titovci," p. 6.

101. Žarko Ljubojev, "Neke činjenice o zločinima Titove klike u Vojvodini," Za socijalističku Jugoslaviju, April 12, 1951, p. 4.

102. Selenić, Pismo/glava, p. 189.

Peter the Great instilled a love of freedom in the soul of the Serb people." Jovan Rajić, Joakim Vujić, Sima Milutinović-Sarajlija, and Dositej Obradović, the leading figures of the Serb Enlightenment, studied or traveled in Russia. Zaharija Orfelin's magazine (1768)— the "first journal not only among the Serbs but among all South Slavs"—was modeled on Russian journals.[103] The Serbian revolution of 1804–1815, an uprising "for the national liberation of the Serb people from under the Turkish yoke," was aided diplomatically and materially only by Russia. This uprising was all too relevant. "When they started the rebellion, the Serbs knew only the tactic of partisan war and brigand attacks. . . . With the coming of Russian units to Serbia, the Serbs started to study the Russian military arts."[104] Field Marshal M. I. Kutuzov, who aided the Serbs during the Russo-Turkish war of 1806–1812, ordered his officers "never to interfere in Serbia's internal affairs."[105] The Ottoman imperial ordinance that gave autonomy to Serbia in 1830 "was the direct result of enormous military, political, diplomatic, and economic aid from the Russian people to the Serb people."[106] Vuk Karadžić, the nineteenth-century Serbian language reformer and chief national ideologist, cleared the Serbian language of Turkisms and filled in the resulting gaps "by adopting Serbianized words from Church Slavonic, and then exclusively by borrowings from the Russian language, or by way of Russian." The true continuers of Karadžić's heritage were not the various gentlemen who wanted to eliminate his reformed Cyrillic and "southern dialect" (the ijekavian reflex in the Serbian literary language) but the working strata of "our people."[107]

The Cominformist sources also gloried in the Serb romantic poets (Jovan Jovanović-Zmaj and Branko Radičević), the Serb "revolutionary democrats" (Živojin Žujović, Svetozar Marković, Mita Cenić, and Vaso Pelagić, all students of the Russian populists), and Laza Lazarević, the translator of N. G. Chernyshevskii.[108] Contrary to the

103. Pero Ivanović, "Duboki su koreni prijateljstva velikog ruskog naroda sa našim narodima," Nova borba, May 15, 1951, p. 4.

104. V. Daničić, "Pomoć Rusije srpskom narodu za vreme Prvog srpskog ustanka," Za socijalističku Jugoslaviju, Dec. 13, 1953, p. 6.

105. "Veliki ruski vojskovodja Mihailo Ilarionović Kutuzov i Prvi srpski ustanak," ibid., Sept. 8, 1954, p. 5.

106. V. Daničić, "Drugi srpski ustanak i Rusija," ibid., May 22, 1954, p. 5.

107. P. Ponjavić, "Velika ličnost našeg nacionalnog preporoda," Nova borba, Jan. 27, 1954, p. 6.

108. V. Karić, "N. G. Černiševski i narodi Jugoslavije," Za socijalističku Jugoslaviju, July 25, 1953, p. 6.

interwar Comintern line, progressive trends of Russian origin even contributed to the establishment of Yugoslavia, as the Bolshevik revolution alone had precipitated the "mighty rise of the revolutionary Yugoslav movement, thus making possible the establishment of the state of the Serbs, Croats, and Slovenes in 1918."[109] Though it was not stated outright, Tito's anti-Serbianism and the foreignness of his policy was implied. The art of the Tito era "was directed by such enemies of the Yugoslav people as Oskar Davičo, Oto Bihalji-Merin, Eli Finci, Oskar Danon, Aleksandar Vučo, Vilko Vinterhalter [and] Branko Ćopić—the willing servant of Tito."[110] Vučo and Ćopić were Serbs, but most of the others were Jews, and Davičo was closely identified with Krleža's *Pečat*. Moreover, just as in the days of Vuk Karadžić and Branko Radičević, Titoist writers "sought to pervert and disfigure the folk language, as was being done by various regime scribblers such as Krleža, the so-called poet Vasko Popa [a Serbian modernist of Romanian origin], and others, whose aim was to separate our people from progressive culture and to impose upon us the notorious 'American way of life.' "[111] Yugoslavia's treaty with Turkey, too, was seen as contrary to the traditions of the Serbs, "who for long centuries were exposed to the barbarian slavery of Turkish military feudalism."[112]

Under the circumstances, it is not surprising that such authoritative observers as Milovan Djilas have referred to Cominformism as primarily a Serb phenomenon, and that the UDB-a often confused the pro-Russianism of the Serb intelligentsia, such as the nationalist poet Desanka Maksimović, with covert Cominformism.[113] Indeed, according to official Yugoslav statistics, Serbia proper had the largest number of *ibeovci*—28,661, or 51.49 percent of all Cominformists in Yugoslavia—and Serbs predominated among the *ibeovci* of Bosnia-Hercegovina, Vojvodina, and Kosmet, and formed a significant portion of the *ibeovci* of Croatia. In Serbia itself, the geographical foci of Cominformism were in the northeast, along the Danube and Timok

109. V. Karasjov [V. G. Karasev], "Veze ruskih i srpskih revolucionarnih demokrata," *Nova borba*, Oct. 14, 1953, p. 4.
110. S. Cekić, "Izrodjavanje književnosti i umetnosti pod režimom beogradskih vlastodržaca," *Za socijalističku Jugoslaviju*, July 7, 1951, p. 4.
111. Z. Nalić, "Povodom stogodišnjice smrti Branka Radičevića," ibid., Oct. 24, 1953, p. 5.
112. P. Ponjavić, "Bratimljenje s vekovnim dušmanima naših naroda," *Nova borba*, July 5, 1954, p. 3.
113. Djilas, *Vlast*, pp. 193, 179.

frontiers with Romania and Bulgaria, where the Soviet army first entered Yugoslav territory in 1944 and where Soviet intelligence agencies swiftly built a considerable network of agents. In Kladovo, across the Danube from Turnu Severin (Romania), the whole county KPJ organization—all the members, including the UDB-a and the militia—opted for the Resolution. The situation in nearby Donji Milanovac, Bor (the major copper mining center), Zaječar, and Negotin was almost as pro-Soviet.[114] Widespread arrests on the Negotin frontier claimed Dragoljub Radisavljević-Stanko, secretary of the KPJ organization in Negotin.[115] Rgotina, near Zaječar, was the center of a Cominformist insurgent group that was destroyed in September 1952.[116] There was also a significant incidence of Cominformism in the Šumadija region of central Serbia and in Vojvodina.[117]

Though KPJ members in the army and among students at the University of Belgrade were most likely to side with the Resolution, pro-Soviet sentiment apparently embraced all kinds of unlikely groups in Serbia. Some Serbian Cominformists were influenced by Dr. Blagoje Nešković, a member of Serbia's KPJ Regional Committee since 1940 and its secretary during the war, who remained at the helm of the party organization in Serbia until January 1949. A strong-willed physician and a veteran of the Spanish Civil War (he was sometimes referred to as "Pašić without the beard," after the crafty Serbian statesman), Nešković always found it hard "to change his position to suit new circumstances."[118] He was reluctant to take a stand on the Resolution ("for months he made no public statements, and he never assumed a decisive and hostile stance toward Moscow"), he openly opposed Tito's decision to stay away from the Bucharest meeting of the Cominform in June 1948, and he was against the idea of fighting the Soviets if they attacked Yugoslavia.[119] Yet, unlike Vojo Srzentić

114. Dedijer, *Novi prilozi*, 3:454. Cf. Danilo Ognjanović and Jovan Coković-Lale, "Usprkos teroru rastu snage za obračun sa ubicama naših naroda," *Nova borba*, Feb. 28, 1950, p. 6.
115. Stanko, "Novi prestaplenija na fašističkata banda na Tito-Rankovič vo Krainska okolija," *Napred*, July 15, 1950, p. 11.
116. "Večna slava na narodnite borci, koi što padnaa vo borbata protiv titofašističkata tiranija!," *Napred*, Nov. 30, 1952, p. 5.
117. Kragujevčanin, "Slobodarska Šumadija u borbi protiv titovskog fašizma," *Nova borba*, June 15, 1950, p. 5; Radnik iz Zrenjanina, "Radnici Zrenjanina uspešnom sabotažom razbijaju titovske planove," ibid.
118. Milovan Djilas, *Memoir of a Revolutionary* (New York, 1973), p. 318.
119. HIA-TC, "Jugoslovenski kominformisti," p. 5; Svetozar Vukmanović Tempo, *Revolucija koja teče: Memoari* (Belgrade, 1971), 2:125, 93–94.

and Milan Kalafatić, the only members of the KPJ CC for Serbia who openly supported the Resolution, Nešković was not immediately expelled.[120] Instead, Petar Stambolić replaced him as secretary of the KPJ organization in Serbia and the KPJ leadership brought Nešković into the Politburo and the federal cabinet, where he could not act independently. Nešković continued to oppose the leadership on a number of important questions (for example, on the decision to seek U.S. credits) and his theoretical statements reflected Stalinist inspiration in the strictest sense.[121] He was finally expelled from the KPJ and deprived of all posts in 1952, but was permitted to work as a researcher at the Oncological Institute of the Medical Faculty in Belgrade.[122]

Whether they were Russophiles, Serbian nationalists, or disaffected members, those who strayed from the party wanted to go on record as supporters of the Resolution. This was to some extent a calculated risk, based on the chance that the USSR might intervene and replace the KPJ leadership, in which case the avowed Resolutionists could

120. HIA-TC, "Centralni komitet Komunisticke [sic] partije Srbije," p. 3. Srzentić, a Montenegrin, joined the party in 1934 and was active in Belgrade, where he participated in various KPJ front groups, including Red Aid, Jedinstvena radnička partija (United Workers' Party), Stranka radnog naroda (Party of the Working People), and sBOTIČ (bank clerks' union). Djilas, who first met Tito in Srzentić's company in 1937, described Srzentić as a well-known leftist who "was cautious and very selective about his contacts" (*Memoir*, p. 258).

121. Vukmanović, *Revolucija*, p. 125. Although Nešković was not the only KPJ leader who uncritically accepted Stalin's thesis about the "sharpening" of class struggle under socialism, his statements on the subject were certainly among the most extreme, especially in the context of the party's decision to foster the collectivization of agriculture after the break with the USSR. See Blagoje Nešković, *O zaoštravanju klasne borbe na selu u sadašnjoj etapi izgradnje socijalizma i o savezu radničke klase i radnog seljaštva* (Zagreb, 1949). Nešković's public criticisms of the Cominform were always balanced by attacks against the West. Speaking at an electoral meeting in Šabac in March 1950, for example, he noted that "capitalist reaction and reaction in the Informburo are united in a struggle against our country": "Naše državno rukovodstvo na čelu s drugom Titom sigurno vodi naše narode u pobedu," *Borba*, March 15, 1950, p. 1. For all that, the Cominformist press never gave Nešković any quarter. He was denounced as a Gestapo agent and—curiously, in an argument later used by Vladimir Dedijer—as a person who "during the whole course of the occupation worked at wrecking the Partisan struggle in Serbia": "Koi se titovski kandidati," *Napred*, March 15, 1950, p. 4.

122. Milan Borković and Venceslav Glišić, eds., *Osnivački kongres KP Srbije (8–12. maj 1945)* (Belgrade, 1972), no. 3, p. 21. Nešković himself always denied that his departure from the party leadership was spurred by disagreements over the Cominform. "That is not correct," he said in 1983. "In 1952 I 'lowered the curtain' over my past career as a 'politician' and picked up where I left off before my departure for Spain." He received the October Prize of the city of Belgrade in 1983 for his contributions to research on the molecular biology of tumors. See Milomir Marić, "Protiv raka i za neka ubedjenja," *Duga*, Nov. 19, 1983, pp. 20–21. Nešković died in 1984.

expect to be rewarded. It also represented a widespread opinion that the primacy of Serbia and the Serbs might be accentuated under Soviet tutelage. This opinion was especially strong among the Serbs of Bosnia-Hercegovina and Croatia, where their minority status (deeply felt as a result of wartime tribulations), as well as the privileges gained through mass participation in the Partisan ranks, inspired feelings of isolation and uneasiness. The security and privileges of these Serb minorities seemed assured only in an authoritarian and Serb-dominated Yugoslavia.

It should be noted that the position of the Serbs in Bosnia-Hercegovina and Croatia was in no way endangered after the Resolution. Nor was the Soviet Union readily identified as the sole guarantor of the kind of Yugoslavia that appealed to these communities. As a result, though Cominformist activity was very strong among the Serbs of western Yugoslavia, it was not their only option. In Sarajevo, where the Bosnian party boss, Djuro Pucar, himself a Serb, remained strongly loyal to Tito, all the KPJ organizations were almost completely changed after the break. Among the many *ibeovci* arrested there were Obren Starović, minister of finance in the government of Bosnia-Hercegovina, and his cabinet colleagues Peko Papić, Vojo Ljujić, Kosta Grubačić, and Ćedo Mijović.[123] Cominformism was widespread in eastern Hercegovina, a largely Serb territory where traditions and wartime experiences paralleled those of neighboring Montenegro, including a tendency toward Left Errors. A significant incidence of Cominformism in this area thus reflected the Montenegrin pattern.

The deepening rift between Moscow and Belgrade seemed to foreshadow genuine democratization and decentralization in Yugoslavia. The KPJ initiated a campaign against Soviet bureaucratism and simultaneously called for more initiative and autonomy in the party's domestic base. The opening up of diplomatic relations with the West, especially the acceptance of United States aid in 1950–1951, accented these processes. As a result, portions of the Communist elites in the minority Serb communities became apprehensive, and Cominformism, largely subdued elsewhere, suddenly rebounded among the Serbs

123. HIA-TC, "Jugoslovenski kominformisti," p. 5. Cf. Lazri and Malo, *Dans les prisons*, p. 19. Cominformism was especially widespread in the old Partisan pivots of heavily Serb northwestern Bosnia. See Jovo, "Bosanska krajina pod terorom titovskih fašista" and "Hapšenja prvoboraca u Zapadnoj Bosni," both in *Nova borba*, October 5, 1949.

of Bosnia-Hercegovina and Croatia. Western observers noted that the Sarajevo administration harbored individuals (all Serbs from north-western Bosnia) with ties to Soviet intelligence.[124] But it was in Croatia that the recidivistic crisis led to a purge of some of the re-public's most influential Serb Communists.

Serbs were heavily represented in Croatia's Central Committee— 28.57 percent of all CC members, including the candidate members elected in November 1948, were Serbs, although Serbs then con-stituted only 14.48 percent of Croatia's population—and this repre-sentation was not seriously undermined by the expulsions.[125] Nev-ertheless, the high status of the defectors was indicative of the Soviet appeal. In 1950, the KPH CC expelled Dušan Brkić, General Rade Žigić, and Stanko Opačić-Ćanica. The KPH also expelled Bogoljub Rapajić. At the time, Brkić was a member and Žigić a candidate member of the KPJ CC. Both also belonged to the Politburo of the KPH CC. All three were reserve generals and prewar Communists who had distinguished themselves during the war in Slavonia and the Kordun.[126] Stanko Opačić, in particular, was a legendary wartime

124. HIA-TC, J., "Izviestaj o jednom kanalu Kominformbiroa preko Beca sa Sarajevom [sic]."
125. The figures are based on an analysis in HIA-TC, "Centralni komitet Komunisticke [sic] partije Hrvatske," pp. 8, 12.
126. Brkić, Žigić, and Opačić were expelled from the KPJ because "they worked against the line of our party and its Central Committee . . . organized themselves as an agency of the Informburo . . . worked against our party's economic measures, against the pace of our socialist industrialization, against the realization of the Five-Year Plan, against our foreign policy line, against the security of our homeland and the building of socialism in the F.P.R. of Yugoslavia. . . . Taking advantage of the fact that they are Serbs, they attempted to present their bogus resignation as an expression of the stand of the Serbs of Croatia, though in fact they were carrying out the Informburo line, which aims to disturb fraternal relations among our peoples, especially among the Serb and Croat peoples": "Rezolucija izvanred-nog plenarnog zasedanja CK KP Hrvatske," Borba, Sept. 11, 1950, p. 1. According to Vladimir Bakarić, the three agitated among the Serb peasants against the obligatory food levies, claiming that insurgent Serb areas should not be subjected to food levies at all. Bakarić noted Brkić's references to the "rich treasure store of Stalinism" in speeches made as late as November 1949. In Bakarić's opinion, the activities of Brkić, Žigić, and Opačić were the "heaviest attack against brotherhood committed since the war": "Završen je rad Sabora Narodne Republike Hrvatske prvog saziva," Borba, Sept. 12, 1950, pp. 1–2.
Brkić was born in Obrovac (Dalmatia), graduated from the Law Faculty of the University of Belgrade, and was one of the organizers of the Partisan movement in Slavonia. He served as the political commissar of the Partisans' First Slavonian Corps in 1943 and was a member of AVNOJ and of the Executive Council of ZAVNOH. He became minister of justice in Croatia's first (Communist-dominated) government, which was formed in Split in April 1945. He later served as vice-president of the Croatian government in Zagreb. Active as the highest-ranking Serb leader in Croatia, Brkić was secretary of the Serb deputies' club of

hero of Croatia's Serbs, known for his operations in the Petrova Gora
mountain range of the Kordun. Serb Partisans sang, "Comrade Ćanica and the Petrova Gora must be remembered until the earth re-
moves."[127] The party leadership accused these Serb leaders of incit-
ing small-scale rebellions among Serb peasants in the Kordun, Lika,
Banija, and the neighboring Cazin area of northwestern Bosnia in
May 1950. Like the better-known incidents in Montenegro, these
disturbances were part of an abortive Cominformist guerrilla movement that emerged among the Serbs of western Yugoslavia. The incidence of Cominformism among the Serb minorities was in part a
reflection of the fact that the "Serb Communists, or at least some of
them, were angered because, despite their great contributions, they
were neglected in the new state, where 'brotherhood and unity,' that

ZAVNOH, and he initiated the Prosvjeta Serb Cultural-Educational Society. See *Narodna
vlada Hrvatske* (Zagreb?, 1945), pp. 99–100. It should be noted that he repudiated "the
falseness and the incorrectness of all slanders heaped on our Party and its leadership by the
Information Bureau and certain Communist parties" from the podium of the Second Congress of the KPH: Dušan Brkić, "Referat o izgradnji socijalizma i narodne vlasti u
Hrvatskoj," *Borba*, Nov. 25, 1948, p. 2. After his dismissal, Brkić lived in relative obscurity
in Belgrade until the wave of Cominformist trials in the 1970s. Charged with "counterrevolutionary conspiracy" and "ties with the Cominformist emigration" in the bloc countries, he was arrested in 1975; on April 12, 1976, he and three other defendants were
sentenced to eight years' imprisonment. Rade Žigić was also a member of AVNOJ and
ZAVNOH. He served as the political commissar of the Sixth (Partisan) Division and remained
in the JA until his dismissal. Of the three, Ćanica Opačić was the most popular among the
Serb masses. A peasant and a veteran of Pribićević's Independent Democratic Party (SDS),
Opačić joined the KPJ in 1940. He headed the first Partisan actions in Croatia during the
summer of 1941. A member of the headquarters staff for Croatia, the presidency of AVNOJ,
and the secretariat of ZAVNOH, he became Croatia's minister of construction in 1945. It is
significant that Većeslav Holjevac, one of the most national Croat Communists of the
postwar period (he was a leader of the uprising in the Kordun and later became mayor of
Zagreb), who certainly had no reason to be sentimental about Opačić's Cominformism or
covert Croatophobia, remained Opačić's friend even after 1950. "After the liberation
different events and circumstances separated our paths and sent us off in different direc-
tions. This is nothing new in life: even the closest sometimes become separated. It is
important for Ćanica and for me that we can always remember with satisfaction those days
when we worked together, because at that time—when the Croat and Serb people were in
the worst straits—we both showed courage and with a series of deeds contributed to the
creation of genuine fraternity between our two peoples": Većeslav Holjevac, *Zapisi iz
rodnoga grada* (Zagreb, 1972), p. 136. Bogoljub Rapajić, a member of the Croatian Sabor,
was a prewar journalist and nationalist activist. He joined the Partisans in 1941, headed the
National Liberation Committee for Lika, and edited *Srpska riječ* (Serb word), the organ of
the Serb members of ZAVNOH.
  127. Stanko Opačić-Ćanica, ed., *Narodne pjesme Korduna* (Zagreb, 1971), p. 237.
Another folk song in the same collection (p. 403) describes Opačić as the "second Prince
Marko," after the principal hero of Serbian epic poetry.

illusive slogan from the war and revolution, were supposed to prevail."[128] The Serb institutions and culture that Hebrang worked to promote, along with his followers Brkić and Žigić, were increasingly eroded after the war. The option for the Cominform was therefore part of a struggle for Serb identity in the distant corners of the Serb national archipelago.

The continuing attraction of Cominformism among the Serbs of Croatia and Bosnia-Hercegovina has been amply demonstrated in recent years.[129] Of the six major Cominformist trials from 1974 to 1978 (excluding the cases of the captured Cominformist émigrés Vladimir Dapčević and Mileta Perović), three—in Belgrade, Novi Sad, and Banja Luka, all during the spring of 1976—involved groups of Serbs from western Yugoslavia. Without doubt, much of the appeal of the USSR in this claustrophobic constituency is a reaction to Yugoslavia's decentralization and the KPJ's nationality policy, which the old-guard Serb Partisans in Croatia and Bosnia-Hercegovina perceive as excessively favorable to the non-Serbs.

The uncertain nature of the Cominformist appeal is evident in the fact that sauce for a centralist goose could also be sauce for a federalist gander. In 1948, when Yugoslav federalism existed in name only and the party's nationality policy was becoming increasingly unitarist, dissatisfaction among the non-Serbs was translated into dividends for the Cominform—despite the fact that Stalinism did not have deep roots in Croatia. The Croats were inclined to view their republic, in the words of Jozo Laušić's alter ego in his novel *Bogumil* (1982), as "yesterday *antemurale christianitatis,* and today *antemurale contra stalinitatem.*"[130] As long as there were actual grounds for complaint against Belgrade's policies, Soviet criticisms of Yugoslavia, even if they did not deal explicitly with the national

128. Mane Pešut, "Djurdjevdanski ustanak Srba u Hrvatskoj—1950 godine," *Glasnik Srpskog istorijsko-kulturnog društva "Njegoš"* 52 (June 1984): 23.

129. At the Second Session of the Central Committee of the League of Communists of Croatia (July 1978), Milutin Baltić, secretary of the CC and himself a Serb, warned against an array of dangers, including the activity of the Cominformists: "Kongresne odluke—glavni zadaci SK," *Vjesnik,* July 12, 1978, p. 5. Baltić's reference to "Cominformist tendencies" was changed to "dogmatic tendencies" in Belgrade's *Politika:* "Afirmisanjem vrednosti našeg sistema protiv neprijateljskih tendencija," *Politika,* July 12, 1978, p. 10.

130. Laušić, *Bogumil,* p. 5.

question, could muster a certain amount of support. Also, of course, criticism cost Moscow practically nothing; it certainly did not commit the Soviet leaders to more enlightened treatment of the non-Russian nationalities of the USSR.

The Cominform's attack on the KPJ certainly seemed to justify those Croats who were dissatisfied with the Croat position in postwar Yugoslavia. According to a high-ranking intelligence operative who defected in 1950, "One can observe rivalry and intolerance between the Serbs and Croats in the party. Since the Soviets in their propaganda against Yugoslavia always claim that there is no democracy in the Yug. party, as there is in theirs, and that privileges exist, Cominformism is fairly strong among the Croats." It is probably more accurate to say that the anti-Cominformist purge claimed a number of Croats who simply resented the disproportionate number of Serbs in the ranking posts, "especially in the army."[131]

Whether by design or as a result of growing disaffection, the purge did embrace a number of Croat Communists. The whole district committee for Hrvatsko Primorje and a part of the district committee for Gorski Kotar came out for the Resolution. The district committee for Istria also was almost entirely for the Resolution.[132] Cominformism was apparently strong in Rijeka, Yugoslavia's principal harbor, and in Pula, the other large urban center of the Istria-Hrvatsko Primorje region.[133] But the most important group among the arrested Croats were party members whose association with the Croat national movement of the early 1930s predated their allegiance to the KPJ, and who were strongly committed to the Hebrang line. This was the case with Šime Balen and Nikola Rubčić, activists of the Croat Peasant Party, who joined the KPJ under Hebrang's influence in the royal prisons and who later took a leading role in ZAVNOH under Hebrang.[134] Balen headed ZAVNOH's propaganda section and Rubčić was editor of Vjesnik (Herald), the ZAVNOH organ.[135]

131. HIA-TC, interviews no. 29, p. 92, and no. 52, p. 124.
132. Dedijer, Novi prilozi, 3:458. Cf. Lazri and Malo, Dans les prisons, p. 19.
133. For the arrests of the Cominformists in Rijeka and Pula, see "Iz pisama uredništvu: Nova hapšenja komunista," Nova borba, June 14, 1949, p. 8; and "Teror Rankovićevih dželata u Istri," ibid., Aug. 8, 1949, p. 2.
134. At the KPJ's initiative, in 1937 Balen and Rubčić edited a paper aimed at stemming the influence of the right in the Croat Peasant Party. Their program is set forth in an editorial in the paper's first issue: "Seljačka misao," Seljačka misao, Jan. 2, 1937, p. 1.
135. Rubčić, a member of the KPH CC since June 1944, was the only CC member of Croat nationality in Croatia to side with the Cominform Resolution: HIA-TC, "Centralni komitet Komunisticke [sic] partije Hrvatske," p. 3. The harsh fate of Šime Balen and his

Several other ZAVNOH activists fell in the purge. Soon after the Resolution the KPH CC expelled Dr. Savo Zlatić, a wartime secretary of the party's committee in Karlovac and the organizer of the famous underground Partisan hospital in Petrova Gora.[136] Expelled and arrested, too, were Andrija Bubanj, Partisan commander of Croatia's Fifth Operational Zone (Hrvatsko Primorje and Gorski Kotar), president of the National Liberation Committee for Gorski Kotar, and the party's secretary in the ZAVNOH apparatus; Dr. Gabro Divjanović, president of the military court for Croatia; Dr. Nikola Nikolić, one of Hebrang's liaisons with the Croat Peasant Party; and Vlado Madjarević, a journalist and former Communist student activist.[137]

The commitment of many of these Croats to the Resolution was

---

wife is described in a roman à clef by Ivan Supek, in which Balen appears under the name of Martin. See Supek, *Krunski svjedok*, pp. 212–19, 237–39, 240–48. Balen repudiated his supposed Cominformist allegiance in June 1949. He did not, however, neglect to hint that his stand had everything to do with Hebrang: "I first acted in the spirit of these letters [Stalin's messages to the KPJ CC] even before the Cominform Resolution, specifically on the question of the KPJ CC Commission of Investigation of Hebrang and Žujović, when I refused to accept both the commission's report and the decision of the KPJ CC about the punishment [of Hebrang and Žujović]": "Izjava Šime Balena," *Borba*, June 29, 1949, p. 2.

136. Zlatić, a physician from Istria, joined the KPJ in 1933. In addition to his wartime functions in Karlovac, he was a member of the Partisan headquarters staff for Croatia and a member of ZAVNOH. Zlatić was elected a candidate member of the KPJ CC at the Fifth Congress, but was not among the KPH CC members four months later. For an incomplete biography see HIA-TC, Biographies: Savo Zlatić. On his activities in the Partisan medical corps see Holjevac, *Zapisi*, pp. 185–87. The ironies of Cominformism are especially notable in Zlatić's case. As Yugoslavia's last envoy to Albania before the Resolution, he earned the hatred of the Albanian leadership for his attempts to bring Albania into union with Belgrade. Tirana's Cominformist leaders apparently prevailed upon the Cominform to name Zlatić among sixteen Yugoslav leaders who were denounced as an espionage ring in the so-called Second Cominform Resolution of November 1949. Another Soviet sympathizer in this group was Dr. Blagoje Nešković. See *White Book on Aggressive Activities by the Governments of the U.S.S.R., Poland, Czechoslovakia, Hungary, Rumania, Bulgaria, and Albania towards Yugoslavia* (Belgrade, 1951), p. 177. Enver Hoxha denounced Zlatić as a "back-room organizer, enemy, and double dealer"; see Hoxha, *Titistët: Shënime historike* (Tirana, 1982), pp. 299–322. And indeed, Zlatić was considered so reliable that the KPJ offered him the position of ambassador to Moscow in the summer of 1948. Apparently he either refused or hesitated, and he was then dismissed from all posts. See "Savo Zlatić odbio položaj ambasadora u Moskvi," *Nova borba*, Dec. 29, 1948, p. 5. Cf. Dedijer, *Novi prilozi*, 3:461. Zlatić recanted his Cominformist allegiance in 1950: "Pismo Save Zlatića redakciji 'Borbe,'" *Borba*, Nov. 18, 1950, pp. 1–2.

137. Other noted Cominformists in Croatia included Djuro Tiljak, Lovro Kurir, Ivan Flec, and Jozo Rusković. Tiljak was a leading leftist painter and a member of AVNOJ and ZAVNOH. His Russophile tendencies led him to Russia in 1919, where he studied briefly under Kandinskii. Kurir was a founding member of the KPH and one of the original members of the KPH CC elected at the congress in the Anindol forest near Samobor in 1937. Flec was a delegate to the Fifth Land Conference of the KPJ in 1940. Rusković was a veteran Communist from Pelješac and an activist of the Croat Peasant Party.

largely an aspect of their commitment to Hebrang. The official link-
age of the Hebrang case with Stalin's policy was really an unexpected
dividend for Stalin. But since Hebrang was always only incidentally a
Cominformist in the official scheme, the time had come for a direct
repudiation of his "Croat chauvinism," which was seen as his real
fault. Hence the dubious quality of much of the alleged Croat Cominformism. As the repentant Žujović pointed out, "My case is entirely
different from Hebrang's. It is interesting that the Cominform campaign [against Yugoslavia] usually connects me with Hebrang,
though they know that Hebrang was an Ustaša agent. It was shown
that they needed such a man and that they still need him."[138]

All the same, the Cominformist propagandists never had a good
sense for mass work among the Croats. Exiled *ibeovci,* among whom
there were very few Croats, never had a good word for Miroslav
Krleža, and so turned their backs on the national traditions of the
Croat left.[139] They denounced the affirmation of Croat identity and
linguistic autonomy in the manner of Yugoslavist unitarists.[140] But
unlike the unitarist forces within the KPJ, unitaristic Cominformists
blamed Tito for toleration of Croat nationalism, a proposition that
was not entirely unrewarding, except among the Croats. Small wonder that, despite the confusion over Hebrang, Croatia had a relatively
small number of *ibeovci,* among whom the Croat contingent was a
group apart.

Much the same pattern obtained among the Bosnian Muslims, the
national group that had the smallest incidence of Cominformism, and
in Slovenia, the republic with the smallest number of *ibeovci.* The
most prominent Slovene party leader identified with Cominformism
was Dragotin Gustinčič, a veteran of the factional struggles of the
1920s and a consistent federalist, who was out of Yugoslavia from
1931 to 1945. Except for the duration of the Spanish Civil War, when
he served first as head censor of the international brigades and later as

138. "Odgovori Sretena Žujovića na pitanja stranih i domaćih novinara," *Borba,* Dec.
2, 1950, p. 2.

139. Krleža was being denounced in the Cominformist press in the most vulgar way. For
a typical example, in which Krleža was portrayed as the "great druid and the supreme
magus of Titoite fascist Parnassus, the old anarchist and Trotskyite," see J. Vadjić,
"Fašistička suština titovske književnosti," *Napred,* April 10, 1953, p. 4.

140. A typical example of this tendency was an attack on Kruno Krstić for his efforts on
behalf of Croat linguistic purity, which was denounced as inspired by the Ustašas. See I.
Marušić, "Mračnjaci i mračnjaštvo u titovskoj 'književnosti,'" *Pod zastavom internacionalizma,* Sept. 24, 1952, p. 2.

the top KPJ representative in Spain, he spent his exile in Moscow, where he worked in various academic institutions. Gustinčič was dismissed from the KPJ Politburo in 1928, during the removal of factional leaders, but was named in absentia to the Central Committee of the newly formed Communist Party of Slovenia in 1937. After his return from Moscow in 1945, in a sort of demotion, he worked as a professor of economics at the University of Ljubljana. Still, Tito considered him dangerous enough to count him among the top anti-party conspirators in 1948. Tito evidently believed that Gustinčič was the source of some of Stalin's arguments in the First Letter, and it is possible that the first trial of the predominantly Slovene former Communist prisoners from Dachau in 1948 was in part an attempt to tar the suspected Soviet informants with the brush of collaboration with the Gestapo. Speaking during a confrontation with Žujović at the plenum of the KPJ CC on April 12, 1948, Tito said, "We wrote the letter [to Stalin] because we suspected that the information was given [to him] . . . [by such] elements as Gustinčič and those who are now being prepared for trial." He added that "for eleven years Crni [Žujović], Hebrang, and Gustinčič have been trying to promote a certain [kind of] leadership—to wreck the [established] leadership."[141] Eleven years earlier, in 1937, Tito was tested with the Comintern mandate to sweep the party clean.

Aside from Gustinčič, who was arrested before the open break and hence was a Cominformist in an attenuated sense, no prominent Slovene party leader defected, although some old cadres and an occasional high-level official did side with the Resolution. Notable among them were Silvester Furlan, a Spanish Civil War veteran; Dušan Kermavner, a noted party historian; Edvin Černej, director of the State Bank in Ljubljana; and Ludvik Mrzel, author, former editor of *Slovenski poročevalec* (Slovene messenger), and head of the National Theater in Maribor. In addition, Dr. Cene Logar (variously identified as a professor of Marxism-Leninism at the University of Ljubljana and as director of the Ljubljana classical gymnasium), the former organizational secretary of Osvobodilna Fronta, spoke publicly in favor of the Resolution and then organized a clandestine Cominformist central committee that included his three brothers, Mirko Gorše,

---

141. "Zapisnik sa sednice CK KPJ od 12. i 13. aprila 1948.," in Dedijer, *Novi prilozi*, 3:381–82.

former secretary of the Slovene branch of SKOJ, and several others. They were all arrested.[142] And Gregor Ravnihar, Yugoslavia's deputy minister of maritime affairs, committed suicide rather than take a stand against Stalin.[143]

Slovenia had two other affairs that were connected with the Cominform. Boris Ziherl (1910–1975), a bookwormish Marxist philosopher of Kardelj's circle, was Slovenia's top waverer. Ziherl, the commissioner for ideology in the KPJ CC Agitprop, wrote a letter in support of Stalin to the KPJ CC. He also complained to Djilas that the whole country and party ought not to suffer on account of Tito. The KPJ leadership, notably Kardelj and Kidrič, treated Ziherl with exceptional forbearance. Kidrič held him incommunicado and argued with him for several weeks until Ziherl changed his stand.[144] A far less serious case was treated with less patience. In February 1949 the Ljubljana court sentenced three important Slovene intellectuals—Dušan Pirjavec-Ahac, Vitomil Zupan, and Jože Jovoršek—to rather stiff sentences for a prank they played on Josip Vidmar, the leading Slovene literary critic and litterateur and later president of the Slovene Academy of Sciences. In the course of a gala party the three telephoned Vidmar, identified themselves as secret policemen, and reported an imminent Soviet invasion. The joke set off a small panic.[145] The most significant of the three was Pirjavec, head of the party Agitprop in Slovenia, who admired cultural autonomy (he sided with Krleža in 1940) but failed to support it when he held power.[146] As the Partisan warlord of Bela Krajina, he was deeply involved in the Left Errors of 1941–1942.[147]

As in Croatia, Cominformist propagandists had little feeling for national aspirations in Slovenia.[148] The KPJ leadership, however,

142. HIA-TC, interview no. 54, pp. 6, 11–14.
143. Dedijer, Novi prilozi, 3:457.
144. Ibid., cf. Djilas, Vlast, p. 156.
145. Ibid., pp. 180–81.
146. Josip Vidmar, not the most objective source on Pirjavec, portrays him as a sort of sectarian who denigrated the worship of France Prešeren, Slovenia's great nineteenth-century national bard and reviver. See Josip Vidmar, Moji savremenici (Sarajevo, 1981), p. 514.
147. This is reported by Jože Javoršek, Pirjavec's codefendant in the 1949 case but later his great denigrator. See Javoršek, Opasne veze (Zagreb, 1980), p. 65.
148. An odd article or two about Slovenia in the émigré Cominformist press made no reference to any specifically Slovene issues. See, e.g., "Ljubljana u redovima aktivne borbe protiv titovaca," Nova borba, Oct. 20, 1949, p. 3.

never challenged the distinctive Slovene Communist movement. For as long as they were unmolested, the Slovenes understood that their aspirations could best be served within the tightly knit federal structure championed by Tito. The Soviet side could better that arrangement only by aiding the unification of Yugoslav Slovenia with the Slovene lands in Italy and Austria. And indeed, for as long as the USSR gave diplomatic support to Yugoslavia's territorial claims to Trieste, Gorizia, and southern Carinthia, the Slovenes, as the principal beneficiaries, applauded the Soviet assistance. The Resolution and the Soviets' inability to dislodge the KPJ leadership changed all that. Moscow's punishment of Yugoslavia included acceptance of Austria's 1938 frontiers, a stand that effectively doomed Yugoslavia's acquisition of southern Carinthia. The Cominformist faction in Trieste, dominated by the Italian Communists, initiated a campaign against Yugoslavia's interests there. Togliatti's Italian Communist Party, which accepted the Resolution, developed an unmistakably irredentist position on the question of Italy's frontiers with Yugoslavia. Under the circumstances, Slovene supporters of the Resolution came into collision with Slovene patriotism. Their influence accordingly plummeted.

Slovenia was a unique case. The logic of Cominformism among the other non-Serb nationalities followed Croatia's pattern. In Macedonia also, the local exponents of Moscow were in effect proponents of a particular national program. Specifically, Cominformist affinities in Macedonia were usually predicated on pro-Bulgarian sentiments. The history of the Macedonian national movement almost unavoidably determined this outcome. Dominated by the Turks until 1912, Macedonia was then divided among Serbia, Bulgaria, and Greece. All three Balkan states claimed the entire territory of Macedonia as their national patrimony, but the native insurrectionary movement was tied above all to Bulgaria. The only serious question was whether the Macedonians were Bulgarians outright or a branch of the Bulgarian people which had developed specific—perhaps separate—national features of its own. But even when they were completely Bulgarophile, as in the case of Todor Aleksandrov's Internal Macedonian Revolutionary Organization (IMRO), Macedonian revolutionaries never ceased to be autonomists; they fought for an autonomous Macedonia within Bulgaria, or within a wider Balkan federation.

Interwar Serbian-dominated Belgrade regimes did not recognize the Macedonian question. Yugoslav (or Vardar) Macedonia was affirmed as Southern Serbia, and its population systematically—but unsuccessfully—Serbianized. As Belgrade outlawed every expression of Macedonian (or Bulgarian) sentiment, opposition was inevitably concentrated in clandestine movements, including the KPJ. Nevertheless, whether they belonged to the KPJ or the Bulgarian Workers' (Communist) Party (BRP), the Macedonian Communists did not conceive of national autonomy within the framework of Yugoslavia, the line backed by the Comintern in 1923. Autonomous Macedonia was envisioned only within Bulgaria, or, briefly after 1928, within a united and independent Macedonian state.[149] In either case, the Macedonian Communists, much like IMRO, sought to detach Macedonia from Yugoslavia.

With Tito's appointment as general secretary in 1937, the KPJ at last took notice of deficient conditions in its Macedonian branch. But as in Croatia, Tito insisted on the abandonment of separatist agitation in the face of the worldwide fascist threat. The secretary chosen to revitalize the Regional Committee for Macedonia was a veteran Communist functionary but hardly the sort of wax enthusiastic over the defense of Yugoslavia's territorial integrity. Metodi Šatorov (Šarlo), born in Prilep in Vardar Macedonia, spent much of the interwar period in Bulgaria, where he joined the BRP and from 1927 served as a member of its Central Committee. An old Comintern hand and a Spanish veteran, Šatorov was not in awe of Tito and would not shed his Bulgarian loyalties: one of his *noms de conspiration* was "Old Bulgarian."

Šatorov first ran afoul of Tito in October 1940, at the KPJ's Fifth Land Conference, clandestinely convened in Zagreb. He rejected the conference theses (drafted by Milovan Djilas) which spoke of a popular front in the narrowest of terms, restricting it to the worker-peasant constituency. Citing the colonial character of Macedonia, Šatorov insisted on a Communist-led national revolutionary front of all Macedonian strata and groups (including the bourgeoisie), which, in the

149. On the Macedonian question in the politics and history of the KPJ, see especially Stephen E. Palmer, Jr., and Robert R. King, *Yugoslav Communism and the Macedonian Question* (Hamden, Conn., 1971). Cf. Aleksandar T. Hristov, *KPJ vo rešavanjeto na makedonskoto prašanje* (Skopje, 1962); and Elisabeth Barker, *Macedonia: Its Place in Balkan Power Politics* (London, 1950), pp. 45–109.

words of the resolution of the KPJ's regional conference for Macedonia (Skopje, September 8, 1940), had to struggle against "Serbian imperialists and oppressors."[150] Šatorov also insisted that the party could not win the Macedonians' confidence unless it came out in favor of expelling the post-1918 Serb settlers from Macedonia. He accused Djilas of a Serb chauvinist stand because Djilas's use of historical analogies to defend the settlers, the Bolsheviks supposedly having protected the Russian colonists in the Caucasus. "We cannot go to the Macedonian peasant," said Šatorov, "and tell him that the colonists are the brothers of Macedonian peasants. Generals, gendarmes, and spies are not brothers. If we opted for an alliance with the colonists, the peasants would give us the shovel. There are some 10,000 settler families with some 70,000 hectares of land. All of them are the oppressors of the Macedonian people and we cannot have good relations with them. In Belorussia *all* the colonists were arrested and their land was taken. We must do the same. Those who know the psychology of the Macedonian peasant know that he is fighting for blood revenge against the colonists."[151] Šatorov's defiant stand was overlooked for the sake of maintaining a semblance of leadership authority in Macedonia. Newly elected to the KPJ CC at the Fifth Conference, Šatorov in fact succeeded in keeping up the KPJ's pre-Tito line in Macedonia, the line predicated on the breakup of Yugoslavia.

Most Macedonians welcomed the Axis occupation and dismemberment of Yugoslavia in April 1941 and Bulgaria's acquisition of most of Vardar Macedonia, but their enthusiasm waned as the Bulgarians displayed their own supremacist ambitions. Initially, at least, Šatorov's sense of Macedonian affinities was proved accurate. Moreover, accepting the new territorial arrangements, Šatorov saw no reason to maintain his ties with the KPJ. He therefore submitted his Regional Committee to the BRP. The jurisdictional dispute that en-

150. The substance of Šatorov's position was expressed in "Rezolucija na Pokrainskata konferencija od KPJ vo Makedonija," *Proleter* 15, nos. 9–11 (1940): 19–21. For Šatorov's debate at the Fifth Land Conference see Pero Damjanović, Milovan Bosić, and Dragica Lazarević, eds., *Peta zemaljska konferencija KPJ (19–23. oktobar 1940)* (Belgrade, 1980), pp. 210–11. For an analysis of his positions see Slavka Fidanova, "Neke specifičnosti pri stvaranju Narodnog fronta u Makedoniji u vreme održavanja Pete zemaljske konferencije KPJ," in Zlatko Čepo and Ivan Jelić, eds., *Peta zemaljska konferencija Komunističke partije Jugoslavije: Zbornik radova* (Zagreb, 1972), pp. 283–85.

151. Damjanović et al., *Peta zemaljska,* p. 210.

sued involved the two Communist parties in an argument over the future Balkan state frontiers and over the most promising insurrectionary tactics. For its own reasons, not wishing to challenge the frontiers of Allied countries, the Comintern decided in favor of the KPJ. Šatorov was expelled from the KPJ and forced into Bulgaria, where the BRP welcomed him into its leadership.[152]

Tito's victory over Šatorov in 1941 did nothing to bolster the KPJ in Macedonia. The Partisan movement lay dormant there throughout much of the war, while the contention between the pro-Yugoslav and pro-Bulgarian Macedonians continued unabated, with Lazar Koliševski at the head of the KPJ loyalists. The KPJ ultimately prevailed, though with considerable difficulties, and Vardar Macedonia became one of Yugoslavia's federal republics in 1946. With the Cominform Resolution, the issues that separated the two groups were clad in new garments. Newly communized Bulgaria, a defeated country that took second place to Yugoslavia in the Communist Balkans, despite the personal prestige of Georgi Dimitrov, was instantly relieved of Yugoslavia's regional tutelage and vindicated in its resentment of the KPJ. The question of Macedonia was conspicuous in the passionate polemics between Belgrade and Sofia after 1948. Before the Resolution, Sofia was obliged to accept Belgrade's thesis that the Macedonians were a separate nationality. After the Resolution, the BRP, in stages, insisted on the Great Serbian character of Titoism, giving its anti-Tito propaganda a decisively nationalistic turn. While loyalty to the USSR and Stalin was important in all Cominformist cases, Macedonian Cominformism depended above all on a positive attitude toward Bulgaria.

If the incidence of Cominformism in Macedonia was less striking than might be expected, it was largely because the KPJ had already removed most of the Bulgarophile elements from Macedonia's party organization, which was on the whole a very youthful one even by KPJ standards.[153] Nevertheless, the cases of a few vacilating veterans

152. Nissan Oren, *Bulgarian Communism: The Road to Power, 1934–1944* (New York, 1971), pp. 190–94. Cf. Lazar Mojsov, *Bugarska radnička partija (komunista) i makedonsko nacionalno pitanje* (Belgrade, 1948), pp. 53–114.

153. Paul Shoup, *Communism and the Yugoslav National Question* (New York, 1968), pp. 174–75. Cf. Palmer and King, *Yugoslav Communism*, p. 127. Speaking from the podium of the First Congress of the Communist Party of Macedonia in late December 1948, Vidoe Smilevski, the organizational secretary who was much resisted by the Macedonian national Communists because he spent most of his party career in Serbia, noted that

who sided with the Resolution illustrate the continuity of nationality allegiances that determined Macedonian Cominformism.

The Cominformism of Bane Andreev, described in the 1940s as "the oldest living Communist in Macedonia who retained his party position until the Fifth Congress [of the KPJ in 1948]," is the best example of political-generational divisions that troubled the Macedonian party throughout the 1940s.[154] Andreev joined the KPJ in his native Veles in 1923 and served as a member of the Veles committee of SKOJ from 1924. He was arrested in the same Communist group with Aleksandar Ranković, shortly after the beginning of the royal dictatorship in 1929, and served at least five years in Mitrovica and Lepoglava prisons. His relations with the imprisoned Croat nationalists were friendly, at least sufficiently so for him to be committed for one month's solitary confinement for attempting to smuggle food to Juco Rukavina, one of the imprisoned Ustaša leaders.[155]

Andreev's rise in the KPJ began in 1935, when he became secretary of the KPJ Skopje district (okrug) committee. Introduced to the Macedonian Regional Committee in 1937, he went along in 1941 with Šatorov's decision to submit the Macedonian party organization to the BRP. Nevertheless, once the Comintern confirmed the KPJ's authority in Macedonia, Andreev was included in the new five-member Regional Committee, which Dragan Pavlović, Tito's field representative, entrusted to Koliševski in mid-September 1941. Despite his association with Šatorov, Andreev was regarded as conciliatory toward the KPJ, perhaps because of his Mitrovica record. With Koliševski's

---

Macedonian Cominformists "did not sincerely apprehend their bad past and failed to mend their ways. Overestimating their abilities, morbidly ambitious, these people looked with envy and hatred at the young, healthy, and trusted party and state functionaries": Smilevski, "Organizacionen izveštaj," in *I Kongres na Komunističkata partija na Makedonija: Izveštai i rezolucii* (Skopje, 1949), p. 198. It is certain that the autonomist veterans were unable to countenance the new cadres schooled in loyalty to a united Yugoslavia. This is not to say that the Resolution did not attract some following among the Communist youth of Macedonia. A group of student Cominformists was arrested at the University of Skopje in November 1948 (HIA-TC, interview no. 22, p. 3). Nevertheless, the struggle over the Resolution in the Macedonian KPJ leadership did assume generational contours, a result of a clash between two traditions: one older, autonomist, and anti-Belgrade, the other imposed toward the end of the war by KPJ representatives and predicated on Tito's slogan "Free Macedonia in Free Yugoslavia," with the stress on the preposition.

154. HIA-TC, Biographies: Andrejev Bane, p. 1. Andreev was born in 1905.

155. Nikola Rubčić, ed., *Robija: Zapisi hrvatskih narodnih boraca* (Zagreb, 1936), p. 43.

arrest on November 7, 1941, Andreev became the party's political secretary for Macedonia. But contrary to the KPJ's expectations, Tito's grip in Macedonia steadily weakened during Andreev's brief five-month tenure.

Andreev was the top Macedonian KPJ official until March 1942. During this period, it is said that he was under the influence of Bojan Bəlgaranov, the BRP emissary in Skopje. The extent of this influence is difficult to determine, although Andreev certainly pursued policies that reflected the views of Bulgarian Communists. He resisted the KPJ's strategy of destabilizing Bulgaria's control of Macedonia by means of partisan war, a strategy the BRP found inappropriate. In late 1941 he disbanded the Prilep Partisan detachment after its poor combat performance. Most important, he avoided all references to Yugoslavia in party publications, preferring to sign declarations in the name of nebulous aggregates—"a group of Macedonians," "honest Macedonians," and the like.[156] According to Svetozar Vukmanović-Tempo. "The leadership after Šarlo [Šatorov] was for the KPJ in words, but actually it threw out the 'J' from the KPJ."[157]

The pressure exerted on Andreev by the KPJ CC and the pro-Tito elements in the Macedonian leadership, some of them veterans of the Communist student movements in Belgrade and Zagreb or from the families of such activists, made Andreev's position untenable.[158] He

156. Mihailo Apostolski et al., eds., *Izvori za osvoboditelnata vojna i revolucija vo Makedonija, 1941–1945*, vol. 1, pt. 1, *Dokumenti na pokrainskiot komitet na Komunističkata partija na Jugoslavija za Makedonija (6 april 1941–22 noemvri 1942)* (Skopje, 1968), pp. 71, 74.

157. Ibid., pt. 3, *Dokumenti na Centralniot komitet na Komunističkata partija na Makedonija* (Skopje, 1970), p. 76.

158. Borko Talevski (1921–1942), a member of the regional committee and a former medical student at Belgrade University, and his wife, Vera Aceva (b. 1919), denounced Andreev to the KPJ CC, claiming that Andreev maintained that the Partisan struggle in Macedonia could not proceed while the masses still had illusions about the liberating role of the Bulgarian authorities (ibid., pt. 1, p. 294). Aceva also held that Andreev was under the influence of Bulgarophile nationalists within IMRO (ibid., p. 190). Mirče Acev (1915–1943), Aceva's brother, another committeeman and a former student activist, criticized Andreev's reluctance to mention Yugoslavia in party documents (ibid., p. 258). Finally, Ljupčo Arsov (b. 1910), a veteran of the Zagreb student movement, denounced Andreev's "divisive stand toward the KPJ CC" (ibid., p. 186). Andreev's legal status in 1941–1942 was also questioned. Although he was arrested briefly by the Germans in 1941, Andreev was not molested by the Bulgarians until 1943, thanks to the protection extended by Jordan Čkatrov and Kosta Cipušev, two active IMRO operatives, the latter an associate of Andreev and the other a Communist from the Mitrovica prison days. Dobrivoje Radosavljević, a KPJ CC emissary in Macedonia, not without reason viewed Andreev's unusual status as "slightly strange, perhaps a unique case in [occupied] Europe, and not only among us"

was deposed by his pro-Tito rivals at the end of March 1942. The new leadership (Provisional Regional Committee), which was duly confirmed by the KPJ CC, did not even include him among its members. Nevertheless, if the changes were meant to widen the KPJ's influence among the Macedonians or to prompt effective partisan warfare, they proved wholly inadequate. Despite Sofia's ill-managed performance, the Macedonians—most Macedonian Communists included—had yet to be lured to Yugoslavia.

Convinced that "autonomism" was the chief source of continued difficulties in Macedonia, in February 1943 Tito dispatched Svetozar Vukmanović-Tempo to bring the Skopje organization into submission.[159] Vukmanović at once began to set the standard autonomist conventions against the autonomist essence of Macedonian aspirations. In a letter to the Macedonian party organization of February 28, 1943, he announced the decision of the KPJ CC "to give autonomy to [the Macedonian Communists] through the establishment of the Macedonian Communist party within the KPJ and under its political control."[160] The central committee of the new party, headed by the imprisoned Koliševski, included Andreev among the committee's five voting members.

The choice of Andreev for the new CC and his subsequent appointment as political commissar at the Partisans' Macedonian headquarters demonstrates his continued influence among the old party cadres and Vukmanović's confidence that the situation in Macedonia was firmly under control. But in Vukmanović's enthusiasm "to gather all

---

(ibid., p. 362). The case was uncommon in that Andreev remained an active party leader. Well-known Communists—indeed, famous ones—occasionally were left alone in Hitler's *Festung Europa,* provided they remained passive. It is not known whether Andreev reciprocated Ckatrov's solicitude after the war. In any case, the IMRO leader was tried and executed only in 1949, after the Resolution and Andreev's own fall. Cipušev emigrated to Bulgaria after the war.

159. In a letter dated January 16, 1943, to the Macedonian organizations, Tito criticized the Macedonian Communists' "liberal" stand toward organizational and national autonomism and warned that "the 'question' of Yugoslavia can no longer be viewed as the *question of the regime* of [interwar] Yugoslavia": *Zbornik dokumenata i podataka o narodnooslobodilačkom ratu jugoslovenskih naroda,* vol. 5, pt. 1, *Borbe u Makedoniji* (Belgrade, 1952), pp. 173–82.

160. Apostolski et al., *Izvori,* vol. 1, pt. 2, *Dokumenti na Pokrainskiot komitet na Komunističkata partija na Jugoslavija za Makedonija i na Centralniot komitet na Komunističkata partija na Makedonija (25 noemvri 1942—3 noemvri 1943)* (Skopje, 1968), p. 113.

Communists in Macedonia," he underestimated the residual suspicion of Yugoslavia.[161] Moreover, Macedonian fears of Serbian supremacy under the guise of Yugoslavism were so profound that even the KPJ CC's legates occasionally adopted autonomist language in order to gain acceptance. The manifesto of the Macedonian CC (June 1943), written by Dobrivoje Radosavljević, a Serbian Communist and Tito's emissary, advocated the unification of all Macedonia with no mention of Yugoslavia, an omission that provoked sharp criticism at Tito's supreme staff.[162] On the other hand, many Macedonians, especially those with Bulgarian affiliations, were not firmly persuaded that Yugoslavia, rather than Bulgaria, was naturally preordained to unify the Macedonians.[163] Their aspirations constrained by Tito's

161. Recently, when asked why Vukmanović included Andreev in the new Macedonian CC, Vera Aceva replied: "It's difficult to answer that question. Besides, this is an unpleasant subject, because Bane [Andreev] is a tragic figure. He landed in jail as a youth and spent more than ten years in prison. Imprisonment left its marks on him; he was somehow muddleheaded. When they appointed him secretary [in 1941], he hesitated, and accepted the post unwillingly. Allow me a small digression: When Tempo [Vukmanović] came and wrote that letter about the forming of the Communist party of Macedonia and the CC, certain objections to his estimates were raised. But Tempo said, 'Comrades, this is no time for discussions. My estimates are based on the information I received!' Tempo wanted to gather all Communists in Macedonia": Darko Stuparić, *Revolucionari i bez funkcija* (Rijeka, 1975), pp. 241–42.

162. The manifesto called for the "realization of the centuries-old ideals of the Macedonian people: *national liberty, equality, and fraternal cooperation with all the Balkan peoples,*" and invoked the right of the Macedonians "*to determine their destiny by [themselves] and to create full people's democratic power in Macedonia.*" It ended with a salute to the Red Army and J. V. Stalin, and to the "fraternal national liberation armies of Yugoslavia, Albania, and Greece," as well as to the Fatherland Front and "the insurgent companies of the fraternal Bulgarian people": *Zbornik dokumenata,* vol. 7, pt. 1, pp. 264–71, 336, 382–83. Readers were left with the unmistakable impression that the cited Balkan states were on an equal footing with Macedonia. There was no mention of Tito or the KPJ.

163. This question was pointedly asked at the BRP regional conference in Gorna Džumaja (now Blagoevgrad, regional center of Pirin [Bulgarian] Macedonia) by Vladimir Poptomov, a veteran Communist from Pirin Macedonia, political secretary of the Communist-front organization IMRO United (1925–1933), an AVNOJ councilman at the Jajce session (1943), who became a member of the BRP Politburo in 1944: "Many [Bulgarians] are asking why the Gorna Džumaja district [Pirin Macedonia] should be united with Macedonia in Yugoslavia rather than the other way around. And why aren't the Caribrod and Bosilegrad districts [non-Macedonian areas of Bulgaria which were allotted to Yugoslavia after World War I] returned to them, while Macedonia is being demanded?" Poptomov also stated that the Macedonian nation was free of national oppression in Fatherland Front–governed Bulgaria and that the question of unification with Vardar Macedonia inside Yugoslavia was not being raised in Bulgarian Macedonia. Moreover, the Bulgarians were completely unprepared for such a step. See Apostolski et al., *Izvori,* vol. 1, pt. 3, p. 443.

increasing successes in Macedonia, they used the Cominform Resolution to mount a counterattack.

Bane Andreev's case was typical of the 1948 attempts to revise the Yugoslav solution to the Macedonian question. Andreev's autonomist past, though useful for Vukmanović's base-building efforts in 1943, became a liability after the war. At the KPJ's Fifth Congress he was not included among the six Macedonians—all with solid pro-Tito records—who were selected for the sixty-three member KPJ CC.[164] Though he had been a party member since 1923 and was "more popular than Koliševski among the old party members," Andreev was relegated to the status of a CC candidate member along with four other Macedonians, all of whom had joined the KPJ only in 1940. This was "actually more than a degradation for him: younger members whom he introduced to communism entered the membership of the KPJ CC."[165]

At the First Congress of the KPJ's Macedonian branch in late December 1948, Andreev was elected to the forty-five-member CC, but not to the Politburo.[166] Rumors of his covert Cominformism soon followed. He denied them in *Borba* on June 16, 1949, stating that he was "taught to love and trust the USSR. . . . That is why the unjustified attacks against our country and Party seriously disturbed me and even confused me, and brought me to take certain steps that were at odds with the firmness, discipline, and dedication of a KPJ member."[167] Despite this disclaimer, he soon developed contacts with the *ibeovci* and was then arrested. Nevertheless, because Andreev's identification with Bulgaria was somewhat conditional, he was not so ready-made a symbol of Cominformist tribulations in Macedonia as some other *ibeovci* there.[168]

164. "Izabran je Centralni komitet Komunističke partije Jugoslavije i Centralna reviziona komisija," *Borba*, July 30, 1948, pp. 1–2.

165. HIA-TC, Biographies: Andrejev Bane, p. 2.

166. Izabran je Centralni komitet Komunističke partije Makedonije," *Borba*, Dec. 25, 1948, p. 1.

167. "Izjava Bana Andrejeva," *Borba*, June 16, 1949, p. 1.

168. Similarly, there was no clear case against Vera Aceva and Ljupčo Arsov, who supposedly were attracted to the Resolution, and Cvetko Uzunovski, who is said to have been dropped from the Macedonian CC because of his Bulgarophile Cominformism (Palmer and King, *Yugoslav Communism*, p. 230, n. 36). Neither Aceva nor Arsov was ever subjected to any known sanctions, and Uzunovski, as Koliševski's brother-in-law, received his share of Cominformist abuse after the Resolution. In any case, none of the three was a suitable symbol for Cominformist agitation; their party records were decidedly Titoist.

Lazar Sokolov (b. 1914) and Pavel Šatev (1882–1952), both of whom were arrested after the Resolution, were far more firmly identified with Bulgarophile autonomism than Andreev. Sokolov joined the SKOJ in 1933 and became a student activist at Zagreb University; he was secretary of the Macedonian student club Vardar. Later, his activities in the Communist-sponsored Macedonian National Movement (MANAPO) in 1936–1938 led to his dismissal from his post as lecturer at the University of Belgrade.[169] He joined the KPJ in 1941, and in late 1943, as a member of the Action Committee of the National Liberation Front for Macedonia, he signed a letter protesting the decision of the headquarters staff to pursue the unification of all Macedonia within Yugoslavia—a decision declared to be inappropriate, as Macedonia could be united only within the framework of a Balkan federation.[170]

Šatev, a veteran Macedonian national revolutionary, was a member of the famous Salonika Gemidžii (Sailors) group, which initiated a terror campaign against the Turks and their Western allies in the wake of the Ilinden Uprising of 1903. (Šatev set the French steamship *Guadalquivir* aflame in Salonika harbor on April 28, 1903.)[171] After exile in Fezzan, Libya, he returned to Bulgaria, where he practiced law and served as editor of a Communist-sponsored "IMRO-United" newspaper.[172] For a brief period after World War II he was minister of justice in the Macedonian republic.[173]

Among the other notable Macedonian *ibeovci,* the most important was the poet Venko Markovski (1915–1988).[174] Markovski's "un-

169. Apostolski et al., *Izvori,* vol. 1, pt. 3, p. 483.
170. Palmer and King, *Yugoslav Communism,* p. 84. Sokolov has been fully rehabilitated and subsequently has headed the Economic Institute in Skopje.
171. Mercia MacDermott, *Freedom or Death: The Life of Gotsé Delchev* (London, 1978), pp. 305, 352–56. Cf. Pavel Šatev, *V Makedonija pod robstvo,* 2d ed. (Sofia, 1968).
172. Apostolski et al., *Izvori,* vol. 1, pt. 3, p. 490.
173. Shoup, *Communism,* p. 174. n. 95.
174. Venko Markovski was the pseudonym of Veniamin Tošev. Other prominent Macedonian Cominformists included Mire Anastasov, a foreign service and Labor Ministry official in Skopje; Panko Brašnarov, a veteran Communist from Veles and commissioner for information of the Antifascist Council of People's Liberation of Macedonia (ASNOM); Boris Gonev, secretary of the KPJ committee in Veles in 1940–1941, delegate to the Fifth Land Conference of the KPJ, and deputy political commissar of a Partisan battalion; Trajko Miškovski, a party leader in Veles and a graduate of Moscow's Communist University of Western National Minorities (KUNMZ), active in Czechoslovakia and loyalist Spain; Rizo Rizov, an IMRO veteran of Delčev's generation; and several trade union officials, among them Blagoj Arizankov, Angele Petkovski, and Koce Zlatev. On the arrests of Miškovski and the Macedonian trade union officials, see Vardarski, "Makedonski sindikati pod terorom UDB-e," *Nova borba,* April 2, 1949, p. 4.

usual fate" (*izključitelna sədba*)[175] was archtypical of Macedonian divisions precisely because his redoubtable communism, Macedonian autonomism, and later Bulgar patriotism were expressed mainly in his verse, which occasionally was more intense than poetic. The Skopje-born "greatest Macedonian poet," as Šatorov called him in 1941—Il'ia Ehrenburg referred to him in 1950 as "simultaneously the Lomonosov and Maiakovskii of Macedonia"—emigrated to Bulgaria after King Aleksandar instituted his royal dictatorship. He spent time in Bulgarian prisons and, after 1941, in concentration camps. In September 1943 he returned to Macedonia and joined the Partisans. Meanwhile, he managed to write several poetic cycles, including *Partizani* (Partisans) and *Robii* (Imprisonments), in which he glorified communism, Partisan struggle, and even Tito.[176] But his principal loyalty was to the BRP, the she-eagle (*orlicata*) of his wartime poem.

175. Pantelej Zarev, ed., *Istorija na bəlgarskata literatura*, vol. 4, *Bəlgarskata literatura ot kraja na pərvata svetovna vojna do Deveti septevri 1944 godina* (Sofia, 1976), p. 662.

176. Curiously, in the prologue to *Partizani* Markovski denounced Šatorov as *zlovešt* (ill-boding). On Markovski's wartime poetry see Dimitar Mitrev, "Za temata na Narodnoosloboditelnata borba vo makedonskata literatura," In Dimitar Mitrev and Aleksandar Spasov, eds., *Borba i literatura: Zbornik od esei i statii* (Skopje, 1961), pp. 31–67. Mitrev recognizes Markovski's literary merits but also points out his stereotyped approach to his heroes. Among Markovski's less successful agitational verses, Mitrev singled out the following section from *Robii*, in which Markovski describes the room of a student militant:

> In the center is an old three-legged stool
> the bed is of pine boards
> next to the window a small table
> on the table arranged books,
> from the left side lies
> *Anti-Dühring* and *Das Kapital,*
> *The Marxist Struggle,*
> *General Theory of Art*
> by Todor Pavlov
> and some foreign-language translations
> from Russian and French.
> From the right: *On Macedonian Affairs*
> by Krsto Misirkov
> and a large-format collection
> by the Miladinov brothers,
> and the still-open volume
> *The National Question*
> by Joseph Stalin.

The reference to Pavlov, a Macedonian who was always Markovski's literary taskmaster, is characteristic. So is the mention of Misirkov's *Za makedonckite raboti* (On Macedonian affairs, published in Sofia in 1903). Misirkov argued for a Macedonian "national separatism" but still considered the Macedonian question part of a larger Bulgar whole, if only for linguistic reasons. The reference to Misirkov testifies to Markovski's autonomist position. He continued to write verses in the south Skopje-Veles dialect of central Macedonia.

Markovski's great prestige as a poet made possible his considerable political role in postwar Yugoslavia. He was a deputy in Yugoslavia's federal assembly (in the Macedonian assembly, too) and at one point was a candidate for the post of Tito's secretary. But he would not conceal his Bulgar national sentiment; he argued that Macedonian identity was but a Bulgar regionalism. Citing an exchange between his mother and Vukmanović-Tempo, a Montenegrin, Markovski declared that Vukmanović "was a Montenegrin, but a Serb. I am a Macedonian, but a [Bulgar]." He opposed the widely practiced oversight of Macedonians who did not hide their Bulgar identity and denounced the privileged position of Serb settlers in Macedonia.[177] Most important, he ran afoul of Milovan Djilas, especially on the question of Macedonian linguistic standardization, which Markovski favored, but not in a way that would create a chasm between standard Macedonian and Bulgarian. At a conference to discuss the Macedonian language, orthography, and alphabet, he opposed the notion that the preferred forms had to be close to the Serbian standard, and earned the reputation of a " 'Bulgarophile,' because his proposal supposedly included Bulgarian linguistic elements." In 1946, his play *Za rodniot kat* (On the native corner) was performed in Skopje, but was quickly banned. According to a Cominformist source, the play addressed the "crimes of the Great Bulgarian as well as the Great Serbian fascists against the Macedonian people and was proscribed only because it did not fail to cite the crimes of the Serbian fascists."[178]

The Resolution found Markovski out of commission. He languished with tuberculosis throughout 1948, but afterward, in the Agitprop, he openly confronted Djilas over the propriety of the increasingly anti-Stalin trend in Yugoslav propaganda. On the sly, however, he passed his satires of Tito, Kardelj, Djilas, Koliševski, and other Yugoslav leaders, mainly Macedonians, to Marko Temnialov, Bulgaria's ambassador to Belgrade.[179] Arrested as a Cominformist in 1949, Markovski and his family were held in the Skopje prison until 1951, though the Yugoslav authorities denied that Markovski was being repressed.[180]

In view of his experiences, Markovski's loyalty to the Soviet Union

177. Venko Markovski, *Goli Otok, the Island of Death: A Diary in Letters* (Boulder, Colo., 1984), pp. 124, 51, 47.

178. Pirin, "Vo zaštita na Venko Markovski," *Napred*, Oct. 10, 1950, p. 3.

179. Markovski, *Goli Otok*, p. 2.

180. "Povodom klevetničkog pisanja bugarske štampe o 'teroru' nad makedonskim pesnikom Venkom Markovskim," *Borba*, April 12, 1950, p. 3.

was tested severely by Khrushchev's overtures to Yugoslavia. Markovski's protest—the poem *Savremeni paradoksi* (Contemporary paradoxes), published illegally in Yugoslavia in August 1955, two months after Khrushchev's visit to Yugoslavia—was directed against Tito. For Markovski, however, Khrushchev was the greater danger. "This wretch of a man precipitated the greatest schism in the history of international communism. . . . Among other things, he forced other Communist parties to pay homage to Belgrade and apologize to the blood-stained, demonic Tito."[181] Betrayed to the authorities by a turncoat Cominformist, Markovski was sentenced to five years in prison, this time at the camp of Goli Otok, previously reserved for the *ibeovci*.[182] In 1966 he "again emigrated to Bulgaria, ever searching for a shelter for an unsatisfied patriotic idea, for an unbroken Communist loyalty." The same source elliptically credits him with "polemics against those who attack the Soviet Union and the Bulgarian Communist party."[183]

Markovski never concealed his disdain for Belgrade and the notion that the Macedonians were outside the Bulgar nation. During the last decade of his life he was at the center of Cominformist activities in Sofia, playing the role of the flame-keeper of unredeemed Macedonia. Markovski wrote poems glorifying figures of the Macedonian and Bulgarian past "who safeguarded Bulgar nationhood" (Kliment Ohridski, Bogomil, Tsar Samuil, Hristo Botev) and more recent Macedonian heroes (Goce Delčev, Jane Sandanski). Despite protests from Belgrade, he was entrenched in Sofia. He seemed to be confident that the USSR would support Bulgaria in the dispute over Macedonia. During one of the periodic Belgrade–Sofia flare-ups he wrote a poem that—in the unmistakable Maiakovskii style—includes the following stanza:

Moskva i Sofija
        kəm slənce ustremeni,
                pod stjag na Lenina
                    prostirat
                        novi
                          dni!

181. Markovski, *Goli Otok*, p. 25.
182. His experiences there are the subject of his *Goli Otok* letters, cited above, which to date have been published only in the United States.
183. Zarev, *Istorija*, p. 662. Another of his poems, "Svet zemli," which glorifies Moscow as the "light of the world," was published in Moscow's *Pravda*, Oct. 7, 1983, p. 3.

Moscow and Sofia
                    directed toward the Sun,
                              under the banner of Lenin
                                        extend
                                           new
                                             days![184]

"Pain from the injustices committed against Bulgaria"—Markovski's principal inspiration, according to a Bulgarian critic[185]—prompted Sofia's campaign against Belgrade after the Resolution. For a while the Bulgarian and Macedonian Cominformist sources continued to recognize the "powerful movement among Macedonians for the right to form a separate Macedonian nation . . . [which] was most actively supported by the Bulgarian Communist party and all progressive people, for whom a Macedonian nation appeared to be a product of historical development and at the same time a political necessity." But where the KPJ saw Macedonian separateness as a step toward the unification of all Macedonians within Yugoslavia, the Bulgarian Communists initially viewed it as a recognition of national duality within the Bulgarophone community and grasped at its potential for blocking further assimilation of Macedonia by the Serbs and Bulgars. But the Serbs, too, held that "it is in the interest of Yugoslavia and especially of the Serb cause in Macedonia that the Macedonians be treated as a separate Macedonian nation."[186] Separated from the Bulgarians, Macedonians would be Serbianized, a development the BRP could not support. Hence the Bulgarian Communists and their Macedonian Cominformist allies countered Yugoslav Macedonism with a version of their own that hinted at the

184. Venko Markovski, *Epopeja na nezabravimite* (Sofia, 1967), p. 161. One of his poems (on the Gemidžii) is dedicated to Pavel Šatev; another glorifies Macedonia's 1903 Ilinden uprising as a movement of the people of Lower Bulgaria (ibid., pp. 79–80, 104–6). In more recent years Markovski was connected with the émigré neo-Cominformist group of Mileta Perović, who was active in Western Europe. In 1918, during the celebrations of thirteen centuries of Bulgarian statehood, Markovski published a poem on Bulgarian history which attacked the recently deceased Tito and alluded to the Cominformist camp at Goli Otok. "Our sole fault," wrote Markovski, "was that we said—Moscow is right!" In March 1985, on his seventieth birthday, he was awarded the order of Hero of the People's Republic of Bulgaria.

185. Zarev, *Istorija*, p. 670.

186. Dino G. K'osev, "Titovskata 'makedonska' politika po patot na kral Aleksandar i Nikola Pašič," *Napred*, Sept. 9, 1950, p. 8.

unification of the three parts of Macedonia within a wider Balkan federation. *Napred* (Forward), the organ of the exiled Macedonian Cominformists, published in Sofia, was printed in a variant of Macedonian that was closer to Bulgarian than the one used in Skopje. The newspaper consistently glorified Macedonian national revolutionary heroes (Goce Delčev, Jane Sandanski, Nikola Karev, Dame Gruev, Kočo Racin), but always in a non-Yugoslav context.[187]

The importance that Sofia attached to its Macedonian policy is seen in the appointment of Vladimir Poptomov (1890–1952), a veteran Communist from Pirin Macedonia, as the Bulgarian foreign minister in 1949. With Poptomov, whom Tito disdainfully described as a man "who sold his [Macedonian] national consciousness for a chicken drumstick," public polemics over Macedonia reached violent proportions.[188] Despite a relatively small number of acknowledged Cominformist cases during this period, there is no reason to doubt that the Resolution created "serious problems among the Macedo-

---

187. Macedonian Cominformists denounced the efforts of Harvard's Slavicist Horace Lunt to provide a Macedonian grammar and primer as an imperialist effort "to prove 'scientifically' that Macedonian and Bulgarian are not the same. . . . The Titoists can hold on to this grammar to help them sing boogie-woogie for their masters. The Macedonian people do not need it": B., "Dolarski lingvist izgotvuvaa 'makedonska' gramatika za lakeite na dolarot," *Napred*, June 1, 1951, p. 4. Sofia adopted all Macedonian oppositionists as its own, even when there was no reason to suspect that Cominformism was at issue. An example of such conspicuous solicitude was the handling of peasant resistance to collectivization in Yugoslav Macedonia. Another was the stand on the so-called Čento Affair. Metodi Andonov-Čento (1902–1954), a very popular Prilep merchant and a member of the interwar Serbian-based Alliance of Agrarian Workers, was drawn to the Partisans in 1943. Because of his political appeal to the noncommunist majority in Macedonia and because he advocated resistance to the Bulgarians, the Communists appointed him president of the Antifascist Council of People's Liberation of Macedonia (ASNOM), Macedonia's Partisan diet. He also was a member of AVNOJ. Andonov took his responsibilities quite seriously and refused to sanction Vukmanović's meddling in Macedonian affairs. (See Vukmanović, *Revolucija,* pp. 411–12.) After the war Andonov objected to some aspects of agrarian reform and then, completely disenchanted with Belgrade's policies, attempted to flee to the West in the hope of raising the issue of a fully "independent Macedonia" at the Peace Conference in Paris. He was arrested in 1946 and sentenced as a Western agent and a covert member of IMRO. Despite this record, Andonov's case was raised after the Resolution in a BRP internal bulletin as an example of a Macedonian militant whose work was denigrated in Skopje: "Klevetnici sami sebe raskrinkavaju," *O kontrarevolucionarnoj i klevetničkoj kampanji protiv socijalističke Jugoslavije* (Belgrade, 1949–50), 1:124–25.

188. "Proslava petogodišnjice Narodne republike Makedonije," in *O kontrarevolucionarnoj i klevetničkoj kampanji,* 2:148. For an example of the intensity of the polemics, including charges that some anti-Belgrade officials in Pirin Macedonia were "fascist scum," see Dimitar Vlahov, *Iz istorije makedonskog naroda* (Belgrade, 1950), pp. 111–18. One can find similar vituperation in Bulgarian publications.

nian population."[189] But even after Stalin's death, on three occasions (1957, 1968–69, 1978) the polemics were resumed, though not so vociferously. The Resolution is of course no longer the main issue (even in 1948 it was for the most part a pretext for the expression of far more fundamental divisions), but it is still invoked.[190] As for the Macedonian question, it remains the most effective vehicle of indirect Soviet pressure on Yugoslavia. The reason is not necessarily that the USSR can readily manipulate Bulgarian foreign policy, as is usually assumed. Rather, for as long as Bulgaria remains in the Soviet bloc, Sofia's historic claims will appear far more menacing than they would if Bulgaria were nonaligned. But even without its bloc partnership, Bulgaria would not let the matter rest.

Apart from the question of Macedonia, the KPJ had to contend with a substantial incidence of Cominformism in Caribrod (Di- mitrovgrad) and Bosilegrad, two districts in eastern Serbia which were unquestionably Bulgarian in national composition. A Bulgarian anticommunist refugee who lived in Caribrod from December 1949 to September 1950 reported that during the time there were numer- ous mass flights to Bulgaria and "even the leading Communists [of Bulgar nationality] were arrested as Cominformists." To the be- wilderment of refugees from Bulgaria, who "under the influence of Cominformist propaganda believed that in coming to Yugoslavia they had already reached a land of Western democracy," their Cari- brod compatriots without exception hoped that these border areas would be returned to Bulgaria.[191] Their motives were not doctrinal, however, but nationalistic. Despite Belgrade's denials of wholesale opposition among the 64,000 Bulgarians of eastern Serbia, there were several publicized cases of Cominformist arrests on the Bulgarian frontier.[192] Even so, the Cominformism of the minority Bulgarians was far less troublesome and difficult to counter then the Comin-

---

189. Palmer and King, *Yugoslav Communism*, p. 141. Vladimir Dedijer is quite wrong in asserting that the "fewest number of individuals opted for the Informburo in Mac- edonia," since, according to his Macedonian informant, "the struggle against the In- formburo meant the struggle for the integrity of Yugoslavia": Dedijer, *Novi prilozi*, 3:453. The incidence of Cominformism was not so great in Macedonia as among the Serbs and Montenegrins, but it was proportiately higher than in Kosovo, Croatia, Bosnia-Her- cegovina, and Slovenia.

190. "Bugarska oživljava rezoluciju Informbiroa u publikaciji CK BKP," *Borba*, March 13, 1970, p. 3.

191. HIA-TC, interview no. 18, p. 1.

192. Shoup, *Communism*, pp. 137–38.

formism in the borderlands with Albania, notably Kosovo and Metohia, or Kosmet, in the acronym of the 1940s and 1950s.

No minority in interwar Yugoslavia was in such deplorable circumstances as the Albanian community (750,431 people in 1948). Subjected to intense discrimination by Serbian officials, regarded as savage, treacherous, and "antinational," the Albanians were denied all minority rights, although their distinctive character was never denied. They were systematically dispossessed and encouraged to emigrate to Albania proper or to Turkey, and their sharecropped lands were in part turned over to Serb settlers. Impoverished, forbidden the use of their language in public life and in the schools, largely illiterate, they nurtured impotent bitterness toward the Serbs and looked to their compatriots in Albania as the only source of relief.

The KPJ had no following in the Albanian minority, but in 1928 (at the Fourth Congress) the party assumed a position consistent with Albanian aspirations and its own nationality policy of the period— that is, "to support the struggle of the dismembered and oppressed Albanian people for *an independent and united Albania*."[193] Tito revised this pledge in the 1930s. At the Fifth Land Conference, which took place more than a year after the Italian invasion of Albania, Tito approved a "struggle for the liberty and equality of the Albanian minorities in Kosovo, Metohia, and the Sandžak" and he approved a direct link between the KPJ CC and the party's Kosovo district (*oblast*) committee, which previously had been under the Montenegrin party organization.[194]

The new treatment of Kosovo, three-quarters Albanian in national composition, foreshadowed its status in postwar Yugoslavia, es-

193. Moša Pijade, ed., *Istorijski arhiv Komunističke partije Jugoslavije*, vol. 2, *Kongresi i zemaljske konferencije KPJ, 1919–1937* (Belgrade, 1949), p. 163.

194. "Rezolucija V zemaljske konferencije Komunističke partije Jugoslavije," in Damjanović et al., *Peta zemaljska*, p. 238. Hence it is not true that the Fifth Land Conference upheld the line of the Fourth Congress on the ceding of Kosovo to Albania, as is often claimed by authors who have not gone to the sources and seemingly have failed to reflect on the fact that Mussolini ruled Albania in 1940. Moreover, where the conference resolution spoke of the struggle for the "equality and self-determination" of the Macedonian and Montenegrin peoples, it limited its commitment to the "liberty and equality" of the national minorities (Albanians, Hungarians, Romanians, Germans, etc.), thereby excluding the possibility of their secession from Yugoslavia. Nor did the Fifth Land Conference recognize the autonomy of Kosovo, as literature from Priština sometimes claims; the question of Kosovo's status was solved only in 1945.

pecially since 1966–1969. Nevertheless, had the Albanians been aware of this inconspicuous decision of an illegal party, they certainly would have regarded it as inadequate, a measure not calculated to permit them to join Albania, as they were determined to do. They were, however, in no position to influence the KPJ: they shunned the Communist organization as an alien "Pan-Slavic" outfit, a judgment that fitted actual conditions in Kosovo, where the KPJ's meager following consisted mainly of Serb and Montenegrin colonists. (The KPJ organization in Kosovo numbered 270 members in April 1941, only 20 of whom were Albanians;[195] the local party leaders were similarly from the ranks of Kosovo's Serb and Montenegrin minority.) As a result, Albanian national aspirations were not asserted within the KPJ.

The situation was not remedied during the war. With the partition of Yugoslavia in 1941, the Axis powers allotted most of Kosovo, all of Metohia, portions of western Macedonia, and several salients on the eastern borders of Montenegro to the Italian protectorate of Albania. This policy won them the support of most Albanians, who regarded the occupiers as liberators. According to a KPJ leader, "as a result of the occupation of Yugoslavia, the Albanian masses of this area [within Italian-sponsored Great Albania] obtained many economic advantages; it can be said that they live[d] several times better than before." But if their new status was "heaven in comparison with the oppression to which they were previously exposed," the Albanians also used it to settle accounts with the Serbs, on whom they turned with bitter fury: "They sought first of all to expel all the Slavs [Serbs and Montenegrins] from Kosovo and Metohia."[196] As a result, Partisan struggle in Kosovo and western Macedonia was largely a Serbian and to a lesser extent Macedonian effort, which attracted only a handful of Albanians. Vukmanović, who was directed to stir up rebellion in these areas, found many problems:

> Conditions for armed struggle were more unfavorable in Kosovo and Metohia than in any other area of [Yugoslavia]. The terrain was flat, surrounded by high mountains, which made maneuvering more difficult. Moreover, the situation was worsened by the hostility toward the

195. *Zbornik dokumenata*, vol. 1, pt. 19, *Borbe na Kosovu, 1941–1944* (Belgrade, 1969), pp. 55 and 37, n. 2.
196. Ibid., pp. 415–16, 510, 59.

Partisans on the part of the Albanian population, which made up three-quarters of the total population.

The occupiers succeeded in winning over the Albanian population by uniting Metohia and a part of Kosovo to Albania. They turned local power in the villages and towns over to the Albanians. The Albanian language was introduced.

The Albanian population remained suspicious toward all those who fought for the resurrection of Yugoslavia, whether it was a question of old or new Yugoslavia. In their eyes, that was less than what they received from the occupiers.

The Serbian and Montenegrin populations, however, found themselves in a position similar to that of the Albanians in old Yugoslavia. That is why they overwhelmingly joined the [Partisan] movement. But their readiness for struggle could not yield comparable results because there were so many fewer Serbs and Montenegrins than Albanians.[197]

Despite these obstacles, the KPJ did not choose to persuade the Albanians with offers of national self-determination. The "sectarianism" of the KPJ's District Committee for Kosovo, which Vukmanović criticized in August 1943, consisted not only of a most debilitating penchant for urban terror but especially of failure to seek common ground with Albanian nationalists, even the antifascist ones.[198] In addition, the KPJ perpetuated an unevenly balanced cadre policy and maintained an indignant and scornful "mass line" toward the "counterrevolutionary" attitude of the Albanian minority.[199]

197. Vukmanović, *Revolucija*, pp. 338–39.
198. *Zbornik dokumenata*, vol. 2, pt. 10, *Dokumenta Vrhovnog štaba NOVJ, 1943* (Belgrade, 1962), p. 152. Cf. ibid., pt 9, pp. 112–13. The KPJ attitude can be seen in the case of Sulejman Riza, an antifascist lawyer and head of an irredentist group that supported the struggle against both German and Yugoslav domination. When approached by the KPJ in 1943 to join the planned People's Committee for Kosovo, Riza agreed provided the committee bore the name Unity—Liberation against Yugoslav Domination. The KPJ considered Riza's group "the most positive [among the active Albanian groups], but at the same time the most dangerous for us." Riza wanted "some sort of independence right now and also [wanted] to separate Kosovo and Metohia from Yugoslavia at once." The KPJ feared this position as well as Riza's "great influence" and his contacts with the British. As a result, the KPJ did not invite Riza to the conference that formed the People's Committee for Kosovo in January 1944, "although earlier it had planned to do so" (ibid., vol. 1, pt. 19, pp. 336, 416–17).
199. KPJ wartime documents contain many examples of invective against the entire Albanian community. The manifesto issued by the KPJ's District Committee on October 1, 1941, the first after the occupation, declared that the Albanians had accepted the advice of the occupiers and their adherents among the Albanian elite, that "you will achieve your national liberty by means of arson, murder, and expulsion of the poor [Serb] colonists. You

In Croatia and Macedonia the KPJ CC imposed a united
Yugoslavia perspective on its branches only after much effort. In
direct opposition, resistance to the centralization of the Partisan
movement was never a problem in Kosovo, because its party organization did not reflect the sentiments of the predominant community
in the region. As in Croatia and Macedonia, Albanian Communists
in Kosovo recognized that the name of Yugoslavia—even in party
publications—repelled potential Albanian supporters.[200] "The Albanian masses," Vukmanović reported, "with one voice [sought] incorporation into Albania."[201] But their opinions mattered little. The
Serb-dominated KPJ District Committee for Kosovo never seriously
contemplated recognition of the region's accession to Albania. Nevertheless, since a modicum of support for Yugoslavia had to be
drummed up among the Albanians, the KPJ found the key to
Kosovo in the nascent Communist movement of old Albania. Accordingly, on November 8, 1941, the emissaries of the KPJ's Kosovo
organization helped forge several mutually estranged Marxist groups
into the Albanian Communist Party (PKSH), headed by Enver
Hoxha.[202]

The KPJ's midwifery in underground Tirana was motivated above
all by the realization that the Kosovo party committee "must work so

did all this and thereby helped fascism" (ibid., p. 20). Some months later, an internal KPJ
resolution of February 1942 assessed the most recent Albanian trends as a shift "from the
positions of counterrevolution to those of wavering" (ibid., p. 58). On the eve of the
Communist victory in Kosovo (October 1944), a KPJ manifesto listed all the Albanian anti-
Partisan actions and concluded that the Albanians had thereby "sullied [their] name and
become accomplices in the crimes committed by the occupiers and their servants against our
[Yugoslav] peoples" (ibid., p. 656). Invective reached truly epic proportions in the words of
Pavle Jovićević, the district party secretary, in November 1944: "Thousands upon thousands of Albanians have fallen and are still falling on the various fronts against the national
liberation struggle. In this fashion, the Albanian people of Kosovo and Metohia have
brought shame on their name, and in the eyes of the other peoples of Yugoslavia they are
only slightly less bad than the German people" (ibid., p. 720).

200. Ali Shukrija, secretary of the KPJ's local committee in Kosovska Mitrovica, noted
in November 1941, "The signature of our leaflet should absolutely not contain the word
'Yugoslavia,' since that way we would only lose rather than win the wide masses. Could I
instead sign with the L[ocal] C[ommittee] of the Communist Party in Kosovo and
Metohia?" (ibid., p. 28).

201. Ibid., vol. 2, pt. 10, p. 154.

202. On the KPJ's role in the formation of the PKSH, see the memoir of Dušan Mugoša,
a member of the KPJ District Committee for Kosovo and one of the two KPJ emissaries who
helped establish the Albanian party: Mugoša, *Na zadatku* (Belgrade, 1973). The official
Albanian version, which minimizes the role of the KPJ, is found in Enver Hoxha, *Kur lindi
Partia: Kujtime* (Tirana, 1981).

that the comrades in Albania take action [against the occupiers], because that would have a strong echo in the orientation of the [Kosovo] masses."203 Not surprisingly, the PKSH's organizers were soon sent to Kosovo, Metohia, and the towns of western Macedonia. But even though the PKSH attracted considerably more Albanians than the KPJ did, Hoxha's party could not abandon its claims to Kosovo and the rest of the Albanian national areas without provoking a bitter reaction from Balli kombëtar (National Front), an influential noncommunist resistance movement that the Communists courted until 1943 over the KPJ's objections.204 The PKSH apparently did not even contemplate such a concession. Its original name, the Albanian Communist Party, suggested jurisdiction over all Albanians, and in 1943 the PKSH CC not only sought to extend its command over the nascent Albanian Partisan units of Kosovo and western Macedonia but actually suggested that Metohia be turned over to the Albanian party.205 Vukmanović allowed that "these measures would indeed facilitate the mobilization of the Albanian masses," but characteristically he rejected them because "we would lose a great deal among the Serb people."206 Moreover, he soon accused the PKSH leadership "of 'unbounded chauvinism' and of 'Great Albania' aspirations" and demanded that Haxhi Lleshi's Albanian Partisans

203. *Zbornik dokumenata*, vol. 1, pt. 19, p. 41.

204. Vukmanović repeatedly accused the PKSH of taking "the opportunist stand that cooperation with Balli kombëtar must be achieved by any means, or at worst wait until differentiation is completed in [Balli's] ranks": ibid., vol. 2, pt. 10, p. 159. Cf. Vukmanović, *Revolucija*, pp. 366–67.

205. It would be interesting to trace the chronology of various changes in the PKSH's name. Despite orthographic distinctions, the term Partija Komuniste Shqiptare (Albanian Communist Party) appeared on the seal of the PKSH's Central Committee in September 1944 (*Zbornik dokumenata*, vol. 1, pt. 19, p. 640). When was the name changed to Partia Komuniste e Shqipërisë (Communist Party of Albania), a term that connotes a far smaller jurisdiction? At the PKSH's First Congress (November 8–22, 1948), the name was changed to Partia e Punës së Shqipërisë (Party of Labor of Albania), which it has retained.

206. Ibid., vol. 2, pt. 10, pp. 154–55. Cf. Vukmanović, *Revolucija*, p. 363. The PKSH occasionally used formulas that detracted from Yugoslavia's claims to Kosovo. A manifesto issued to the Albanians of Kosovo in March 1942 (signed jointly by the PKSH and the KPJ's Kosovo District Committee) exhorted the people to join their struggle "with the struggle of [their] brothers in Albania and with the struggle of the neighboring peoples of Montenegro, Serbia, and Greece." This passage, which made no mention of Yugoslavia, placed Kosovo on an equal footing with the areas it named, all of which maintained elements of statehood under the New Order (*Zbornik dokumenata*, vol. 1, pt. 19, p. 77). Several KPJ documents from Macedonia contain references to "the indecisive stand of the Albanian Partisans [of Haxhi Lleshi] toward Great Albanian reactionaries" (Apostolski et al., *Izvori*, vol. 1, pt. 2, pp. 309, 382).

either quit the Debar (Dibra) district in Macedonia or accept Yugoslav command. "Otherwise, there will be clashes in which the Communists, too, will take part."[207]

The KPJ's resistance withered the hopes for Albanian national unification under Communist auspices. The short-lived accord that the PKSH reached with Balli kombëtar on August 1–2, 1943, in Mukje, included a provision that obliged the Communists to support the establishment of "ethnic Albania," including Kosovo and Çamëria (Tsamouria in northern Greece). Hoxha, however, rejected this agreement—in part, it is thought, under pressure from the KPJ.[208] Instead, he declared that the territorial issue "will be resolved after the war by the Kosova and Çamëria population themselves, who will decide their future according to their wishes."[209] The plebiscites in fact did not take place, because after 1935 the KPJ in reality never considered ceding Kosovo.

Aside from an occasional elliptical phrase, the maintenance of the interwar border with Albania was an unspoken axiom within the KPJ. All departures from this policy, however minor, were sternly rebuffed. In October 1943 the Kosovo party organization created a special committee for Metohia, which was by party decision referred to by its Albanian name—*Rrafshë Dukagjini,* or Dukagjin Plateau. Writing on behalf of the Supreme Staff, Milovan Djilas discouraged this usage because "the term Dukagjin includes areas beyond the former frontiers of Yugoslavia," and he warned that while hostilities continued, the frontier with Albania should not become a source of friction "with the Albanian comrades."[210] This was clearly a response to the resolution of the newly created Kosovo People's Com-

207. Institute of Marxist-Leninist Studies at the CC of the Party of Labor of Albania, *History of the Party of Labor of Albania* (Tirana, 1971), p. 224. The editorial board responsible for the publication of Yugoslavia's wartime documents has claimed that Vukmanović's two letters to the PKSH leadership are not in its possession: *Zbornik dokumenata,* vol. 7, pt. 2, *Borbe u Makedoniji* (Belgrade, 1952), p. 32, nn. 2 and 6.

208. In response to the Mukje agreement, the KPJ CC sent a letter to the Albanian party leadership at "the end of summer of 1943," opposing any discussion of the transfer of Kosovo and Metohia to Albania. The KPJ claimed that minority and territorial inequities could not exist between New Yugoslavia and "democratic and anti-imperialist Albania": Vladimir Dedijer, *Jugoslovensko-albanski odnosi, 1939–1948* (Belgrade, 1949), pp. 82–83.

209. Enver, Hoxha, *Selected Works,* vol. 1, *November 1941–October 1948* (Tirana, 1974), p. 167.

210. *Zbornik dokumenata,* vol. 1, pt. 19, p. 462.

mittee, which was dominated by Albanians. In the sole departure from the KPJ line on the question of the status of Kosovo, this mass political front of the Partisan movement, at a meeting in Bujan, in prewar Albanian territory, on January 2, 1944, declared that "Kosovo and Metohia are areas that are inhabited mostly by the Albanian people, who, now as earlier, wish to unite with Albania. . . . The only way the Albanians of Kosovo and Metohia can unite with Albania is by joining the struggle of the other peoples of Yugoslavia against the occupiers and their hirelings, because this is the only way to achieve liberty, when all peoples, including the Albanians, will be able to decide their own future through the right of self-determination, up to the point of secession."[211]

Quite apart from the remote possibility that the status of Kosovo might be revised, it was not even certain that the KPJ would permit Kosovo's semi-autonomous status within Serbia. Djilas vetoed the unilateral decision of the KPJ District Committee to elevate its status to that of a regional committee (hence making itself equal to Serbia), because Kosovo was "not some special compact region." And during the same period (late April 1944), a KPJ leader in Gnjilane wanted a clarification on whether the Albanians would be treated as a minority

211. Cited in Zvonko Simić, "Kako je Kosovo dobilo autonomiju," *NIN*, May 31, 1981, p. 53. Simić notes that Ali Hadri, author of a monograph on the Partisan movement of Kosovo, failed to cite this passage in the Bujan resolution, despite his extensive treatment of the conference. More poignant, the official series of Partisan documents includes the milder manifesto of the Bujan conference, but only an excerpt from the resolution, without reference to the means by which the Kosovars would be able to unite with Albania. See *Zbornik dokumenata*, vol. 1, pt. 19, pp. 377–78.

In the wake of the Kosovo crisis of 1981, the Bujan conference has become a subject of considerable controversy. Enver Hoxha has given an extensive evaluation of this meeting, citing it as a correct and confident step and a source of great joy for the PKSH. He has contrasted it with the AVNOJ sesion at Jajce, where decisions on the integrity of Yugoslavia were reached without the participation of or consultation with Yugoslavia's Albanians, indeed without the courtesy of informing the KPJ's own committee in Kosovo and Metohia. See Hoxha, *Titistët*, pp. 106–11. Recent Yugoslav comments have focused on the location of the conference (Albania proper), the overwhelming predominance of Albanians among the participants (51 Albanians vs. 7 Serbs-Montenegrins), and the fact that some of the Albanian participants (apparently at least 10) were not Yugoslav subjects at all. The academic nature of sovereignty and citizenship under Kosovar conditions in January 1944, when there was no spot of Partisan territory on which to hold a conference, underscores the fact that Serbian claims to Kosovo are really based on the historical right of Serbia (or Yugoslavia)—one might even say its linear legitimacy—which no Kosovar assembly, Communist or otherwise, could change. See "Zloupotreba jednog ratnog dokumenta," *NIN*, Dec. 11, 1983, pp. 11–14; "Secesionistički deo dokumenta bio je ilegalan," "Ipak nije objašnjeno," and "Granice su nepovredive," ibid., Dec. 25, 1983, pp. 3–4.

after the war. In other words, the KPJ offered the Albanians an undefined place in a federated Yugoslavia in which "all peoples . . . would be free and equal," but it systematically avoided any discussion of any special minority provisions, especially if it touched on frontier and political arrangements with Albania.[212]

The overwhelming majority of Albanians understood that the KPJ's plans pointed to a diminution of their sovereignty. Although Yugoslavia's Communist leaders vowed that their nationality program differed substantially from that of the Great Serbian Chetniks, the Albanians were not impressed: "For the Albanian masses, Serbs are Serbs: enemies of Albanians, no matter what one calls them, Communists or Chetniks."[213] Except for occasional tolerance of strictly Albanian units, the Albanian people actively resisted the Partisans, and even the Albanian Partisans—"Serbian agents"—encountered increasing antagonism.[214] Albanian commanders of the Emin Duraku Partisan unit reported in April 1943 that they had to be on guard not only against the villagers but against "dogs, shepherds, and even goats."[215] Despite warnings that their response to the Partisans would be the sole standard by which their future status would be determined, the Albanians of former Yugoslavia opted for the 1941 arrangements and relied on the Germans after the capitulation of Italy.

Kosovo's resistance to Tito's forces was weakened in 1944 by Hoxha's units, which crossed into Metohia at Yugoslavia's urging. The combined operations of Yugoslav and Albanian Partisans and of the Second Bulgarian Army rid Kosovo of retreating Germans and their Albanian allies in November 1944. But the indigenous Albanian resistance managed to regroup and staged an uprising a few weeks later, and some Kosovo-Albanian Partisan units (4,000 men under the command of Shaban Polluzha) refused to participate in opera-

212. *Zbornik dokumenata,* vol. 1, pt. 19, pp. 462, 481–82, 656.
213. Ibid., p. 24.
214. According to Vukmanović, "the chauvinist hatred of the Albanians for the Serbs can be clearly seen from the fact that one of our units, which is composed of Albanians, was surrounded by more than two thousand armed Albanian peasants. The struggle lasted several hours until the Albanians [peasants] saw that this was an Albanian [Partisan] unit. When they established this, they dispersed, leaving the Italians to their own devices" (ibid., vol. 2, pt. 10, p. 153).
215. Ibid., vol. 1, pt. 19, p. 205.

tions against the insurgents.[216] Only with the introduction of martial law, direct military intervention, and much bloodshed was the rebellion suppressed by March 1945. There followed a period of slow pacification which exposed the Albanian minority to severe tests. The spirit of the times is revealed in a statement by Pavle Jovićević, secretary of the KPJ's Kosovo District Committee, in November 1944: "The Albanian people bought the continuation of their [reactionary] path . . . bloodily and with their own skin. Their blind falling into line behind various beys, their service to the occupiers, and their struggle against the People's Liberation Movement were avenged in blood. In this way the Albanian people of Kosovo and Metohia put their own future in doubt."[217]

As the war ended, the KPJ, perhaps out of sheer impatience with the stubborn Albanian resistance, unwisely made its position worse by hammering away at the centralist line. The district leaders of the party in Kosovo were solidly Serb and Montenegrin (the district party secretary, Djoko Pajković, was imported from Montenegro). At the First Congress of the Serbian party organization (to which Kosovo belonged) in May 1945, only one Albanian (Xhavid Nimani-Patrija) was elected to the forty-three-member CC. Two Montenegrins and a Serb were the other Kosovars in this forum. (Similarly, the forty-five-member Macedonian CC of December 1948 included only one Albanian.) The Serbian party organization then decided to dissolve the Kosovo District Committee, thus making the county and town committees in Kosovo directly subject to the Serbian CC, with whom they could correspond only in Serbian. This decision was too much for even the most loyal Albanian members. The entire county committee in Kosovska Mitrovica, the town committee in Vučitrn, and many individual Communists resigned from their offices and quit the party. The scandal was somewhat mitigated when a special commission of the KPJ CC, headed by Milovan Djilas, annulled the Belgrade deci-

216. Ali Hadri, *Narodnooslobodilački pokret na Kosovu, 1941–1945* (Priština, 1973), p. 388. According to Dedijer, "Tito's greatest worry at the end of the war and in the first days of peace was Kosovo." Dedijer cites the testimony of General Savo Drljević, who was sent by Tito to head the military administration of Kosovo, that the area had perhaps as many as 20,000 to 30,000 Albanian insurgents: Dedijer, *Novi prilozi,* 3:156, 159.

217. *Zbornik dokumenata,* vol. 1, pt. 19, p. 720. Tirana has claimed that the Yugoslavs liquidated 36,000 Albanians in the postwar period, under the false claim of eliminating Balli kombëtar and "war criminals": Lazri and Malo, *Dans les prisons,* p. 130.

sion and permitted special district and regional organizations in Kosovo and Vojvodina.[218] As was officially disclosed after the 1966 fall of the UDB-a directorate of Aleksandar Ranković, abuse of power by the security police was especially notable in Kosovo, which is still the most undeveloped and unschooled area of Yugoslavia.

Hoxha's Albania was in no position to assist the Albanians of Yugoslavia during the difficult postwar years. The Tirana leadership, uncertain of its status in the Communist world, was greatly hampered by the ubiquitous Belgrade advisers, who were doing all they could to impose Yugoslavia's economic and political supremacy on Albania. As for the question of Kosovo, Hoxha has claimed that his entreaties for the unification of Kosovo with Albania met with Tito's approval in the summer of 1946. The Yugoslav leader felt that the timing was still inauspicious, however, "because the Serbs would not understand us."[219] Hoxha was therefore understandably relieved when Stalin's action freed him of Yugoslavia's tutelage. In a swift display of support for the Resolution, Albania became the first Communist-governed state to denounce its treaties with Yugoslavia and the first to purge a Titoist faction from its party ranks.

The open hostility toward Belgrade—in which Tirana particularly excelled—only worsened the situation of Yugoslavia's Albanian minority and strengthened Belgrade's already pronounced tendency to view all Albanians as potentially subversive. But the break between the two countries permitted the PKSH to intercede publicly for the first time on behalf of the Albanian minority in Yugoslavia. Though

218. HIA-TC, "Centralni komitet komunisticke [sic] partije Srbije," pp. 2–3.
219. Hoxha, Titistët, p. 260. Hoxha has also claimed that earlier, in 1943, he drew Tito's attention to the fact that the KPJ insisted on the prewar frontiers in Kosovo, while simultaneously calling for revision of the prewar frontiers with Italy in Istria. Tito saw the apparent contradiction as false, because Istria had a developed revolutionary movement. But then, as Hoxha could not fail to note, the Partisan movement in Istria was not led by Italians (ibid., p. 96). Yugoslav commentators have denied that Tito ever agreed, even in principle, to cede Kosovo to Albania. According to Josip Djerdja, Yugoslavia's ambassador to Albania in 1946 and a participant in the Belgrade talks between Tito and Hoxha, the Albanian leader himself noted on that occasion that the "entrance of Albania into the Yugoslav federation was only natural and a matter that will be resolved in the near future." But Albania's efforts in that direction "would be significantly facilitated if [Tirana] could get a clearer picture of what the fate and position of the Kosovar Albanians will be in such a federation" (cited in Pero Zlatar, Gospodar zemlje orlova [Zagreb, 1984], p. 126). On Yugoslavia's policies in Albania see Nicholas C. Pano, The People's Republic of Albania (Baltimore, 1968), pp. 67–87, 91–95; Peter R. Prifti, Socialist Albania since 1944: Domestic and Foreign Developments (Cambridge, Mass., 1978), pp. 196–201; and Stefanaq Pollo and Arben Puto, eds., Histoire de l'Albanie (Roanne, 1974), pp. 307–10.

the PKSH does not acknowledge that it ever "accepted the fascist slogan of 'Great Albania,'" much of its anti-Belgrade propaganda deals with the subject of Kosovo.[220] Albania claims that its acceptance of the status quo in Kosovo was based on the PKSH's positive assessment of Yugoslavia's wartime Marxist-Leninist qualities. Since Albania never rescinded its totally negative assessment of "Yugoslav revisionism," it may be concluded that—despite the maintenance of state relations with Yugoslavia—the Albanian leadership views Belgrade's rule over a third of the Albanian nation as fundamentally illegitimate. This was certainly what the Albanians of Yugoslavia thought, and the degree of Cominformism among them and the continuous support of Hoxha's government by a significant portion of this minority must be attributed to national rather than ideological impulses.

In 1948 the KPJ had only a modest number of Albanian cadres, most of them thoroughly screened, and unpopular in their community as exponents of alien rule. These people stood behind the KPJ after the Resolution. Thus, although the Kosovo party branch "remained monolithic,"[221] its loyalty was no indication of the minority's political reliability, since at that time the Albanians were not in the majority within the KPJ's regional organization. Furthermore, a number of key Albanian KPJ leaders sided with the Resolution. They included Lieutenant Colonel Qamil Brovina-Bujku, a popular wartime youth organizer, the only Albanian in Kosovo's Regional Committee of SKOJ in 1942, and a political commissar of several Albanian Partisan units from Kosovo (Zejnel Ajdini, Bajram Curri, Emin Duraku, and the Kosovo battalion), who studied in Soviet military schools after the war; Major Faik Pruti-Telli, one-time secretary of the KPJ's committee in Djakovica; Xhelladin Hana, political commissar of several Kosovar Partisan units and later editor of *Rilindja* (Awakening), the chief Albanian-language newspaper, published in Priština;[222] Omer Çerkezi, a member of Kosovo's Regional Committee; Xhafer Vokshi, secretary of SKOJ in Kosovo from 1945 to 1949, when he escaped to

220. *History of the Party of Labor*, p. 225.
221. Stuparić, *Revolucionari*, p. 56.
222. V. Kesmanović, "Pronásledování narodnostních menšin v Jugoslavii," *Slovanský přehled* 26, no. 6 (1950): 255–56. The same Cominformist article mentions the mistreatment of the Slovak minority in Vojvodina. Michal Kardelis, one of its leaders and a Partisan veteran, supposedly was liquidated.

Albania;[223] Nexhat Agolli, a deputy minister in the government of Macedonia; and others.[224]

Owing to the profound sympathies for Albania among the Albanian Kosovars as a whole, the majority were somewhat Cominformist, but this allegiance had little to do with any significant appreciation of Albania's radical political system. Nor could it be considered a gain for the Soviets, with whom Hoxha broke as soon as they renewed their ties with Yugoslavia. It may be argued that the Albanians of Yugoslavia might have been all the more attracted to a more humane government in Tirana, provided, of course, that such a government maintained a clear distance from Belgrade. But if we may judge by the Kosovo crisis of 1981, when student demonstrations and a wave of protest forced the Yugoslav government to purge the Albanian leadership of the province and impose martial law, the Hoxhist version of Marxism-Leninism will continue to provide the language, concepts, and political culture of the Albanian national movement in Yugoslavia.[225]

Like the Kosovo Albanians, the Hungarian minority in Vojvodina and some other areas along the Drava frontier (496,492 people in 1948) became the focus of a concerted anti-Belgrade drive, spearheaded by the Budapest Communist leadership of Mátyás Rákosi after the Resolution. Although the primary theme of this drive was not irredentism, there are nevertheless indications that Budapest

223. Vokshi came from a prominent Albanian Communist family. A leader of the Kosovar émigrés in Albania, he apparently was liquidated in Hoxha's purge of the pro-Soviet group of Dali Ndreu and Liri Gega in 1956. See Zlatar, *Gospodar,* pp. 210–11.

224. Vasile Luca, "Fašistička suština Titove klike u nacionalnom pitanju," *Za socijalističku Jugoslaviju,* April 1, 1951, p. 7; Kosovac i Jašar, "Starite i novite prestaplenija na titovcite vo Kosmet," *Napred,* May 31, 1950, p. 4; P. Dragila, "Titovci istrebljuju albansku nacionalnu manjinu," *Nova borba,* June 2, 1952, p. 3. Of course, many completely innocent Albanians were repressed as Cominformists. The use of sly insinuations by Ranković's police to justify the persecution of loyal Kosovar KPJ members is described in the case of the fictional Lis ("Oak"), who stands for all the longsuffering Albanians of Yugoslavia, in the novel by Sinan Hasani, *Vetar i hrast* (Sarajevo, 1976). Hasani is a member of Yugoslavia's collective presidency for the current mandate (1984–1989). He served as president of the presidency in 1986–1987.

225. On the Kosovo crisis of 1981 see Jens Reuter, *Die Albaner in Jugoslawien* (Munich, 1982), pp. 79–101; *Mbi ngarjet në Kosovë* (Tirana, 1981); *Shtypi botëror rreth ngjarjeve në Kosovë* (Tirana, 1981); *Šta se dogadjalo na Kosovu* (Belgrade, 1981); Muhamed Kešetović, *Kontrarevolucija na Kosovu* (Belgrade, 1984); Sinan Hasani, *Kosovo: Istine i zablude* (Zagreb, 1986).

considered the possibility of a more activist territorial revisionist policy.[226] Since the Hungarian minority in Yugoslavia never accepted the truncation of "historic Hungary" in 1918 and the resulting Serbian rule, the Budapest government rightly anticipated that territorial claims on Yugoslavia might prove popular among the minority Hungarians; their attraction to the motherland surfaced periodically, most notably in 1941, after Hungary's annexation of Bačka, Baranja, Medjimurje, and Prekmurje.

The restoration of these areas to the new Belgrade administration precipitated many incidents of retribution against both the Hungarians and the large German minority that was expelled from Yugoslavia after the war. Memories of that period were still fresh, and Rákosi's championing of the Hungarian minority elicited considerable approval even among the Hungarians, who had no illusions about the record of Rákosi's government. Vojvodina thus became a relatively receptive locale for the recruitment and propaganda activities of Hungarian security organs.[227] At the same time, the Hungarian legation in Belgrade maintained contacts with some Cominformist groups, including the Subotica group of Sándor Ivános, in which Hungarians predominated.[228] The effect of this policy is difficult to establish, although a former pilot who served in the JA's base at Batajnica (northwest of Belgrade) reported that KOS, the counterintelligence service, uncovered Cominformist agents among the Hungarians in the 111th Storm Regiment. "Of all the national minorities," he noted, "it's the Hungarians who are the most dangerous."[229] The only major Cominformist among the Hungarians was István Dobos, a deputy from Vojvodina and an old party member. Dobos was a graduate of Moscow's party schools and spent many years in the USSR, where he belonged to the CPSU. Cominformist

226. An arrested Cominformist confirmed that Hungarian diplomats in Belgrade collected information on the attitudes of the Hungarian minority in Yugoslavia and on their potential reaction to Hungary's acquisition of Bačka. When asked by the prosecutor whether this constituted a territorial revisionist policy, he replied that it did. See "Sudjenje grupi špijuna u Novom Sadu: Optuženi su vršili razne špijunske poslove i sprovodili lažnu protivnarodnu propagandu," Borba, June 4, 1949, p. 4.

227. "Reč ministra unutrašnjih poslova Slobodana Penezića," Borba, Feb. 19, 1949, p. 2.

228. "Sudjenje," p. 4. The Romanian embassy, too, sought the services of Yugoslavia's minority Romanians for the distribution of Cominformist propaganda. See "Potpuno je dokazana krivica optuženih izdajnika," Borba, Sept. 6, 1950, p. 3.

229. HIA-TC, interview b.b. [PV], p. 16.

sources say that he was murdered in the Stara Gradiška penitentiary.[230]

Neither the Albanians nor the Hungarians were as troubled by the
authorities as the Russians, a minority without roots in Yugoslavia.
Mainly veterans of various anti-Bolshevik units (especially those of
Baron Wrangel), their families, and other émigrés, these Russian
Whites numbered some 20,000 people in 1948, over 65 percent of
them in Serbia. In the 1920s and 1930s, the leaders of this community, still plotting to overthrow the Soviet regime, applauded and in
some cases administered the government's anticommunist decrees,
which frequently were extended to all opposition groups. Activist
émigrés also engaged in anti-Partisan warfare and served in German
volunteer units against the Soviet army on the eastern front and in
German auxiliary units in occupied Serbia. On the whole, however,
Russian refugees in Yugoslavia were a highly skilled and peaceful lot;
they tended to mind their own affairs but retained their opinions
about bolshevism. Their children, born in Yugoslavia, were casting
off much of the older generation's rather flamboyant Russian style, or
at least the peculiarities of speech and behavior that set them apart.

Most Whites were disturbed by the victory of Bolshevik disciples in
Yugoslavia and headed for the West. Those who remained were
quickly exposed to various pressures by Soviet representatives in
Yugoslavia, who wanted to enlist their services to gather intelligence.
They were promised Soviet citizenship on petition, and many accepted this option, which gave them immunity to actual or potential
unpleasantness with Yugoslav officialdom. The Soviet reparation
commissions, which administered the processing of citizenship pa-
pers, were not meant to repatriate potentially troublesome exiles to
the USSR but simply to set up a sort of clearinghouse for Soviet
intelligence operations in the Russian community.[231]

Yugoslavia's security police undoubtedly had some inkling of the
extent of the community's entrapment but could initiate no counter-
measures before the Resolution. Shortly thereafter, the exiles became
the subject of a concentrated campaign that exactly fitted
Yugoslavia's requirements: the Soviets were depicted as master spies
and intriguers, their sole instruments the "discarded" remnants of

230. Lazri and Malo, *Dans les prisons,* pp. 34–36.
231. *White Book,* p. 40.

Russian counterrevolutionary forces—some of them said to be former royalist police agents or Gestapo operatives, or collaborators in Nazi massacres.[232]

To some extent, Belgrade seems to have believed its own propaganda, at least to the extent of mistrusting the whole Russian community as a group of spies or potential spies. The mistrust even extended to the Ukrainian (Rusyn) community that had resided in Vojvodina and northern Croatia since the times of Maria Theresia. Russians were systematically harassed and discriminated against, if only to prompt their emigration. Whether they held responsible and sensitive posts (as did Colonel Gavrichenko, a former royalist officer who continued to head the artillery school in Zagreb) or minor administrative positions, thousands of Russians were thrown out of work as unreliable elements. Many were also imprisoned.[233]

Some attempt was made to confuse the Russian *ibeovci* with ordinary spies, and they were often branded as antisocial.[234] Ideological Cominformism was not inconceivable among the former Whites, as the exiled Russian community included militant communists. Patriotism, nostalgia for the homeland, the futility of exile, Russia's obvious rise among the powers, and its wartime distress induced a change of heart among some Russian émigrés. These inducements were strongest among their children, helped along by intergenerational rivalries. The novelist Meša Selimović recalled the case of one Arkadii R., the son of a tsarist colonel, who became a Communist at the gymnasium of Tuzla. Imprisoned during the war, he taunted his Ustaša tormentors with claims that the Red Army was the best and strongest military force in the world. "The restless Arkadii was true to his nature in 1948," concludes Selimović, "and was again imprisoned."[235]

Moscow proved exceptionally sensitive to the plight of the Russian community. Certainly no Soviet note caused greater worry in Belgrade than one dated August 18, 1949, which cited Yugoslavia's conduct toward the Russian minority and warned that the Soviet

232. Ibid., pp. 120–22, 374–77. Slobodan Penezić, Serbia's minister of the interior, noted in his report to the Serbian assembly in February 1949 that "White Guard Russians, who served even the black devil, are now eager adherents of the Cominform Resolution": "Reč ministra unutrašnjih poslova," p. 2.
233. HIA-TC, interviews no. 29, p. 82; no. 12, p. 5.; no. 44, p. 4.; no. 19, p. 3.
234. *White Book,* p. 122.
235. Meša Selimović, *Sjećanja* (Belgrade, 1976), pp. 128–31.

government "will not reconcile itself to such a state of affairs and . . . will be compelled to resort to other, more effective means, indispensable for the protection of the rights and interests of Soviet citizens in Yugoslavia, and to take to task the fascist tyrants who have gone beyond all limits."[236]

236. *White Book*, p. 126.

5

Groups, Organizations, Actions

The *ibeovci* were swayed by far too many influences and interests—some historical, some factional, some nationally based, some
centralist, some autonomist and special—to develop a single movement, leadership, or program. Their only real common denominator
was that they all found some comfort in the Resolution. What they
were against was far clearer than what they were for, aside from such
generalities as socialism and workers' power. And as the generalities
were also part of the KPJ's arsenal, it was hard to claim them as a
unique program, especially since Belgrade remained strictly orthodox
well into the 1950s.

Straight Cominformist appeals based on the primacy of Moscow,
Stalin's charisma, and the unity of the world's "democratic front"
seemed less interesting than denunciations of Belgrade's sociopolitical
practices and restatements of the KPJ's Popular Front line of the
1930s, aimed now at Yugoslavia's leadership. Of course, unlike the
situation in the interwar period, openly seditious groups had absolutely no leeway under communism. *Ibeovci* might have organized
earlier, at least among party members—no one else was likely to see
the allure of an alternative Marxist-Leninist model—but they saw no
reason to do so; they certainly did not expect to be arrested. Once the
UDB-a's steamroller got moving, many of the pro-Resolution forces
were identified, and any attempt to fashion an organization became
all the more difficult.

Even with the narrowness of their appeal, however, the Cominformists seemed remarkably unimaginative in their efforts to promote
the Soviet view. From the very beginning of the crisis, they assumed

that their cause was not only theirs but above all the cause of the
USSR and the other bloc countries. This was their opinion and
Moscow's as well; they had no reason to set up an anti-Titoist Communist party of Yugoslavia. Therefore the question of the most
efficacious political and organizational course for the pro-Soviet
forces did not arise. That would have been precisely the "nationalism" that defined Tito's deviation. Despite some inconsistencies, especially when the territorial claims of Sofia, Tirana, and
Budapest were involved, Moscow directed the strategy of confrontation with the KPJ. The growing Cominformist émigré centers and the
domestic underground groups merely reflected this authority.

Fear of arrest and a desire to fight the KPJ from outside prompted
the growth of the Cominformist emigration. The first exiles found
refuge in Albania. These were mostly Montenegrin participants in the
Cominformist rebellions of the summer and autumn of 1948. Montenegrins also provided the first émigré leaders, among them Radonja
Golubović, Yugoslavia's ambassador to Romania. But even though
several leading figures responded to the Soviet beckoning by attempting to flee to the bloc countries (Arso Jovanović and his group), the
flight could not be organized in any massive or systematic way; key
Cominformists continued to trickle across the borders, but most escape attempts failed or were too difficult to contemplate. As a result,
the overwhelming majority of émigré Cominformists were persons
who were outside Yugoslavia at the beginning of the conflict. Besides
Golubović, they included a number of diplomats, most notably
Slobodan-Lale Ivanović, press attaché in Washington; Lazar
Brankov, consul at the legation in Budapest and chargé in the absence
of Ambassador Mrazović; Colonel Slobodan Ćekić, military attaché
in Stockholm; and Momčilo Ješić, an official at the embassy in Oslo.

The contests between Titoists and Stalinists, common in most of
Yugoslavia's legations, were well matched, since the Cominformists
were not at a disadvantage on foreign soil. Occasionally, as in Washington, Ottawa, and Cairo, they almost succeeded in driving the KPJ
loyalists out of the embassy compounds.[1] The defection of mostly
lower-echelon diplomatic officers left the KPJ leadership unper-
turbed, though press campaigns were carried out to discredit the

---

1. Bože Šimleša, "Sve Vuletićeve alke," *Start*, Aug. 23, 1978, p. 43; Boro Krivokapić,
"Srdja Prica: Sasvim lično," *NIN*, Sept. 9, 1979, p. 32.

deserters as unworthy or hostile elements who had been appointed too carelessly.[2] There was concern, however, when a large number of hand-picked students sent to study various military and technical subjects in the bloc countries, primarily in the USSR and Czechoslovakia, refused to return home. These trainees, 475 of whom were highly visible in various activities in the bloc capitals, made up the bulk of the émigré *ibeovci*.[3] Their allegiance had been cultivated by their hosts well before the Resolution.

According to Belgrade sources, the entire Cominformist emigration numbered 4,928 persons, of whom some 2,400 fled abroad after the Resolution, most of them Serbs (1,120) and Bulgars (1,060).[4] They were divided into three distinct groups—propagandistic, military, and activist—depending on the sector (*liniia*) of work assigned to individual émigrés. By its nature, propaganda work received the most public attention. Following Lenin's dictum on the overriding importance of the revolutionary press, the Soviets and their bloc partners encouraged and assisted the establishment of a Cominformist press, but in the absence of a central organization, there was no central organ. Belgrade tried to make light of their efforts by saying that the émigrés were printing "four sheets for two hundred Trotskyists," but the roster of exile newspapers climbed to eight biweeklies, all intended primarily for clandestine distribution in Yugoslavia.

The first voice of the Cominformist emigration was *Nova borba*

2. All the notable Cominformist defectors were denounced as hitherto unsuspected traitors. Slobodan-Lale Ivanović was called the "personal secretary of the kulak leader Dragoljub Jovanović," head of the Serbian left agrarians, who was arrested in 1947 after the KPJ decided to abolish all parliamentary opposition. Ivanović was also denounced as a persecutor of Communists in Kosovska Mitrovica early in Nedić's collaborationist regime: "Pravo lice jednog izdajnika i špijuna," *Borba*, Dec. 9, 1948, p. 2. Lazar Brankov was accused of working for the Hungarian police organs in occupied Bačka: "Agent-provokator i špijun Brankov—glavni svedok na budimpeštanskom procesu," *Borba*, Sept. 22, 1949, p. 2. Ratomir Andrić and Momčilo Ješić were described as accomplices of the Chetniks, and several others as immoral, dissolute, and cowardly characters: "Četnički jatak—junak Informbiroa," *Borba*, Aug. 7, 1949, p. 4; "'Revolucionari' i 'patrioti' koje brani sovjetska nota," *Borba*, June 15, 1949, p. 3. Vladimir Dedijer has suggested that this was a propaganda tactic. When he challenged the notion that Ivanović was an agent during the war, he was told "by a responsible comrade not to create problems for the UDB-a, which is fighting a life-and-death battle": Vladimir Dedijer, *Novi prilozi za biografiju Josipa Broza Tita*, vol. 3 (Belgrade, 1984), pp. 481–82.

3. The names of the 475 activists are listed in HIA-TC, "Vijesti iz Jugoslavije: Jugoslovenska kominformisticka [*sic*] emigracija," pp. 1–3. The list was compiled in July 1950.

4. Dragan Marković, *Istina o Golom otoku* (Belgrade, 1987), pp. 56, 59.

(New struggle), issued in Prague. Its name underscored the émigré
tenet that *Borba,* the KPJ central organ, had lost its revolutionary
function. (A generation later, European Maoists distinguished their
press in precisely the same way—hence *L'Humanité nouvelle, Nuova
unità,* etc.). The appearance of *Nova borba* drew an immediate protest from the Yugoslav embassy, which rightly held the Czechoslovak
government responsible for providing the necessary facilities.[5] Perhaps because its founders were "Americans" (Slobodan-Lale Ivanović
and Pero Dragila, from the staff of Yugoslavia's embassy in Washington), *Nova borba* devoted much space to the life of South Slavic
immigrants in the United States and elsewhere overseas. *Nova borba*
was the keystone of an extensive émigré center in Prague, closely
connected with Bedřich Geminder, head of the Foreign Section of the
Czechoslovak Communist party and later one of the victims in the
Slanský trial. The Pressmen's Club, to which the émigré propagandists belonged, also issued *Mladi revolucionar* (Young revolutionary),
a newspaper aimed at young people.

   Although it retained a measure of its importance, *Nova borba* was
soon eclipsed by *Za socijalističku Jugoslaviju* (For a socialist
Yugoslavia), published in Moscow. Several leading *ibeovci*
(Popivoda, Golubović, Ćekić) wrote extensively for this newspaper.
So did several exiles whose stature the Soviets underscored by ap-
pointing them to the leading organs of the various international Communist fronts; among them were Anton Rupnik, a member of the
executive committee of the World Trade Unions Federation, and
Bosiljka Marjanović, a member of the executive committee of the
International Federation of Democratic Women. Momčilo Ješić, Vik-
tor Vidmar, Asim Alihodžić, and Aleksandar Opojević were among
other frequent contributors. Other émigré newspapers included *Pod
zastavom internacionalizma* (Under the banner of internationalism),
Bucharest; *Napred* (Forward, published mainly in Macedonian),
Sofia; *Za pobedu* (For victory), Warsaw; *Za slobodu* (For liberty),
Tirana; and the Slovene-language *Za ljudsko zmago* (For people's
victory), Budapest.[6] The work of émigré journalists also appeared

   5. *White Book on Aggressive Activities by the Governments of the U.S.S.R., Poland,
Czechoslovakia, Hungary, Rumania, Bulgaria, and Albania towards Yugoslavia* (Belgrade,
1951), pp. 109–10. Between 1948 and 1951 the Yugoslav government addressed 14 notes
to the USSR and its bloc partners protesting the aid they extended to the Cominformist
exiles.
   6. HIA-TC, "Jugoslovenski kominformisti," pp. 7–8; "Vijesti iz Jugoslavije," pp. 2–2a.

frequently in the principal newspapers of the host countries, in various organs of the Slavic Committee, and in *For a Lasting Peace, For a People's Democracy,* the prodigiously titled central organ of the Cominform, which was shifted from Belgrade to Bucharest after the Resolution. The exiles also got sixty minutes of air time for daily radio transmissions to Yugoslavia from Bucharest (Radio Free Yugoslavia), and they frequently participated in the regular anti-KPJ broadcasts from the bloc countries.[7] A small group of notable exiles served Soviet propaganda in another way: Lazar Brankov and Blagoj Hadži-Panzov were, respectively, the most damaging witnesses at the rigged trials of László Rajk in Hungary (September 1949) and Trajčo Kostov in Bulgaria (December 1949).[8]

While the journalists were paving the way for the political downfall of the Belgrade government, others in the émigré group were preparing for more drastic action. These were the military men, graduates of Soviet military schools, led by General Pero Popivoda. Popivoda deployed his subordinates from the USSR to Hungary, Romania, and Bulgaria, in anticipation, it seemed, of invasion. Soviet strategy clearly pointed in this direction. The establishment of three international brigades, stationed in Hungary, Romania, and Bulgaria, was especially ominous, and their aim was certainly Yugoslavia, even

7. According to Yugoslav statistics, the daily length of radio transmissions aimed at Yugoslavia in July 1950, including special Sunday programs, was: Radio Moscow, 5 hrs. 45 min.; Radio Sofia, 3 hrs. 30 min.; Radio Prague, 3 hrs. 15 min.; Radio Budapest, 1 hr. 35 min.; Radio Bucharest, 45 min.; Radio Tirana, 45 min.; Radio Warsaw, 30 min.: *White Book,* pp. 477–78. Yugoslavia's minority nationalities could in some cases, of course, follow the regular broadcasts from the neighboring countries in their mother tongues.

8. László Rajk, Hungarian foreign minister and deputy general secretary of the Hungarian Working People's (Communist) Party, was tried in September 1949 as a criminal conspirator, charged with attempting to overthrow the socialist order in Hungary. His taskmasters were supposed to be Tito and Ranković, who acquainted Rajk with their plots to take over the people's democracies on behalf of the United States. Brankov testified that he attended conspiratorial meetings at which Tito and Ranković gave instructions to Rajk. It is not clear whether Brankov willingly submitted to the role assigned to him by the stage managers of Rajk's trial; he denied it after his flight from Hungary in 1956.

The trial of Trajčo Kostov, Bulgaria's deputy prime minister and a member of the BRP Politburo, was almost identical. Kostov's part in a "conspiracy" with Belgrade and the West was attested to by Blagoj Hadži-Panzov, a Macedonian Bulgarophile Communist who served as a councilor of Yugoslavia's embassy to Sofia before his defection in the wake of the Cominform Resolution. Belgrade accused Hadži-Panzov of supporting "the Great Bulgarian ideas of [the IMRO leader] Vančo Mihajlov." He was a cosigner of the protest letter of Skopje's Action Committee, drafted by Lazar Sokolov in late 1943: *O kontrarevolucionarnoj i klevetničkoj kampanji protiv socijalističke Jugoslavije,* vol. 2 (Belgrade, 1950), pp. 344–46.

though the brigades did not consist solely of émigrés. (The Second International Brigade, with headquarters in Blagoevgrad, Pirin Macedonia, included 6,000 "volunteers" from the German Democratic Republic.) The Blagoevgrad brigade coordinated its activities with the "Pirin *komita* [guerrilla] units" of Ivan Aleksiev, which were a frequent source of border incidents. The brigade, which included a battalion of parachutists, was stationed on the right bank of the Struma, from Radomir to the Greek frontier, along the border with Yugoslavia. The brigade's commander was General Aleksa Mićunović, the former head of the Operational Staff of the First Yugoslav Army.[9] A unit of Yugoslav Cominformist airmen, too, was organized in the Urals.[10]

The bulk of the exiles, who were in neither the propaganda nor the military group, occupied themselves mainly with training in various specialties. For the first time in the history of the KPJ, "Moscow [was] massively constructing a new KPJ leadership according to a plan and methods that suited its convenience."[11] Whether they attended party schools or regular universities, the exiles were taught all the skills necessary to run party and state agencies, the military, and economic, scientific, and cultural institutions, all according to Soviet prescriptions. The process of "cadre building" went on even among the least talented émigrés, who were put to work in factories. Though the entire effort was part of the "exceptional measures" taken to train exiles who would "tomorrow lead the peoples of Yugoslavia, once the 'Tito clique' was overthrown," the immediate effect of specialization was felt especially in the sabotage campaign carried out by graduates of various intelligence courses in the bloc countries.[12] According to Belgrade sources, "the fact that by 1955 several thousand terrorists, saboteurs, spies, and others were liquidated, captured, or surrendered is sufficient indication of the weight and dimensions of this struggle."[13]

9. HIA-TC, "Vijesti iz Jugoslavije," pp. 1–2.

10. X-2 [Ivan Očak], "O Informbirou s one strane," in Dedijer, *Novi prilozi*, 3:505.

11. HIA-TC, "Jugoslovenski kominformisti," p. 8.

12. See "Povodom note Vlade SSSR Vladi FNRJ," *Borba*, June 4, 1949, p. 1; "Kako žive i šta rade 'politemigranti' u Rumuniji," *Borba*, Sept. 9, 1949, p. 4.

13. Savo Kržavac and Dragan Marković, *Informbiro—šta je to: Jugoslavija je rekla ne* (Belgrade, 1976), p. 181. According to an earlier Belgrade source:

The Yugoslav authorities in the course of the last three years [1949–1951] have captured 504 persons, infiltrated into Yugoslavia from neighboring countries of the

Saboteurs (*diverzanty*) were trained in special schools of various bloc security agencies and were infiltrated into Yugoslavia with assignments ranging from distribution of literature to assassinations and bombings of industrial facilities. Though material damage was encouraged, the terrorists were supposed above all to arouse panic and uncertainty. Their success can only be guessed at. The evidence is misleading, but perhaps as many as twenty-seven security operatives and militiamen were killed in struggles with infiltrators between 1949 and 1953 (see table 4). As there were also some thirty-four other unexplained deaths of secret police and militiamen in the same period, the total may well be higher.[14] In addition, Yugoslav sources claim that infiltrators killed "more than a hundred citizens and soldiers of our Army who defended the frontiers. More than 700 émigrés were infiltrated across the frontiers with arms, mines, leaflets, with spying and terrorist assignments. Around 160 were captured, and 40 were killed in direct conflict with our security organs."[15] Such skirmishes claimed the lives of some notable UDB-a operatives, including Lieutenant Colonel Pane Djukić-Limar, killed on June 30, 1952, near Leskovac in combat with infiltrators from Bulgaria.[16]

The bloc services devoted considerable attention to infiltration. Though not all the candidates were political refugees—they included a scattering of fleeing criminals, displaced citizens familiar with Yugoslavia, and the odd representative of Yugoslavia's various dis-

---

Soviet bloc, to organise and commit subversive and terroristic acts and organise espionage. Although the number of arrested persons infiltrated into Yugoslavia from Hungary, Rumania, Bulgaria, and Albania is high, the number of those who, after committing their crimes, succeeded in returning to the territories from which they had come is also considerable.

Apart from this, the proceedings have established that during the past three years more than 400 persons have been recruited for intelligence and subversive activities by the intelligence services of the U.S.S.R., Hungary, Bulgaria, Albania, Rumania, Czechoslovakia, and Poland.

Concerning these acts of terrorism and sabotage, organised by the authorities of neighboring countries, the Yugoslav Government possesses distressing proofs also in the many Yugoslav officials and citizens who have fallen victims to such activities. [*The Threat to Yugoslavia: Discussion in the Ad Hoc Political Committee of the United Nations Organisation, Sixth Session* (Belgrade, 1952), pp. 58–59]

14. During the same years 19 more were killed by unidentified outlaws, 14 succumbed under unexplained circumstances, and one died simply "while on assignment": Selim Numić, ed., *Pali nepobedjeni, 1944–1964* (Belgrade, 1965), pp. 355–429.

15. Kržavac and Marković, *Informbiro—šta je to,* p. 317.

16. Živojin Gavrilović, *Pane Limar: Životni put Rasinca i udbovca Pana Djukića-Limara,* 2d ed. (Belgrade, 1982), pp. 171–81.

Table 4. Number of Yugolav security personnel killed in confrontations with infiltrators from three Soviet-bloc countries, 1949–1953

Infiltrated from	1949	1950	1951	1952	1953	Total
Albania	4	3	1	4	1	13
Bulgaria	1	1	4	4	3	13
Hungary	1	0	0	0	0	1
Total	6	4	5	8	4	27

Reconstructed from Selim Numić, ed., *Pali nepobedjeni, 1944–1964* (Belgrade, 1965), pp. 355–429.

affected minorities—they were given appropriate training, sometimes by prominent leaders of the host countries. Major General Haxhi Lleshi, chairman of the Albanian Control Commission and Albania's nominal head of state from 1953 to 1982, supervised the work of his country's intelligence training center at Peshkopi, across the frontier from Debar in Yugoslavia. He personally gave directives to the under-cover *ibeovci* in Debar, the area of his wartime Partisan exploits. Training centers in Stari Vrač (now Sandanski) and Knjaževo (a sub-urb of Sofia) in Bulgaria and in Szeged in Hungary also equipped and dispatched large numbers of infiltrators.[17] Although the UDB-a at first handled the cases of uncovered Soviet operatives with discretion, the escalation of hostilities by Cominformist infiltrators soon obliged it to take extreme measures.[18]

All the various functions assigned to the émigré groups were of course secondary to their main task: the slow building of a Sovietized Communist movement that would come to power in Yugoslavia. For as long as they assumed that the takeover would come as a direct result of Soviet pressures or even military intervention, the exiles neglected the domestic *ibeovci,* who were feeling the blows of police repression. But as Yugoslavia strengthened its ties with the West, so that Soviet intervention became increasingly risky and increasingly unlikely, a strong domestic front became necessary. Plans had to be

17. *White Book,* pp. 389–90, 393–406. Cf. *O kontrarevolucionarnoj i klevetničkoj kampanji,* 2:334–37; and *Testimonies Which Cannot Be Refuted: Statements by Refugee Soldiers of the Soviet Satellite Armies* (n.p., 1952?). For a comment on the activities of Ratomir Andrić-Kmet, commander of the Niš military district, who deserted to Bulgaria and became the operational head of the Cominformist infiltrators from that country, see Arso Milatović, "Negativan odjek," *NIN,* Dec. 28, 1985, p. 18.

18. HIA-TC, interview no. 29, pp. 8, 11.

made to establish a Cominformist party in Yugoslavia. To prepare for the "overthrow of the criminal gang of Tito-Ranković," as early as the second half of 1949 *Nova borba* urged the reestablishment of the "true Marxist-Leninist Communist party of Yugoslavia."[19] Pero Popivoda, by then the émigrés' undisputed leader, joined this campaign in September 1950, but cautiously, noting that "in the struggle against the Tito-Ranković clique for the establishment of a vanguard Communist party, the working class of Yugoslavia relies on the fraternal aid of the international proletariat and Communist parties, on their rich revolutionary experience, and above all on the experience of the heroic Russian working class and the great party of Lenin-Stalin." Since the "popular masses of Yugoslavia are coming forward against the clique, it is necessary to stand at the head of the struggle, to organize it. But that can be done only by a militant Marxist-Leninist party of a new type. Such a party must and will come into being in Yugoslavia!"[20] Finally, in 1951, the leaders of the Cominformist emigration dispatched a secret directive to the clandestine groups in Yugoslavia. The domestic cells, the directive noted, had "already passed the most difficult phase of development, both in regard to the choice of work methods and forms of struggle against Tito's fascist regime and from the point of view of creating effective organizational forms." Now the time was ripe: "The basic task that now confronts all illegal Communist groups is the establishment of mutual ties and the transformation of these groups into an appropriate organizational system. The timetable for the creation of a new—genuinely Marxist-Leninist—party depends on the carrying out of these tasks. Again, the success of the Yugoslav peoples' liberation struggle depends on the creation of such a party."[21]

As it happened, the new party was still "being established" when Popivoda addressed the Nineteenth Congress of the Soviet Communist party in October 1952 on behalf of the cumbersomely named League of Yugoslav Patriots for the Liberation of the Peoples of Yugoslavia from the Yoke of the Tito-Ranković Clique and Imperi-

19. "Ponovno uspostaviti Komunističku partiju—osnovni zadatak jugoslovenskih komunista," *Nova borba*, Aug. 8, 1949, p. 1; "Ka višem stupnju organizovane borbe za slamanje fašističkog titovskog režima," ibid., Jan. 15, 1950, p. 1.

20. Pero Popivoda, "Za ponovno stvaranje revolucionarne, prave komunističke partije Jugoslavije," *Za socijalističku Jugoslaviju*, Sept. 22, 1950, p. 6.

21. HIA-TC, "Jugoslovenski kominformisti," p. 9.

KAKO ŽIVE

JUGOSLAVENSKE »ZDRAVE SNAGE« U BUKUREŠTU

alist Slavery.[22] And Popivoda, president of the League (its name now somewhat curtailed to League of Yugoslav Patriots for the Liberation of the Peoples of Yugoslavia), continued to advocate the establishment of a Yugoslav Stalinist party even after Stalin's death ("the conditions for the establishment of such a party exist in Yugoslavia").[23] In 1954, in the wake of the Djilas affair, Popivoda's Moscow organ still attacked "Tito's government" (no longer "clique") but suggested that the "normalization of relations between [Yugoslavia] and the countries of the democratic camp" was still possible if Tito were to take an anti-Western stand.[24] Talk of a new Yugoslav Communist party subsided.

In fact, whatever the exigencies of Soviet policy vis-à-vis the émigrés, conditions that might have favored an alternative Communist party never existed in Yugoslavia. Divided into disconnected cells throughout the country, often with different ideological predispositions and nationality bases, totally unable to influence the course of

22. Pero Popivoda, "Pozdrav XIX kongresu SKP(b)," *Pod zastavom internacionalizma,* Oct. 18, 1952, p. 2.
23. Pero Popivoda, "Oslobodilačka borba jugoslovenskih naroda za nacionalnu nezavisnost i zadaci Saveza patriota," *Za socijalističku Jugoslaviju,* June 3, 1953, p. 2.
24. "Za ponovno uspostavljanje bratskih veza Jugoslavije sa zemljama tabora mira i demokratije," *Za socijalističku Jugoslaviju,* Feb. 13, 1954, p. 5.

---

7. "How the Yugoslav 'Healthy Forces' Live in Bucharest." This cartoon by Zagreb's famous cartoonist Otto Reisinger, published in the satirical weekly *Kerempuh* in October 1949, covers all the Cominformist themes of Yugoslav counterpropaganda. At top right, Cominformist émigrés make their way to a cashier. A sign announces the evening's "ideological political lecture" and warns that the use of firearms is prohibited. On the floor below, the editors of *Pod zastavom internacionalizma* (Under the banner of internationalism) crank out their sheet—"today's circulation is 87." On the ground floor, in the Two Principles Tavern of the Political Émigré Central Committee, a sign announces that the cadre section has moved behind the bar and a message urges a tart to wait for the imminent return of the organizational secretary. At bottom right, a truck is transferring suborned Cominformist witnesses from Budapest to Sofia for new anti-Titoist show trials. The lamppost signs direct anyone interested in a top job in Yugoslavia, a speedy academic degree, or vodka to the tavern. At bottom left, in a lefthanded jab at Soviet satellites, a Catholic priest is erecting a church financed by "our friend good sheep Bierut," an allusion to the relative toleration of religion in Poland. The Überchelovek movie house, at the center, is showing "Rákosi and Ana Pauker in *Struggle Near Kuibyshev.*" The film's title, with its reference to the Soviet wartime capital on the Volga, alludes to the lack of a credible war record among satellite leaders. In front of the theater a group of émigrés, some dressed in Chetnik and Ustaša uniforms, are singing the "Internationale" to welcome Comrade Popivoda, the foremost exile. The great leader is driven in a horse carriage with diplomatic plates beneath a sign reading "There Is No Room for Titoists in Our Ranks."

Soviet and émigré politics, the underground *ibeovci* caused enormous problems for Belgrade, but only because they burrowed into the very heart of Yugoslavia's policy-making institutions. Cominformist cells were uncovered on the staff of *Borba* and in the Ministry of Foreign Affairs. There were *ibeovci* "whom Tito called 'spies–time bombs,' who received special instructions not to take a stand for the Cominform Resolution, to sit where they were, and to inform their contacts on what was happening in Yugoslavia."[25] Instead of a Leninist party, Popivoda himself seemed to prefer a "grandiose intelligence organization that with almost no effort 'would penetrate the whole apparatus of those over there [in Yugoslavia] and destroy them from within.' "[26] More important, that was the Soviet preference.

Nevertheless, Cominformist cells, varying in size from whole sections of KPJ organizations to fractions within them to territorial networks, caused considerable damage to the KPJ. Obviously, the scope of these groups, which began to operate soon after the Resolution, is difficult to determine. We have only marginal knowledge of the uncovered cells. Nevertheless, there are strong indications that such cells existed in many party organizations and that "their channels reached to the very summits of the legal KPJ, from which they drew sensitive information."[27]

Some units consisted largely of foreign Communist émigrés, such as the Italian group formed in Rijeka by Alfredo Bonelli; at the opposite extreme were units carefully put together by the security agencies of neighboring bloc countries. A few groups of university students functioned almost publicly: at the Philosophy Faculty of the University of Belgrade, "Cominformists were occasionally caught when they sang Soviet songs or when they held some of their secret organizational meetings late in the evening." In April 1952, a secret Cominformist organization at the Technical Faculty in Belgrade decided to show its strength at a public meeting called by the faculty council and the party bureau for the purpose of expelling three students branded as Western propagandists. Despite the diametrically opposed political sentiments of the accused, the Cominformists interrupted the proceedings with exhortations: "Comrades, how long are we going to

25. Dedijer, *Novi prilozi,* 3:460–61, 448.
26. Slobodan Pauljević, *Strašno budjenje* (Rijeka, 1982), p. 98.
27. HIA-TC, "Jugoslovenski kominformisti," p. 9.

allow Tito and his gang to expel our colleagues from the university and deny them an education? We must openly fight against this." The wild brawl that erupted was stopped only by truckloads of armed militiamen. Injuries and arrests were extensive, and one student reportedly was killed. At the University of Zagreb, the UDB-a uncovered several groups of *ibeovci*. The student Communist leaders at the Technical Faculty expelled their organizational secretary, the secretary of SKOJ, and three other leading members as Cominformists. Outspoken *ibeovci* were physically assaulted at the Forestry Faculty. Their colleagues at the Economics Faculty created a highly successful thirty-member secret organization, called the Young Bolshevik Faction, which disseminated large quantities of Cominformist newspapers and leaflets. The group was discovered and arrested late in 1948.[28]

The secret Cominformist cells in the armed forces were especially dangerous, as they could threaten a military seizure (as in the aborted plot of the Popović-Malešević-Rodić group in Sarajevo and Novi Sad) and maintain channels for the escape of prominent *ibeovci*, especially air force officers, to the bloc countries. Some of these networks operated through Soviet agents in the JA.[29] They were also skillful at sabotage, and that was their main activity.

Sensationalist and occasionally fabricated tales of terror and sabotage disseminated by the bloc countries to underscore the chaos wrought by Yugoslavia's domestic opposition helped Belgrade's efforts to downplay actual incidents.[30] In recent years, however, various spokesmen have admitted that "there was terror and sabotage or attempts of that sort" during the period of confrontation with the USSR.[31] On two occasions in the late summer of 1951 military conspirators attacked supply depots at the Batajnica air base. During a

28. Ibid., interviews no. 66, p. 84, and no. 56, pp. 117–18; "Zagrebacko sveuciliste u eri komunistickog rezima u Jugoslaviji [sic]," pp. 19–20, 42–44. In an apparent attempt to damage the reputation of Savka Dabčević-Kučar, a party leader in Croatia purged in 1971, Dedijer cites a claim by one of her opponents to the effect that a "certain female student, later a well-known political worker, reported 836 of her colleagues (economics majors), charging them with speaking against Tito and in favor of the Cominform": Dedijer, *Novi prilozi*, 3:451–52. If there is any truth to the account, the number is obviously exaggerated.

29. HIA-TC, interview no. 56, pp. 18, 29, 197.

30. A typical example of official disparagement of sensationalist news coverage can be found in *Borba*, March 30, 1949, p. 1.

31. Maroje Mihovilović, Mario Bošnjak, and Sead Saračević, *Sukob s Informbiroom* (Zagreb, 1976), p. 69.

third attack, in September, they burned a clothing depository that also held oxygen bottles for high-altitude flights. The saboteurs were never discovered, although suspected culprits were thoroughly investigated. Large groups of saboteurs eluded detection for several years after the Resolution. Major Krste Vukčević, a Montenegrin and the commissar of the Messerschmitt regiment at the Zemunik air base near Zadar, organized some twenty officers from his unit and the technical battalion. They bombed twelve planes in Zemunik in 1951, although some were saved. All were arrested as *ibeovci*.[32]

The scope of Cominformist sabotage is difficult to assess. Other underground groups in Yugoslavia were committing terrorist acts at the same time. For example, though the authorities believed that arson in some six factories in Osijek (Croatia) was the work of the *ibeovci*, most citizens credited remnants of the Ustaša and Chetnik groups with these actions.[33] Yet, however widespread, sabotage could not destroy the government. Marxist assessments of terrorism seem especially valid when they concern Marxist groups. But mass actions were not a good alternative in the circumstances, considering the effectiveness of the UDB-a and the Cominformists' reliance on bloc aid. Guerrilla engagements, which had to rely on mass support, and even occasional rebellions did occur from time to time, however. They were usually suppressed quickly, but they detracted from the government's prestige, caused considerable damage, and generated further discontent. The most successful of them were based on a wide spectrum of grievances beyond the narrow Cominformist issues, usually wrongs that the peasants considered intolerable. And inasmuch as the Serbs were the main participants, they demonstrated that even conservative nationalists in the Serb community relied on the Soviets as the only hope for an improvement in Yugoslavia's political climate.

The extent of Montenegrin Cominformist insurgency has already been noted. The rebellions in Montenegro continued in several waves. Mobile UDB-a forces suppressed the strongest outbreaks during the summer and autumn of 1948. The following year the security units of Komnen Cerović destroyed the Cominformist strongholds in the Montenegrin portion of the Sandžak.[34] Rebellions also broke out in

32. HIA-TC, interview b.b. [VP], pp. 14–15, 19.
33. Ibid., interview no. 60, p. 1.
34. Ibid., "Jugoslovenski kominformisti," p. 5. Cf. ibid., Biographies: Komnen Cerović, p. 1.

the Zeta valley, between Nikšić and Titograd, the capital of Montenegro; most party members there sided with the insurgents and fought alongside them. The participation of leading Cominformists from other areas—such as Miloš Stojaković, former forestry minister in Bosnia-Hercegovina—indicates that some *ibeovci* thought of Montenegro as a possible base area from which partisan warfare could spread to the other republics, especially Bosnia-Hercegovina and eventually Serbia.[35] Nevertheless, despite its intensity, the Montenegrin movement was successfully halted.

Other instances of Cominformist insurgency took place in Slovenia, Croatia, and Bosnia-Hercegovina. Except for a small group of Slovene Cominformists, who took to the mountains only to be decimated by the army and the UDB-a,[36] these outbreaks were but a continuation of traditional primitive rebelliousness. And even the group led by the mysterious Major Petar "Šubara" (Fur Hat) was little more than a more sophisticated Cominformist version of a sort of Robin Hood band that roamed Slavonia in the early 1920s. Following the pattern of Jovo Stanisavljević Čaruga, a notorious cutthroat whose gang originally espoused primitive egalitarian socialism, Major Šubara mixed politics with traditional outlawry, relying on local accomplices (*yataks*) for shelter, food, and information.

So little is known about Šubara that his activities can be reconstructed only in the broadest of strokes. Even his name is not certain. Šubara was a nickname inspired by his characteristic headgear. It is certain, however, that he was a Serb from a village between Borovo and Vinkovci, in Slavonia, a major in the JA, and a Partisan veteran. After the Resolution he deserted with a group of followers and took to roaming central and eastern Slavonia, from the Papuk highlands to the Dalj collective farm, the former estate of the Serbian metropolitanate of Karlovci, on the banks of the Danube. His purpose clearly was to rouse the peasants by propaganda broadcast by his mobile radio station, by broadsheets printed on his small press, and by exemplary liquidations of party and security officials.[37]

The peasants, especially the Serbs of the Dalj area, apparently re-

---

35. Ibid., interview no. 56, p. 4a.
36. Sofokli Lazri and Javer Malo, *Dans les prisons et les camps de concentration de la Yougoslavie* (Tirana, 1960), p. 19.
37. HIA-TC, "Jugoslovenski kominformisti," p. 5. Cf. ibid., interviews no. 52, pp. 5–6, and no. 60, p. 10.

sponded positively and actively aided Šubara's group. They were completely disaffected by the forced collectivization, which the government launched in 1948–1949 in a misguided effort to disprove Moscow's charges that rural Yugoslavia was held in thrall by "kulaks." Since the rebels disseminated the most elementary propaganda ("Brothers and sisters, rise up against the bloodsuckers of our people who steal and kill, etc.") the peasants took the message as a protest against collectivization.[38] Observers reported that the slogan "Long live Šubara" could be seen on the collective farms in the environs of Dalj and Bijelo Brdo. When asked about these inscriptions, the peasants replied that they referred to a man who would save them. Šubara's band never incited a mass insurrection and it was finally liquidated, but before that happened his followers certified his reputation by attacking several UDB-a outposts and reportedly killing not only a handful of security officers but also a unit of six counterinsurgency specialists.[39]

Developments in northwestern Bosnia and the adjoining areas of Croatia were more violent and dramatic but equally ephemeral. On May 6, 1950—St. George's Day (Djurdjevdan), which in Balkan peasant tradition signaled the beginning of the annual *hajduk* (outlaw) actions against the Turks—the predominantly Muslim peasants of the Cazin frontier mutinied. The leaders of the rebellion were Milan Božić and Mile Devrnja, Serb Partisan veterans and demobilized officers of the JA, who promised the peasants that the Yugoslav kingdom would be restored under King Petar II and that compulsory deliveries of grain and produce, collective farms, and taxes would all be abolished. The peasants tried to seize the town of Cazin and also

38. Ibid., interview no. 60, p. 10. Cominformist propaganda in fact exploited the unpopular collectivization drive in Yugoslavia, a measure provoked by the KPJ's self-defeating urge to prove to the Soviets that "kulaks" were not thriving in Yugoslavia. But instead of praising the Yugoslav efforts, the Cominformists claimed that the collective farms in Yugoslavia were "kulak collectives" and the food levy nothing but "fascist plunder." For characteristic examples of the Cominformist position on the Yugoslav land question, see D. Nikolić, "Sve oštrija borba radnog seljaštva protiv plačke i nasilja," *Nova borba*, June 29, 1951, p. 5; "Sačuvati hleb za narod!" ibid., Aug. 5, 1951, p. 5; B. Urošević, "Eksploatatorski karakter zemljoradničkih zadruga," ibid., May 17, 1954, p. 4.

39. HIA-TC, interview no. 60, p. 1. No record of this incident is found in Numić, *Pali nepobedjeni*. We do, however, find a reference to a train wreck in Vinkovci, not far from Dalj, in which six Belgrade militiamen lost their lives (pp. 409–10). If the incident took place on the date given, November 6, 1951, it could not have been a camouflaged version of the clash with Šubara, which certainly occurred before August 1950, when the person who reported it emigrated to Trieste.

marched to Bihać. They burned the archives of local authorities, pillaged food depots, and cut telephone wires. In another version of the mutiny, Cominformists roused the army units in Cazin with the intention of using the tank units to extend the rebellion in the direction of Banja Luka, the administrative center of this part of Bosnia, and nearby Mount Kozara, a Partisan base area during the war. The rebellion was quickly subdued and nine participants were killed in the mop-up action. The authorities arrested 714 persons; 288 of them were tried by a military tribunal, which meted out stiff punishments, including 17 death sentences. The 426 other participants were given administrative punishments.[40]

During the same period, in coordination with the developments in the Cazin area, a group of Serbs from the neighboring Kordun, in Croatia, attacked and held Ladjevac and Rakovica. They were dispersed and pursued for a month over the highlands of the Kapela Range.[41] Though these dramatic events were not organized by the Cominformists, the Yugoslav authorities, according to Djilas, were "afraid of a pro-Stalin disturbance."[42] As we have seen, several top Serb leaders from Croatia (Žigić, Brkić, Opačić) were held responsible for unrest among the Serb peasants.[43] Perhaps it is best to conclude that the volatile situation could have developed in a Cominformist direction, as the *ibeovci* clearly sensed.[44]

Any consideration of Cominformist groups would be incomplete without a discussion of international Cominformism. Of course, ex-

40. Sava Dautović, "Cazinska krajina godine 1950.," *NIN,* April 20, 1986, pp. 30–31; Murat Tatarević, "Bilo je istraživanja," *NIN,* April 27, 1986, p. 6; HIA-TC, interview no. 56, p. 4a.
41. The most detailed account of the disturbances published to date is in Mane Pešut, "Djurdjevdanski ustanak Srba u Hrvatskoj—1950 godine," *Glasnik Srpskog istorijsko-kulturnog društva "Njegoš"* 52 (June 1984): 19–34.
42. Milovan Djilas, *Tito: The Story from Inside* (New York, 1980), p. 80.
43. According to one Chetnik source, the rebels rejected the overtures of Rade Žigić, Dušan Brkić, and Stanko Opačić-Ćanica because the "insurgents were Chetniks": Pešut, "Djurdjevdanski ustanak," p. 30. Another of Pešut's sources cites projected aid from abroad that did not materialize because infiltrators from Austria were captured at the frontier (ibid., pp. 24–25). And indeed, Yugoslav authorities announced the capture of ten infiltrators from Austria, eight of them former Chetniks, who supposedly were directed by the "official service of [ex-King] Petar Karadjordjević . . . in close collaboration with Mačekist elements": "Saopštenje Ministarstva unutrašnjih poslova FNRJ," *Borba,* June 24, 1950, p. 1.
44. "Još jedanput o krvavim zločinima titovskih janičara u Cazinu," *Za socijalističku Jugoslaviju,* Dec. 29, 1950, p. 3.

cept for a few insignificant Titoist factions, from 1948 to 1955 the entire Communist movement was Cominformist. Nevertheless, Cominformist activity in Trieste and Carinthia and among Yugoslavia's nationals overseas proceeded independently of Yugoslavia's native *ibeovci* and constituted a separate chapter in the anti-Tito campaign.

The Free Territory of Trieste (FTT), established in 1947 and subsequently divided into Zone A (Trieste and its environs, under U.S.-British military administration) and Zone B (the districts of Koper and Buje, south of Trieste, under Yugoslavia's military control), had its separate Communist party (CP FTT), which was in fact an extension of the KPJ until the Resolution. Triestine communism, rooted in the Italian Communist Party (PCI), with traditions dating to the socialist movement of Austria-Hungary, survived under Mussolini as a harmonious coalition of Italian working-class militants and the persecuted Slovenes and Croats, victims of fascist cultural genocide. But this unity was severely strained by the harsh policies pursued by Yugoslavia during its brief occupation of Trieste in 1945, by the rival claims of Rome and Belgrade on the Julian region, and by the further circumstance that Trieste became a focal point of irredentist Italian forces after Yugoslavia occupied Istria and Rijeka.

The Cominform Resolution split the executive committee of the CP FTT. The majority of six, headed by Vittorio Vidali (1900–1983), the party's general secretary, sided with the Resolution. Branko Babič (b. 1912), a Slovene Communist from the Triestine commune of San Dorligo (Dolina), led the pro-Belgrade minority of four. Subsequently, the Babič group mustered its majority in the party's CC to expel Vidali and his adherents. In response, Vidali held a congress of Triestine Cominformists, who elected a new party leadership. Both groups claimed to represent the "genuine" CP FTT. In fact, by the end of August 1948, the Tito–Stalin split was complete in Trieste.[45] Babič's party enjoyed a privileged position in Zone B, but Vidali's men were banned there. The pro-Soviets were hardly the favorites of the Western military government in Zone A, but at least they were legally protected there. Safe among the Americans and the British, they harassed Babič's party, which retaliated in kind. Internecine Vi-

45. Bogdan C. Novak, *Trieste, 1941–1954* (Chicago, 1970), pp. 299–300. Cf. "Komunistička partija slobodne teritorije Trsta poziva svoje članove da povedu odlučnu borbu protiv frakcionaša, oportunista i izdajnika," *Borba*, Sept. 4, 1948, p. 5.

dali–Babič struggles weakened the Communist movement in Zone A, and thus contributed to the outcome of the Trieste dispute.

It would be an oversimplification to claim that the Vidali–Babič split disguised a rupture between Italians and Slavs. Babič's party was indeed an agency of the KPJ, but it is not obvious that the Italian national cause was Vidali's first concern. Vidali, an old-line Stalinist, was a charter member of the PCI. He left Italy after the Fascist takeover and continued his party work among Italian immigrants in Chicago, where he edited a Communist newspaper and served as secretary of a mass anti-Fascist organization. He subsequently served as a Comintern instructor to Mexican Communists, underwent intensive training in Moscow, and held a commanding position in the international brigades in Spain. As a Soviet intelligence operative— indeed, a liquidator—he apparently participated in Soviet plots against the lives of Trotsky and several Italian anti-Fascists. After Franco's victory he returned to Latin America, where he remained until 1947. He then returned to his native Trieste, perhaps as a prelude to Stalin's intrigue on the Yugoslav frontier.[46] Like many Italian Communists, Vidali had fought under Stalin's banner long before Tito's rise, and he saw no reason to switch his allegiance. The same held true for his CC, which included twenty-four persons (more than half) with obvious Slavic names, though not all of them necessarily had a highly developed national consciousness.[47] Most of Trieste's veteran Communists, including those who played key roles under Yugoslavia's brief military rule in 1945 (Giorgio Jaksetich, Alessandro Destradi, Giuseppe Gustincich), sided with the Resolution. Furthermore, during the first elections in Zone A (June 12 and 19, 1949), the Cominformists received 42,587 votes (23 percent) to Babič's 5,344 (2.94 percent). According to one calculation, a sixth to a fourth of all Cominformist votes came from the Slovene community, which gave almost half of its votes to Vidali and only a fifth to

46. The best short account of Triestine Cominformism and Vidali's role in its operations can be found in Eric R. Terzuolo, *Red Adriatic: The Communist Parties of Italy and Yugoslavia* (Boulder, Colo., 1985), pp. 144–54. On Vidali's role in the assassination plots against Trotsky, see Robert Conquest, *The Great Terror: Stalin's Purge of the Thirties* (London, 1968), pp. 446–47.

47. HIA-TC, J: "Clanovi CK KP (Kominformisti) slobodnog teritorija Trsta su slijedeci [sic]," pp. 1–2. Sixteen of the 44 CC members, including Vidali, had Italian passports, issued in Udine, Gorizia, and Milan.

Babič. "Thus the solidarity manifested between Italian and Slovenian Communists during the entire period from the end of World War I was not seriously damaged by Tito's schism."[48]

Vidali's position on Trieste was a restatement of the Soviet posture. The CP FTT (Vidali) wanted to maintain the Free Territory. The Cominformists opposed a partition between Italy and Yugoslavia and demanded that just as the Western powers should vacate Zone A, Tito's forces should get out of Zone B, "since Yugoslavia [was] no longer a socialist country." Belgrade maintained that the Cominformists were nothing but covert Italian irredentists who cooperated with patent Fascist forces in an anti-Yugoslav chorus, designed to prove the *italianità* of the entire Julian region.[49] But it is likely that Yugoslavia's resolve to partition the Free Territory, influenced by Babič's poor showing at the 1949 elections in Zone A, was interpreted as a serious threat to Slovene minority rights, since partition implied full Italian sovereignty over Zone A. In any case, although practically all Triestine Titoists were Slovenes, the Cominformists also had a sizable Slovene following. The results of the 1952 elections in Zone A showed that matters remained much the same four years after the split. On the other hand, considerable absenteeism (9.61 percent) and a large number of invalid ballots (8.75 percent) in the 1950 elections in Zone B indicated the continuation of Italian and Cominformist opposition to Yugoslavia's military occupation.[50]

The PCI and Vidali did not perceptibly lessen Yugoslavia's chances to acquire Trieste, but their anti-Tito campaign and ill-natured attacks on Belgrade certainly improved their standing among Italian nationalists. Vidali also hoped to carry the Cominformist message into Yugoslavia with his Slovene-language newspaper *Delo* (Labor). Most dramatic, according to a recent revelation by Vladimir Dedijer, Vidali was very successful in infiltrating the Yugoslav navy. He directed his officer agents "to organize a putsch in . . . the navy, seize the city of Split, and call in the Soviet fleet for help."[51] For all these

---

48. Novak, *Trieste*, p. 308; see pp. 305–9.

49. *O kontrarevolucionarnoj i klevetničkoj kampanji protiv socijalističke Jugoslavije* (Belgrade, 1949), 1:489–90.

50. Novak, *Trieste*, pp. 394, 326.

51. Dedijer, *Novi prilozi*, 3:464–65. Terzuolo, in contrast, feels that the Italian Communists, though not Vidali, were "lukewarm toward work in the direction of Yugoslavia"; the Cominformist apparatus in the provinces along the Italo-Yugoslav border, he says, was small and was concerned with little but information gathering and propaganda: Terzuolo,

reasons, Yugoslavia's press reserved special odium for the Triestine Cominformist leader. There are reports that the UDB-a even contemplated kidnaping him.[52] After Khrushchev's reconciliation with the KPJ, Vidali remained unconvinced of the wisdom of the new Soviet policy.[53] Though he remained active in the PCI's leadership from the 1956 unification of the Triestine party with the rest of Italy's Communists till his death, his dogmatic views were largely out of harmony with Berlinguer's line.

The Cominformist leadership of the Austrian CP welcomed Soviet support for Austria's 1938 frontiers. The Slovene minority in Carinthia apparently resisted this position, and a bitter dispute ensued. While Belgrade rediculed the claims of Austrian Cominformists that the Slovene minority in Carinthia "fought to remain in Austria," the Austrians felt obliged to terminate their ties with *Slovenski vestnik* (Slovene messenger) and *Die Einheit* (Unity), Slovene minority organs that were printed at a Communist printing plant in Klagenfurt.[54] As a result, the influence of the Resolutionists remained negligible among the Slovene minority in Austria. The situation of the Croat and Serb minorities in Hungary and Romania was very different. The Democratic Alliance of South Slavs, the minority organization in Hungary, and its equivalent in Romania were turned into instruments against Yugoslavia.

Finally, Communist party members and sympathizers among the overseas emigrants in the Americas and Oceania frequently followed the Cominform line and remained faithful to their pro-Moscow parties. This position was reflected on the pages of *Napredak* (Progress), the Croat leftist biweekly published in Sydney, Australia. Croat *ibeovci* in Argentina had a Slobodna Jugoslavija (Free Yugoslavia) association, which published a newspaper of the same name. Argentine Cominformists also published *Iseljenička reč* (Emigrant word). The Montevideo newspaper *Bratstvo* (Fraternity) reflected the views

---

Red Adriatic, pp. 133–38. Terzuolo's account is based on the manuscript memoirs of Alfredo Bonelli, one of the leaders of an underground Cominformist group in Rijeka. On the Cominformist activities of Italian Communist workers from Monfalcone (Tržič) at Rijeka, see Mladen Plovanić, "O nekim zbivanjima u Rijeci vezanim uz objavljivanje Rezolucije Informbiroa 1948. godine," *Dometi* 18, no. 11 (1985): 57–70.

52. HIA-TC, interview no. 14, p. 5.

53. Branko Lazitch and Milorad M. Drachkovitch, *Biographical Dictionary of the Comintern* (Stanford, 1973), p. 427.

54. *O kontrarevolucionarnoj i klevetničkoj kampanji*, 2:103–4.

of Croat Cominformists in Uruguay. Most important, the two oldest
Communist newspapers of the South Slavic immigrants in North
America, the Pittsburgh *Narodni glasnik* (People's herald, founded in
1913) and the Toronto *Jedinstvo* (Unity, founded in 1931), broke
with the KPJ and joined the American and Canadian CPs in opposing
Tito.[55]

55. HIA-TC, "Jugoslovenski kominformisti," p. 8.

6

The Marble Isle

Cominformism was not a fringe movement, yet it had no tangible successes and its chances of victory were never great. This was not simply the fault of the Cominformists themselves. Unequivocal Soviet support was always indispensable for their morale; and the ambiguity created by Khrushchev's détente with the KPJ certainly harmed the *ibeovci*. But during Stalin's lifetime, when full Soviet commitment was not in doubt, the chief obstacle to the domestic *ibeovci* was less a lack of encouragement than unyielding police repression, which escalated as the rift deepened. Tito's decision to treat the Cominformists in the same way as noncommunist foes gave the KPJ leadership a clear advantage over the opposition. And persecution exerted a prophylactic influence.

The decision to go after the Cominformists was made in piecemeal fashion. At the beginning of the dispute, the KPJ encouraged its basic organizations to engage in candid discussion of Stalin's letters and the Cominform Resolution. Many took this suggestion at face value, only to learn that equivocal or pro-Soviet sentiments prompted schoolmasterly dissuasion. Those who were "won over" in these "struggle sessions" were then left alone. The recusants were isolated, demoted, or expelled. At first these sanctions were viewed as merely disciplinary. They did not imply infringements of the kind usually ascribed to "class enemies," though it was understood that the Cominformists were "actually either enemies or a drag on socialist construction."[1]

1. "Pojačajmo budnost u borbi za čvrstinu partiskih redova," *Borba*, Aug. 21, 1948, p. 1.

As Tito himself noted, at first the KPJ was confident that the dispute would be smoothed over. But as the conflict intensified, more and more Cominformists were arrested, and in January 1949 Tito publicly set the new tone in the struggle against the Resolution. Propaganda against the KPJ, he said, "must be called by its proper name: this is hostile propaganda, counterrevolutionary propaganda, because it is carried out against a socialist state."[2]

"Counterrevolution" meant all-out war against the *ibeovci*. In time the Cominformists were viewed as the principal enemy, far more dangerous than the anticommunists. "Listening to foreign [radio] stations is not formally prohibited," an émigré observed, "but listeners nevertheless avoid tuning in the obviously Cominformist stations. So far as the other stations are concerned, they have nothing to worry about."[3] Still, some ambiguity remained. Yugoslavia was a profoundly troubled country during the period of confrontation with the USSR. Yesterday's associates became enemies overnight. Uncertainty rent the entire political system: "It is characteristic that [in Yugoslavia's postwar history] most political rumors . . . circulated at the time of the Cominform Resolution."[4] Not surprisingly, even an occasional KPJ leader viewed the ferreting out of *ibeovci* as an ordeal of true loyalty.[5] When ideological arguments proved ineffective, coercion was applied without restraint. The situation was not without irony, as a Serbian philosopher has pointed out:

> Sartre said in another context: "It is a lasting truth that man must become the same as his opponent in order to fight successfully against him." . . . In the case of Yugoslavia in 1948, this required no special effort, because the situation was to a large degree a conflict of like against like. That is why Yugoslav resistance [to Moscow] for a long time had the earmarks of *Stalinist anti-Stalinism*. Although the struggle against domestic Stalinists was and still is justified, explicitly Stalinist *methods* of struggle against them offer ample testimony in this regard.[6]

2. "Govor druga Tita na Drugom kongresu Komunističke partije Srbije," *Borba,* Jan. 22, 1949, p. 1.

3. HIA-TC, interview b.b. [SS], p. 2.

4. Slobodanka Ast and Milan Milošević, "Opasna šaputanja," *NIN,* June 18, 1978, p. 17.

5. This was apparently the stand of Colonel General Ivan Gošnjak, who explained the arrests of the Cominformists among the JA's officers as a test of their loyalty: HIA-TC, interview no. 29, p. 9.

6. Svetozar Stojanović, "Od postrevolucionarne diktature ka socijalističkoj demokratiji: Jugoslovenski socijalizam na raskršću," *Praxis* 9, nos. 3–4 (1972): 380–81.

Much as Stalin looked upon his state as the embodiment of socialism and thought that in strengthening control he was strengthening socialism, Yugoslavia's ideologists thought that the Cominformist alternative to their model of socialism could best be repulsed through a rapid increase in state power. There is an echo, too, of Stalin's belief that class struggle actually becomes more acute under socialism in Edvard Kardelj's political pronouncement of July 1948:

> The process of struggle for the socialist road of development is unavoidably accompanied by a sharpening of resistance of those classes that are disappearing from the stage of history. That resistance is also reflected in various forms and in various elements inside the Popular Front [NFJ], and even in the Party. . . . The sharpening of class struggle, based on socialist construction, causes wavering among such elements; they become double-dealers and tend to desert to the enemy camp.[7]

In conformity with this theory, loyal party members were prepared to accept the legitimacy of placing the Cominformists "under lock and hasp."[8] Though Communists could ordinarily not be arrested unless their party membership were terminated, an exception was made for *ibeovci*.[9] Curiously, the UDB-a treated these arrests as an intraparty affair, as a matter not covered by civil procedure. Ranković made no secret of the fact that most of the arrested *ibeovci* were sentenced by UDB-a investigators, or, as he put it, "by administrative procedure" (*po administrativnom postupku*).[10] His figures for 1952 seem to indicate that only 18.77 percent of all arrested Cominformists were tried by regular military or civilian courts.[11] Only a few of these trials were publicized, usually for calculated political effect. Various persons who cooperated with bloc intelligence agencies and a few infiltrators were given public trials. Vladimir Dapčević and Branko Petričević, the survivors of Arso

7. Edvard Kardelj, "KPJ u borbi za novu Jugoslaviju, za narodnu vlast i socijalizam," *Borba*, July 27, 1948, p. 2.

8. Darko Stuparić, *Revolucionari i bez funkcija* (Rijeka, 1975), p. 97.

9. HIA-TC, interview no. 51, p. 6.

10. Aleksandar Ranković, "O predlogu novog Statuta Komunističke partije Jugoslavije i nekim organizacionim pitanjima Partije," *Šesti kongres KPJ (Saveza komunista Jugoslavije)* (Belgrade, 1952), p. 123.

11. "Between 1948 and today [November 1952], 11,128 persons were sentenced by administrative procedure. . . . So that it would not be thought that many more were sentenced by the courts, I stress that up to now, 2,572 persons were sentenced by regular military or civil courts" (ibid.).

Jovanović's attempt to flee to Romania, were given a much-publicized trial, but only some two years after their capture, by which time they had become fairly docile.[12] Obren Blagojević, Žujović's deputy in the Ministry of Finance and governor of Yugoslavia's National Bank, was also publicly tried, on the charge of having attempted to flee to Albania with 1.2 million dinars and $5,240 embezzled from the state treasury.[13] And the authorities were preparing—but then gave up on—a show trial for Andrija Hebrang.

The lack of publicity given the majority of these trials and arrests was all part of an effort to downplay the significance of the opposition. Public knowledge of the imprisonment of scores of people, such as the mass arrest of students at the middle mining school in Bor (Serbia) in October 1951, would have been very damaging.[14] The means employed to uncover the Cominformists also had to be kept secret, since entrapment played an important role in detection. Undercover agents of the KOS, for example, would sometimes be "expelled" from the party in order to strengthen their credentials with the Cominformists, who it was assumed would contact them through the underground. Some agents even went through the forms of arrest in order to obtain compromising evidence against fellow prisoners.[15]

After arrest, the accused underwent an investigation that often lasted several months. The object was to establish all possible links between the prisoners and the *ibeovci* at large. Afterward a UDB-a commission usually sentenced the accused to a term of "socially useful labor" (*društvenokoristan rad*), which was almost never less than two years. Most prisoners, especially the leading Cominformists, received considerably longer terms, from four to sixteen years; the average sentence was ten years. Some were sentenced to death, but executions were delayed and then commuted.[16] A concerted decision

12. Savo Kržavac and Dragan Marković, *Informbiro—šta je to: Jugoslavija je rekla ne* (Belgrade, 1976), pp. 154–58.

13. "Obren Blagojević osudjen na osam godina lišenja slobode," *Borba*, Dec. 20, 1950, p. 3. After serving seven years of his sentence, Blagojević became a professor of economics at the University of Belgrade, and later at the University of Niš. His election to regular membership in the Serbian Academy of Sciences in May 1981 aroused considerable opposition and led to the resignation of Bogdan Bogdanović, the unofficial secretary of the party *aktiv* in the academy and a well-known sculptor and architect. See Bogdan Bogdanović, "Zašto sam napustio akademiju," *NIN*, Nov. 22, 1981, pp. 30–33.

14. HIA-TC, IIa, "Povjerljive vijesti iz Jugoslavije," p. 2.

15. Ibid., interview no. 29, pp. 24–25, 163.

16. Sofokli Lazri and Javer Malo, *Dans les prisons et les camps de concentration de la Yougoslavie* (Tirana, 1960), pp. 48–49. The average prison terms were established on the basis of the cases in this volume. There is no indication that all terms were served in full.

was clearly taken not to use the maximum penalty. "Our revolution," said Tito, "does not eat its children. The children of this revolution are honest."[17] Rather, the confinement of the *ibeovci* was viewed as the beginning of their total debasement, which would become the first step on the road to potential "reeducation and rehabilitation."

In other words, arrest was not merely for prevention and punishment. The arrested Cominformists had to be broken, their attitude revised, their loyalty to the party restored. The procedures necessarily differed from those used against political prisoners who had never shared common ground with the authorities. As a result, the treatment accorded the *ibeovci* was paternalistic even at its most brutal.

The prisoners were confined in various special camps left over from former regimes: in Croatia, Sisak, Lonjsko Polje, Ugljan, Vis, and Korčula; in Bosnia-Hercegovina, Zenica, Vareš, and a refurbished Bileća; in Serbia, Srijemska Mitrovica, Banjica, and the old city prison (Glavnjača) in Belgrade. Military officers were held in the old Ustaša concentration camp at Jasenovac, at the Petrovaradin fortress (Vojvodina), and especially in Stara Gradiška (Croatia).[18] The old Lepoglava prison in Croatia served as a transit center for 200 army officers in 1949. Most of them were then sent to the secret detention camp in Stara Gradiška, which housed some 280 officers until February 1951.[19]

Still, the Cominformist challenge required something unique. The solution was found in two rocky reefs between the island of Rab and the mainland in the northern Adriatic—the uninhabited islands of Goli and Sveti Grgur (Saint Gregory). The felicitiously named Goli Otok (literally Naked Island) has acquired a legendary reputation. Recent attempts to humanize it as "liberty surrounded by the sea" ring hollow, despite the fact that Goli has long since been transformed into a detention center for young delinquents.[20] Goli and Sveti Grgur have entered Yugoslavia's folklore as "the Marble Isle," "Hawaii," and "our Alcatraz." Several major works of imaginative literature on the theme of Goli have been published since 1981.[21] In

---

17. Kržavac and Marković, *Informbiro—šta je to*, p. 58. According to Djilas, Tito actually followed a policy of "hitting them over their heads, but not the taking of heads." See Milovan Djilas, *Vlast* (London, 1983), p. 192.
18. HIA-TC, "Jugoslovenski kominformisti," p. 6.
19. Ibid., interviews no. 59b, p. 4, and no. 63, p. 18.
20. Mića Adamović, "Sloboda okružena morem," *Susret*, Nov. 17, 1971, pp. 11–13.
21. Most of these works have been cited in Part I. The Cominform split and particularly the traumatic theme of Goli Otok have received a great deal of attention in the literatures of

1949, however, Goli was a completely barren limestone reef of some 4.74 square kilometers, dominated by a rocky cliff 230 meters high. Before the war a marble quarry operated on the island; there was virtually no soil. Sveti Grgur, with an abandoned bauxite mine, was slightly larger (7 sq. km.) and was covered by some shrubs. The archipelago received its first Cominformist visitors in July 1949.

The testimony of former inmates permits a summary of the busiest period in Goli's history, until February 1951. In those first eighteen months Goli received some 8,250 inmates in eight groups. The first two groups were the largest, 2,000 and 1,500 prisoners, respectively. They stayed for a mere two months. After relatively liberal treatment, they were dispatched in brigades to various public works projects on the mainland. It was assumed that these *ibeovci* were cured of their political malady before release.[22]

Those were the early days, before the application of methods that destroyed the prisoners' morale. The third group got its first psychological shocks immediately after disembarkation. The prisoners were greeted by menacing shouts; some were pushed into the shallow sea. This was the origin of the famous *stroj* (line), the most dreadful aspect of camp life after April 1950.

As the ship approached the shore in the early-morning hours, the packed prisoners could hear distant cries of "*Ti*-to! Par-ti-*ja!*"—a loud trochee and an anapest—or "*Ti*-to! *Mar*-ko!" (Marko was the *nom de révolution* of Aleksandar Ranković), swelling in wild unison. Once on shore, they were forced to run a gauntlet of crazed prisoners who were obliged to demonstrate their reform by beating the newcomers. Depending on the account one reads, the *stroj* was as short as 500 meters or as long as 1,500. By the end of the ordeal, the victims were dazed and staggering:

> I no longer know what they did with me. I only know I was wrenched, bloodied, my skin pounded to a pulp, and that I ran the gauntlet of

Yugoslavia, especially in Serbian literature and drama. Ljuba Tadić, a leading man of the Belgrade stage, recently has noted that the Serbs got stuck on two themes, Serbianism and the Informburo; "we don't have too many theater works dealing with contemporary themes": Sava Dautović, "Jedna velika moda," *Politika*, March 3, 1984, p. 11. For a critical analysis of early Yugoslav literary works on the Cominformist theme, see Ante Kadić, "The Stalin-Tito Conflict as Reflected in Literature," *Slavic Review* 37, no. 1 (1978): 91–106. On more recent works on Goli see Predrag Matvejević, "Literatura Golog otoka," *Književnost* 37, no. 10 (1982): 1534–38.

22. HIA-TC, interview no. 54, pp. 9–10.

4,000 prisoners barefoot and naked—because we had to take off our
shoes and clothes—over the rocks for a kilometer and a half. Somewhere halfway stood Dr. Mihelčič, a physician and himself a prisoner,
formerly the chief of sanitation of the Slovenian UDB-a. He examined
our heartbeat and then we had to go on. At the end of the gauntlet we
were given prisoners' uniforms and moccasins. Many fell unconscious
along the way, but I saw with my own eyes that those who fell were
picked up and beaten. Many wanted to kill themselves and leaped headlong upon the rocks.[23]

Nobody escaped the gauntlet, not even former generals. Petričević
and Dapčević were apparently led through the barracks, from room
to room. In some rooms they were beaten, in others spat upon.[24]
There were also individual inquisitions as newcomers explained their
background and reasons for siding with the Resolution. A manager,
for example, would state his case and be shouted down: "So you were
a director of a socialist enterprise! You, Stalinist lickspittle! Weren't
you paid well?"[25] And woe to him who refused to cooperate. Such
"bandits" were placed under boycott, which meant the worst and
heaviest work, no rest, practically no food or other necessities, nightly
runs through their compound's mini-*stroj*, and other forms of torture,
among them *krug* (beating in a circle) and "barking at the bulb"
(several victims grasp each other as if to dance while the others beat
them).[26]

For all that, two aspects of Goli were a source of particularly
painful wonder. First, the prisoners were tormented with endless and
aimless Sisyphean toil. For example, they would be obliged to carry
rocks from the quarry to the top of a nearby hill. This enterprise
would continue ceaselessly until the command was given to carry
them back. "Worse than the rocks on burning backs was the realization of the total uselessness of this work. Labor divested of all meaning killed them more spiritually than bodily."[27] Second, to all ap-
pearances the camp was governed by the prisoners themselves. The
Principle of the Heated Hare, which in inmate slang signified the
ordeal of the *stroj*, through which all had to run before gaining

23. Ibid., pp. 7–8.
24. Ibid., interview no. 63, p. 9.
25. M.K.M., "Tajne Golog Otoka," in *Jugoslovensko krvavo proleće 1945.*, ed. Bor. M.
Karapandžić (Cleveland, 1976), p. 347.
26. HIA-TC, interview no. 63, p. 7. Cf. Lazri and Malo, *Dans les prisons*, pp. 72–73.
27. Branko Hofman, *Noč do jutra* (Ljubljana, 1981), p. 137.

the right to beat new runners, operated everywhere. The prisoners saw their investigators, but they were never in touch with the UDB-a colonel who commanded the camp or with most of his staff. Nor did they have much to do with the 150 militiamen who guarded the premises. All the torments were carried out by the prisoners themselves. Indeed, the camp was managed by an inmate hierarchy dominated by the president of the conference of room chiefs. Of course, these people were appointed by and responsible to the administration. But the overseeing of reform was exclusively in their hands and they pursued it with the vigor of converts.

The *stroj* was said to be an inmate invention. "That is your self-initiative," says an investigator to Antonije Isaković's Man of Šid in the novel *Tren 2*. "You created that. You have full freedom of behavior here on the island. This, too, is your right. I understand, the Principle of the Heated Hare is taken to an extreme."[28] In order to become a member of the "collective," a newcomer had to repudiate his allegiance to the Resolution and declare his loyalty to the KPJ leadership. He had to "revise his stand" and join the ranks of the *revidirci* (revisers). "The sooner you are cured, the sooner you are healthy," a survivor commented.[29]

It was in fact impossible to remain loyal to the Resolution. Intransigent "bandits" were packed to compound R-101, the quarantine for the ranking *ibeovci*, where they were exposed to systematic mistreatment.[30] In Stara Gradiška, Colonel Dapčević organized a group of resisters, mainly Montenegrins.[31] They were discovered and subjected to stern sanctions. No secrets could be kept at Goli and resistance was futile. Recusants and would-be fugitives were occasionally lynched.[32] And even the *revidirci* were not safe. The slightest sign

28. Antonije Isaković, *Tren 2: Kazivanja Čeperku* (Belgrade, 1982), p. 72.
29. HIA-TC, interview no. 63, p. 9.
30. Dragan Marković, *Istina o Golom otoku* (Belgrade, 1987), pp. 113–18.
31. HIA-TC, interview no. 63, p. 17.
32. Lazri and Malo mention several such cases. This was, according to one version, the fate of Rade Žigić: Venko Markovski, *Goli Otok, the Island of Death: A Diary in Letters* (Boulder, Colo., 1984), p. 105. Djilas remembers the case of Blažo Raičević, an old Montenegrin Communist: "In 1950 Ranković told me that Raičević had been lynched in the concentration camp at Goli Otok by a mob of prisoners who had 'repented.' I must admit that none of us leaders felt sorry for him. True enough, Ranković issued orders that a detailed report be submitted in order to exonerate the role of his own people. There was a feeling of relief that Raičević had met his end in a way which absolved us of 'guilt' and excused us from any further concern for him. I thought that way myself": Milovan Djilas,

of wavering, refusal to beat newcomers, leniency toward "bandits," or shortfalls in work quotas subjected one to boycott. "You are clean only as long as you remain active," says a survivor.[33] Personalities were changed as the prisoners were divided into three groups: activists (*revidirci*), passives, and "bandits." These divisions created a psychosis of constant fear, spying, and denunciations. Passive *revidirci* were boycotted as insincere. In the end 343 (perhaps 394) prisoners died in the camps, 175 of them when a typhus epidemic struck Goli in 1951.[34]

As there was no comradeship on Goli, all commitment to the Cominform was quickly suppressed. Guilt set in. One former prisoner remembered how he felt when others confessed to withholding information about their hostile thoughts: "I thought of escaping across the frontier, but I never mentioned it. When some of the *revidirci* mentioned the same thing, that they wanted to escape, or if somebody was criticized for not admitting it and was therefore placed under boycott, I became extremely uncomfortable. I felt that my conscience wasn't clear, and I found it hard to look the others in the eye; I looked down."[35]

Repentance did not imply freedom. Only after repeated ordeals were prisoners declared "clean." They could then join the shock brigades, which were the first step toward release. One prisoner who was sentenced to two years spent two months in investigation and eight and a half on Goli, and was then sent with his brigade to help in the construction of the Breza-Vareš railroad in Bosnia. After three more months he was formally released, but was obliged to work as a civilian until the project was completed.[36] Those *revidirci* who slackened during the last phase were returned to Goli.[37] Noncommunist prisoners at other work sites remembered the *revidirci* with distaste. An involuntary woodsman who cleared the Sandžak forests in 1950 noted that repentant Cominformists worked as privileged overseers and were as heartily hated as the guards.[38] The most reso-

Memoir of a Revolutionary (New York, 1973), p. 64. Cf. M.K.M., "Tajne Golog Otoka," pp. 353–55.

33. HIA-TC, interview no. 63, p. 17.
34. Marković, *Istina*, p. 89.
35. HIA-TC, interview no. 63, p. 12.
36. Ibid., interview no. 54, pp. II1–2; interview no. 63, p. 15.
37. Ibid., interview no. 54, pp. II7–8.
38. Ibid., interview b.b. [MH], p. 4; cf. interview b.b. [HB], p. 11.

lute or distrusted *ibeovci* remained on Goli, but the lesser offenders soon returned to their homes and occasionally reentered the party; some even rejoined the lower officialdom. One of the conditions of release was silence about Goli. Just as the camp at Goli was never mentioned in the press (the authorities went to great lengths to camouflage its purpose),[39] the *revidirci* were required not to relate their experiences there. Not that this precaution was necessary. Every former inhabitant of the Marble Isle was reluctant to discuss it. "He is disinclined to talk, makes long pauses, and skips something, as if he is unwilling to speak through to the end. Is this because of the humiliations that he experienced, and of what sort? Or is it because the humiliation was inflicted by fellow prisoners? I do not know. But that covert shame, or fear, is something that I have noticed with all the Cominformists that I know."[40] The back of domestic resistance was successfully broken.

According to Ranković, by November 1952, 7,039 former Cominformists had been released from detention. Their loyalty seemed reliable, since only 1.9 percent of the released had been rearrested by the same date.[41] Notables among the *revidirci* made public statements repudiating the Cominform Resolution. These statements were publicized with considerable relish in the party press and were used to demoralize the recusants. Sreten Žujović made the most famous of these confessional declarations.[42] On the whole, swift arrests and repression effectively halted the spread of Cominformism.

Who thought up the Marble Isle and what is its meaning for the history of postwar Yugoslavia? These questions, which can cause fists to fly in post-Tito Yugoslavia, have importance beyond the context of the struggle against Cominformism. Clearly, the Yugoslav state had to defend itself against an actual or potential fifth column. Clearly, too, the responsibility was Tito's.[43] But the method of self-defense as

---

39. For example, when a group of *revidirci* were sent to the Zagreb-Belgrade highway work sites in October 1949, they sent a note of thanks to the militiamen of the "Marble" enterprise, expressing gratitude for the role of the guards in their rehabilitation. See "Pozdravno pismo bivših kažnjenika Narodnoj miliciji pri preduzeću 'Mermer,'" Oct. 26, 1949, p. 2.

40. Žarko Komanin, *Prestupna godina* (Belgrade, 1982), p. 132.

41. Ranković, "O predlogu novog Statuta," p. 123.

42. Others included Savo Zlatić, Bane Andreev, Šime Balen, and Niko Pavić.

43. Vladimir Dedijer has cited several reports to the effect that the idea for the concentration camp at Goli Otok originated with Antun Augustinčić, a Croat sculptor who was surveying quarries that could produce marble of Carrara quality, and Ivan Krajačić

practiced at Goli Otok says something about the nature of the Yugoslav system in the 1940s and early 1950s. It is an uncomfortable reminder of Yugoslavia's systemic links with the countries of the Soviet bloc—a reminder that has proved especially telling for the outspoken opponents of Soviet communism.[44] "Goli Otok, in my opinion," writes Milovan Djilas, "is the darkest and the most shameful event in Yugoslav communism. Goli Otok is even worse and more horrifying than that. It is an unanticipated stumble and an unimaginable humiliation."[45] And commenting on the fact that official Yugoslav sources often point out that no Cominformists were sentenced to death or executed, Dr. Gojko Nikoliš, a retired general and former head of the army's sanitary administration, has written that the "goings-on at Goli Otok were more amoral than the death penalty, more difficult to bear than a bullet or a guillotine blade. I am no pacifist; I am for the 'sword of the revolution,' let it cut where and when it is necessary. But I am a humanist and wish to remain one, at least to the extent of not being obliged to hold that the sharp edge of the sword ought to be exchanged for the systematic humiliation of people, in fact, below the zero point."[46] The defenders of the system reply that "if there had been no Goli Otok, the whole of Yugoslavia would have been a Goli Otok."[47]

Perhaps the most judicious appraisal of Goli Otok, and one that puts it in its historical context, was provided by Zlatko Čepo, a former head of the Institute for the History of the Workers' Movement of Croatia. Writing about Vladimir Dedijer's third volume of

---

(Stevo), Croatia's minister of the interior. Their suggestion got the ear of Kardelj, and finally Tito's approval. See Vladimir Dedijer, *Novi prilozi za biografiju Josipa Broza Tita*, vol. 3 (Belgrade, 1984), p. 465. But this is a selective version that exculpates the movers and shakers of Ranković's security apparatus.

44. Djilas has even suggested that Soviet propaganda and exiled *ibeovci* closed their eyes to the camp at Goli Otok, presumably because it was so similar to Soviet camps: Milovan Djilas, *Vlast* (London, 1983), p. 194. That, of course, is not the case. For a sample of Cominformist articles on Goli Otok, see "U logoru smrti," *Za socijalističku Jugoslaviju*, Feb. 14, 1952, pp. 4–5; D. B., "Goli Otok—titovski Majdanek," *Nova borba*, Dec. 22, 1952, p. 5; D. G. Kamenov, "Mačilišteto na Goli Otok," *Napred*, April 30, 1953, p. 2; "Protiv policijskog nasilja i terora," *Za socijalističku Jugoslaviju*, Jan. 30, 1954, p. 5; "Istina o udbovskim logorima smrti," *Nova borba*, July 12, 1954, p. 4.

45. Djilas, *Vlast*, p. 195.

46. Gojko Nikoliš, "Još jedna varijacija na temu polu odevenog otoka," *Književna reč*, May 10, 1982, p. 3.

47. Dedijer, *Novi prilozi*, 3:478. This is the opinion of Ante Raštogorac, one of the UDB-a operatives at Goli Otok.

contributions to Tito's biography, Čepo notes that Dedijer failed to provide an estimate of overall Yugoslav conditions in the postwar period:

> There is no mention of the fact that our first socialist system was rather crude, the use of force notable, laws severe, and prisons quite full—and not just with war criminals, but also with speculators, saboteurs, and other class enemies. The obligatory food levy and later the establishment of collective farms were carried out with a notable use of force. Everything that happened in the first postwar years was in part a historical necessity, but there were also subjective, arbitary actions. In that context, the attitude toward the Cominformists was nothing exceptional, apart from the fact that it concerned "one's own," and not the reaction. That circumstance perhaps contributed to the fact that—at least at the start—their treatment was even harsher.[48]

Even more apposite to the whole argument, the anti-Cominformist repression strengthened Yugoslavia's revolutionary dictatorship in precisely the same way that the Soviet regime established its absolute hegemony in the 1930s under Stalin. "It is only seemingly paradoxical," writes Svetozar Stojanović, "to say that only Stalinists, men in Stalin's confidence and persons who understood Stalinism from the inside, could assume positions in which they had some chance to resist Stalin successfully."[49] The search for pragmatic alternatives to the *ideology* of Stalinism could therefore proceed without significant concessions to political pluralism.

48. Zlatko Čepo, "Prilozi za biografiju, ali čiju," *Vjesnik—Sedam dana,* July 26, 1984, p. 5.
49. Stojanović, "Od postrevolucionarne diktature," p. 381.

7

Conclusion

The Communists who sided with Stalin in 1948 were not without active intelligence. They were swayed by a variety of influences and interests, some historical, some nationally based, some centralist, and some autonomist and special. These circumstances, coupled with the history of factional struggle within the KPJ, played a role in every individual or group decision to support the Resolution. Some people reacted in haste and never made a conscious decision, and some were hardly Cominformists in any real sense—simply confused people who made inopportune statements at the wrong time. Most important, they were far too scattered in motivation to develop any single movement, leadership, or program. Any study of the political line of demarcation in 1948 and immediately thereafter (see figure 8) will identify the queer contours of Yugoslav Communist cleavages. Milovan Djilas's leftist extremism of the 1940s had far more in common with the psychology of equally leftist Montenegrin Cominformists than the latter were likely to develop with Andrija Hebrang. Žujović's moderate leftism was structurally similar to that of Kardelj but could not hold together a house that was splitting apart. Nor could allegiance to the Cominform bridge the gap between the centralist unitarism of many *ibeovci* and the national communism of a Hebrang of any of Yugoslavia's national orientations. Matters were complicated further by the ostensibly leftist stand of the otherwise "rightist" Stalin, whose adherents were more likely to be to the right of the KPJ than to its left.

The Cominformist forces found a modicum of agreement over one issue alone—a favorable, or at least dutiful, stand on the Soviet cri-

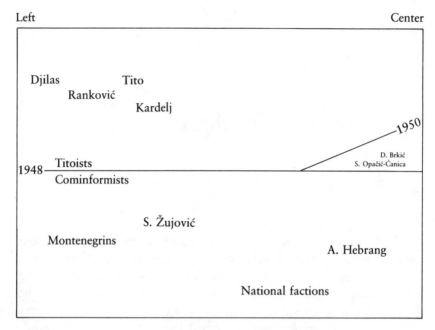

Left   Center

Djilas   Tito
      Ranković
                   Kardelj

                                                            1950

1948   Titoists   D. Brkić
        Cominformists   S. Opačić-Ćanica

                        S. Žujović
        Montenegrins
                                        A. Hebrang

                        National factions

8. The Cominform split, 1948–1950

tique of the KPJ. As the Cominformists did not really constitute a
movement, as they had no single leadership and no consistent program, it can fairly be concluded that they shared little common
ground besides reliance on the USSR or—in some cases—on Soviet
satellite states. This is a clue to the larger question of the roots of
Cominformism. My own research convinces me that the Yugoslav
Communist movement was always very diverse, as diverse as
Yugoslavia itself. We err when we see a monolith even in the late
1930s and especially during the war. Cominformism was therefore no
less factionalized than the larger Yugoslav Communist movement.
Moreover, significant sections of the Cominformist camp were to a
large extent continuations of prewar and wartime party factions.

The *ibeovci* failed to seize power not because they were numerically
insignificant (we have seen that they commanded very significant
forces) but because they lacked internal coherence and a program.
They also lacked strategic initiative, which they needed in ample
supply in view of Stalin's decision not to intervene militarily in
Yugoslavia. Finally, though the Cominformists seriously undermined

Yugoslavia's military and police forces, these services were kept loyal to the KPJ leadership. This last matter is highly important because it demonstrates that even Communist methods of revolutionary struggle are no match for the quartz crushers of a Communist security system.

The crushing of the Cominformist threat had enormous implications for Yugoslavia's internal development. Even Communists who reject the Soviet model of socialism frequently hold that centralist—and therefore bureaucratic—management of the public administration and of the economy, party vanguardism, and a form of revolutionary terror are necessary features of the first stages of socialist development. In Yugoslavia this stage was not reached during the Partisan war, when political pluralism was still in evidence, or to a considerable extent during the immediate postrevolutionary dictatorship. Its full apogee became possible only during the confrontation with Stalin between 1948 and 1950. A struggle against Cominformism and the Cominformists was inevitable because Yugoslavia's party and state apparatus was not Soviet handiwork. It kept Yugoslavia separate from the rest of the bloc and, thanks to Western aid, assured it of an autonomous place in Europe. Yet the conflict with Stalin played the same part in the shaping of Yugoslavia's political system that collectivization and the purges of the 1930s played in the history of Soviet communism. The frank accounting for this period which the Yugoslavs will ultimately have to provide is made more difficult by Western analysts who assume that every manifestation of anti-Stalinism or anti-Sovietism within a socialist state is necessarily a sign of emerging political pluralism.

The Yugoslav leaders were fully aware that their struggle against the Cominformists was won at a cost. They were constantly reminded that the control and unanimity they achieved after 1948 mirrored the Soviet system. And that system, according to Tito's analysis, led the USSR onto the "road of state capitalism with a hitherto unheard-of bureaucracy," rule by a "bureaucratic caste," imperialism, and, indeed, fascism.[1] The best way to avoid the Soviet "blind alley" was

1. Josip Broz Tito, "Borba komunista Jugoslavije za socijalističku demokratiju," in *Šesti kongres KPJ (Saveza komunista Jugoslavije)* (Belgrade, 1952), pp. 27–28. The Soviet leaders, said Tito at the Sixth Congress of the KPJ in November 1952, slandered the Yugoslavs in various ways, "most frequently by resorting to the term 'fascists,' although their own practice accords with that term in full measure" (ibid., p. 35).

not, however, to embrace "bourgeois society," that is, a multiparty democracy and private initiative in production. Yugoslavia's "authentic socialist road" meant the decentralization of the economy, greater worker participation in industrial decision making, and the steady curtailment of state functions. These improvements on the Soviet model were the features of what later would be called "socialist self-management," which, together with the federal system and the policy of nonalignment, came to constitute one of the three pillars of Yugoslavia's political system after the split.

Caught between the Soviet and Western systems, Yugoslavia increasingly nurtured aspects of a market economy (its link with the West) but at the same time maintained many features of the Soviet system, thereby becoming a half-tide basin of Communist reform. Full enlightenment about the malignant side of the Soviet model was not sufficient to stem the caution with which the KPJ/SKJ leadership circumscribed every concession to market mechanisms and to political pluralism—caution born of the realization that the path to liberalization leads through dangerous political territory. This caution, perfectly understandable in a leadership dominated by relatively young people who had been schooled in a highly dogmatic environment, brought Tito to accept Khrushchev's overtures after Stalin's death. This caution also provided the Cominformists with a new lease on life, fitting them first for the role of a genuine left opposition and lately, in their most recent metamorphosis, for that of aspiring partners in a broad coalition pressing for democratic reforms.

The evolution of Cominformism followed the tortuous road of Soviet–Yugoslav relations. Khrushchev's policy seemed to augur complete restoration of friendly ties between Moscow and Belgrade. State relations between the two countries certainly improved. The Belgrade Declaration, signed by the two sides at the end of Khrushchev and Bulganin's momentous visit to Belgrade in May and June 1955, bound the Soviet leaders to recognize Yugoslavia's sociopolitical practice as a legitimate variant of socialism. Relations were further improved with the Twentieth Congress of the CPSU (February 1956), the beginning of the de-Stalinization campaign, and the dissolution of the Cominform in April 1956. For all that, the Yugoslav leadership balked at the idea of ideological unity with the CPSU as long as the Soviets refused to accept pluralism in socialist models and insisted on imposing bloc allegiance on the Yugoslavs.

Yugoslavia's Cominformist exiles and the leaders of the East European countries, especially those of Hungary, Bulgaria, and Albania, continued to pressure the Soviet hierarchy, itself divided on the question of détente with Yugoslavia, not to permit excessive concessions to Tito. And even Khrushchev, who spearheaded Soviet initiatives toward Belgrade, did not wish to abrogate the Cominform Resolution of June 28, 1948, or to break with the Cominformist emigration. The Soviets wanted to present the entire past conflict with Yugoslavia as strictly ideological: Belgrade committed certain doctrinal errors and Stalin unnecessarily exacerbated the dispute. In any case, Moscow did not want to accept the notion that the clash was essentially one of opposing national interests. Moscow therefore continued to treat the *ibeovci* as "Communist internationalists," while Belgrade viewed them as foreign agents. Although the Soviets terminated all émigré newspapers, radio broadcasts, and organizations in 1954, new relations beween Moscow and Belgrade nevertheless remained most sensitive on the question of the *ibeovci*.

One of the concluding points of the Belgrade Declaration was an agreement to initiate measures for the repatriation of nationals of either Yugoslavia or the USSR who lived in the other signer state. Though it was specified that questions of citizenship should be resolved "with respect for humanitarian principles," it was obvious that the USSR, and certainly the Cominformist exiles themselves, hoped for full rehabilitation of the *ibeovci*. The convention signed by the USSR and Yugoslavia in May 1956 left the matter of repatriation to each individual exile's choice. With amnesty of domestic *ibeovci* already in effect, it was unlikely that returning exiles would be subjected to legal sanctions even if they were considered to have committed offenses against the state. Yugoslavia did not demand extradition of any exile, but it was clear that the offer of repatriation and legal protection did not imply that all was forgiven.[2]

---

2. At the Seventh Congress of the SKJ in April 1958, Ranković noted:
During recent years great efforts have been made to find employment [for former *ibeovci*] suitable to their qualifications, although we have had great problems, because it was necessary to overcome the resistance that the working people displayed toward them. The great majority [of *ibeovci*] correctly understood our position and took advantage of it. They must continue to be helped not only in employment and in the solution of their personal problems but also so that they can find a place in our socialist community. The most they can expect from our working people is that they will be given a chance to prove themselves loyal to socialist Yugoslavia and to socialism in

The Soviet government did not actually want the exiles to return, however, partly because they could provide Yugoslavia with embarrassing details of the various anti-Belgrade actions during the period of confrontation and also because future developments might require their services again. In one way and another, Moscow made things difficult for exiles who wanted to go home. During Tito's visit to the USSR in the summer of 1956, the Soviets rather high-handedly pressured Tito into receiving a delegation of exiles. The exiles, following the Soviet example, asked not only for full amnesty but for employment fully comparable to the jobs they held in the USSR, such as similar ranks in the armed forces or the security apparatus. They also demanded assurance of housing and employment for their dependents (often Soviet nationals) and a promise that they would retain Soviet citizenship until all their demands were actually fulfilled. According to Veljko Mićunović, Yugoslavia's ambassador to Moscow, the exile leadership, "certainly in agreement with the Russians, in effect demanded that [Belgrade] reward them for the national treason they committed in 1948 and afterward."[3]

Yugoslav leaders were not plagued by these importunate demands for very long. Relations between Moscow and Belgrade worsened noticeably after the Hungarian revolution. "Yugoslav revisionism" was once again pilloried and Belgrade was held responsible for the Hungarian independence struggle, despite Tito's acquiescence in Soviet intervention. Domestic Cominformists, taking heart, began new activity, though they risked arrest. Three recently released Cominformists, Vladimir Dapčević, Mileta Perović, and Momčilo Djurić (later replaced by Milan Kalafatić), set up a center for the establishment of a new pro-Soviet Communist Party of Yugoslavia, and by mid-1958 they had succeeded in forming six clandestine cells (two in Belgrade and one each in Kosovo, Sarajevo, Zagreb, and Ljubljana).

---

general in everyday work and life. Many of them will quite likely follow that road and again find their place in the SKJ. However, there are completely demoralized individuals who will not choose this road, who stand aside, who are aloof, and who even act in a hostile manner, regardless of the service they receive. They seem to have forgotten their traitorous role and acts toward the people and our socialist country. [Aleksandar Ranković, "O organizaciono-političkim zadacima Saveza komunista Jugoslavije," *Sedmi kongres SKJ (22–26 aprila 1958, Ljubljana)* (Belgrade, 1958), p. 132]

3. Veljko Mićunović, *Moskovske godine 1956/1958.* (Zagreb, 1977), pp. 64–65, 117–18.

When the bloc delegates (with the exception of the Poles) staged a walkout at the Seventh Congress of the SKJ in April 1958 and subsequently denounced the new SKJ program, the underground Cominformists decided the time had come to transfer their base to the Soviet bloc, where support of the *ibeovci* was once again as determined as in Stalin's time. Accordingly, in June 1958, Dapčević, Perović, and their closest associates fled to Albania; so did the members of the Sarajevo cell. Other underground Cominformists escaped to Italy and Hungary. Dapčević, Perović, and Kalafatić were recognized by the Albanian leadership as the Central Committee of the Communist Party of Yugoslavia. In Albania during the next two years they initiated various propaganda efforts against Belgrade and helped to publish information about Goli Otok. They sailed for the USSR in late May 1960—just at the crisis point in Soviet–Albanian relations, which were becoming increasingly tense as a result of Tirana's support for China during the earliest stages of the Sino–Soviet rift.

The split between Moscow and Peking complicated all previous differences in the Communist movement. Soviet disagreements with the SKJ were pushed into the background. Khrushchev sought allies in the struggle against Mao Zedong and found them in Belgrade. Tito portrayed the Chinese leadership as a warmaking Stalinist agency, while hoping that Moscow's confrontation with Peking would strengthen Khrushchev's reformist faction in Moscow. Although the Soviets accepted Yugoslavia as a legitimate socialist state, thus removing the Cominformists' grounds for existence, Tito's alignment with the Russians against China was not without risks. The Soviet leadership, even under Khrushchev, never abandoned the idea of reclaiming Yugoslavia for the East. The SKJ's full acceptance in the bloc councils, on Tito's own terms notwithstanding, thus increased the danger of Soviet possessiveness and possible meddling in less amicable times. Nevertheless, Belgrade's relations with Moscow remained rather warm until the disquieting dismissal of Khrushchev in October 1964.

The dismissal of Aleksandar Ranković from all of his posts in July 1966 marked a further decline of the domestic dogmatists in the SKJ, significantly weakened Soviet influence in Yugoslavia, and initiated the country's decisive drift toward a more democratic socialism. Various political and economic reforms were renewed on a broader scale. The SKJ branches in the various republics, increasingly independent of the Belgrade center, were operating more and more as autonomous—even competing—springboards for each republic's national interests. In most republics, reform forces were in full control, their dominance having been assured by the decisions of the SKJ's Ninth Congress (March 1969). Ties with the USSR were gradually loosened and a more balanced foreign policy evolved, always in the direction of genuine nonalignment. Belgrade continued to deride the excesses of Mao's Cultural Revolution, but it was no longer to be counted on as the leader of a collective interdict on China. Moreover, Yugoslavia's vigorous reform prompted similar endeavors in the bloc countries, especially in Czechoslovakia, where the democratic gains of the Dubček period went beyond those in Yugoslavia.

After the invasion of Czechoslovakia, Belgrade's vociferous objections provoked the Soviets and their bloc allies to charge that "the leaders of Yugoslavia had joined the imperialist chorus."[4] It looked as if Yugoslavia and Romania might be the next objects of attention under the newly articulated Soviet doctrine of "limited sovereignty," which the SKJ did not hesitate to label "neo-Stalinist."[5] In addition, Yugoslavia's relations with Bulgaria declined drastically with the beginning of a new uproar over the national status of Macedonia. Belgrade saw Bulgaria's position as transparent irredentism. The New Left sparked student demonstrations at the University of Belgrade in June 1968, but it was not they that benefited from the new Soviet offensive; rather, the decade-long silence of the original Cominformists was coming to an end, as Moscow apparently authorized their new mobilization.

In 1968 the fear of an imminent Soviet invasion was so great that the Yugoslavs had reason to be apprehensive about this reversal in Soviet policy toward the émigré Cominformists. In 1968 the Soviets started to permit émigré *ibeovci* to return to Yugoslavia, some only as visitors but others as permanent repatriates. In all, 1,300 such persons returned to Yugoslavia with their families; Belgrade refused the applications of only 200.[6] Many of the repatriates no doubt resumed their lives in Yugoslavia with no thought of political engagement,

4. "Antijugoslovenska kampanja: U službi nasilja," *Borba*, Sept. 2, 1968, p. 2.
5. For a typical example of Yugoslavia's rebuttals of the so-called Brezhnev doctrine, see Obren Milićević, "Na stazama neostaljinizma," *Borba*, March 18–19, 1969, p. 2.
6. Savo Kržavac and Dragan Marković, *Informbiro—šta je to: Jugoslavija je rekla ne* (Belgrade, 1976), p. 318.

much less participation in clandestine activities, but some undoubtedly acted as Soviet agents, and of course many of the 1,300 had served in the Soviet army or the intelligence apparatus. At the same time—that is, after the invasion of Czechoslovakia—many undercover domestic *ibeovci*, including some military officers, fled to the Soviet bloc, presumably under the impression that the Soviet Union would welcome their assistance if it was contemplating action against Yugoslavia. Most important, some of the new émigrés joined in the revival of the exile Cominformist organization, which Mileta Perović reactivated in 1968 in Kiev.

By 1971 the center of political attention in Yugoslavia had shifted to the struggle for a new model of the Yugoslav federation and less attention was paid to the Cominformists. This was the high point of the Yugoslav reform movement that had begun in the 1960s and ended in the autumn of 1972, when Tito—for reasons that are beyond the scope of this study—completed his purge of Croatian and Serbian reformers. This sharp change left Yugoslavia's political spectrum dangerously unbalanced. With the reformers and the various nonconformists they protected on the run, the dogmatists and diverse "democratic centralists" undid many of the post-1966 party reforms, though they could not turn the clock back all the way. Naturally, a freer atmosphere for the restrictive left also proved to be a boon for the *ibeovci*. Perović's organization became increasingly active in 1973. Perović now had ties with the exiles in Romania and Czechoslovakia and also, since 1972, with a West European center in Paris. The moment had come to establish direct contacts with the Cominformist underground in Yugoslavia and to hold the founding congress of the new KPJ.

The clandestine congress that took place at the Adriatic harbor of Bar (Montenegro) in April 1974, the subsequent uncovering of the conclave's documents, and the mass arrests of domestic *ibeovci* constituted the swan song of organized Cominformism. Two consequences of this affair ought to be noted. The first (and on the surface the more important) concerns a major change in Soviet policy. In September 1974 Edvard Kardelj was dispatched to Moscow, where he negotiated with the Soviets for almost a fortnight. The contents of these talks have not been revealed. By 1975, however, leading Cominformists living in the USSR, including Mileta Perović, were obliged to leave the country and resettle in the West. And then, on November

27, 1975, a *Pravda* editorial (signed "I. Aleksandrov") attacked "various émigré groups and individual renegades, both inside Yugoslavia and outside its frontiers, who demagogically attempt to portray themselves as the 'most orthodox' adherents of socialism in the SFR Yugoslavia, but who in fact work against the policy of the SKJ and the unity of the peoples of Yugoslavia in the struggle for socialism." *Pravda* added that the Western press was trying to implicate the USSR in this activity. Vigorously denying these charges, the editorial stressed that such "inventions" were aimed at "poisoning relations between the fraternal socialist countries." As for the Cominformists, these "small conspiratorial sectarian groups represent no one but themselves."[7]

The uncovering of the congress at Bar had another important consequence. In 1977 Mileta Perović, acting as general secretary of the new KPJ, brought out the new Cominformist program. This document is characteristic in several ways. Perović's principal aim was to create a broad popular front of all forces opposed to Tito and eventually to form a government in exile. As a consequence, his unwaveringly Marxist-Leninist program nevertheless included elements attractive to noncommunist forces. The agitational edge of Perović's program was aimed squarely at Tito's personal rule: "In its present form the Titoist dictatorship is not a people's or parliamentary democracy at all, but it is also not fascism, though very similar to it as a result of the introduction of corporatism and leaderism. Its essence is the securing of Marshal Tito's real power. This is, therefore, a counterrevolutionary regime of personal rule." Contrary to the sort of internally consistent class analysis that the Cominformists had often attempted in the past, Perović's program was based on the expectation of winning the "Yugoslav People's Army and the other organs of repression" to the side of a "broad popular anti-Titoist front." In that case, it would be possible to topple the regime by peaceful means (a general strike and mass demonstrations), although violence was not ruled out entirely.[8]

The program attacked the SKJ as a "nationalist" and "militarized" party, which should be disbanded unless it underwent reform after

7. I. Aleksandrov (pseud.), "Otpor protivnikam kursa X s'ezda SKIU i sovetsko-iugoslavskoi druzhby," *Pravda*, Nov. 27, 1975, p. 4.

8. Centralni komitet Komunističke partije Jugoslavije, *Program Komunističke partije Jugoslavije* (n.p., 1976), pp. 33, 52–53.

Tito's death, in which case its members could join Perović's KPJ. It promised full rule of law, amnesty for all political prisoners, and the abolition of the secret police. Its position on the crucial question of nationality relations in Yugoslavia was expressed in charges that the "national question has once again surfaced and intensified under the sway of a counterrevolutionary regime of personal rule." The program did not, however, go beyond a call for the "liquidation of the undevelopment that exists among the nations and national minorities of Yugoslavia" and the realization of their social and ideational homogeneity (*istovetnost*).[9]

Though Perović effectively called for Yugoslavia's reintegration within the Soviet bloc ("The KPJ will fight for . . . Yugoslavia's contribution to the defensive capability of the world socialist system. . . . The KPJ will forever remain an indivisible, organic part of the international Communist and workers' movement"), he did not fail to chide the Soviets for their conciliatory attitude toward Tito: "Most of the socialist countries and fraternal parties meet the Titoists halfway in an effort to keep them from going over to the side of imperialism 'beyond recall'; they cling to the belief, which has no basis in fact, that their return to the Marxist-Leninist line is still possible. In this connection the KPJ openly states that it is an illusion to expect that the Titoists will ever return to the Marxist-Leninist path."[10]

The principal features of Perović's program could appeal only to a very narrow base. Despite its democratic pretensions, it had no hope of enlisting support among the Slovenes and Croats, who could not possibly respond to a program that disparaged self-management as anarchistic because of its decentralizing tendencies. (In fact, Perović's program denounced Tito's role in 1971, when the Yugoslav leader supposedly "was initially on the side of Croat nationalists, the adherents of the establishment of a new Independent State of Croatia, whom he amply helped and encouraged.") Nor could his program find much response among the Montenegrins and Serbs, who alone constituted the minuscule base of the Cominformist KPJ.

The decline of Cominformism from a large coalition to an insignificant handful paralleled the general decline of revolutionary vigor in Yugoslavia. The old *ibeovci* represented a variety of political and

9. Ibid., pp. 93–94.
10. Ibid., p. 44.

nationality interests and hence had no coherent program. The new Cominformists had a program of 121 pages with no internal contradictions. The old *ibeovci* incongruously represented both the KPJ's left and its right. The new Conformists stemmed only from the SKJ's dogmatic factions. Many of the old *ibeovci* were young rebels. The younger generation of Cominformists, especially their Montenegrin core (all the leaders of the new KPJ were Montenegrins), were the children of old *ibeovci*. The old *ibeovci* had no formal leadership, but counted among their number two members of the KPJ Politburo and numerous other instantly recognizable party leaders. The new Cominformists had no "personalities," but maintained a party, a central committee, and a general secretary. Still, the old and the new Cominformists had at least one thing in common. Among the many disadvantages they shared, the most poignant was the fact that Moscow never reciprocated their devotion. From the beginning the USSR had the power to destroy them. What the Cominformists interpreted as protection was in the Soviet view simply the economic management of doctrine.[11]

The arrest and subsequent imprisonment of Mileta Perović in the summer of 1977 was official Cominformism's lowest point. It never recovered. Variants of Cominformism will continue to play some role as long as Bulgaria (acting as a member of the Soviet bloc) and

11. Some former *ibeovci* came to believe that the USSR abandoned the Yugoslav Cominformist movement as a troublesome liability. This view was allegorically rendered in a poetic cycle, *Knjaževska kancelarija* (Princely chancellery), by Radovan Zogović (Titograd, 1976). The subject was Prince Miloš Obrenović, who ruled Serbia as a Turkish vassal and contended with radical rivals who looked to Russia for full liberation. In one passage Zogović's Miloš muses:

Rebellions. Rebellions. Yes, "all the émigrés in Iaşi
must be sent somewhere to Russia, quickly and far away!"
And he who explains, who entreats, will not remain unheard
(because Russia also fears rebellions and puts out their flames
where'er they flare—that they may not burst into a conflagration!),
and Count Nesselrode writes me:
"that a sharp command was issued to the governor of Bessarabia that he should sternly watch the Serbian chiefs, of whom some are away from the frontier, and others under guard, and all in such a state that they will no longer be able to intrigue against the Prince's wise administration and against the peace-loving endeavors of the Emperor . . ."
. . .
"Russia! Russia!" Here's Russia for you!
. . .
You are no longer of use to Russia. And I am a "Turkish footman."
So—where will you now? [Pp. 69–70]

Albania (acting as a heterodox Communist state) pursue their respective policies in regard to the status of Macedonians and Albanians in Yugoslavia. Indeed, the use of "Marxist-Leninist" in the names of illegal Albanian groups uncovered in Kosovo has been noticeable since the beginning of the crisis there in 1981.[12] Specific nationality problems have also contributed to forms of "private" Cominformism, as among some fringe contingents of the Croat emigration. Nevertheless, the Soviet-style *ibeovci* have no hope of becoming a substantial force as long as their nationality base remains almost completely uninational and their initiatives can be changed to suit Moscow's policy in southeastern Europe. Despite the deep economic, political, and structural crisis of post-Tito Yugoslavia, with all the attendant opportunities for Cominformist mischief, Gorbachev's *perestroika* in international relations may yet sound the death knell of the old cause. When it becomes essential for the educator to educate himself, does he forget the materialist doctrine that men are the products of their upbringing?

12. The names of some of these organizations are highly suggestive: Group of Marxists-Leninists of Kosovo, Communist Marxist-Leninist Albanian Movement in Yugoslavia, Marxist-Leninist Party of Albanians in Yugoslavia, Revolutionary Socialist Movement of Albanians in Yugoslavia.

Appendix: Backgrounds of the Ninety Emigrants Cited in the Dinko A. Tomašić Collection

	Croats		Serbs		Slovenes		Ukrainians		Albanians		Czechs		Russians		Macedonians		Bulgars		Hungarians		Montenegrins		Muslims (nationality)		Slovaks		Romanians		Other	
	M	F	M	F	M	F	M	F	M	F	M	F	M	F	M	F	M	F	M	F	M	F	M	F	M	F	M	F	M	F
Age																														
15–20	1		2	1	3														2											
20–25	8	1	3					1	2		2		1						2		1									
25–30	7	4	6		7		1	1	1				1		1						1						1		2	
30–35	3		2				1	1	1		1																			
35–40			1																										1	
40–	1	2			1				2		1		1												1					
Unknown	2	1	4												1															
Regional origin																														
Bosnia-Hercegovina	3		2				2														1								1	
Croatia	19	5	2				1												1										1	
Kosovo			1																											
Macedonia									1						1															
Montenegro			1																		1									
Serbia	1		6										1																1	
Slovenia					12	2					1																			
Vojvodina			2												1				1						1					
Foreign							2		2		2		1		1		2										1			
Unknown			3	1																										
Religion																														
Roman or Greek Catholic	21	8			12	2	3[a]		1		2[b]								1[c]										2	
Eastern Orthodox			18	1									1	2	2		2				1						1			
Muslim	1								1														1							
Other																													1	
Unknown							2		1		1								1						1					
Education																														
Elementary	1		1		4		1												1											
Trade school	4	1	5		1	2									2															
Gymnasium	2		1	1	2				1																					
University	6	3	5		1				1		2		1		1	1	2										1		1	
Other			1																											
Unknown	7	4	5		4				3		1		1						1		1		1		1				1	
Occupation																														
Professional	2		1				1		1																					
Other nonmanual	4	3	4	1			2	1	1				1		2	1											1		1	
Student	3		2						2				1				2										1		1	
Military	4		2																		1									
Artisan	3	1	4		2						1		2										1							
Worker	8		4		1										1				1											
Peasant	3		2		6		3																		1		1			
Other			3		1																									

269

	Croats M	F	Serbs M	F	Slovenes M	F	Ukrainians M	F	Albanians M	F	Czechs M	F	Russians M	F	Macedonians M	F	Bulgars M	F	Hungarians M	F	Montenegrins M	F	Muslims (nationality) M	F	Slovaks M	F	Romanians M	F	Other M	F
Wartime allegiance																														
Ustaša units or regular Croat army	3																													
Slovene collaborationist units					2																									
Partisans																														
1941–1943	4		2		3																									
1944	2		1		1																									
Membership																														
KPJ	6		5		3														1											
SKOJ	3		4		2		1						1																	
Imprisoned since 1945	2		4	1	2		1																							
Emigration																														
To West, Yugoslav passport																														
1952	1	2	2																											
1953	1		1																											
To West, foreign passport or as stateless	2	6					1	3	3		3		1	2	1		1		1										1	
Illegal																														
1950	1																													
1951	8		5		8		1										1		1						1		1			
1952	9		7	1	2	1	1												1		1									

a One certain, two probable.
b One certain, one probable.
c Uncertain.

Bibliography

BOOKS

Adamic, Louis. *The Eagle and the Roots*. Garden City, N.Y.: Doubleday, 1952.

Alexander, Stella. *Church and State in Yugoslavia since 1945*. Cambridge: Cambridge University Press, 1979.

Apostolski, Mihailo, Velimir Brezoski, Vlado Ivanovski, Rastislav Terzioski, and Mile Todorovski, eds. *Izvori za osvoboditelnata vojna i revolucija vo Makedonija, 1941–1945*. Vol. 1, pts. 1–3. Skopje: Institut za nacionalna istorija, 1968–1970.

Armstrong, Hamilton Fish. *Tito and Goliath*. New York: Macmillan, 1951.

Avakumovic, Ivan. *History of the Communist Party of Yugoslavia*. Vol. 1. Aberdeen: Aberdeen University Press, 1964.

Averoff-Tossizza, Evangelos. *Le Feu et la hache: Grèce 46–49*. Paris: Breteuil, 1973.

Banac, Ivo. *The National Question in Yugoslavia: Origins, History, Politics*. Ithaca: Cornell University Press, 1984.

Barker, Elisabeth. *British Policy in South-East Europe in the Second World War*. London: Macmillan, 1976.

———. *Macedonia: Its Place in Balkan Power Politics*. London: Royal Institute of International Affairs, 1950.

Bass, Robert, and Elizabeth Marbury, eds. *The Soviet-Yugoslav Controversy, 1948–58: A Documentary Record*. New York: Prospect Books, 1959.

Bebler, Aleš. *Kako sam hitao: Sećanja*. Belgrade: NIRO Četvrti jul, 1982.

Belinić, Marko. *Do naših dana*. Zagreb: Republika, 1966.

———. *Put kroz život*. Zagreb: August Cesarec, 1985.

Benes, Vaclav L., Robert F. Byrnes, and Nicolas Spulber, eds. *The Second Soviet-Yugoslav Dispute*. Bloomington: Indiana University Publications, 1958.

Bilandžić, Dušan. *Borba za samoupravni socijalizam u Jugoslaviji 1945–1969*. Zagreb: Institut za historiju radničkog pokreta Hrvatske, 1969.

_____. *Društveni razvoj socijalističke Jugoslavije*. 2d ed. Zagreb: Centar društvenih djelatnosti SSOH, 1976.

_____. *Historija Socijalističke Federativne Republike Jugoslavije: Glavni procesi*. Zagreb: Školska knjiga, 1978.

Blažević, Jakov. *Brazdama partije*. Samobor: Zagreb, 1986.

_____. *Suprotstavljanja . . . i ljudi: Za novu Jugoslaviju po svijetu*. Zagreb, Belgrade, and Sarajevo: Mladost, Prosveta, and Svjetlost, 1980.

_____. *Tražio sam crvenu nit*. Zagreb: IPP Zagreb, 1976.

Borković, Milan, and Venceslav Glišić, eds. *Osnivački kongres KP Srbije (8–12. maj 1945)*. Belgrade: Institut za istoriju radničkog pokreta Srbije, 1972.

Borowiec, Andrew. *Yugoslavia after Tito*. New York: Praeger, 1977.

Brzezinski, Zbigniew K. *The Soviet Bloc: Unity and Conflict*. Cambridge: Harvard University Press, 1960.

Burks, R. V. *The Dynamics of Communism in Eastern Europe*. Princeton: Princeton University Press, 1961.

Campbell, John C. *Tito's Separate Road: America and Yugoslavia in World Politics*. New York: Harper & Row, 1967.

Cenčić, Vjenceslav. *Enigma Kopinič*. 2 vols. Belgrade: Rad, 1983.

Centralni komitet Komunističke partije Jugoslavije. *Program Komunističke partije Jugoslavije*. N.p., 1976.

Čepo, Zlatko, and Ivan Jelić, eds. *Peta zemaljska konferencija Komunističke partije Jugoslavije: Zbornik radova*. Zagreb: Institut za historiju radničkog pokreta Hrvatske, 1972.

Ciliga, Ante. *La Yougoslavie sous la menace intérieure et extérieure*. Paris: Plon, 1951.

Claudín, Fernando. *The Communist Movement: From Comintern to Cominform*. Vol. 2, *The Zenith of Stalinism*. New York: Monthly Review Press, 1975.

Clissold, Stephen. *Yugoslavia and the Soviet Union*. London: Institute for the Study of Conflict, 1975.

_____. *Yugoslavia and the Soviet Union, 1939–1973: A Documentary History*. London: Royal Institute of International Affairs, 1975.

Čolaković, Rodoljub. *Kazivanje o jednom pokoljenju*. 3 vols. Sarajevo: Svjetlost, 1964–1972.

_____, Dragoslav Janković, and Pero Morača, eds. *Pregled istorije Saveza komunista Jugoslavije*. Belgrade: Institut za izučavanje radničkog pokreta, 1963.

Conquest, Robert. *The Great Terror: Stalin's Purge of the Thirties*. London and Toronto: Macmillan, 1968.

Damjanović, Pero, Milovan Bosić, and Dragica Lazarević, eds. *Peta zemaljska konferencija KPJ (19–23. oktobar 1940)*. Belgrade: Komunist, 1980.

Dedijer, Vladimir. *Dnevnik*. 3 vols. Belgrade: Državni izdavački zavod Jugoslavije, 1945.

_____. *Dnevnik*. 2d rev. ed. Belgrade: Prosveta, 1970.

_____. *Izgubljena bitka J. V. Staljina*. Sarajevo: Svjetlost, 1969.

———. *Josip Broz Tito: Prilozi za biografiju.* Belgrade: Kultura, 1953.

———. *Jugoslovensko–albanski odnosi, 1939–1948.* Belgrade: Borba, 1949.

———. *Novi prilozi za biografiju Josipa Broza Tita.* Vol. 2. Rijeka: Liburnija, 1981.

———. *Novi prilozi za biografiju Josipa Broza Tita.* Vol. 3. Belgrade: Rad, 1984.

———, ed. *Dokumenti 1948.* 3 vols. Belgrade: Rad, 1980.

Dimitrov, Georgi. *Selected Works.* 2 vols. Sofia: Foreign Languages Press, 1967.

Djilas, Milovan. *Članci, 1941–1946.* Zagreb: Kultura, 1947.

———. *Conversations with Stalin.* New York: Harcourt Brace & World, 1962.

———. *Memoir of a Revolutionary.* New York: Harcourt Brace Jovanovich, 1973.

———. *Tito: The Story from Inside.* New York: Harcourt Brace Jovanovich, 1980.

———. *Vlast.* London: Naša reč, 1983.

———. *Wartime.* New York: Harcourt Brace Jovanovich, 1977.

Doder, Milenko. *Kopinič bez enigme.* Zagreb: Centar za informacije i publicitet, 1986.

Eudes, Dominique. *The Kapetanios: Partisans and Civil War in Greece, 1943–1949.* New York: Monthly Review Press, 1972.

Farrell, R. Barry. *Jugoslavia and the Soviet Union, 1948–1956: An Analysis with Documents.* Hamden, Conn.: Shoe String Press, 1956.

Fejtö, François. *Histoire des démocraties populaires.* Paris: Seuil, 1952.

Gabelić, Andro. *Tragovima izdaje.* Zagreb: Naprijed, 1951.

Gardiner, Leslie. *The Eagle Spreads His Claws: A History of the Corfu Channel Dispute and of Albania's Relations with the West, 1945–1965.* Edinburgh: William Blackwood, 1966.

Gavrilović, Živojin. *Pane Limar: Životni put Rasinca i udbovca Pana Djukića-Limara.* 2d ed. Belgrade: Nolit, 1982.

Gibianskii, L. Ia. *Sovetskii Soiuz i novaia Iugoslaviia, 1941–1947 gg.* Moscow: Nauka, 1987.

Godina, Ferdo. *Molčeči orkester.* Maribor: Obzorja, 1981.

Gorkić, M. *Novim Putevima (Pouke iz provala).* Brussels: Radnička biblioteka, 1937.

Gregorić, Pavle. *NOB u sjeveroistočnoj Hrvatskoj 1942. godine.* Zagreb: Stvarnost, 1978.

Hadri, Ali. *Narodnooslobodilački pokret na Kosovu.* Priština: Zavod za istoriju Kosova, 1973.

Hahn, Werner G. *Postwar Soviet Politics: The Fall of Zhdanov and the Defeat of Moderation, 1946–53.* Ithaca: Cornell University Press, 1982.

Halperin, Ernst. *The Triumphant Heretic: Tito's Struggle against Stalin.* London: Heinemann, 1958.

Hasani, Sinan. *Kosovo: Istine i zablude.* Zagreb: Centar za informacije i publicitct, 1986.

———. *Vetar i hrast.* Sarajevo: Svjetlost, 1976.

Hoffman, George W., and Fred W. Neal, *Yugoslavia and the New Communism.* New York: Twentieth Century Fund, 1962.

Hofman, Branko. *Noč do jutra.* Ljubljana: Slovenska matica, 1981.

Holjevac, Većeslav. *Zapisi iz rodnoga grada*. Zagreb: NZ Matica Hrvatska, 1972.

Hoxha, Enver. *The Anglo-American Threat to Albania: Memoirs of the National Liberation War*. Tirana: 8 Nëntori, 1982.

――――. *Kur lindi Partia: Kujtime*. Tirana: 8 Nëntori, 1981.

――――. *Selected Works*. 5 vols. Tirana: 8 Nëntori, 1974–1985.

――――. *Titistët: Shënime historike*. Tirana: 8 Nëntori, 1982.

――――. *With Stalin: Memoirs*. Tirana: 8 Nëntori, 1979.

Hristov, Aleksandar T. *KPJ vo rešavanjeto na makedonskoto prašanje*. Skopje: Kultura, 1962.

Hurem, Rasim. *Kriza narodnooslobodilačkog pokreta u Bosni i Hercegovini krajem 1941. i početkom 1942. godine*. Sarajevo: Svjetlost, 1972.

Institute of Marxist-Leninist Studies at the CC of the Party of Labor of Albania. *History of the Party of Labor of Albania*. Tirana: Naim Frashëri, 1971.

Isaković, Antonije. *Tren 2: Kazivanja Čeperku*. Belgrade: Prosveta, 1982.

Isusov, Mito. *Komunističeskata partija i revoljucionnijat proces v Bəlgarija 1944/1948*. Sofia: Partizdat, 1983.

Jareb, Jere. *Pola stoljeća hrvatske politike*. Buenos Aires: Knjižnica Hrvatske revije, 1960.

Javoršek, Jože. *Opasne veze*. Zagreb: Globus, 1980.

Jelić, Ivan. *Komunistička partija Hrvatske, 1937–1941*. Zagreb: IHRPH, 1972.

――――. *Komunistička partija Hrvatske, 1937–1945*. 2 vols. Zagreb: Globus, 1981.

Jelić-Butić, Fikreta. *Hrvatska seljačka stranka*. Zagreb: Globus, 1983.

Jenšterle, Marko. *Skeptična levica*. Maribor: Založba Obzorja, 1985.

Johnson, A. Ross. *The Transfiguration of Communist Ideology: The Yugoslav Case, 1945–1953*. Cambridge: MIT Press, 1972.

Jovanović, Dragoljub. *Ljudi, ljudi . . . (Medaljoni 56 umrlih savremenika)*. 2 vols. Belgrade: Author, 1973–1975.

Jovanović, Dušan. *Karamazovi*. Belgrade: Nezavisna izdanja, 1984.

Kalajdžić, Dragan. *Otok gole istine*. Zagreb: Globus, 1985.

Kardelj, Edvard. *Borba za priznanje i nezavisnost nove Jugoslavije: Sećanja*. Belgrade: NIRO Radnička štampa, 1980.

Kešetović, Muhamed. *Kontrarevolucija na Kosovu*. Belgrade: NIRO Zadruga, 1984.

King, Robert R. *Minorities under Communism: Nationalities as a Source of Tension among Balkan Communist States*. Cambridge: Harvard University Press, 1973.

Kirjazovski, Risto. *Narodnoosloboditelniot front i drugite organizacii na Makedoncite od Egejska Makedonija (1945–1949)*. Skopje: Kultura, 1985.

Kljakić, Dragan. *Dosije Hebrang*. Belgrade: Partizanska knjiga, 1983.

――――. *General Markos*. Zagreb: Globus, 1979.

Kofos, Evangelos. *Nationalism and Communism in Macedonia*. Salonika: Institute for Balkan Studies, 1964.

Kolakowski, Leszek. *Main Currents of Marxism: Its Origins, Growth, and Dissolution*. Vol. 3, *The Breakdown*. Oxford: Oxford University Press, 1978.

Komanin, Žarko [Žarko Jovanović]. *Prestupna godina*. Belgrade: Srpska književna zadruga, 1982.

Korać, Vitomir. *Povjest Radničkog Pokreta u Hrvatskoj i Slavoniji*. Vol. 1. Zagreb: Radnička Komora za Hrvatsku i Slavoniju, 1929.

Korbel, Josef. *Tito's Communism*. Denver: University of Denver Press, 1951.

Koštunica, Vojislav, and Kosta Čavoški. *Stranački pluralizam ili monizam: Društveni pokreti i politički sistem u Jugoslaviji, 1944–1949*. Belgrade: Institut društvenih nauka Univerziteta u Beogradu, 1983.

Kousoulas, D. George. *Revolution and Defeat: The Story of the Greek Communist Party*. London: Oxford University Press, 1965.

Kovač, Mirko. *Vrata od utrobe*. Belgrade: BIGZ, 1971.

Kovačević, Branislav. *Komunistička partija Crne Gore, 1945–1952. godine*. Titograd: NIO Univerzitetska riječ, 1986.

Kreft, Ivan. *Spori in spopadi v spominih in dokumentih*. 3 vols. Maribor, Ljubljana, Koper, Murska Sobota: Založba Obzorja, Državna založba Slovenije, Založba Lipa, and Pomurska založba, 1981–1984.

Kremenšek, Slavko. *Slovensko študentovsko gibanje, 1919–1941*. Ljubljana: Mladinska knjiga, 1972.

Krivokapić, Boro. *Dahauski procesi*. Belgrade: Prosveta and Partizanska knjiga, 1986.

Krnić, Zdravko, ed. *Drugi kongres KPJ: Materijali sa simpozija održanog 22. i 23. VI 1970. povodom 50-godišnjice Drugog (Vukovarskog) kongresa KPJ 1920*. Slavonski Brod: Historijski institut Slavonije, 1972.

Kržavac, Savo, and Dragan Marković. *Informbiro—šta je to: Jugoslavija je rekla ne*. Belgrade: Sloboda, 1976.

Lasić, Stanko. *Krleža: Kronologija života i rada*. Zagreb: Grafički zavod Hrvatske, 1982.

———. *Sukob na književnoj ljevici, 1928–1952*. Zagreb: Liber, 1970.

Laušić, Jozo. *Bogumil*. Zagreb: Globus, 1982.

Lazitch, Branko, and Milorad M. Drachkovitch. *Biographical Directory of the Comintern*. Stanford: Hoover Institution Press, 1973.

Lazri, Sofokli, and Javer Malo. *Dans les prisons et les camps de concentration de la Yougoslavie*. Tirana: Mihal Duri, 1960.

Lešnik, Avgust. *Spor med Jugoslavijo in Informbirojem*. Ljubljana: Zveza delavskih univerz Slovenije, 1978.

Ličina, Djordje. *Izdaja*. Zagreb: Centar za informacije i publicitet, 1986.

Livadić, Stjepan [Stjepan Cvijić]. *Politički eseji*. Zagreb: Author, 1937.

Lukač, Dušan. *Radnički pokret u Jugoslaviji i nacionalno pitanje, 1918–1941*. Belgrade: Institut za savremenu istoriju, 1972.

McCagg, William O., Jr. *Stalin Embattled, 1943–1948*. Detroit: Wayne State University Press, 1978.

MacDermott, Mercia. *Freedom or Death: The Life of Gotsé Delchev*. London: Journeyman Press, 1978.

Marić, Milomir. *Deca komunizma*. Belgrade: NIRO Mladost, 1987.

Marinko, Miha. *Moji spomini*. Ljubljana: Mladinska knjiga, 1974.

Markov, Mladen. *Isterivanje boga: Seljačka tragedija.* 2 vols. Belgrade: Prosveta, 1984.

Marković, Dragan. *Istina o Golom otoku.* Belgrade: Narodna knjiga and Partizanska knjiga, 1987.

——— and Savo Kržavac. *Zavera Informbiroa.* Belgrade: Narodna knjiga and Partizanska knjiga, 1987.

Marković, Milivoje. *Preispitivanja: Informbiro i Goli otok u jugoslovenskom romanu.* Belgrade: Narodna knjiga, 1986.

Marković, Sima. *Nacionalno pitanje u svetlosti marksizma.* Belgrade: Grafički institut Narodna misao, 1923.

Markovski, Venko. *Epopeja na nezabravimite.* Sofia: Nacionalnija səvet na Otečestvenija front, 1967.

———. *Goli Otok, the Island of Death: A Diary in Letters.* Boulder, Colo.: East European Quarterly, 1984.

Mastny, Vojtech. *Russia's Road to the Cold War: Diplomacy, Warfare, and the Politics of Communism, 1941–1945.* New York: Columbia University Press, 1979.

Mbi ngarjet në Kosovë. Tirana: 8 Nëntori, 1981.

Mićunović, Veljko. *Moskovske godine, 1956–1958.* Zagreb: SN Liber, 1977.

Mihovilović, Maroje, Mario Bošnjak, and Sead Saračević. *Sukob s Informbiroom.* Zagreb: IP August Cesarec, 1976.

Milatović, Arso. *Pet diplomatskih misija.* 2 vols. Ljubljana: Cankarjeva založba, 1985.

Milatović, Mile. *Slučaj Andrije Hebranga.* Belgrade: Kultura, 1952.

Mitrev, Dimitar, and Aleksandar Spasov, eds. *Borba i literatura: Zbornik od esei i statii.* Skopje: Kultura, 1961.

Mojsov, Lazar. *Bugarska radnička partija (komunista) i makedonsko nacionalno pitanje.* Belgrade: Borba, 1948.

Morača, Pero. *Istorija Saveza komunista Jugoslavije: Kratak pregled.* Belgrade: Rad, 1966.

——— and Dušan Bilandžić. *Avangarda, 1919–1969.* Belgrade: Komunist, 1969.

———, ———, and Stanislav Stojanović. *Istorija Saveza komunista Jugoslavije: Kratak pregled.* Belgrade: Rad, 1976.

Mugoša, Dušan. *Na zadatku.* Belgrade: Četvrti jul, 1973.

Muhić, Fuad. *SKJ i opozicija.* Subotica: Radnički univerzitet Veljko Vlahović, 1977.

———. *Staljinizam: Teorijski pogled na jedan fenomen.* Sarajevo: NIŠRO Oslobodjenje, 1981.

Narodna vlada Hrvatske. Zagreb?: Državno nakladno poduzeće Hrvatske, 1945.

Neal, Fred Warner. *Titoism in Action.* Berkeley: University of California Press, 1958.

Nešković, Blagoje. *O zaoštravanju klasne borbe na selu u sadašnjoj etapi izgradnje socijalizma i o savezu radničke klase i radnog seljaštva.* Zagreb: Naprijed, 1949.

Nešović, Slobodan. *Bledski sporazumi: Tito-Dimitrov (1947).* Zagreb: Globus, 1979.

_____, and Branko Petranović, eds. *AVNOJ i revolucija: Tematska zbirka dokumenata, 1941–1945.* Belgrade: Narodna knjiga, 1983.
Nikoliš, Gojko. *Korijen, stablo, paventina: Memoari.* Zagreb: Liber, 1981.
Novak, Bogdan C. *Trieste, 1941–1954.* Chicago: University of Chicago Press, 1970.
Numić, Selim, ed. *Pali nepobedjeni, 1944–1964.* Belgrade: Savezni odbor za proslavu dvadesete godišnjice Službe unutrašnje bezbednosti, 1965.
Očak, Ivan. *U borbi za ideje Oktobra: Jugoslavenski povratnici iz Sovjetske Rusije, 1918–1921.* Zagreb: Stvarnost, 1976.
O kontrarevolucionarnoj i klevetničkoj kampanji protiv socijalističke Jugoslavije. 2 vols. Belgrade: Borba, 1949–1950.
Opačić-Ćanica, Stanko, ed. *Narodne pjesme Korduna.* Zagreb: Prosvjeta, 1971.
Oren, Nissan. *Bulgarian Communism: The Road to Power, 1934–1944.* New York: Columbia University Press, 1971.
Pajetta, Gian Carlo. *Le crisi che so vissuto: Budapest Praga Varsavia.* Rome: Riuniti, 1982.
Palmer, Stephen E., Jr., and Robert R. King. *Yugoslav Communism and the Macedonian Question.* Hamden, Conn.: Archon, 1971.
Pano, Nicholas C. *The People's Republic of Albania.* Baltimore: Johns Hopkins Press, 1968.
Pauljević, Slobodan. *Strašno budjenje.* Rijeka: Otokar Keršovani, 1982.
Perović, Latinka. *Od centralizma do federalizma: KPJ u nacionalnom pitanju.* Zagreb: Globus, 1984.
Pešić, Desanka. *Jugoslovenski komunisti i nacionalno pitanje, 1919–1935.* Belgrade: Rad, 1983.
Peti kongres Komunističke partije Jugoslavije: Izveštaji i referati. Belgrade: Kultura, 1948.
Petković, Aleksandar. *Gospodo i drugovi.* Belgrade: Pres Kliping, 1981.
Petranović, Branko. *Politička i ekonomska osnova narodne vlasti u Jugoslaviji za vreme obnove.* Belgrade: Institut za savremenu istoriju, 1969.
_____, Ranko Končar, and Radovan Radonjić, comps. *Sednice Centralnog komiteta KPJ (1948–1952).* Belgrade: Komunist, 1985.
_____ and Čedomir Štrbac. *Istorija socijalističke Jugoslavije.* 3 vols. Belgrade: Radnička štampa, 1977.
_____, _____, and Stanislav Stojanović. *Jugoslavija u medjunarodnom radničkom pokretu.* Belgrade: Institut za medjunarodni radnički pokret, 1973.
Pijade, Moša. *Izabrani spisi.* Tome 1, 5 vols. Belgrade: Institut za izučavanje radničkog pokreta, 1966.
_____, ed. *Istorijski arhiv Komunističke partije Jugoslavije.* Tome 2, *Kongresi i zemaljske konferencije KPJ, 1919–1937.* Belgrade: Istorijsko odeljenje CK KPJ, 1949.
Pirjevec, Jože. *Tito, Stalin, e l'Occidente.* Trieste: Stampa Triestina, 1985.
Pleterski, Janko. *Komunistička partija Jugoslavije i nacionalno pitanje, 1919–1941.* Belgrade: Komunist, 1971.
_____. *Nacije—Jugoslavija—revolucija.* Belgrade: IC Komunist, 1985.
Pollo, Stefanaq, and Arben Puto. *Histoire de l'Albanie.* Roanne: Horvath, 1974.

Popović, Aleksandar. *Mrešćenje šarana i druge drame.* Belgrade: BIGZ, 1986.
Popovski, Jovan. *General Markos: Zašto me Staljin nije streljao?* Belgrade: Partizanska knjiga, 1982.
Pribićević, Branko. *Sukob Komunističke partije Jugoslavije i Kominforma.* Belgrade: Komunist, 1972.
Prifti, Peter R. *Socialist Albania since 1944: Domestic and Foreign Developments.* Cambridge: MIT Press, 1978.
Prvo redovno zasedanje Saveznog veća i Veća naroda: Stenografske beleške 15 maj—20 jul 1946. Belgrade: Narodna skupština FNRJ, n.d.
Ra'anan, Gavriel D. *International Policy Formation in the USSR: Factional "Debates" during the Zhdanovshchina.* Hamden, Conn.: Archon, 1983.
Radonjić, Radovan. *Izgubljena orijentacija.* Belgrade: Radnička štampa, 1985.
———. *Sukob KPJ sa Kominformom i društveni razvoj Jugoslavije (1948–1950).* 2d ed. Zagreb: Narodno sveučilište grada Zagreba and Centar za aktualni politički studij, 1976.
Rad zakonodavnih odbora Pretsedništva Antifašističkog veća narodnog oslobodjenja Jugoslavije i Privremene narodne skupštine DFJ (3 aprila–25 oktobra 1945). Po stenografskim beleškama i drugim izvorima. Belgrade: Prezidium Narodne skupštine FNRJ, n.d.
Ralić, Prvoslav. *Dogmatizam kao kontrarevolucija.* Belgrade: Komunist, 1976.
Ranković, Aleksandar. *Izabrani govori i članci: 1941–1951.* Belgrade: Kultura, 1951.
Reale, Eugenio. *Avec Jacques Duclos au banc des accusés à la réunion constitutive du Kominform à Szklarska Poreba (22–27 Septembre 1947).* Paris: Plon, 1958.
Reuter, Jens. *Die Albaner in Jugoslawien.* Munich: R. Olenbourg, 1982.
Richter, Heinz. *British Intervention in Greece: From Varkiza to Civil War (February 1945 to August 1946).* London: Merlin, 1985.
Rothberg, Abraham, ed. *Anatomy of a Moral: The Political Essays of Milovan Djilas.* New York: Praeger, 1959.
Rubčić, Nikola, ed. *Robija: Zapisi hrvatskih nacionalnih boraca.* Zagreb: Editor, 1936.
Rusinow, Dennison. *The Yugoslav Experiment, 1948–1974.* Berkeley: University of California Press, 1977.
Šatev, Pavel. *V Makedonija pod robstvo.* 2d ed. Sofia: Bəlgarski pisatel, 1968.
Sedmi kongres SKJ (22–26 aprila 1958, Ljubljana). Belgrade: Kultura, 1958.
Selenić, Slobodan. *Pismo/glava.* Belgrade: Prosveta, 1982.
Selimović, Meša. *Sjećanja.* Belgrade: Sloboda, 1976.
Šepić, Dragovan. *Vlada Ivana Šubašića.* Zagreb: Globus, 1983.
Šesti kongres KPJ (Saveza komunista Jugoslavije). Belgrade: Kultura, 1952.
Seton-Watson, Hugh. *The East European Revolution.* New York: Praeger, 1951.
Shoup, Paul. *Communism and the Yugoslav National Question.* New York: Columbia University Press, 1968.
Shtypi botëror rreth ngjarjeve në Kosovë. Tirana: 8 Nëntori, 1981.
Sidran, Abdulah. *Otac na službenom putu.* Belgrade: NIRO Mladost, 1985.
Sirotković, Hodimir, ed. *Zemaljsko antifašističko vijeće narodnog oslobodjenja*

Hrvatske: Zbornik dokumenata 1943–1944. 3 vols. Zagreb: IHRPH, 1964–1975.

Smodlaka, Josip. *Partizanski dnevnik.* Belgrade: Nolit, 1972.

Stalin, I. V. *Sochineniia,* 3 vols. Stanford: Hoover Institution on War, Revolution, and Peace, 1967.

Stalin's Correspondence with Churchill and Attlee, 1941–1945. New York: Capricorn, 1965.

Šta se dogadjalo na Kosovu. Belgrade: Politika, 1981.

Štaubringer, Zvonko. *Titovo istorijsko ne staljinizmu.* Belgrade: Radnička štampa, 1976.

Stavrakis, Peter J. *The Soviet Union and the Greek Civil War, 1944–1949.* Ithaca: Cornell University Press, 1989.

Stilinović, Marijan. *Sumrak u Pragu.* Zagreb: Naprijed, 1952.

Stojanović, Stanislav, ed. *Istorija Saveza komunista Jugoslavije.* Belgrade: IC Komunist, Narodna knjiga, and Rad, 1985.

Štrbac, Čedomir. *Jugoslavija i odnosi izmedju socijalističkih zemalja: Sukob KPJ i Informbiroa.* Belgrade: Institut za medjunarodnu politiku i privredu, 1975.

Stuparić, Darko. *Revolucionari i bez funkcije.* Rijeka: Otokar Keršovani, 1975.

Sudebnyi protsess Traicho Kostova i ego gruppy. Sofia: Press Dept., 1949.

Supek, Ivan. *Krivovjernik na ljevici.* Bristol: BC Review, 1980.

_____. *Krunski svjedok protiv Hebranga.* Chicago: Markanton, 1983.

Terzuolo, Eric R. *Red Adriatic: The Communist Parties of Italy and Yugoslavia.* Boulder, Colo.: Westview, 1985.

Testimonies Which Cannot Be Refuted: Statements by Refugee Soldiers of the Soviet Satellite Armies. n.p.: Yugoslav Newspapermen's Assn., 1952?

The Soviet-Yugoslav Dispute. London: Royal Institute of International Affairs, 1948.

The Threat to Yugoslavia: Discussion in the Ad Hoc Political Committee of the United Nations Organization, Sixth Session. Belgrade: IUP Jugoslavija, 1952.

Tito, Josip Broz. *Borba i razvoj KPJ izmedju dva rata.* Belgrade: Komunist, 1978.

_____. *Govori i članci, 1941–1957.* 12 vols. Zagreb: Naprijed, 1959.

_____. *Sabrana djela.* 20 vols. Belgrade: Komunist, 1977–1984.

Tomasevich, Jozo. *War and Revolution in Yugoslavia, 1941–1945: The Chetniks.* Stanford: Stanford University Press, 1975.

Tomasic, D. A. *National Communism and Soviet Strategy.* Washington, D.C.: Public Affairs Press, 1957.

Topalović, Živko. *Začeci socijalizma i komunizma u Jugoslaviji.* London: Peasant Jugoslavia, 1960.

Torkar, Ivan [Boris Fakin]. *Umiranje na rate: Dachauski procesi.* Zagreb: Globus, 1984.

Treće redovno zasedanje Saveznog veća i Veća naroda: Stenografske beleške 26. III–26. IV 1947. Belgrade: Narodna skupština FNRJ, n.d.

Treći kongres Saveza komunista Hrvatske (16.–28.V.1954.). Zagreb: Kultura, 1956.

Ugrinov, Pavle. *Carstvo zemaljsko.* Belgrade: Nolit, 1982.

_____. *Zadat život.* Belgrade: Nolit, 1979.

Veselinov-Žarko, Jovan. *Svi smo mi jedna partija*. Novi Sad: SUBNOR SAP Vojvodine, 1971.

Vidmar, Josip. *Moji savremenici*. Sarajevo: Svjetlost, 1981.

Vlahov, Dimitar. *Iz istorije makedonskog naroda*. Belgrade: Prosveta, 1950.

Vlajčić, Gordana. *Jugoslavenska revolucija i nacionalno pitanje 1919–1927*. Zagreb: Centar za kulturnu djelatnost SSO Zagreb, 1984.

———. *KPJ i nacionalno pitanje u Jugoslaviji*. Zagreb: August Cesarec, 1974.

———. *Osma konferencija zagrebačkih komunista*. Zagreb: Školska knjiga, 1976.

———. *Revolucija i nacije: Evolucija stavova vodstava KPJ i Kominterne, 1919–1929*. Zagreb: Centar za kulturnu djelatnost SSO Zagreb, 1978.

Voznesenskii, N. *Voennaia ekonomika SSSR v period Otechestvennoi voiny*. Moscow: OGIZ, 1948.

Vucinich, Wayne S., ed. *At the Brink of War and Peace: The Tito–Stalin Split in a Historic Perspective*. Brooklyn: Brooklyn College Press, 1982.

———, ed. *Contemporary Yugoslavia: Twenty Years of Socialist Experiment*. Berkeley: University of California Press, 1969.

Vukmanović-Tempo, Svetozar. *Borba za Balkan*. Zagreb: Globus, 1981.

———. *Revolucija koja teče: Memoari*. 2 vols. Belgrade: Komunist, 1971.

Warriner, Doreen. *Revolution in Eastern Europe*. London: Turnstile, 1950.

White, Leigh. *Balkan Caesar: Tito versus Stalin*. New York: Scribner's, 1951.

White Book on Aggressive Activities by the Governments of the U.S.S.R., Poland, Czechoslovakia, Hungary, Rumania, Bulgaria, and Albania towards Yugoslavia. Belgrade: Ministry of Foreign Affairs, 1951.

Woodhouse, C. M. *The Struggle for Greece, 1941–1949*. London: Hart-Davis, MacGibbon, 1976.

Yindrich, Jan. *Tito v. Stalin: The Battle of the Marshals*. London: Ernest Benn, 1950.

Zakonodavni rad Pretsedništva Antifašističkog veća narodnog oslobodjenja Jugoslavije i Pretsedništva Privremene narodne skupštine DFJ (19 novembra 1944–27 oktobra 1945). Belgrade: Prezidium Narodne skupštine FNRJ, n.d.

Zarev, Pantelej, ed. *Istorija na bəlgarskata literatura*. Vol. 4, *Bəlgarskata literatura ot kraja na pərvata svetovna vojna do Deveti septevri 1944 godina*. Sofia: BAN, 1976.

Zatezalo, Djuro, ed. *Četvrta konferencija KPH za okrug Karlovac 1945*. Karlovac: Historijski arhiv, 1985.

———, ed. *Treća konferencija KPH za okrug Karlovac 1943*. Karlovac: Historijski arhiv, 1979.

Zbornik dokumenata i podataka o narodnooslobodilačkom ratu jugoslovenskih naroda. Vols. 1, pt. 19; 2, pts. 10–14; 5, pt. 1; 7, pts. 1–2. Belgrade: Vojnoistoriski institut, 1951–1982.

Zečević, Momčilo. *Na istorijskoj prekretnici: Slovenci u politici jugoslovenske države, 1918–1929*. Belgrade: Prosveta, 1985.

Živković, Dušan, ed. *Hronologija radničkog pokreta i SKJ, 1919–1979*. Vol. 2. Belgrade: Narodna knjiga and Institut za savremenu istoriju, 1980.

Zlatar, Pero. *Gospodar zemlje orlova*. Zagreb: Grafički zavod Hrvatske, 1984.

Zogović, Radovan. *Knjaževska kancelarija*. Titograd: NIP Pobjeda, 1976.

ARTICLES

Banac, Ivo. "The Communist Party of Yugoslavia during the Period of Legality (1919–1921)." In *The Effects of World War I: The Class War after the Great War; The Rise of Communist Parties in East Central Europe, 1918–1921,* ed. Ivo Banac, pp. 188–230. Brooklyn: Brooklyn College Press, 1983.

———. "South Slav Prisoners of War in Revolutionary Russia." In *Essays on World War I: Origins and Prisoners of War,* ed. Samuel R. Williamson, Jr. and Peter Pastor, pp. 119–48. Brooklyn: Brooklyn College Press, 1983.

Bilić, Jure. "Otvoreno i kritički—ne samo o 'kriznim' situacijama." In *Jugoslavija, samoupravljanje, svijet—danas,* ed. Ante Gavranović et al., pp. 86–99. Zagreb: Društvo novinara Hrvatske, 1976.

Blagojević, Obren. "Neki momenti iz rada Izvršnog odbora ZAVNO Crne Gore i Boke." *Istorijski zapisi* 24, nos, 3–4 (1971): 555–66.

Dašić, Jaroslav. "Privredna delatnost u oslobodjenom Čačku 1941. godine." In *Užička Republika,* 2 vols., ed. Života Marković, 2:55–68. Belgrade and Titovo Užice: Muzej ustanka 1941, Institut za istoriju radničkog pokreta SR Srbije, and NIRO Eksport-pres, 1978.

Defilippis, Josip. "The Development of Social Holdings in Yugoslavia." In *The Yugoslav Village,* ed. Vlado Puljiz, pp. 69–81. Zagreb: Institut za ekonomiku poljoprivrede i sociologiju sela Poljoprivrednog fakulteta Sveučilišta u Zagrebu, 1972.

"Deklaracija Hrvatskog Seljačko-Radničkog Bloka." In *Poruka Hrvatskom seljačkom narodu pred izbore za Oblasnu Skupštinu,* pp. 14–16. Split: Ivo Brodić, 1926.

Filipič, France. "Moša Pijade: Martovska revolucija." In *Poglavja iz revolucionarnega boja jugoslovanskih komunistov, 1919–1939,* pp. 44–97. Ljubljana: Založba Borec, 1981.

Gorkić, Milan. "Problemi i zadaće Narodne Fronte u Jugoslaviji." *Klasna borba* 10, nos. 1–2 (1937): 56–76.

Hammond, Thomas T. "Foreign Relations since 1945." In *Yugoslavia,* ed. Robert F. Byrnes, pp. 18–41. New York: Praeger, 1957.

Hough, Jerry F. "Debates about the Postwar World." In *The Impact of World War II on the Soviet Union,* ed. Susan J. Linz, pp. 253–81. Totowa, N.J.: Rowman & Allanheld, 1985.

Huljić, Veseljko. "Medjupovezanost razvitka NOP-a u Dalmaciji i Bosni i Hercegovini do kapitulacije Italije." In *AVNOJ i narodonooslobodilačka borba u Bosni i Hercegovini (1942–1943),* pp. 206–26. Belgrade: Rad, 1974.

Iatrides, John O. "Civil War, 1945–1949: National and International Aspects." In *Greece in the 1940s: A Nation in Crisis,* ed. John O. Iatrides, pp. 195–219. Hanover, N.H.: University Press of New England, 1981.

Jadranski [Rajko Jovanović]. "Nacionalreformističke punktacije i borba za hegemoniju nad revolucionarnim pokretima masa u Jugoslaviji." *Klasna borba* 8, nos. 19–20 (1933): 35–45.

Jovanović, Jadranka. "Borba Jugoslavije protiv pritiska SSSR-a i istočnoevropskih država u Organizaciji ujedinjenih nacija (1949–1953): Glavni momenti." *Istorija 20. veka* 2, nos. 1–2 (1984): 85–111.

Jovanović, Nadežda. "Je li u razdoblju 1934–1937. M. Gorkić bio protiv jedinstvene jugoslovenske države?" *Časopis za suvremenu povijest* 15, no. 1 (1983): 77–89.

——. "Milan Gorkić (Prilog za biografiju)." *Istorija 20. veka* 1, no. 1 (1983): 25–57.

Kadić, Ante. "The Stalin–Tito Conflict as Reflected in Literature." *Slavic Review* 37, no. 1 (1978): 91–106.

Kermauner, Taras. "Dijalog o razlikovanju (VI)." *Književnost* 44, nos. 1–2 (1988): 55–62.

Kesmanović, V. "Pronásledování narodnostních menšin v Jugoslavii." *Slovanský prehled* 26, no. 6 (1950): 255–56.

Kociper, [Stanko?]. "Pomembnost in plodovitost sodelovanja osnovnih skupin v O.F." *Slovenska revolucija* 1, no. 4 (1942): 33–39.

Kolar-Dimitrijević, Mira. "Put Stjepana Radića u Moskvu i pristup Hrvatske republikanske seljačke stranke u Seljačku internacionalu." *Časopis za suvremenu povijest* 4, no. 3 (1972): 7–29.

Kolendić, Antun. "Racin na robiji (I)." *Književnost* 41, nos. 1–2 (1986): 231–40.

Končar, Ranko. "Problem autonomije Vojvodine u kontekstu odluka Drugog zasedanja AVNOJ-a." In *AVNOJ i narodnooslobodilačka borba u Bosni i Hercegovini (1942–1943)*, ed. Nikola Babić, pp. 622–31. Belgrade: Rad, 1974.

Koštunica, Vojislav, and Kosta Čavoški. "Opozicione stranke u Narodnom frontu Jugoslavije (1944–1949)." *Istorija 20. veka* 1, no. 1 (1983): 95–116.

Krleža, Miroslav. "Dijalektički antibarbarus." *Pečat* 1, nos. 8–9 (1939): 1–232.

Lakić, Zoran. "Neke karakteristike konstituisanja i rada CASNO-a." *Istorijski zapisi* 24, nos. 3–4 (1971): 577–603.

——. "Zemaljsko antifašističko vijeće narodnog oslobodjenja Sandžaka." In *AVNOJ i narodnooslobodilačka borba u Bosni i Hercegovini (1942–1943)*, ed. Nikola Babić, pp. 678–94. Belgrade: Rad, 1974.

Lazitch, Branko. "Cominformists in Yugoslavia." *Eastern Quarterly* 6, nos. 3–4 (1953): 25–26.

McClellan, Woodford. "Postwar Political Evolution." In *Contemporary Yugoslavia: Twenty Years of Socialist Experiment*, ed. Wayne S. Vucinich, pp. 119–53. Berkeley: University of California Press, 1969.

Matvejević, Predrag. "Literatura Golog otoka." *Književnost* 37, no. 10 (1982): 1534–38.

Miladinović, Milan M. "Marksističko obrazovanje i vaspitanje u Užičkoj Republici." In *Užička Republika*, 2 vols., ed. Života Marković, 2:295–307. Belgrade and Titovo Užice: Muzej ustanka 1941, Institut za istoriju radničkog pokreta SR Srbije, and NIRO Eksport-pres, 1978.

M. K. M. "Tajne Golog Otoka." In *Jugoslovensko krvavo proleće 1945*, ed. Bor. M. Karapandžić, pp. 338–60. Cleveland: Editor, 1976.

Nikolić, Milan [Milan Gorkić]. "Prodiranje Hitlerizma u Jugoslaviju." *Klasna borba* 10, nos. 1–2 (1937): 22–38.

Pappas, Nicholas. "The Soviet-Yugoslav Conflict and the Greek Civil War." In

At the Brink of War and Peace: The Tito-Stalin Split in a Historic Perspective, ed. Wayne S. Vucinich, pp. 219–37, 324–32. Brooklyn: Brooklyn College Press, 1982.

Pelicon, Ivo. "Sovjetski blok godinu dana bez Staljina." *Naša stvarnost* 8, no. 3 (1954): 97–104.

Pešut, Mane. "Djurdjevdanski ustanak Srba u Hrvatskoj—1950 godine." *Glasnik Srpskog istorijsko-kulturnog društva "Njegoš"* 52 (1984): 19–34.

Petranović, Branko. "KPJ i društveno-političke promene u Jugoslaviji od AVNOJ-a do Ustavotvorne skupštine." *Institut za izučavanje istorije Vojvodine. Istraživanja* 1 (1971): 351–410.

——. "O levim skretanjima KPJ krajem 1941. i u prvoj polovini 1942. godine." *Matica srpska. Zbornik za istoriju,* no. 4 (1971): 39–80.

——. "Osnivački kongres Komunističke partije Srbije." *Medjunarodni radnički pokret* 16, no. 4 (1973): 108–20.

——. "Položaj Sandžaka u svetlosti odluke Drugog zasedanja AVNOJ-a o izgradnji Jugoslavije na federativnom principu." *Istorijski zapisi* 24, nos. 3–4 (1971): 567–75.

Petrovich, Michael B. "The View from Yugoslavia." In *Witnesses to the Origins of the Cold War,* ed. Thomas T. Hammond, pp. 34–59. Seattle: University of Washington Press, 1982.

Pirjevec, Jože. "Die Auseinandersetzung Tito–Stalin im Spiegel britischer diplomatischer Berichte." *Südost-Forschungen* 40 (1981): 164–74.

"Plenum Društva književnika Hrvatske (24. lipnja 1985)." *Republika* 41, no. 6 (1985): 3–73.

Plovanić, Mladen. "O nekim zbivanjima u Rijeci vezanim uz objavljivanje Rezolucije Informbiroa 1948. godine." *Dometi* 18, no. 11 (1985): 57–70.

Popović, Milentije. "O ekonomskim odnosima izmedju socijalističkih država." *Komunist* 3, no. 4 (1949): 89–146.

Ranković, Aleksandar. "O predlogu novog Statuta Komunističke partije Jugoslavije." In *Šesti kongres KPJ (Saveza komunista Jugoslavije),* pp. 109–45. Belgrade: Kultura, 1952.

Resis, Albert. "The Churchill–Stalin Secret 'Percentages' Agreement on the Balkans, Moscow, October 1944." *American Historical Review* 83, no. 2 (1978): 368–87.

Šitin, Tonči. "Borba KPJ za primjenu marksističkog stava u nacionalnom pitanju s posebnim osvrtom na ulogu Splitskog plenuma CK KPJ 1933. [1935.] godine." *Naše teme* 19, nos. 10–11 (1975): 1605–41.

Smilevski, Vidoe. "Organizacionen izveštaj." In *I Kongres na Komunističkata partija na Makedonija: Iveštai i rezolucii,* pp. 147–245. Skopje: Kultura, 1949.

Smith, Ole L. "The Problems of the Second Plenum of the Central Committee of the KKE, 1946." *Journal of the Hellenic Diaspora* 12, no. 2 (1985): 43–62.

Stanojević, Gligor. "Stvaranje kulta Rusije u Crnoj Gori." In *Istorija Crne Gore,* bk. 3, *Od početka XVI do kraja XVIII veka,* ed. Milinko Djurović et al., 1:325–71. Titograd: Editorial Board, 1975.

Stojanović, Svetozar. "Od postrevolucionarne diktature ka socijalističkoj demokratiji: Jugoslovenski socijalizam na raskršću." *Praxis* 9, nos. 3–4 (1972): 375–98.

Supek, Ivan. "Obnovljeni humanizam: Povodom obljetnice Kongresa kulturnih radnika Hrvatske, Topusko, 25–27. [lipnja] 1944." Unpublished article, 1984.

Tucker, Robert C. "Stalinism as Revolution from Above." In *Stalinism: Essays in Historical Interpretation*, ed. Robert C. Tucker, pp. 77–108. New York: Norton, 1977.

Vujović, Djuro. "O lijevim greškama KPJ u Crnoj Gori u prvoj godini narodnooslobodilačkog rata." *Istorijski zapisi* 20, no. 1 (1967): 45–113.

Zhdanov, A. "O mezhdunarodnom polozhenii," *Bol'shevik* 24, no. 20 (1947): 10–26.

Životić, M. [Sreten Žujović]. "Ugledajmo se na Francusku Narodnog Fronta." *Klasna borba* 10, nos. 1–2 (1937): 78–93.

"Značajan istorijski dokumenat iz ratne arhive K.P.J." *Naša reč* 33, no. 313 (1980): 10–12.

Zogović, Radovan. "Devet pjesama." *Forum* 4, no. 3 (1965): 391–403.

——. "O našoj književnosti, njenom položaju i njenim zadacima danas." In *Na poprištu*, pp. 182–204. Belgrade: Kultura, 1947.

DISSERTATION

Cicak, Fedor I. "The Communist Party of Yugoslavia between 1919–1924: An Analysis of Its Formative Process." Indiana University, 1965.

ARCHIVAL SOURCES

Arhiv Instituta za historiju radničkog pokreta Hrvatske (AIHRPH, Archive of the Institute for the History of the Workers' Movement of Croatia), Zagreb, Fond Kominterne (Comintern Collection).

Hoover Institution Archives, Stanford, Calif., Dinko A. Tomašić Collection.

NEWSPAPERS, BULLETINS, AND MAGAZINES

Borba (Zagreb, Užice, Drinići, Belgrade), legal organ of Komunistička partija Jugoslavije (KPJ) (1920s), central organ of KPJ (1941–1954), and central organ of Socialist Alliance of the Working People of Yugoslavia (since 1954)

Danas (Zagreb), weekly newsmagazine

Duga (Belgrade), biweekly magazine

Intervju (Belgrade), biweekly magazine

Izvestiia (Moscow), Soviet government daily

Književna reč (Belgrade), biweekly of Literary Youth of Serbia

Književne novine (Belgrade), biweekly of Writers' Society of Serbia

Književne sveske (Zagreb), KPJ's polemical collection on questions of art, literature, and philosophy

Napred (Sofia), organ of Yugoslav Communists—Political Émigrés in the People's Republic of Bulgaria

Naprijed (Otočac, Partisan liberated territory, Zagreb), organ of Komunistička partija Hrvatske (KPH)

New York Times

NIN (Belgrade), weekly newsmagazine

Nova borba (Prague), organ of Yugoslav Revolutionary Émigrés in the People's Republic of Czechoslovakia

Pod zastavom internacionalizma (Bucharest), organ of Yugoslav Communists—Political Émigrés—in the People's Republic of Romania

Politika (Belgrade), leading Serbian daily

Pravda (Moscow), Soviet party daily

Proleter (Zagreb, Vienna, Prague, Paris, Brussels, Belgrade, Foča, Drinići), organ of KPJ CC

Radničko jedinstvo (Belgrade), "independent workers' newspaper," organ of Života Milojković group

Radnik-Delavec (Belgrade), central organ of Independent Workers' Party of Yugoslavia (legal front organization of KPJ)

Srpska riječ (Otočac, Partisan liberated territory, Zagreb), organ of Serb Club of Councillors of Zemaljsko antifašističko vijeće narodnog oslobodjenja Hrvatske (ZAVNOH)

Štampa (Zagreb), legal organ of KPJ

Start (Zagreb), biweekly magazine

Susret (Belgrade), youth magazine

Vjesnik (Zagreb), organ of Socialist Alliance of the Working People of Croatia, leading Croatian daily

Vjesnik—Sedam dana (Zagreb), weekly supplement to *Vjesnik*

Za socijalističku Jugoslaviju (Moscow), organ of Yugoslav Communists—Political Émigrés—in the USSR

Zeta (Podgorica, now Titograd), weekly newspaper

Index

Administration of State Security. *See* Uprava državne bezbednosti

Albania: and Cominform split, 132–33, 147–48, 159–60, 185n, 222, 227–28, 245, 259; and Kosovo, 206–12, 214–16; and Soviet Union, 26, 28, 32, 38–40; and Yugoslav Communists, 17, 19, 29–30, 32, 35, 38–43, 208–10, 214; mentioned, 4n, 30, 40n, 41n, 103, 123, 205, 216, 261, 267

Albanian Communist Party. *See* Partia Komuniste e Shqipërisë

Albanians: and Cominformism, 151, 160n, 174–75, 215–16, 218, 267; in Yugoslavia, 79, 83, 105, 126, 205–16, 218

Allies and Yugoslavia, 6, 79

Andreev, Bane, 193–95, 197–98, 252n

Antifašističko vijeće narodnog oslobodjenja Jugoslavije (AVNOJ, Antifascist Council of People's Liberation of Yugoslavia): founding of, 11, 99, 103n; 2d session of (Jajce), 12, 18, 99–100, 102–3, 109, 211n; in Tito-Šubašić agreement, 15; in Yalta agreements, 16; mentioned, 31n, 85, 101–3, 182, 203n

Austria, 17, 137, 189, 237n, 241

Austria-Hungary. *See* Habsburg Monarchy

AVNOJ. *See* Antifašističko vijeće narodnog oslobodjenja Jugoslavije

Axis: and Yugoslavia, 4–6 *passim;* mentioned, 8

Babič, Branko, 238–40

Bačka, 4n, 107–8, 154, 170, 217

Bakarić, Vladimir, 72, 77, 93, 95n, 98, 121n, 135, 181n

Balen, Šime, 115, 184–85, 252n

Baljkas, Ivo, 59, 70, 115

Balli kombëtar (National Front), 209–10

Banija, 84, 89, 106n, 128, 182

Baranja, 4n, 104, 107–8, 217

Belgrade, 15, 52, 57, 65n, 102, 104, 117, 131, 162, 167, 170, 173, 178, 232, 247, 262

Bilandžić, Dušan, 172

Biljanović, Vojislav, 35, 158

Bogdanov, Vaso, 72

Bornemissa, Vladimir, 48

Bosnia-Hercegovina: Cominformism in, 157, 173, 177, 180–81, 183, 204n, 235–37; in Croat banate (1939), 76; Serbs in, 173, 180–81, 183; in World War II, 4, 79, 81; and Yugoslav federation, 100–101, 103, 106; mentioned, 22, 50–51, 128, 151, 174–75, 182

Bosnian Muslims, 79, 100–101, 105, 150n, 151, 160n, 186

Brankov, Lazar, 222–23, 225

Brkić, Dušan, 98, 115, 181–83, 237

Broz, Josip. *See* Tito, Josip Broz

BRP. *See* Bəlgarska rabotničeska partija

Brudniak, Gejza, 48

Bukšeg, Vilim, 46

Bulgaria: and Cominform split, 121–22, 133, 225–28, 259; and liberation of Serbia, 14, 212; and Macedonian question, 36–37, 189–90, 192, 194–97, 199–204, 262, 266; and occupation of Yugoslavia, 4, 79, 191; postwar policies of, 18–19, 21–22; and Soviet Union,

287

Library of Congress Cataloging-in-Publication Data

Banac, Ivo.
  With Stalin against Tito.

  Bibliography: p.
  Includes index.
  1. Communism—Yugoslavia—History.   2. Communist Information Bureau—History.   3. Tito, Josip Broz, 1892–1980.   4. Stalin, Joseph, 1879–
1953.   5. Yugoslavia—Politics and government—1945–   . I. Title.
HX365.5.A6B36 1988   335.43′44   88-47717
ISBN 0-8014-2186-1 (alk. paper)